The Economics of Technological Diffusion

D0814154

The Economics of Technological Diffusion

Paul Stoneman
Warwick Business School

Copyright © Paul Stoneman 2002

The right of Paul Stoneman to be identified as the author of this work has been asserted in accordance with the Copyright, Designs and Patents Act 1988.

First published 2002

2 4 6 8 10 9 7 5 3 1

Blackwell Publishers Ltd
108 Cowley Road
Oxford OX4 1JF
UK

Blackwell Publishers Inc.
350 Main Street
Malden, Massachusetts 02148
USA

British Library Cataloguing in Publication Data
A CIP catalogue record for this book is available from the British Library.

Library of Congress Cataloging-in-Publication Data
Stoneman, Paul.
        The economics of technological diffusion/Paul Stoneman.
           p.   cm.
        Includes bibliographical references and index.
        ISBN 0–631–21976–5 (alk. paper) — ISBN 0–631–21977–3 (pb.: alk paper)
        1. Technological innovations—Economic aspects.   2. Diffusion of innovations.   I. Title.

     HC79.T4 S864 2001
     338′.064—dc21   2001018130

Typeset in 10/12pt Ehrhardt
by Graphicraft Limited, Hong Kong
Printed in Great Britain by TJ International, Padstow, Cornwall

This book is printed on acid-free paper.

Contents

Figures

Tables

Preface

I have been fascinated by the question of what determines the diffusion or take up of new technology since the completion of my PhD thesis on this topic in the early 1970s. Since then I have continued to work, publish and teach in this field. In teaching graduate and under-graduate students I have become aware that there is no obvious place for students interested in this issue to turn for a comprehensive treatment of the relevant literatures. Originally, to meet this need, I proposed to the publishers a book of my collected papers on the Economics of Technological Diffusion. Blackwell suggested instead that I produce a book that is a mix of past papers and new material. This mixing has provided an opportunity to present the theory of diffusion in a more accessible way than would have been possible just using past papers. However, the inclusion of past papers themselves provides a level of sophistication that would have been unlikely if all the text were to be written from scratch. By organizing the past papers under themes and writing introductory chapters on each theme, I hope also to have provided accessible overviews of the literatures upon the themes. The mix of new mater-ial and past papers provides a volume that goes beyond a text book. Although much of the material is accessible to third year undergraduate and graduate level students, often I have had in mind that I am talking to other researchers in the field. I believe that they will find much of interest here. I also believe that policy makers will find much of the material relevant.

Many of the papers included in this book, and also much of my research over the last 25 years, has been the product of myself and a series of co-authors. I would like to thank these co-authors both for their involvement in the research and also their permission to include the papers reproduced. The co-authors are: Professors Norman Ireland and Mike Waterson of the Department of Economics at the University of Warwick and Professor Paul David of Stanford University and All Souls College, Oxford; Otto Toivanen, Paul Diederen, Myung Joong Kwon, Massoud Karshenas and Giuliana Battisti, who were research associ-ates and assistants who worked with me over the years in the Warwick Economics Depart-ment and Warwick Business School; and Florian Zettlemeyer who was a Masters student at Warwick whose research I supervised. In addition I wish to thank the following journals for their permission to reproduce the papers included below: the *Economic Journal*, *Oxford Economic Papers*, the *Rand Journal of Economics*, the *International Journal of Industrial Organisation* and the *Economics of Innovation and New Technology*. I would also like to thank Paul Geroski and Giuliana Battisti as well as an anonymous reviewer for comments on the first draft of the volume. Of course, all errors that may remain are my responsibility alone.

Part I

Introduction and Empirical Observations on the Diffusion Process

Chapter one

By Way of an Introduction and Guide

1.1. Introduction

This book is concerned with the process by which new technologies spread across their potential markets over time. It is commonly observed and will be illustrated below that for most new technologies it takes many years for the extent of ultimate use to be attained. The main aims of this book are to explore potential reasons for this, to test the various explanations, explore policy issues and analyse the implications for economic analysis more generally. The key question is essentially why, if a new technology is superior to previous technologies, do not all potential users adopt the new technology immediately? As will be seen there are many different and varied answers.

The relevance of the topic is obvious. Although much of the literature on technological change is concerned with the generation of new technology exploring, for example, research and development and the launch of new technologies (innovation strictly defined), it is only as new technologies are used and spread widely in an economy that any real welfare gains arise from those technologies. The benefits that can be realized from new technologies are well documented and understood (see, for example, Stoneman, 1995). Thus to understand the diffusion process is to understand the process by which new technology generates these economic benefits.

The modern analysis of technological change in economics is often considered as originating with the work of Schumpeter (1934). His classic contributions on the importance of technological change as the driving force behind the long (Kondratieff) trade cycle can be considered as the origin of interest in the diffusion process. Post war, however, it was the pioneering work of Griliches (1957) and Mansfield (1968) on the diffusion of new process technologies in agriculture and industry that really began theoretical and empirical exploration of diffusion phenomena in economics. Over the last 45 years the literature in economics has grown considerably as has the understanding of the diffusion process. In marketing, geography and sociology there has been similar, although often unrelated, growth of interest in diffusion, but, except where such literature has impacted upon economics, these approaches are outside the remit of this volume.

Appreciation of the nature and determinants of the diffusion process has not been widespread in economics. Within the field of technological change its importance is recognized and past findings are part of the standard literature. In other parts of economics, however, this is less the case (although hopefully there is some change occurring here). One of the most influential developments in economics in the last 15 years has been the renaissance of interest in growth theory and especially the development of what is known as 'new growth' theory. The dominant approach in this rapidly developing field is endogenous growth models which analyse the macro economics of the growth process with an emphasis on the role played by technological change (see, for example, Jones, 1998). In particular the very influential Romer (1990) variant of this approach sees economic growth in the (world) economy as driven by the generation of new technologies in a research and development (R&D) sector that are then used in a final goods producing sector. Balanced growth paths exhibit a given allocation of the work force to the R&D sector (determined by consumer preferences or saving rates, the growth rate of the labour force and the underlying research technology) and as a result a given flow of new technologies to the final goods sector. In nearly all such models, however, it is assumed that new technologies coming from the R&D sector are adopted by all producers immediately and to the limit of their potential; that is, the existence of a time-intensive diffusion process is not recognized. Although not true for all such models, the failure to realize that adoption of new technologies takes time suggests that as yet the analysis of diffusion phenomena has not fully penetrated the psyche of the economics profession. The limited new growth theory literature that explicitly considers diffusion processes includes Grossman and Helpman (1991), Sala-i-Martín and Barro (1995), and Escot (1998).

Although one may decry this failing of the new growth theory, it must be accepted that such theory has brought issues of growth and technological change to the fore of interest for many more economists. This is thus an appropriate time to attempt to bring together in one volume much of the knowledge on the economics of technological diffusion that has been developed in the post-war era.

1.2. Defining Technological Change

For the purposes of this volume new technology is widely defined. By technology is meant the goods and services produced and the means by which they are produced in a firm, an industry or an economy. Technological changes mean changes in the goods and services produced and the means by which they are produced. Technological advances are changes where the new in some sense is considered superior to the old. Technological advances in the nature and types of products produced are product innovations. Technological advances in the techniques used in production, whether they relate to the types of machinery employed, the layout of the factory, the raw material and intermediate inputs employed or the management methods used would all be considered as process innovations.

These definitions emphasize the actual products and processes in an economy at a point in time. It is not unusual in the literature, however, to think of technology as information or knowledge and in particular information upon what products and processes could but are not necessarily used in the economy.[1] For the purposes of analysing diffusion the former definition is more useful. However, the information approach also has some benefit. One might consider that the information set provides a menu of technological possibilities from which firms and households select preferred technologies, which they then acquire. The step from knowledge to actual use is not an automatic one. Incorporating information or knowledge into a production process may require the purchase of capital equipment, the training of labour or many other expenditures. However, the process of moving from knowledge to actual use is a major part of what the diffusion process encompasses. In strict terms, the analysis of diffusion is the analysis of the process by which knowledge is incorporated into an economy post first incorporation (or innovation). The analysis of the generation of information is not strictly within the remit of this volume except as it is endogenous to, or joint with, the diffusion process itself.

Recent analysis of technology as information has emphasized certain characteristics of information that are worth stating at an early stage. First, information is non-rivalrous in the sense that one person's ownership of a piece of information does not affect another person's ability to also hold that piece of information. In this sense information is different to normal goods. This, it should be noted, does not imply that there is no potential rivalry in the use of information. There may in fact be considerable rivalry in use. Secondly, information is at least to some degree excludable, in the sense that the owner can charge a fee for its use. Excludability can come through secrecy, patenting, copyright or the ownership of joint inputs. Non-rivalrous goods that are essentially unexcludable are often called public goods (e.g. defence services) and thus information that cannot be protected may be considered a public good. In general, however, information is at least partly excludable and as such will not be a public good.

The term 'technology' can apply equally to households and firms. In a household there is a production technology that underlies both the supply of labour services and the process of generating consumer services. The technology will encompass washing machines, vacuum cleaners, televisions, cars, video recorders, cookers and so on. In a wider sense the technology will also encompass how the use of these is organized and managed according to the family's needs and preferences. To a considerable degree technological change in the household will be primarily concerned with updating the machinery employed and/or adding to the stock of technologies incorporated. The household will largely innovate by reacting to new technologies offered to it by suppliers and deciding whether and or when to acquire those new technologies. Only rarely will the household be generating its own new technologies.

For firms, the sources of innovations to be diffused is wider. Firms may obtain new technologies from their own R&D efforts, through learning by doing, by licensing (or even stealing) from other firms (whether they are rivals or not), or by buying new technologies embodied in capital equipment from capital equipment suppliers. The relative importance of these sources will differ across industries and firms. Some firms for example will produce most technology in house, especially product technologies (e.g. electronics firms), whereas others (e.g. service sector firms) may rely more upon outside suppliers. Pavitt (1984) has produced a useful taxonomy that shows what sources are most important to what industries. At the economy-wide level, in some economies domestic sources will be more important whereas in other economies technology importation may be of greater relevance. As should be clear, however, technologies sourced from outside a firm or an economy may well be subject to different factors impacting on the diffusion process than those produced internally or imported.

Although it is very useful for the purposes of organizing one's thoughts, technologies very rarely exhibit a stand-alone character. New technologies more frequently will be introduced into an existing production process alongside other existing or new technologies. A new machine, for example, may need to be operated alongside an old machine. One new technology may also be introduced with another new technology and there may be spill-over effects from one technology to another. Some new technologies may also require complementary inputs in order to function efficiently; for example, computer hardware also requires computer software. A new technology might also be introduced into an existing supply chain and thus have to integrate with current flows of materials and other inputs. New products may require new processes for their production – for instance, the introduction of a new car model is often accompanied by the laying down of a new production line. The introduction of new technologies may require new organizational or management forms if they are to be fully exploited (see Milgrom and Roberts, 1995), it being argued, for example, that the full potential of information technology (IT) for the firm can only be realized with accompanying organizational innovation. New technologies may also only generate their greatest benefits when there are a number of other users and mature supporting markets for inputs and services have developed fully. There are a myriad of such 'network' or interaction effects in existence in the real economy that suggest that although a single technology perspective can clarify thought processes, analysis restricted solely to the latter would be incomplete.

Some technologies are more important than others. Some new technologies may well have only a small impact on a production process, or be responsible for only a small share of total costs, or have only a very limited area of application. Other technologies may well be of greater significance, their introduction impacting significantly on costs or household utility and/or having a very wide area of application. Recently the term 'general purpose technologies' has been coined to encompass such widely applicable technologies. Such technologies exemplified by, for example, steam power, electrification or IT, are essentially technologies that are very widely applicable and through the introduction of a large number of products and processes incorporating the technology in a very wide area of use will have considerable impact upon the economy. Such general purpose technologies may well be particularly subject to network externalities.

General purpose technologies, like most technologies, rarely stand still. New technologies after first being introduced go through many significant improvements and changes during their life. One has only to look at the development of computers over the last 50 years to see that the year 2000 computer is very different from its forebears first launched in the late 1940s. The differences are obvious in terms of capabilities, size and price. For the analyst of diffusion processes this creates a problem. The problem is whether one should analyse the diffusion of an improving technology as one continuous process partly, at least, driven by the improvements, or alternatively consider each improvement as generating a new technology and then analyse a number of separate but linked individual diffusion processes. For example, it is commonly observed that computers and steam engines have been or went through a number of 'generations', each later generation being better than the previous generation. One could analyse the diffusion of steam engines or computers as one continuous process with an improving technology being diffused, or alternatively consider the appearance of each new generation as the start of a new diffusion process. There is no simple answer to what is the most appropriate approach, but it is fair to state that most literature concentrates on the single diffusion process approach rather than modelling according to generations. This will emphasize the role of technology improvement in the diffusion process. The reason for doing so is, I feel, often a desire to consider the big question rather than the little question.

1.3.   Diffusion: Some Initial Organizing Thoughts

Whatever the source or nature of a technology it is clear that the adoption of technology takes time. An individual firm will rarely completely transform its production process at a single point in time from an old to a new technology. In general one will observe a gradual process of transition with, for successful technologies, a greater and greater proportion of output gradually being produced using the new technology. This internal diffusion process is called intra-firm diffusion. One may see a similar intra-household diffusion process, for example, the switch from vinyl-based music service flows to CD-based music service flows has been gradual in most households with the complete switch to CDs being conditioned on the rate at which vinyl sources are replicated. At the industry level it is generally observed that the number of firms using a particular new technology grows over time, this is the process of inter-firm diffusion. Similarly, the adoption of a new technology across house-holds also takes time. At the economy-wide and international level one may also observe similar diffusion processes taking place, with technologies taking time to spread across different industries and also across national boundaries. Diffusion may thus be analysed at a large number of different aggregative levels.

The lower the level of aggregation being addressed the greater will be the emphasis on firm and household heterogeneity. Unlike much literature in economics, the analysis of diffusion has emphasized that households differ from each other and firms (even in the same industry) differ from each other. Technologies also differ in characteristics. Such hetero-geneity is an important part of diffusion modelling.

Most household technologies and many producer technologies will be acquired through the purchase of capital equipment that embodies such technologies; for example, a house-hold may buy a tumble drier or a firm may buy a robot production line. To some degree at least, the number of buyers of these new technologies at a point in time will depend upon the quality adjusted price of the capital goods on offer. This immediately leads one to consider that the structure and behaviour of the industries supplying the new technology will influence the diffusion process. For example, one might expect that a monopoly sup-plier may charge higher prices than a competitive supplier and as such slow down the diffusion process. Suppliers may also attempt to intertemporally price discriminate in order to maximize their profit over time. In addition suppliers may use advertising and other information spreading mechanisms to make buyers aware of the new technologies. The study of diffusion is thus also a study of the supply of technologies. One should note, however, that for the supplier the new technology will be a product innovation. To a considerable extent, therefore, the study of supplier behaviour is also the study of the launching and pricing of new products.

The supply side has its own momentum. When a completely new technology appears there may be only a few suppliers, especially if the intellectual property in the technology is heavily protected, say through patents. As time proceeds, however, the number of suppliers may increase and as it does so prices and technology might change. Alternatively, a new technology may be initially produced by a very large number of firms, but as time goes by many firms leave the market and the number of suppliers decreases. An example here could be the motor car industry. From early days, almost as a cottage industry with a large number of small suppliers, over time, the number of suppliers has dwindled and the size of the average supplier increased markedly. However, economies of scale and the use of new mass production techniques still enabled the price of cars to decline over time. Either pattern is thus feasible. The full analysis of a diffusion phenomenon thus encompasses the development of the supplying industry.

With a large number of suppliers entering a market one may well expect product differentiation. Such product differentiation may be vertical or horizontal (in the former case all consumers agree on the quality ordering of the goods on offer, in the latter case different consumers value goods differently). As potential buyers of new technology may well have different preferences or income, the greater the degree of horizontal or vertical product differentiation the more likely the buyer is to find a product variant matching his/her requirements and thus the more likely is he/she to acquire that product.

A multiplicity of product variants, however, is not always going to speed diffusion. Many new technologies will appear in different forms that are not compatible. For example, video recorders appeared with three different formats, VHS, BETAMAX and Video 2000. The three formats were not compatible in that software produced for one was not readable on another. A potential purchaser of such technologies may well be deterred by the uncertainty induced by many differing formats, in that a decision to buy a format that eventually becomes obsolescent would leave the purchaser with software that cannot be used. In the presence of such compatibility problems, product differentiation may thus actually slow the diffusion process rather than speed up that process. The issue of compatibility (and by implications standards) is another example of the network aspects of new technologies discussed above.

The inability to be sure as to which standard or format of a technology is likely to dominate in the future is an example of the uncertainty that is inherent to technological change and the risk that new technology buyers have to face. Uncertainty is apparent in a number of different forms. The potential acquirers of new technology may be uncertain as to how that technology will perform, how long lived it will be in a physical sense or when it might be superseded and become obsolescent. For suppliers of new products similarly, there will be uncertainty as to the market's reaction to those products, the economics of production and the reaction of competitors. In addition there will be general uncertainty as to how economies will develop and grow over time and thus how individual markets will grow. It is not uncommon to define two basic types of uncertainty: technological uncertainty relating to how technologies perform and their physical or economic life; and market uncertainty relating to the development of demand for products and incorporating the reaction of rival producers. Both need to be considered.

If there is uncertainty, then the decision-making processes of potential buyers and suppliers of new technology will reflect this. It has long been realized that economies do not offer a complete set of insurance markets (see Arrow, 1962) and as such risk aversion may affect the diffusion of new technology and/or the speed with which new technologies are improved. In addition, in the face of uncertainty, firms and consumers may well undertake a search for information better to inform purchasing decisions, and a commitment to search may slow the acquisition process. It is not unrealistic to consider that the potential purchaser of new technology does not face a decision between just two alternatives, adopt or not adopt, but between three alternatives – adopt, not adopt, or search and reconsider the decision on adoption at a later date. In addition, as the diffusion of a new product proceeds it is possible that potential acquirers may well learn from past acquirers and this will influence the diffusion process. It is even possible that firms and households acquire a small amount of a technology to learn about it prior to a full commitment to that technology and this may be one of the reasons generating time-intensive intra-firm and intra-household diffusion.

1.4.   The Way Ahead

The study of diffusion is exciting. One reason for this excitement is that issues that might be considered 'sexy' are being addressed (new technologies, new industries, new know-ledge). More relevant for the economist, however, is that diffusion concerns issues that are among the more difficult to analyse adequately. Time is involved. Uncertainty is inherent. Change is the main topic. Imperfect markets abound. All such characteristics mean that the analysis of diffusion stands apart from much of the standard fare of economic textbooks where perfect competition, full information, static models tend to hold sway. However, the fact that economic analysis can contribute so much to our understanding of diffusion phenomena should be taken as evidence of the robustness of such analysis.

The rest of this book is structured as follows. The chapter that immediately follows presents a review of a number of empirical observations upon the nature of the diffusion process. In particular it explores patterns of inter-firm, intra-firm, intra-household and economy-wide diffusion processes illustrating time profiles of adoption and the character-ization thereof. This is supplemented with some empirical observations on how new tech-nologies change and develop over time, post initial introduction, to illustrate the points made above relating to technological improvement. A discussion and illustration of inter-temporal patterns of changes in the cost of acquiring new technologies is then provided. Finally, this chapter looks at the developments on the supply side, analysing how supply industries change as technologies mature. This chapter closes the first, introductory, part to the book.

Part II of the book is concerned with the theory of diffusion. Here an attempt is made to provide an accessible and often non-technical overview of the different theoretical approaches to the analysis of technological diffusion found in the economics literature. The approach starts with the demand for stand-alone technologies and includes a discussion of the role of horizontal and vertical product differentiation. Uncertainty and risk are then addressed. The discussion is then extended to interrelated technologies, standards, compat-ibility and general purpose technologies, before this part of the book closes with an analysis of the interaction between supply and demand in the diffusion of new technologies.

The next part of the book is concerned with testing theory. The empirical relevance of theory is a main means by which one may discriminate between theories and come to some view as to what factors are more important and what factors are of lesser importance in the diffusion process. This section of the book starts with an overview of the techniques appropriate to empirical work on diffusion and past results. This is then followed by three papers, previously published by the author, that reflect the detail of empirical analysis. These papers are more technical than the earlier part of the book partly because they are designed, in addition to illustrating empirical issues, to also show how the earlier theoretical work can be formalized, and partly because such technicality is part of placing academic work in the best journals.

The fourth part of the book is concerned with policy. The intention is to illustrate how one may analyse the need for and instruments of government intervention in the diffusion process. After an initial introduction four previously published papers are again included. The first of these presents an overview of the diffusion policy debate, the second illustrates how theory can be developed to address policy issues, the third considers the theory of policy instruments and the fourth represents an empirical investigation of the impact of certain diffusion policy tools.

The final part of the book considers applications, extensions and implications. The main purpose is to argue that the existence of diffusion phenomena should be more generally recognized and taken more account of in the analysis of key economic issues. After a general discussion of examples of how this has been and can be done, three further papers are presented that look at how, by using diffusion analysis, one may more realistically explore the impact of technological change upon productivity growth, employment and gross investment. The book is closed with a discussion of possible future research agendas.

The informed reader may consider that there are two bodies of literature that are given less attention in this volume than they may deserve. The first of these is the growing 'evolutionary' analysis of diffusion. This is discussed in chapter 3 alongside other theoretical approaches, but the extent of coverage may not satisfy the evolutionists. It is fair to state that the majority of this book reflects the neoclassical bias in the author's own work. The second 'omission' is the large body of 'institutional' literature especially as it relates to policy issues. This has been played down partly on the grounds of space, but also because much of the relevant material has been addressed in another recent co-authored book, Diederen *et al.* (1999).

The material in this book to some degree overlaps with material presented in Stoneman (1983, 1987 and 1995). However, here the topic of diffusion is analysed in much greater depth than in those previous volumes and in addition a conscious attempt has been made, especially in Part II, to make the theoretical material more accessible. If, as a result of this work, the general awareness of diffusion phenomena is raised within the economics profession and/or more research into diffusion phenomena is encouraged then the book will be seen by the author as a success.

Note

1   To some readers the distinction between the two approaches may be getting close to the distinction between science and technology. Personally, however, I am more convinced by the view that science is an activity producing output for the public domain whereas technology produces output for the private domain (see Dasgupta and David, 1987). In this approach either the actual products and processes or information may be technology. As a whole this book has little to say about science thus defined.

References

Arrow, K.J. (1962) 'Economic Welfare and the Allocation of Resources for Invention', in R.R. Nelson (ed.), *The Rate and Direction of Inventive Activity*, Princeton, NJ: Princeton University Press.

Dasgupta, P. and David, P. (1987) 'Information Disclosure and the Economics of Science and Technology', in G. Fiewal (ed.), *Arrow and the Ascent of Modern Economic Theory*, New York: New York University Press.

Diederen, P., Stoneman, P., Toivanen, O. and Wolters, A. (1999) *Innovation and Research Policies: An International Comparative Analysis*, Cheltenham: Edward Elgar.

Escot, L. (1998) 'Technological Catch Up: Gradual Diffusion of Technology and Convergence in the Neo-classical Growth Model', *International Advances in Economic Research*, 4(1), 24–33.

Griliches, Z. (1957) 'Hybrid Corn: An Exploration in the Economics of Technological Change', *Econometrica*, 48, 501–22.

Grossman, G.M. and Helpman, E. (1991) *Innovation and Growth in the Global Economy*, Cambridge, MA: MIT Press.

Jones, C. (1998) *Introduction to Economic Growth*, New York: W.W. Norton & Co.

Mansfield, E. (1968) *Industrial Research and Technological Innovation*, New York: W.W. Norton & Co.

Milgrom, P. and Roberts, J. (1995) 'Complementarities and Fit: Strategy, Structure and Organisational Change in Manufacturing', *Journal of Accounting and Economics*, 19(2/3), 179–208.

Pavitt, K. (1984) 'Sectoral Patterns of Technical Change: Towards a Taxonomy and a Theory', *Research Policy*, 13, 343–73.

Romer, P. (1990) 'Endogenous Technological Change', *Journal of Political Economy*, 98, S71–S102.

Sala-i-Martín, X. and Barro, R.L. (1995) 'Technological Diffusion, Convergence and Growth', Yale Economic Growth Center, Discussion Paper No. 735, June.

Schumpeter, J.A. (1934) *The Theory of Economic Development*, Cambridge, MA: Harvard University Press.

Stoneman, P. (1983) *The Economic Analysis of Technological Change*, Oxford: Oxford University Press.

Stoneman, P. (1987) *The Economic Analysis of Technology Policy*, Oxford: Oxford University Press.

Stoneman, P. (ed.) (1995) *Handbook of the Economics of Innovation and Technological Change*, Oxford: Basil Blackwell.

Chapter two

Empirical Patterns in the Diffusion of Innovations

2.1.   Introduction

This chapter explores observed patterns in the diffusion of new technology, making observations on key facts as the chapter proceeds. The initial section looks at the diffusion of process innovations, that is, new technologies adopted by firms in their production processes. Differences across firms, technologies, industries and countries are all illustrated. This is then followed by a section on the diffusion of new technologies across households. The chapter then moves to consider the launching of new products that embody new technology, the market structure of technology supplying industries and the pricing of new technologies. The factors that underlie the observed patterns are discussed in the following chapters.

2.2.   Process Innovations

The classic observations with respect to diffusion refer to the inter-firm diffusion of new process technology. Griliches' (1957) work on the diffusion of hybrid corn in different US states is a convenient starting point. Griliches observed that if one plotted the proportion of total corn acreage in a state i that is planted with hybrid seed ($P_i(t)$, usefully labelled the extent of market penetration), against time, then the resulting plot is usually found to be S shaped as per figure 2.1. This S shape suggests that the rate at which the new technology is being used starts at a low level and at first increases slowly. The rate of increase then gets larger until a point of inflection, after which the level of use is still increasing but at a decreasing rate. As time goes to infinity the level of use approaches some asymptote (often unity). Griliches (1957) characterized the observed pattern as being represented by the logistic curve written as

$$P_i(t) = P_i^*/(1 + \exp(-\eta_i - \phi_i \cdot t))$$

or

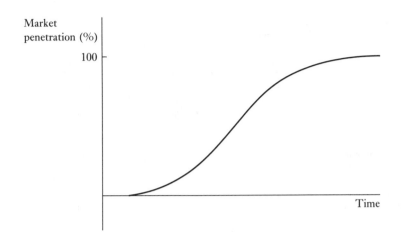

Figure 2.1 The S-shaped diffusion curve

$$\mathrm{d}P_i(t)/\mathrm{d}t = \phi_i \cdot P_i(t)\{1 - P_i(t)/P_i^*\}$$

where P_i^* is the asymptotic level of use, η_i locates the diffusion curve on the horizontal axis and ϕ_i is a measure of the speed of diffusion. Griliches finds that the parameters of this curve, including the asymptote, differed across states. He finds positive correlations between both the speed of diffusion and the size of the asymptote with the profitability of adopting the new technology. Dixon (1980) looks again at the Griliches data and adds a number of later data points. He then finds that in all states the asymptote is unity. He also suggests that the Gompertz curve is a better representation of the diffusion process than the logistic curve, where the Gompertz can be written as

$$\mathrm{d}P_i(t)/\mathrm{d}t = \phi_i \cdot P_i(t)\{\log P_i^* - \log P_i(t)\}$$

although Dixon finds again that profitability impacts positively on the diffusion process. The Gompertz curve is again S shaped but whereas the logistic has a point of inflexion at $0.5P_i^*$ for the Gompertz the inflection point is at $P_i^*/3$. In the literature a number of other S-shaped curves are also used to represent the diffusion process. Among the more common are the cumulative normal and cumulative log normal which have the advantage of a parameter determined, rather than fixed, inflection point.

This work on hybrid corn illustrated that the diffusion path differs across states. Alderman and Davies (1990) also show how, within the UK, the diffusion of a number of different manufacturing technologies differs across regions. Equivalently one may also illustrate that the diffusion process differs across industries. In table 2.1 some data is presented on the use of advance manufacturing technologies in Canada in 1989 (Vickery and Northcott, 1995). The inter-industry differences are marked.

Mansfield has made a number of significant contributions to the understanding of empirical patterns of diffusion processes. Table 2.2 presents some data from Mansfield (1989) indicating not only the length of time that the diffusion process may take, but also how it differs across technologies. The following table (table 2.3) from Stoneman and Toivanen

Table 2.1   Use of advanced manufacturing technology by industry: Canada, 1989

	CAD/ CAE	NC/ CNCMT	FMS/ FMC	Pick and place robots	Storage, retrieval	Final inspection, testing	Factory LAN
Food, beverages, tobacco	14	7	11	3	5	12	14
Leather, textiles, clothing	10	14	6	3	4	3	6
Wood	13	7	9	3	4	10	8
Furniture and fixtures	7	7	4	1	1	5	7
Paper and allied products	27	11	7	7	10	30	22
Printing, publishing and allied	14	12	1	3	6	3	2
Petroleum and chemicals	18	3	6	1	8	8	16
Rubber and plastics	10	8	10	3	6	9	6
Non-metallic mineral products	11	13	12	1	14	12	14
Primary metal	28	20	14	6	4	20	20
Fabricated metal products	21	25	7	1	1	8	13
Machinery	36	35	13	5	3	6	9
Electrical and electronic products	42	18	9	2	1	14	12
Transportation equipment	34	19	13	12	9	21	18
Other manufacturing	7	9	5	2	1	7	3
All manufacturing:							
Establishment weighted	17	14	7	3	4	8	9
For comparison:							
Shipment weighted	49	30	21	15	15	35	37

Establishment-weighted percentages estimated for all manufacturing plants in each industry
CAD/CAE: computer-aided design/computer-aided engineering;
NC/CNCMT: numerically controlled/computer numerically controlled machine tools;
FMS/FMC: flexible manufacturing system/flexible machining centre;
LAN: local area network.
Source: Vickery and Northcott (1995, p. 264).

Table 2.2   Diffusion indicators: United States

Innovation	No. of years taken for half of potential adopters to acquire
Industrial robots	12
Numerically controlled machine tools	5
Diesel locomotives	9
Centralized traffic control	14
Car retarders	13
Continuous wide strip mill	8
By-product coke oven	15
Continuous annealing	13
Shuttle car	5
Trackless mobile loader	6
Continuous mining machine	3
Tin container	1
High-speed bottle filler	6
Pallet loading machine	5

Source: Mansfield (1989).

Table 2.3   Adoption of technologies by 1986

Technology	Sample size	Number of adopters	%
CNC	733	362	49.4
Computers	733	466	63.6
NC	733	214	29.2
Carbide tools	733	289	39.4
Microprocessors	733	214	29.2

Source: Stoneman and Toivanen (1997, p. 13).

Table 2.4   The diffusion of technologies

Innovation	% of output product using new technology	Years from own date of innovation		
		UK	West Germany	Sweden
Special presses (paper making)	10	3	2	2
Tunnel kilns (brick making)	10	n/a	2	8
Basic oxygen process (steel)	20	5	8	9
Gibberalic acid (brewing)	50	4	n/a	3
Continuous casting	1	6	9	3
Shuttleless looms (textiles)	2	6	6	9
Automatic transfer lines (vehicles)	30	10	1	2

Source: Nabseth and Ray (1974, p. 17).

(1997) summarizing data from a 1986 survey of the use of new technologies in the UK engineering industry undertaken by the Centre for Urban and Regional Development Studies (CURDS) at the University of Newcastle upon Tyne, further reinforces the view that diffusion differs across technologies. This is further illustrated in table 2.4 from Nabseth and Ray (1974) which shows not only differences across technologies but also differences across countries. Vickery and Northcott (1995) review a number of national surveys of the diffusion of advanced manufacturing technologies (AMT) that further illustrate differences across countries. An overview of their results are presented in figure 2.2 which plots the proportion of firms (in their sample) using AMT. They observe that the traditionally found S shape can be observed again. The authors also note that such surveys clearly indicate that diffusion tends to start with larger plants and then to move down the firm size distribution.

To illustrate that it is not only technological innovations that follow time-intensive diffusion paths, Ruigrok et al. (1999) present some evidence on organizational innovations comparing the level of use of different innovations in 1996 and 1992. Some of their data is presented in table 2.5.

Data on intra-firm diffusion are not widely available. Table 2.6 presents Mansfield's (1968) data on the intra-firm diffusion of diesel locomotives in US railroads. One may note that Mansfield finds that the intra-firm diffusion of technologies also follows an S-shaped curve (specifically a logistic curve for Mansfield).

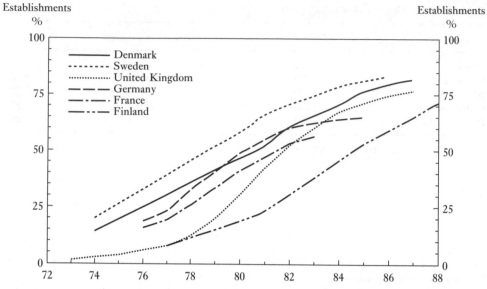

Figure 2.2   The introduction of advanced manufacturing technology
Source: Vickery and Northcott (1995, p. 259).

Table 2.5   The use of organizational innovations in Europe

	(% of sample reporting)				
Innovation	*Extensive decentralization of strategic decisions*		*Vertical R&D networking linkages*		*Internal labour market growth*
	1992	*1996*	*1992*	*1996*	*1996*
Region					
Europe	10.2	17.9	22.5	43.7	67.4
UK	8.0	13.6	16.0	38.2	57.5
German speaking	16.5	26.8	37.8	57.4	65.1
Southern	4.8	9.5	17.4	43.7	85.7
Northern	12.2	22.4	34.9	46.5	80.1

Source: Based on data reported in Ruigrok *et al.* (1999).

Table 2.6   Dieselization in US railroads: time intervals between 10 and 90 per cent usage

Time interval (years)	*Number of firms*
14 or more	3
11–13	7
8–10	11
5–7	3
3–4	6

Source: Mansfield (1968, p. 178).

Table 2.7   Utilization of computer assets by federal government agencies, 1987 and 1992

Measure	Mean		Annual growth %
	1987	1992	
Computer assets per employee ($)	1619	2623	6
No. of mainframes	11	12	0
No. of minicomputers	102	326	17
No. of PCs per employee	0.13	0.85	55
No. of terminals per employee	0.35	1.19	32

Source: Lehr and Lichtenberg (1998, p. 267).

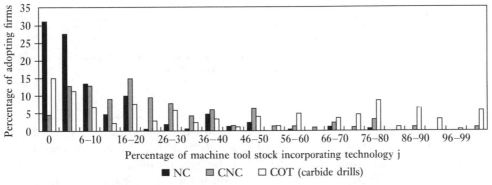

Figure 2.3   Intra-firm diffusion patterns, three technologies, 1993
Source: Stoneman and Battisti (1997, p. 272).

Lehr and Lichtenberg (1998) provide some data on computer use in federal government agencies in 1987 and 1992 illustrating that public non-market sectors also experience an intra-firm diffusion process – see table 2.7. Stoneman and Battisti (1997) also illustrate how intra-firm diffusion of a number of new technologies differed across firms in 1993 (see figure 2.3).

Overall, these empirical observations indicate that the rate of diffusion of new process technologies differs across technologies, industries, firms and nations. It is generally found, however, that the diffusion pattern follows an S-shaped curve when percentage use is plotted against time. There are also some regularities concerning the impact of profitability and firm size upon the diffusion process.

2.3.   Household Diffusion

Many of the empirical patterns found in the diffusion of new process technologies across firms are also found in the diffusion of new product technologies across households. Karshenas

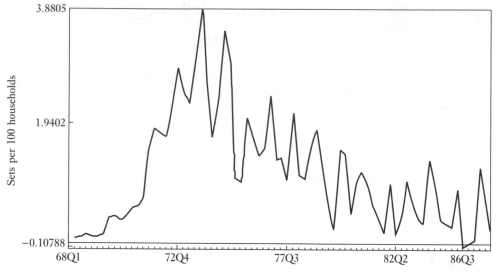

Figure 2.4   UK colour television ownership: one quarter lagged difference (percentage of households)
Source: Karshenas and Stoneman (1992, p. 589).

and Stoneman (1992) for example, illustrate the diffusion of colour television ownership in the UK. Plotting the change in the ownership of colour televisions in the UK against time they generate data as shown in figure 2.4. As can be seen, the diffusion starts slowly, then the rate of ownership increases quickly after which the rate of increase declines. The common S-shaped pattern is revealed again. Jha and Majumdar (1997) provide information on how household diffusion differs across countries. In this case they present data on the diffusion of mobile (or cellular phones) in different countries in 1992 (table 2.8). These data also reveal international differences in the diffusion of an older technology, land-line telephones. The international differences (e.g. Finland versus Austria) are marked.

2.4.   Product Innovation

It would be of interest to observe how the supply of product innovations embodying new technologies (and product differentiation) develop over the diffusion process or alternatively how the quality of products and product performance change as diffusion proceeds. Unfortunately data on indicators of the former do not seem to be available. What are available, however, and these are not quite the same thing, are (1) some indication of how the introduction of new technologies into products can develop; (2) some indicators of how the performance of products embodying new technology can develop; and (3) some indicators of how the number of suppliers of new technology develops. The third of these is considered in the next section. Vickery and Northcott (1995) provide some data upon the first by looking at the introduction of microelectronics in products. Exploring a sample of 1200 firms, their data reproduced in table 2.9 maps out the 'diffusion' of microelectronics in

Table 2.8   The diffusion of cellular phones, 1992

Country	Mainlines	Mainlines per 100 persons	Cellular subscribers	Ratio of cellular subscribers to mainlines
Australia	8,540,000	48.72	689,000	0.0807
Austria	3,466,493	43.97	172,000	0.0496
Belgium	4,264,342	42.54	65,000	0.0152
Canada	16,246,600	59.20	1,133,000	0.0697
Denmark	3,002,848	58.08	206,453	0.0688
Finland	2,742,000	54.38	359,761	0.1312
France	30,100,000	52.46	435,000	0.0145
Germany	35,400,000	43.94	982,000	0.0277
Greece	4,496,544	43.66	0	0.0000
Iceland	140,031	53.86	15,896	0.1135
Ireland	1,113,000	31.38	34,000	0.0305
Italy	23,709,000	41.03	783,011	0.0330
Japan	57,652,000	46.37	1,712,545	0.0297
Luxembourg	206,205	60.65	1,100	0.0053
Netherlands	7,395,000	48.72	166,000	0.0224
New Zealand	1,516,600	44.42	93,000	0.0613
Norway	2,268,486	52.93	292,918	0.1291
Portugal	3,014,173	30.61	37,262	0.0124
Spain	13,792,000	40.46	180,000	0.0131
Sweden	5,919,000	68.21	685,000	0.1157
Switzerland	4,184,841	60.61	215,000	0.0514
Turkey	9,471,881	16.12	61,395	0.0065
United Kingdom	26,193,130	45.28	1,445,000	0.0552
United States	143,324,900	56.14	11,032,750	0.0770

Source: Jha and Majumdar (1997, p. 28).

products (with an implicit S shape again) and figure 2.5 provides an international comparison. The data indicates that the incorporation of new technologies into products shows (again) time intensity and differences across countries.

A well-documented example of product performance development is microelectronics. Stoneman and Toivanen (1997) explore the development of a particular computer memory chip (EPROMs) and detail the history of the changing size of the chip with the best cost-performance ratio. This size increases from 1 K capacity in 1973 through 4 K (1976), 8 K (1978), 16 K (1981), 64 K (1982), 256 K (1985) and 1024 K (1990). This illustrates how the nature of the product has changed as the product matured. Such changes could be a major factor in the diffusion process.

2.5.   Market Structure

One of the issues addressed in the chapters below is the interconnection between demand and supply in the diffusion of new technology. A key factor here is the market structure of

Table 2.9 Introduction of microelectronics into products: United Kingdom, 1973–1987

	Products	
	Starting in year	*Cumulative total*
Sample base	1200	1200
1973	1.4	1.4
1974	0.3	1.7
1975	0.6	2.3
1976	1.0	3.3
1977	0.2	3.4
1978	1.2	4.6
1979	1.3	5.8
1980	2.1	7.9
1981	1.8	10.5
1982	2.3	12.8
1983	2.9	15.7
1984	2.6	18.3
1985	1.1	19.4
1986	0.6	20.0
1987	0.3	20.3

Percentages of all establishments in sample starting production during the year, and cumulative percentages.
Source: Vickery and Northcott (1995, p. 260).

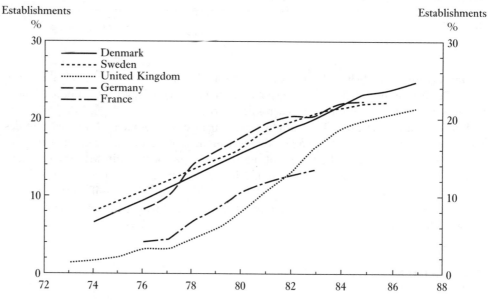

Figure 2.5 Introduction of microelectronics in products
Source: Vickery and Northcott (1995, p. 259).

the industry that supplies the new technology. One might well expect that the number of suppliers (and their size composition) will change over the lifetime of a technology. For example, Utterback (1993) has shown that in the US automobile industry in the first half of the twentieth century an early radical product innovation (the motor car) led to many new entrants to the industry and to several competing designs. However process innovation and the scaling up of production led to the emergence of a dominant robust design, mergers and bankruptcies followed and eventually an oligopolistic market structure of a few firms was established. It is further argued that this was typical of other industries as well, such as typewriters, bicycles, sewing machines, televisions and semiconductors. Sutton (1998) explores the development patterns of other industries that also reflect a similar time profile (e.g. the aircraft sector) exploring the main causal factors over time.

This pattern is not necessarily always realized. In the xerography industry, for example, there was for many years only one supplier, the Xerox Corporation, because of the patent protection that it enjoyed. Once patent protection expired there were a number of new entrants, with the industry currently being oligopolistic. In this case, however, oligopoly was approached from monopoly rather than from a position with many firms.

There is a growing literature on the evolution of industries (see for example, Gort and Klepper, 1982; Hannan and Carroll, 1992; Jovanovic and Macdonald, 1994; and Klepper, 1997). For present purposes the work of Klepper and Graddy (1990) is particularly illustrative. They explored the evolution of the number of producers of a sample of 46 new products in the US from initial commercial introduction up to 1981 with the products having initial commercial introductions from 1887 on. They characterize industry development as having three stages. In stage 1 the number of firms supplying the new product grows. This stage is defined to finish when the maximum number of producers is reached. In stage 2 there is a decline or shakeout of firms. Stage 3 is a period after the shakeout when the number of firms stabilizes. In table 2.10 the Klepper and Graddy data on the number of years spent by each industry in each of the three stages is reproduced. As can be seen, with some products the peak number of suppliers occurs very early (fluorescent lamps), whereas other products show an increasing number of suppliers for a very long period (e.g. gyroscopes and electrocardiographs). Some industries (e.g. nylon) have not reached the second stage even after many years.

In stage 1 the number of suppliers may be increasing but the rate of increase differs across industries. The average mean annual change in the number of suppliers in stage 1 is 3.8, but in some industries it is low for a long time and in yet others high for a short time. Thus, for example, in rocket engines the number of suppliers increases for 37 years at an annual average rate of 0.4, while in fluorescent lamps stage 1 only lasts two years but in those two years the number of firms increased by 32. By construction the number of suppliers changes little in stage 3, an average increase per annum of only 0.2. The extent of the shakeout in stage 2 also differs across industries, for example in tyres, of a peak number of 275 suppliers, 211 left in stage 2, whereas in shampoo, of 114 suppliers at the peak, only 5 left in stage 2.

Klepper and Graddy also go on to analyse annual average percentage changes in output in each five-year interval of life of the sample industries. On average they find that the average annual percentage rates of change, for the first six five-year periods they can identify are: 49.8, 15.5, 8.6, 3.4, 2.7, 1.9. Although this does not necessarily reflect the standard S shape of a diffusion curve it does illustrate that the fastest rates of growth are in the early years of a product's life. These rates of growth varied across industries. Whereas in the first five-year

Table 2.10 Number of years in each stage of industry life cycle

Product name	Period	Stage 1	Stage 2	Stage 3
Baseboard radiant heating	1946–1981	25	10	
Compressors, freon	1935–1981	45	1	
Computers	1935–1981	46		
Crystals, piezo	1936–1981	31	4	10
DDT	1943–1981	9	22	7
Electrocardiographs	1914–1981	50	17	
Electric blankets	1911–1981	51	13	6
Electric shavers	1930–1981	8	4	39
Engines, jet-propelled	1943–1981	21	8	9
Engines, rocket	1944–1981	37		
Fluorescent lamps	1938–1981	2	1	40
Freezers, home and farm	1929–1981	25	18	9
Gauges, beta ray	1955–1981	18	8	
Gyroscopes	1911–1981	55	15	
Lasers	1960–1981	21		
Machinery, adding and calculating	1889–1981	38	19	35
Missiles, guided	1950–1981	12	19	
Motors, outboard	1908–1981	9	6	58
Nylon	1939–1973	34		
Paints, rubber and rubber base	1933–1981	33	15	
Penicillin	1943–1981	7	23	8
Pens, ball point	1945–1981	36		
Photocopy machines	1940–1981	25	11	5
Polariscopes	1906–1981	50	11	14
Pumps, heat	1953–1981	28		
Radar	1940–1981	22	19	
Radio transmitters	1922–1981	40	13	6
Reactors, nuclear	1942–1981	22	17	
Readers, microfilm	1929–1981	49	3	
Records, phonograph	1887–1981	36	9	45
Saccharin	1906–1972	12	9	45
Shampoo	1898–1981	51	1	31
Streptomycin	1945–1981	8	19	9
Styrene	1935–1981	45	1	
Tanks, cryogenic	1959–1981	8	1	13
Tape recording	1947–1981	32	2	
Telemeters	1928–1979	34	17	
Television receivers, monochrome	1929–1973	26	18	
Tents, oxygen	1926–1981	32	23	
Tyres, automobile	1896–1981	26	10	49
Transistors	1948–1981	33		
Trees, artificial christmas	1912–1981	52	17	
Tubes, cathode ray	1922–1981	37	7	15
Turbine, gas	1936–1981	45		
Windshield wipers	1914–1981	11	9	47
Zippers	1904–1981	55	13	9
Average (across products attaining the next stage)		29.3	10.5	

Source: Klepper and Graddy (1990, p. 30).

period fluorescent lamps showed an annual percentage rate of growth of output of 107 per cent, for outboard motors it was −2.6 per cent. In the fifth five-year period rates of growth varied from 22 per cent to −36 per cent.

These data of Klepper and Graddy illustrate the evolution of industries. They show how the number of suppliers changes over time and how the actual path of evolution is different in different sectors. Although the dominant pattern is one where there is an initial phase with an increasing number of firms followed by a phase with a decreasing number then reasonable constancy, the length of these phases differs considerably across products. Moreover some industries have never reached stage 2 after a long period of time (rocket engines after 37 years) whereas others reached it quickly and did not stay long (e.g. outboard motors which spent only 15 years in stages 1 and 2 in total). There is thus considerable heterogeneity across industries even if the general pattern observed in this sample is common.

2.6.   The Pricing of New Technologies

It is commonly observed that during the diffusion process technologies become cheaper and/or improve in quality. Although this may not always be the case, the prime example must be in the computer and related industries. In Stoneman and Toivanen (1997) some quality-adjusted price series for computers and microprocessors in the UK are calculated that illustrate the point. These are reproduced in table 2.11.

Although this example may be extreme, it illustrates that such reductions in prices and improvements in quality are sufficiently significant to probably impact markedly on the diffusion process.

Further information on prices can be obtained from the Klepper and Graddy (1990) study discussed above. For their sample of 46 new products they calculate annual average percentage changes in constant dollar implicit prices (sales divided by output and then deflated by the consumer price index) for each five years of the life of a product. Their data is reproduced in table 2.12.

Although these prices are not quality adjusted, Klepper and Graddy observe that the mean average percentage change in price is generally negative but with considerable

Table 2.11   Quality-adjusted prices for computers and microprocessors in the UK, 1960–1992

Year	Computers (1972 = 100)	Microprocessors (1981 = 100)
1960	2088.2	n.a.
1965	525.0	n.a.
1970	177.9	n.a.
1975	79.2	1093.2
1980	29.7	228.1
1985	26.5	32.0
1990	12.8	4.1
1992	6.6	1.9

Source: Stoneman and Toivanen (1997, p. 116).

Table 2.12   Annual average percentage change[a] in product prices by five-year intervals[b]

Product name	Period	Order of five-year interval							
		1	2	3	4	5	6	7	8
Computers	1955–1971	−16.5	−0.8	−0.6					
Crystals, piezo	1963–1971	−9.0							
DDT	1944–1970	−26.3	−8.5	−5.1	−7.5	−3.8			
Electrocardiographs	1961–1972	9.6	−0.9						
Electric blankets	1946–1972	−4.5	−9.2	−9.7	−3.8	−2.9			
Electric shavers	1931–1972	−6.5	−1.9	−2.5	1.6	−4.0	−6.3	−4.2	−3.3
Fluorescent lamps	1938–1972	−23.5	−5.2	3.2	0.8	−0.6	−4.7	−1.9	
Freezers, home and farm	1947–1972	1.6	−0.9	−8.4	−4.6	−5.9			
Gyroscopes	1962–1972	−15.6	−3.0						
Lasers	1963–1971	−1.9							
Motors, outboard	1925–1974	4.0	−8.1	−0.3	5.9	11.2	0.2	1.7	
Nylon	1940–1971	−12.2	−6.2	−2.1	−4.7	−1.3	−4.2		
Penicillin	1945–1972	−55.7	−29.3	−1.0	−39.0	−6.8			
Pens, ball point	1951–1972	−2.2	−17.2	−3.0	−3.2				
Records, phonograph	1914–1972	−11.6	−4.5	−1.7	−1.4	−2.7	2.7	−9.0	
Streptomycin	1946–1965	−63.4	−30.6	−17.0	−18.2				
Styrene	1943–1971	−17.9	7.8	−4.5	−7.3	−9.1			
Tape, recording	1961–1972	2.9	−14.0						
Television receivers	1939–1972	−10.6	−4.4	−7.6	−2.6	−5.8	−7.5		
Tyres, automobile	1915–1972	−3.0	−4.1	−6.8	6.9	0.7	0.2	−2.5	−1.0
Transistors	1954–1972	−11.4	−18.2	−19.8	−15.1				
Tubes, cathode ray	1948–1972	−3.5	−5.3	−2.3	−6.8	−2.6			
Zippers	1920–1972	−1.8	6.7	−20.7	−2.3	−5.9	−1.5	0.8	
Average		−12.6	−8.1	−6.6	−6.0	−3.2	−2.6	−2.9	−2.2

[a] Percentage changes are computed as the first differences in logarithms.
[b] In some instances the intervals exceed five years because of the unavailability of data or because there is less than a four-year interval at the end of a product's history (in which case the residual years are included with the previous five).
Source: Klepper and Graddy (1990, p. 34).

variations across products. The annual percentage change in price is most negative in the first five years of the product's life, after which the rate of decline reduces. However, there are considerable variations across products, in 41 of 86 pair-wise comparisons between consecutive five-year intervals the percentage price fall is greater in the later period. It would not, however, be stretching reality too far to say that these data give strong support to the view that new technologies experience reductions in price over their lifetime.

2.7.   Conclusions

This chapter illustrates a number of empirical regularities (or stylized facts) relating to the diffusion process. The first of these is that the diffusion of new technologies takes time, and often a considerable period of time. This time intensity applies to the intra-firm and inter-firm diffusion of new process technologies and also the inter-household diffusion of new product technologies. It was also shown that diffusion rates differ across industries, regions (or states) and countries and also across technologies. A commonly found empirical regularity is that if one plots market penetration of a technology against time then the resulting curve is, in many cases, S shaped, illustrating a low initial rate of growth of ownership followed by faster rates up to a point of inflection after which, although still positive, rates of growth decline.

It was shown that as new technologies mature they tend to exhibit both improved performance and reduced prices. The nature of the product may also change. This is allied with and may be partly due to changes in the structure of the industries supplying new technologies. It has been illustrated how such industries tend to have their own life cycles with changing numbers of firms as the industry matures.

These observations represent a set of empirical regularities that much of the rest of this book is designed to both explain and build upon. The next part of the book begins this by considering the theory that has been developed over the last 30 years to provide such explanations.

References

Alderman, N. and Davies, S. (1990) 'Modelling Regional Patterns of Innovation in the UK Metal-working Industries', *Regional Studies*, 24(6), 513–28.

Dixon, R. (1980) 'Hybrid Corn Revisited', *Econometrica*, 58, 1451–61.

Gort, M. and Klepper, S. (1982) 'Time Paths in the Diffusion of Product Innovations', *Economic Journal*, 92, 630–53.

Griliches, Z. (1957) 'Hybrid Corn: An Exploration in the Economics of Technological Change', *Econometrica*, 48, 501–22.

Hannan, M. and Carroll, G. (1992) *Dynamics of Organisational Populations*, Oxford: Oxford University Press.

Jha, R. and Majumdar, S. (1997) *Cellular Technology Diffusion in OECD Countries and Telecommunications Sector Productivity*, mimeo, University of Michigan Business School, December.

Jovanovic, B. and Macdonald, E. (1994) 'The Life Cycle of a Competitive Industry', *Journal of Political Economy*, 102, 322–47.

Karshenas, M. and Stoneman, P. (1992) 'A Flexible Model of Technological Diffusion Incorporating Economic Factors with an Application to the Spread of Colour Television Ownership in the UK', *Journal of Forecasting*, 11, 577–601.

Klepper, S. (1997) 'Industry Life Cycles', *Industrial and Corporate Change*, 6, 145–82.

Klepper, S. and Graddy, E. (1990) 'The Evolution of New Industries and the Determinants of Market Structure', *Rand Journal of Economics*, 21(1), 27–44.

Lehr, W. and Lichtenberg, F. (1998) 'Computer Use and Productivity Growth in US Federal Government Agencies, 1987–1992', *Journal of Industrial Economics*, XLVI(2), 257–79.

Mansfield, E. (1968) *Industrial Research and Technological Innovation*, New York: Norton.

Mansfield, E. (1989) 'Industrial Robots in Japan and the USA', *Research Policy*, 18, 183–92.

Nabseth, L. and Ray, G.F. (1974) *The Diffusion of New Industrial Processes: An International Study*, Cambridge: Cambridge University Press.

Ruigrok, W., Pettigrew, A., Peck, S. and Whittington, R. (1999) 'Corporate Restructuring and New Forms of Organising: Evidence from Europe', *Management International Review*, 1999/2, 41–64.

Stoneman, P. and Battisti, G. (1997) 'Intra Firm Diffusion of New Technologies: The Neglected Part of Technology Transfer', *International Journal of Industrial Engineering*, 4(4), 270–82.

Stoneman, P. and Toivanen, O. (1997) 'The Diffusion of Multiple Technologies: An Empirical Study', *Economics of Innovation and New Technology*, 5, 1–17.

Sutton, J. (1998) *Technology and Market Structure: Theory and History*, London: MIT Press.

Utterback, J.M. (1993) *Mastering the Dynamics of Innovation*, Boston: Harvard Business School Press.

Vickery, G. and Northcott, J. (1995) 'Diffusion of Microelectronics and Advanced Manufacturing Technology: A Review of National Surveys', *Economics of Innovation and New Technology*, 3, 253–76.

Part II
The Theory of Technological Diffusion

Chapter three

The Intertemporal Demand for Stand–Alone Technologies

3.1. Introduction

This chapter initiates the discussion of the theory of technological diffusion. The diffusion patterns illustrated in the previous chapter will be the result of the interaction of the forces of both supply and demand. This chapter concentrates on the demand side leaving supply side considerations until later. This chapter also concentrates on stand-alone technologies, leaving considerations of multiple technologies and network effects until a later chapter. Here the analysis is restricted to a world without uncertainty, that again being considered in a later chapter. The material is presented in an almost historical ordering, the history being determined by the date at which approaches became part of the standard literature. The approach taken is, as far as possible, to minimize formal theorizing and mathematical content and to rely upon diagrams and verbal reasoning, although, on occasion, for future purposes some simple mathematics is used. More formal theorizing is provided in later chapters.

3.2. Epidemic Models

The earliest modelling of technological diffusion processes relied largely on the use of so-called 'epidemic' models. Such models, as their name implies, have their origins in the analysis of the spread of infectious diseases. Technology is thus being considered to spread as might an infection in a population. Early examples of such an approach are Griliches (1957) and Bain (1964) where similar models were used to explain both the diffusion of producer and household technologies.

The essence of such models is that there is assumed to exist a population of potential adopters of a given new technology that is usually taken as invariant over time. At the start of the diffusion process there will be a given number of users of the new technology. Users and non–users mix socially and make contact over time. In its simplest form the approach assumes that on making contact with a user of the technology a non–user becomes a user. Thus when a non–user meets a user the non–user also becomes a user. Over time the number of users increases and with constant mixing of the population there is a greater chance of a non-user meeting a user and becoming a user. However, over time, the number of non-users will decrease and thus the number that can convert to become users will decline. The growth in the number of users over time, resulting from an increasing probability of contact and a declining number of non-users, will generally map out an S-shaped curve over time of the number of users as a proportion of the total number of potential adopters.

A particular issue relating to this approach is: what is actually happening when a non-user meets a user that will lead to the non-user becoming a user? A common interpretation is that the contact leads to a transfer of information from the user to the non-user. For example, it could be that on meeting a user the non-user learns that the new technology exists. Then, given the knowledge of existence the non-user proceeds to acquire the technology. This has some appeal, however, as discussed above, some diffusion processes take many years, and it seems unreasonable to allow that the only reason why late adopters have not acquired a technology is because they do not know of its existence.

Alternatively, one could argue that it is not existence of the technology *per se* that is important. It could be assumed that all potential adopters know that the technology exists but knowledge of the performance characteristics of the technology is limited and it is such knowledge that is transferred through contact. Such an approach enables one to construct a more general model whereby a single contact between a user and a non-user is not of itself going to lead to adoption. One might argue that the non-user needs to meet many users before all necessary performance information is acquired and only then will he/she convert to become a user. Then a number of contacts between a non-user and users is required for a non-user to convert, or to put it alternatively, a contact with a user would only lead the non-user to adopt with a probability less than unity.

This slight variation on the simple model can be mathematically expressed as follows. Let the number of potential adopters be N and the number of adopters at time t be $M(t)$. Allow that contact between a user and a non-user is linearly related to the proportion of users in the population of potential adopters, such that in a time period individuals will make contact with $\delta M(t)/N$ users of the technology. Letting γ be the probability that contact will lead to adoption, the addition to the number of users in time t is given by

$$\mathrm{d}M(t)/\mathrm{d}t = \phi \cdot M(t)/N \cdot \{N - M(t)\} \tag{3.1}$$

where $\phi = \delta \cdot \gamma$ (the probability of 'effective contact').

Equation (3.1) is a first order differential equation which can be solved as

$$M(t) = N/(1 + \exp\{-\eta - \phi t\}) \tag{3.2}$$

which is the standard expression for a logistic curve. The time profile of diffusion processes are commonly argued (see chapter 2) to follow a logistic shape. In (3.2) the value of η defines the starting date of the diffusion process, N determines the end level of use and ϕ, commonly referred to as the diffusion speed *per se*, determines the speed of approach to the end point. The logistic curve is symmetric in that the growth rate of the number of users starts low, then increases up to a point of inflection at $0.5N$, after which it slows to approach zero asymptotically at N.

This formulation illustrates two main points about the epidemic model that make it somewhat different to other models considered below.

1   In the epidemic model the diffusion process is self-perpetuating. Use of the technology, through the contact between users and non-users, leads to further use. That use in turn stimulates even further use. The process is thus self-propagating and once started will only finish when all potential users have the technology.
2   This is a disequilibrium model. In this model the equilibrium level of use is N. Along the diffusion path, therefore, the actual level of use is always less than the equilibrium level of use. The diffusion path is in fact the path of adjustment from an initial disequilibrium point to the equilibrium or end point. The speed of adjustment is determined by the frequency of personal contact and the amount of contact required to switch a non-user to being a user.

Although most commonly used to approach issues of inter-firm or inter-household diffusion, the epidemic approach can also be used to model intra-firm (and if desired intra-household) diffusion. In such approaches a firm or household would learn from its own past experience. As experience leads to more knowledge this leads to increased use. The Mansfield (1968) model discussed in chapter 4 falls into this category.

The epidemic model has been subjected to many criticisms over the years. These may be classed into sins of commission and sins of omission. The sins of commission largely relate to the modelling of the process of interpersonal contact. The point has been made (see Davies, 1979 for example) that, as modelled, this process assumes that the population of potential adopters is homogeneous and unitary. If there are non-mixing subgroups in the population then information spreading may stop before diffusion is complete (see, for example, Karshenas and Stoneman, 1992). In addition it is being assumed that users live forever. If a user drops out of the population for some reason then his/her past adoption will not affect future adoption. Amendments can be made to the model to allow for such factors (see, for example, Zettlemeyer and Stoneman, 1993, reproduced as chapter 10, for a model with subgroups in the population) but this is only one of the many fixes that might have to be made for the model to be really acceptable.

In terms of sins of omission there are many criticisms.

1   The model as constructed assumes that interpersonal contact is the only source of information. Clearly this is very limiting. In the marketing literature the epidemic model as formulated by Bass (1969) plays a major role in diffusion analysis. It is, however, very common in that literature to include a non-endogenous information source to the model so that the diffusion process is no longer completely self-propagating (see, for example, Mahajan and Wind, 1986). Such other sources, especially advertising by suppliers, may be an important source of information about a technology. In the literature on technology transfer there is also considerable emphasis on how knowledge is embodied in individuals, and as individuals transfer from one firm to another so information spreads. This is quite a different mechanism to that being discussed in the epidemic model and will generate quite a different diffusion model (see, for example, Acemoglu, 1993).
2   The essence of the model is that information is being disseminated and driving the use of a technology. However, no clear picture is given as to what the information refers. It could be, as considered above, that potential adopters are reluctant to buy a technology

until they have more detail on the performance characteristics of that technology. But if it is such information that is being spread then why are potential buyers not actively searching for information rather than waiting to acquire it passively? If they actively seek information then a very different diffusion model should be applied (see below in the next chapter on uncertainty). Secondly, if it is information that is being passed between individuals, this implies that buyers are in a world of uncertainty. This ought to be considered explicitly.

3   In many ways the epidemic model contains no behavioural content and no explicit consideration of economic behaviour. In particular: (a) there is no explicit theory of technique choice. Kapur (1995) shows that if there are information externalities as illustrated in the epidemic story, then a rational theory of technique choice would indicate that potential buyers would rather wait until others have purchased before purchasing themselves. Such considerations do not appear in the epidemic story. (b) There is no explicit consideration as to how what is delivered from the interpersonal contact impinges upon technology choice. (c) There is no explicit consideration as to the factors that determine the number of potential adopters. As a result the number of potential adopters, N, is usually taken as predetermined and fixed. Although it is possible to construct an epidemic model in which N changes over time according to some theory of technique choice (see Chow, 1967) that is again a patch on the model rather than a formal consideration of the main underlying issue.

4   In many of the applications of this model it is assumed (often implicitly rather than explicitly) that the technology being diffused does not change over the diffusion process in terms of price or performance. As seen in chapter 2 most new technologies do get cheaper over time and also offer improved quality or performance over time. This could lead to changes in the number of potential adopters N, over time, and also change buyers' decisions on whether to adopt the technology. Such factors are not however explicitly considered in the epidemic model.

Further objections to the epidemic approach can be raised. Rather than doing so, however, one might instead note that the core of the epidemic model, that information and self-propagating information spreading processes may have some role to play in the diffusion process, should not be discarded completely. Although one may well wish to model these things in a different way this basic insight is a useful one. One might even argue that the epidemic approach may be quite appropriate to the diffusion of a cheap short-lived technology that is diffused very quickly, say a fad or fashion. It seems unlikely, however, that it is going to provide a full explanation of the long-term diffusion of an important household or industrial technology.

The following sections therefore consider alternative modelling frameworks. These frameworks differ from the epidemic approach in a number of ways. The first difference is that each includes an explicit theory of technology choice, that is, the acquisition decision of individuals is explicitly considered and modelled. In each case the gain from acquisition, be it profit (for the firm) or utility gain (for the household) is compared to the cost of acquiring the technology in the modelling of the acquisition decision. At each moment in time the number of users of the technology is determined as that number for whom there is a net gain from acquisition. The models thereby generated are thus equilibrium models as opposed to the disequilibrium epidemic model. In addition, in these alternative models the diffusion process is not self-propagating. Diffusion proceeds as the equilibrium level of use changes. However the change in the equilibrium level of use will result from exogenous stimuli rather than endogenous forces (although when the supply side is added one may be able to endogenize some of these exogenous influences). The various models discussed largely differ in terms of how the benefits from adoption are determined.

3.3.   The Probit or Rank Approach

Putting aside any issues relating to knowledge or information upon a technology, consider that all firms or households (depending on the type of technology being discussed) know of the existence of a technology. Let the population be of size N. Within the population, for reasons to be discussed further below, allow that there is heterogeneity, so that different members of the population would get different benefits if they acquired the technology. This heterogeneity is shown in figure 3.1 as a frequency distribution of gross benefit of acquisition, B, plotted against population proportion. The bell shape plotted is one of many possible shapes but is commonly seen or hypothesized.

An individual considering acquisition of the technology will compare gross benefit against the cost of acquisition (the exact definition of this cost is considered further below). Any theory of technique choice (in the absence of uncertainty) will predict that the acquirer will buy the technology if the gross benefit is greater than the cost. Let the cost of acquisition in time t be $c(t)$, which is assumed to be the same for all members of the population (which is reasonable, if for the moment, one considers that each member of the population would only ever acquire the same number of units of the technology). The acquisition rule is thus that the technology is acquired if $B(t) \geq c(t)$. In terms of figure 3.1, the proportion of the population for whom $B(t) \geq c(t)$ in time t is equal to the area under the frequency distribution to the right of $c(t)$, labelled $m(t)$, and thus the level of use or ownership of the technology in time t will be $M(t) = m(t) \cdot N$.

However, this is not yet a diffusion model. Thus far the model only establishes what proportion of the population will own the technology in time t. To generate a diffusion path one needs to generate changes in $M(t)$ over time. Such changes can come about in two ways:

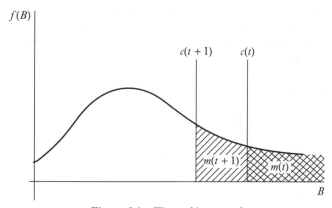

Figure 3.1   The probit approach

(1) the most common argument is that the cost of acquisition, $c(t)$, changes over time; (2) less commonly discussed, although just as feasible, is for the gross benefits (or at least perceived gross benefits) from adoption to change over time. For the model to produce increasing levels of use it is necessary that the cost of acquisition falls and/or the benefits increase over time. If the cost of acquisition rises over time (or benefits decrease) then the level of use may well fall. However, declining technologies are rarely analysed in diffusion studies. Moreover it is generally argued that investment in new technologies may well be irreversible, at least in the short term, and in such circumstances the only effect of a rising cost of acquisition will be that diffusion ceases but does not go into reverse.

In terms of figure 3.1 if the cost of acquisition in $t + 1$, $c(t + 1)$ is less than $c(t)$, the number of users will increase to $M(t + 1) = m(t + 1) \cdot N$. As $c(t)$ declines or benefits increase with time, a diffusion path for $M(t)$ will be mapped out.

As can be clearly seen from the figure, the shape of the diffusion path (plotting $M(t)$ against time) will depend on the shape of the benefit distribution, how that distribution shifts over time and the time path of $c(t)$. The speed of diffusion will thus depend upon both the rate of change of benefits and costs. Any final level of use will be determined by where benefits and costs stop changing. One may also note that, obviously, if all users have the same cost of acquisition at a point in time, then the early users of the technology are the ones that would get the greatest gross benefit from its use whereas the later users are the ones that get the least gross benefit. Finally, one may note that different technologies, or the same technologies in different populations will show different diffusion curves if the benefit distributions are different or the time path of acquisition costs is different.

This framework, generally labelled the probit model (because of its affinity to other probit models in the economics literature such as models of unemployment) or the rank model (because the population can be ranked in terms of the benefits from adoption), needs more flesh to be added to be fully appreciated. Consider first the benefits from adoption.

3.3.1. Benefits from adoption

Consider a firm for whom the new technology is a process innovation. Allow that by introducing this process innovation the production costs of the firm will be reduced. This cost reduction will yield an increase in gross profits. The new technology generally will have a life longer than a single time period and as such the profit increase will last for a number of years. Although the technology may become physically obsolescent and need replacing at some date necessitating a further acquisition cost, it is simpler, and not misleading, to set aside issues of physical obsolescence and thus assume that any technology acquired will have an infinite physical life. In the absence of the technology being superseded by a newer, better technology (economic obsolescence) the present value in time t of acquiring the technology at time t, $V(t, t)$, will be the discounted sum of the annual profit gains from adoption. Define the expected annual profit gain in time τ from the adoption of technology in time t as $\Pi(t, \tau)$, $t < \tau$. Defining r as the discount rate then yields

$$V(t, t) = \int_{\tau = t}^{\infty} \Pi(\tau, t) \exp(-r\tau) d\tau \tag{3.3}$$

Of course there is always the possibility that the technology could be made obsolescent by further technological changes. If one allows that the chance of this happening in any time period is a constant, then by an appropriate redefinition of r, the discount rate, to incorporate the constant hazard rate that economic obsolescence might occur in a given time period, this formulation can include obsolescence (see Ireland and Stoneman, 1986). However if one wishes to be more refined and allow that as time proceeds there is an increasing probability of economic obsolescence then a more sophisticated approach would be necessary.

A basic requisite of the rank model is that $\Pi(t, \tau)$ is not affected by the number of users or acquirers of the technology either at the date of acquisition or at any time t (such possibilities are considered in other frameworks below). It is, however, possible that the profit gain from adoption might be different in different periods (i.e. different τ) because of different macroeconomic or market conditions. Life is made considerably simpler if one assumes that for a given firm, $\Pi(\tau, t)$ is a constant for each year τ after adoption has occurred. This formulation will still allow that prior to adoption technology could be improving and thus the potential profit gain increasing, but once adoption has occurred the firm is locked into the technology purchased and would not benefit from further improvements. Let the benefit to the firm be fixed in this way so that $\Pi(\tau, t) = \Pi(t)$, then the present value in time t of adopting the technology in time t may be simply written as

$$V(t, t) = \Pi(t)/r \tag{3.4}$$

Consider now why the gross benefit of adoption, that is $V(t, t)$, may differ across firms. In general the reason is that firms are different and thus will be able to get different profit gains from a technology. Particular examples of factors that might affect the returns from adoption would be:

1 *Location.* Some geographical sites are preferred to others and may suit certain technologies better than others – for example, for water power, sites with fast flowing streams are preferred. In addition factor prices for inputs, say wage rates, may differ across locations.
2 *Previous investments.* Some firms may have older existing technology, some may have newer. The potential gain from the latest technology may be less for those who have only recently changed technology than for those with much older capital equipment. Some firms may also have technologically complementary technologies in place that enable them to better exploit the new. Some firms may have experience in the new technology others may not.
3 *Other inputs.* Some firms may have better management than others and are able to work the new technology more productively. Other inputs into the firm (such as skilled labour) may also be better. Firms that do R&D and acquire much information may be better able to use new technology (see, for example, Cohen and Levinthal, 1989).
4 *Market factors.* Some firms may be operating on buoyant or growing markets some may be operating on declining markets. The former are likely to generate greater returns.
5 *Organizational factors.* Some firms may be more bureaucratic than others. Some may have a more appropriate organizational form.
6 *Expectations.* The concept of annual profit gains is forward looking and as such firms with buoyant expectations may see larger profit gains than firms with pessimistic expectations. Similarly, as the annual expected profit gain will depend on the performance of

the technology at the date it is installed, firms may have different estimates of the expected profit gains to be realized from installation at different dates depending on their views of how the technology will improve.

Equation (3.4) contains a term in r, the discount rate. Just as characteristics may differ across firms, so the discount rate may also differ across firms. It has already been argued that r might include an allowance for the possibility of technological obsolescence and as such firms that consider obsolescence more likely will have a higher discount rate and thus a lower expected present value from adoption and will be less likely to adopt. However firms may also face different discount rates for other reasons:

1   One possibility is that the discount rate will reflect risk aversion. Strictly, this is a world of certainty, but uncertainty is sometimes introduced simply by considering that greater uncertainty means a higher discount rate.
2   Firms may have different access to finance. Firms having difficulty raising finance may have to pay higher interest rates implying higher discount rates and as such be less likely to adopt. Other firms may borrow cheaply and easily implying lower discount rates and a greater probability of adoption. It is quite possible that large, or at least successful and profitable firms, will be of this kind. It is, however, quite rare in theory modelling to consider how financial factors might impinge on the diffusion process, but this is one simple way to do so. Santarelli (1995) and Goodacre and Tonks (1995) are interesting places to look for a further discussion of finance and technological change.

Clearly there are many factors that can impinge upon the return to the firm from acquisition. In the literature, however (see, for example, David, 1969 and Davies, 1979) one factor stands out as of major importance – firm size. It is usually considered that larger size yields greater returns. Sometimes this is because firm size is considered as a proxy for other factors (on the basis that good firms that are going to get a high return will be successful firms and therefore large) but it might also be considered as indicative of returns to scale.

There are two potential concepts of size that are relevant. The first is size immediately prior to adoption of the technology and the second is size after the adoption of the technology, it being possible that by adopting the new technology the firm takes market share from its rivals and becomes larger. However, as stated above, this particular modelling approach rules out any feedback from adoption by the firm on its own characteristics and thus profit gains and as such only size at the date of adoption is considered.

Letting firm size (output) at the date of adoption be written as $Q(t)$, and all other firm characteristics (at time t) that impinge upon the determination of profit gains be represented by the vector $\mathbf{C(t)}$ a reasonable summary of the literature on the determinants of the gross benefits to adoption would be given by (3.5) below.

$$V(t, t) = \Pi(t, Q(t), \mathbf{C(t)})/r \tag{3.5}$$

Building on this discussion of the determinants of net benefits it is not difficult to see why the benefit distribution might change over time. How market conditions might change, or how the technology might improve have been referred to above. It could also be that discount or interest rates change or firm characteristics change or expectations change. In particular firm sizes may increase (or decline) as firms in an industry grow (or decline). In fact firm sizes may change over time in such a way that the whole benefit distribution not only shifts but also changes shape.

3.3.2.   Costs of adoption

Having discussed the benefits of adoption, now consider the cost side. The main cost that is usually discussed in such diffusion models is the price that has to be paid to acquire new capital goods that embody the new technology. Let the cost of one unit of the technology in time t be $P(t)$. In many variants of this modelling framework it is often assumed that the firm only needs to buy one unit of the technology to equip all its production. This is a useful simplification with which to proceed. In this case, ignoring any other costs, one may define the net present value in time t of the benefits of adopting the technology in time t, $NV(t, t)$ as

$$NV(t, t) = V(t, t) - P(t) = \Pi(t)/r - P(t) \tag{3.6}$$

In early versions of the probit model it was then considered that the firm would acquire the new technology in time t (if it had not acquired at an earlier date) if the net present value of adoption was positive – if $\Pi(t) \geq rP(t)$ i.e. if the annual profit gain from adoption is greater than the annual cost of having the technology. Such a condition is, however, only a necessary and not a sufficient condition.

Consider a world in which the cost of acquiring a technology is falling over time and thus $P(t + 1) < P(t)$. In such a world a potential purchaser of the technology may find it worthwhile to adopt the technology in time t, but even more worthwhile to adopt the technology in time $t + 1$ when the cost of buying the technology is lower. Any person who has considered investment in a personal computer cannot fail to have thought about waiting until some later date before committing to purchase in order to take advantage of lower expected prices.

In fact there are two conditions that have to be met for adoption in time t:

1   It must be profitable to adopt in time t, that is the net present value of adoption must be positive.
2   It must not be more profitable to postpone until a date later than t.

These are called the profitability and arbitrage conditions (see Ireland and Stoneman, 1986). The first condition requires that

$$\Pi(t) \geq rP(t) \tag{3.7}$$

The second condition is most simply stated if one allows that the potential adopter is only considering a one-year horizon (rather than all future time) and is thus comparing the net benefits of acquiring today compared to the benefits of acquiring one period ahead. The net present value in time t of acquiring in time t will be $V(t, t)$. The net present value in time t of acquiring in time $t + 1$ will be $V(t, t + 1)$ where $V(t, t + 1)$ will be equal to $V(t + 1, t + 1)$ discounted back to time t, that is

$$V(t, t + 1) = (V(t + 1, t + 1))/(1 + r) \tag{3.8}$$

For the arbitrage condition to be satisfied it is thus necessary that

$$\Pi(t)/r - P(t) \geq (\Pi^e(t + 1)/r - P^e(t + 1))/(1 + r) \tag{3.9}$$

where $\Pi^e(t + 1)$ is the expectation at time t of the annual profit gain to be realized if adoption takes place in time $t + 1$ and $P^e(t + 1)$ is the expected cost at time t of buying the technology in time $t + 1$.

The arbitrage condition can be tidied to yield

$$\Pi(t) - rP(t) \geq \Pi^e(t + 1)/r - P^e(t + 1) - (\Pi(t)/r - P(t))$$
$$= (\Pi^e(t + 1)/r - \Pi(t)/r) - P^e(t + 1) + P(t) \tag{3.10}$$

that is, the firm will wish to acquire in time t rather than time $t + 1$ if the extra gain from having the technology a year early, $\Pi(t) - rP(t)$, is greater than the benefit of waiting $(\Pi^e(t + 1)/r - \Pi(t)/r) - P^e(t + 1) + P(t)$, that is, the gain in present value that comes from generating a higher annual gross profit gain or paying a lower price for the technology.

If $\Pi^e(t + 1) = \Pi(t)$ and $P^e(t + 1) = P(t)$ then the arbitrage and profitability conditions coincide. Thus if buyers are completely myopic (i.e. they expect today's prices and returns to hold in all future periods), the profitability condition is both necessary and sufficient to determine the number of adopters. If the annual profit gain is increasing with the date of adoption, $\Pi^e(t + 1) > \Pi(t)$, and/or the cost of buying the technology is falling with the date of adoption $P^e(t + 1) < P(t)$ (so $- P^e(t + 1) + P(t)$ is always positive) then the arbitrage condition is the binding condition determining the date of adoption (with the profitability condition binding in the opposite case). Given that one expects in most cases that the performance of new technology will improve with time and/or its purchase price will decline with time, in most cases the arbitrage condition will be the dominant condition and it is on this case that the following concentrates.

Using the arbitrage condition it is now possible to be explicit as to exactly what is meant in the early part of this section by the comparison of costs and benefits of adoption. Using the arbitrage condition, the firm will adopt the new technology in time t iff

$$\Pi(t) \geq rP(t) + \Pi^e(t + 1)/r - \Pi(t)/r - P^e(t + 1) + P(t) \tag{3.11}$$

that is, the firm will adopt the technology in time t if the annual profit gain (assumed constant post adoption i.e. for all $\tau > t$) from adoption in time t is greater than the annual interest cost $rP(t)$ plus the expected gain from waiting until the next time period before adoption. The right-hand side of this expression may then be considered as the appropriate definition of $c(t)$, the cost of adoption, in the earlier part of this section.

On this basis it is clear that the use of the technology in time t will depend upon expected annual profit gains, expected changes in gross profit gains to be realized through waiting, the cost of buying the technology in time t and expected changes therein. As discussed above (apart from the cost of buying the technology in time t) all these may differ across firms and thus at any moment in time some firms may be adopters and others may not.

In presenting this formulation it was assumed that in order to acquire the technology each firm had to buy only one unit of the technology. This is an extreme assumption. It would be more reasonable to assume that the number of units of the technology required by the firm to equip all its production would be related to the output of the firm. For example, allowing that the number of units of technology required per unit of output is α, and that output in time t is $Q(t)$, then to equip the whole firm the total purchase cost would be $\alpha Q(t)P(t)$. The analysis above can then be adapted to allow for this.

However, proceeding in this way assumes that when the technology is acquired the firm equips all of its production with the new technology at the same time. In fact it was shown in chapter 2 that most firms experience an intra-firm diffusion process whereby acquisition is spread over time. Within the model discussed here there are no particular factors that would generate a time intensive intra-firm diffusion process. Such factors are discussed later in this chapter. For present purposes therefore, assume that firms equip their whole production process at one time, and thus take the acquisition cost for the firm (i.e. the cost of purchasing the capital goods embodying the new technology) as $\alpha Q(t)P(t)$.

3.3.3. Costs and benefits

The benefits to a firm from ownership of the technology may be summarized by equation (3.5). Setting aside differences between firms other than size, the annual profit gain from adoption, $\Pi(t)$, is given by $\Pi(t, Q(t))$, which for simplicity is written as (3.12):

$$\Pi(t, Q(t)) = A(t)Q(t)^{\beta} \tag{3.12}$$

where $A(t)$ is a time shifter and β is usually considered ≥ 1. Substituting into the arbitrage condition (3.11) for both the cost of acquisition $\alpha Q(t)P(t)$ and the annual profit gain from (3.12) yields that the firm will acquire the technology in time t, iff (3.13) holds.

$$A(t)Q(t)^{\beta} \geq r\alpha Q(t)P(t) + A(t+1)Q(t+1)^{\beta}/r - A(t)Q(t)^{\beta}/r$$
$$- \alpha Q(t)P^e(t+1) + \alpha Q(t)P(t) \tag{3.13}$$

where $Q(t+1)$ is the expected output of the firm in time $t+1$ (if it does not adopt the technology in time t). To make life simple, assume that the firm does not expect its output to change over time and thus $Q(t) = Q(t+1) = Q$. Condition (3.13) may then be written as that the firm will adopt the technology in time t iff (3.14) holds

$$Q \geq \{(r\alpha P(t) - \alpha P^e(t+1) + \alpha P(t))/(A(t) - A(t+1)/r - A(t)/r)\}^{1/\beta} \tag{3.14}$$

Labelling the right hand side of (3.14) as a critical or threshold value of Q, $Q^*(t)$, if in time t the firm has output greater than $Q^*(t)$ it will be a user of the technology in time t and if its output is less than $Q^*(t)$ it will not be a user in time t. The determinants of the critical value of Q are the technological requirements of the technology (α), the cost per unit of the technology and expected changes therein ($P(t)$ and $P^e(t+1)$), the payoff from the technology, $A(t)$ and changes therein, and the discount rate.

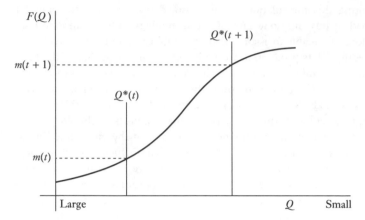

Figure 3.2   Firm size distribution

Following a similar model commonly used (e.g. Davies, 1979), allow that the size distribution of firms in an industry is represented by some bell-shaped distribution (say a log normal). In figure 3.2 the cumulative distribution of firm sizes is plotted with firm size measured largest to smallest on the horizontal axis. At time t all firms of a size greater than $Q^*(t)$ will be users of the technology. As time proceeds, the cost of acquiring the technology $P(t)$ may well reduce, the performance of the technology as represented by $A(t)$ may well increase, and also expected changes in performance and price may change. This will generate changes in $Q^*(t)$ and thus changes in the level of use. In figure 3.2 such changes are mapped out by $m(t)$ and the number of users of the technology by $M(t) = m(t) \cdot N$. As long as $Q^*(t)$ is falling over time, the diffusion of the technology will proceed.[1]

3.3.4.   Household technologies

The above discussion has largely referred to firms acquiring a new process technology. The model can, however, be simply extended to the diffusion of a household technology. In this case potential adopters will be maximizing their utility and choosing that date of adoption when the net utility gain is greatest. Households will differ in terms of preferences, discount rates, expectations and income. A reasonably standard rank model of household diffusion would consider income as the main characteristic of interest and, by letting income play the role for households that firm size plays for firms, generate a diffusion model similar to that immediately above for the firm (see, for example, Bonus, 1973). A rank type consumer diffusion model is used by Stoneman and Battisti (2000), reproduced below as chapter 15, with the interesting property that the model predicts the logistic diffusion curve that is usually found in epidemic models.

Whether one is talking of households or firms, however, this approach can be taken a step further. In the discussion it was implicitly assumed that firms (or households) acquired the technology by buying a capital good that embodies the technology (e.g. a robot production line or a washing machine). This may be too simple minded. When firms acquire new technology they may need to invest in labour training, they may need to adjust other production activities, vary their organizational form or in general incur additional expenditures to the straight purchase cost. The probit framework can be adapted to allow for such factors (see for example, Stoneman, 1990) by redefining Π as net of such costs and proceeding as before. The model can thus be made even richer than presented above.

3.3.5. *Product differentiation*

Thus far it has been implicitly considered that the technology available at a point in time is homogeneous and available at a common price with common performance (although different payoffs) to all the population. It may well be that at a moment in time the technology is available in many different forms – that is, there is product differentiation.[2] Thus, for example, with household technologies there may be washing machines available with different spin speeds, different load capacities, with and without dryers and so on. For the firm at a moment in time there may be computers with many different configurations available. This section addresses how such differentiation is going to impact on the diffusion path.

Economics distinguishes two types of product differentiation – horizontal and vertical (see, for example, Ireland, 1987). Consider the former first. In a heterogeneous population two products are considered horizontally differentiated if at a common price some buyers prefer one variant whereas other buyers prefer the other variant. The different preferences may reflect tastes for households or characteristics for firms.

For the sake of the argument assume that buyers are myopic (and thus expectations may be ignored) and that all differences between potential buyers can be modelled in a simple way. In particular, assume that each buyer places the same value upon a product as every other buyer when that product exactly matches his/her own preferences or requirements. However, as different buyers have different preferences or requirements different product variants are valued differently by different buyers. Allow that the requirements or preferences of buyers are equally distributed around a unit circle.

At this stage it is useful to consider an analogy. Think of potential buyers of a uniform type of ice cream who are equidistantly placed around a lake (figure 3.3). Each has the same

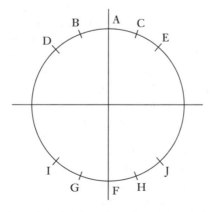

Figure 3.3 Horizontal product differentiation

implicit valuation of ice-cream but the further they are from a supplier the greater is the distance to be travelled to acquire an ice-cream. The full cost of buying an ice-cream is thus the purchase price plus the travel cost. The analogy is that potential purchasers of a new technology consider the cost of buying a particular variant upon the market as the price to be paid plus the valuation of the extent to which the variant does not completely meet their needs. Alternatively one might think that buyers of a technology will adapt that technology to meet their needs. The cost of adaptation would be equivalent to the travel costs.

Let a single product variant be available upon the market in location A (figure 3.3) at a price $P(t)$. At this price some potential buyers (in the arc BAC) who have preferences or requirements close to those of the variant on offer will buy the technology. As the price falls those with preferences less close to the model variant (in the arc DAE) will also become buyers in a manner similar to that considered above. Let there now be two product variants upon the market located at A and F both offered at price $P(t)$. At this price the number of buyers will be double that when there was only one variant, for those buyers with preferences or requirements around F (in the arc GFH) will find that the total cost of purchase ($P(t)$ plus travel costs) is less than when only A was on the market. Clearly it is not only the price of the technology that affects the demand for the technology but also the extent to which the technologies available match preferences or requirements. It can thus be argued that if there are many differentiated products on the market there is likely to be a higher demand for the technology. Also, if during the diffusion process, more differentiated variants of the product are launched this differentiation is likely to advance the extent of use of the technology.

Vertical product differentiation is rather different. Two products are considered vertically differentiated in a heterogeneous population if all members of the population have the same quality ordering for these products. In many ways the modelling above has assumed that over time as technology improves it improves in a vertically differentiated way. This year's technology is considered by all to offer higher quality than last year's technology. However, one can use the concept of vertical product differentiation to illustrate further. If two vertically differentiated products are available on the market it will be agreed that one is of higher quality than the other. The high quality one will be of higher price than the low quality. Potential purchasers may have different incomes or preferences that cause some to demand the high quality product and some the low quality product. If only the high quality product, say, were on the market, some purchasers may not demand that product because of preferences or too low resources (income). The addition of the low quality product increases the demand for the product class in total. One can see again that the more quality variants on the market the greater is the demand. Also, if over time more differentiated products are being placed on the market, *ceteris paribus*, diffusion will extend.

By way of an example one might think of firms buying computers. If the only machines available were very expensive, large and of military quality only large firms with considerable resources or vital computing need would acquire them. However, if smaller, cheaper 'lower quality' machines were to become available, other firms may well acquire such machines (while the initial buyers stuck to the higher quality model) and as such the usage of the technology will extend. The point is that the lower quality machine need not offer a lower quality adjusted price, it may have a higher quality adjusted price. It is that the lower quality machine is more suited to the needs and preferences of different buyers.

3.3.6.   Intra-firm diffusion

The emphasis so far in this section has been on the inter-firm or inter-household diffusion of new technology. It is also possible to construct an intra-firm model of diffusion based upon rank principles. The purpose is to illustrate why different firms have different rates of intra-firm diffusion. The approach here is built upon Battisti (1999).

In the neoclassical theory of investment one assumes that the firm faces a production function with output (Q) as a function of capital input K and labour input L, ($Q = AK^{\alpha}L^{1-\alpha}$) with given output prices $p(t)$, wage rates $w(t)$, discount rates/interest rates $r(t)$, and a cost of buying capital goods $P(t)$. The profit maximizing firm will demand capital to the point where (3.15) holds

$$K^*(t) = \alpha p(t)Q(t)/c(t) \tag{3.15}$$

where $c(t)$ is the user cost of capital defined, in the absence of depreciation as

$$c(t) = r(t)P(t) - dP(t)/dt \cdot (1/P(t)) \tag{3.16}$$

that is, the annual interest cost less capital gains.

To construct a theory of intra-firm diffusion one may allow that there are two types of capital goods, the new and the old, labelled with N and O subscripts. The production function is then rewritten as (3.17)

$$Q = AK_N^{\alpha N}K_O^{\alpha O}L^{1-\alpha} \tag{3.17}$$

allowing both old and new technologies to contribute to production. One may then specify demand for each type of capital as (3.18) and (3.19)

$$K_N^*(t) = \alpha_N p(t)Q(t)/c_N(t) \tag{3.18}$$

$$K_O^*(t) = \alpha_O p(t)Q(t)/c_O(t) \tag{3.19}$$

where N and O are used as subscripts for the two types of capital goods. A simple measure of intra-firm diffusion is given by $K_N(t)/(K_O(t) + K_N(t))$ which using (3.18) and (3.19) yields (3.20)

$$K_N(t)/(K_O(t) + K_N(t)) = \alpha_N/c_O(t)/\alpha_N/c_N(t) + \alpha_O/c_O(t)$$
$$= \alpha_N c_O(t)/(\alpha_N c_O(t) + \alpha_O c_N(t)) \tag{3.20}$$

From (3.20), the extent of the use of the new technology by the firm will be driven by the user cost of capital. As the user cost for the new technology falls (or the old increases) so the proportion of the capital stock that is new increases and intra-firm diffusion proceeds. Differences between firms in an industry in the extent of the use of the technology will be related to the different values of α_N and α_O that one may expect in firms of different characteristics. Empirical analysis of such a model is to be found in Battisti (1999).

3.3.7.   Overview of the rank model

The rank or probit model of diffusion is rich and can be made richer. It has been shown that the model is built upon rational profit maximizing or utility maximizing behaviour. It includes an explicit theory of technique choice. The model is not self-propagating. Instead it is a model in which at each point in time there is an equilibrium number of owners (or level of use) of new technology, that equilibrium is assumed to be established at each date, but over time exogenous factors change this equilibrium number and trace out the diffusion path. The analysis above has shown that factors that impinge on the diffusion path are (1) firm characteristics widely defined to include size, location, history and so on; (2) discount rates and attitudes to risk; (3) price, technology and market expectations; (4) the number of product variants on the market; and (5) changes in all the above.

In a later chapter attempts that have been made to endogenize some of these influences through the addition of the supply side are discussed. Before doing that, however, here an alternative diffusion model is considered. In the rank model, as emphasized above, it is necessary to assume that the return to a firm from adopting a new technology is independent of its own use and the number of other users of that technology. For reasons discussed below, this is difficult to accept as always reasonable and as such alternative diffusion models have been proposed in which relaxing this assumption actually generates the diffusion path.

3.4.   The Stock Model, Schumpeter and Evolutionary Economics

When a firm installs a new process technology one might expect that technology to impact on (reduce) its costs. That reduction in costs may lead to a change in the price charged for its products and thus in its output levels and also the output levels of other firms in the industry. The inclusion of such reasoning into the diffusion story would impact in two ways on the previous probit or rank framework. First, as the benefits that the firm will obtain from new technology may well depend upon its output levels, such benefits will be related to output levels after adoption, which may well differ from the output level at the time of adoption considered previously. Secondly, the firm's output level will be dependent on the adoption behaviour of other firms. In determining the gain from adoption, the relevant comparison therefore is between the firm's profits having adopted the new technology and the firm's profits without the new technology (when other firms may well adopt). If a firm is operating in an industry when other firms are adopting the new technology and it is not, that firm's profits may well be falling over time rather than staying at a constant level as implicitly implied in the previous framework. A variety of modelling approaches have been developed that incorporate such reasoning. We consider three such approaches. The first is attributable in general terms to Reinganum (1981) but see also Quirmbach (1986), the second to Schumpeter (1984) and the third to the Evolutionary School.

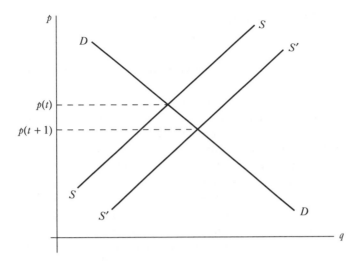

Figure 3.4   The stock model of diffusion

3.4.1.   *The Reinganum model*

Following the Reinganum approach, assume that prior to initiation of the diffusion process all firms are the same in terms of output, characteristics and costs and that all firms have perfect information regarding the technology. Also assume that firms are myopic in their expectations (this is not crucial but makes the presentation easier). More real world expectations formulations could be introduced into this framework without changing the essence of the approach. Let the new technology reduce the costs of the firm.

In figure 3.4 let DD be the industry demand curve and SS the industry supply curve. Industry price will be established at $p(t)$ in time t where demand and supply intersect. As firms in the industry adopt the new technology and generate lower (marginal) costs the industry supply curve will shift downwards. Thus the position of the supply curve is dependent on the extent of use of the technology in time t, $M(t)$. As $M(t)$ increases, the industry price will fall. This change in industry price with increasing use is the key to understanding the stock model.

Let the old technology generate cost per unit of output of c_0 and the new technology costs per unit of output c_1. The annual profits of a user of old technology in time t will thus be

$$\Pi_0(t) = (p(t) - c_0)q_0(t)$$

and the profit of a user of new technology will be

$$\Pi_1(t) = (p(t) - c_1)q_1(t)$$

where $q_1(t)$ and $q_0(t)$ are the outputs of the firm in time t with and without the new technology and dependent upon $p(t)$ and costs. The profit difference between a user and a non-user in time t will thus be

$$\Pi_1(t) - \Pi_0(t) = (p(t) - c_1)q_1(t) - (p(t) - c_0)q_0(t)$$
$$= p(t)(q_1(t) - q_0(t)) - c_1q_1(t) - c_0q_0(t)$$

Given that the new technology is superior to the old, $c_1 < c_0$ and thus $q_1(t) > q_0(t)$ and so $\Pi_1(t) - \Pi_0(t) > 0$.

As the number of users increases along the diffusion path $p(t)$ will fall over time. As it does so two things happen. First the profits of a non-user decline and second the profits of a user also decline. Under certain conditions relating to the shape of the demand curve,[3] which are assumed to hold, the profits of a user fall faster than the profits of a non-user and as such the difference in profits also decline. Thus as diffusion proceeds the difference in profits between a user and a non-user gets smaller.

As the decision to install a new technology is an investment decision, that decision will be dependent upon the present value of profit gains rather than the annual profit gain *per se*. Allowing that the technology has an infinite physical life, defining a discount rate r, adjusted if necessary to account for potential economic obsolescence, the present value of the profit streams for a firm adopting in time t and a non-adopter at time t are given by

$$V_1(t, t) = \int_{\tau=t}^{\infty} \Pi_1(\tau, t)\exp(-r\tau)d\tau$$

and

$$V_0(t, t) = \int_{\tau=t}^{\infty} \Pi_0(\tau, t)\exp(-r\tau)d\tau$$

The present value of the profit stream depends, as can be seen, on the whole time profile of the number of users over the life of the technology, for as the number of users increases annual profits decline. However, for the sake of simplicity, let us assume that potential buyers of the new technology hold myopic expectations, thus at time τ for all $\tau > t$, they expect the number of users ($M(t)$) at that point in time to be the same at as time t. As the profits realized in time $\tau > t$ depend on the number of users at that point in time, they will thus expect that for all $\tau > t$ the profits they generate will be the same. One may then write the profits for users and non-users to be

$$\Pi_1(\tau, t) = \Pi_1(M(t))$$
$$\Pi_0(\tau, t) = \Pi_0(M(t))$$

which yields that

$$V_1(t, t) - V_0(t, t) = (\Pi_1(M(t)) - \Pi_0(M(t)))/r$$

and upon the basis of the discussion above this is declining in $M(t)$. Figure 3.5 plots the curves of $V_1(t, t)$, $V_0(t, t)$ and $V_1(t, t) - V_0(t, t)$ against $M(t)$ assuming linearity. One may note that the last of these curves is rather similar to that seen in the probit model. Benefits to the adopter are plotted against the number of users. However, the underlying story here

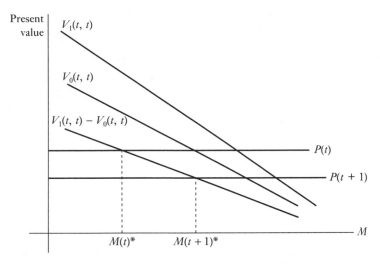

Figure 3.5 Profit gains in the stock model

is very different. There, benefits differed because firms were different. Here, benefits differ because the profits vary as the number of users changes. Given the present value of the gross benefits from adoption one may now compare these with the costs of acquisition ($P(t)$). Again one could include non-myopic expectations (and this would lead as above to consideration of profitability and arbitrage conditions) but for the sake of simplicity, assume that firms have myopic expectations on the cost of acquisition. Then the firm will acquire the technology in time t iff

$$V_1(t, t) - V_0(t, t) = (\Pi_1(M(t)) - \Pi_0(M(t)))/r \geq P(t)$$

In terms of figure 3.5, the number of firms for whom adoption at or by time t is profitable is given by $M(t)^*$.

$M(t)^*$ is the equilibrium number of firms for whom adoption at or by time t is profitable. If $M^*(t) + 1$ firms adopt the technology then all or some would not achieve an increase in net present value. If less than $M(t)^*$ firms adopt, then more firms could profitably adopt. Without discussing how $M(t)^*$ is established it is assumed that the number of adopters at or by time t is given by $M(t)^*$. One may note that as all firms are the same, one cannot say which firms in the industry adopt first and which adopt later.

This reasoning establishes the number of users of the technology in time t. To generate a diffusion path it is necessary to have some external forces impacting. These external forces can impact on either profits (e.g. the quality of the technology) or on the cost of acquisition. The simplest approach is to argue that $P(t)$ will fall over time. As it does so a diffusion path will be mapped out. The lower cost of acquisition means that more firms can profitably adopt.

This model is basically saying, therefore, that as adoption proceeds the profit gain from adoption (comparing profits with and without the new technology) falls. At any moment in time this means that it is not profitable for all firms to adopt. The number of adopters is limited by comparing profit gains to the cost of adoption. As the cost of adoption falls (or profit gains increase as a result of technology improvement) more firms will adopt.

This story has been explored implicitly assuming that the number of firms in the industry is fixed. The model could be adapted to allow firms to enter or exit the industry (either temporarily or permanently). One might also note that the free entry equilibrium number of firms in the industry may be different under the new and old technology. The full diffusion story would only be told once the number of firms in the industry is equal to that number which would exist in a zero profit equilibrium and all those firms have the new technology.

3.4.2.   Schumpeter

This stock model of diffusion (labelled such because the return to adoption depends on the stock of users at any point in time) has many parallels to the seminal discussion of diffusion by Schumpeter (1984). The essence of the Schumpeter story is as follows. An 'entrepreneur' observes a profitable opportunity for the use of new technology and pursues this opportunity by innovating. The innovation leads the entrepreneur to generate excess or entrepreneurial profits. These profits then act as a signal to other potential users of the technology who follow the lead of the entrepreneur in the search for profit gains. In the full Schumpeter story this process is placed in the context of increasing credit availability and also macroeconomic spillovers. In a more limited conception, however, as the new technology is used more widely and output expands in the industry there is an increasing demand for inputs in limited supply. The price of such inputs increases reducing the profits of users and also non-users. The increased prices may then cause non-users to leave the market or find the switch to the new technology more attractive. The story clearly is very similar to that already told.

3.4.3.   The Evolutionary School

A modern parallel of Schumpeter's analysis is the Evolutionary School. This school offers a theory of diffusion very similar to the story told above (see, for example. Metcalfe, 1995). Main characteristics of the evolutionary approach are a rejection of full information, perfect competition models in which economic actors are rational, maximizing agents. Instead the emphasis is upon satisficing behaviour, limited information and bounded rationality. This in itself does not lead to enormous differences in the modelling as compared to the more neoclassical models concentrated upon here. For example the Davies (1979) probit model is very much in such a mould but yields a very similar outcome to the David (1969) probit model which is not.

The evolutionary approach does, however, produce some new insights that are worth exploring. In particular it emphasizes (1) that firm sizes are endogenous to the diffusion process (as in the standard stock model) but (2) that through firm size change, diffusion may have its own dynamic and thus reflect more of the self-generating nature seen in the epidemic model.

In the evolutionary approach, at any moment in time there is assumed to be a number of potential production technologies that the firm may use (and this pool is being continually replenished through R&D for example). Investing firms will select from this pool in a framework of limited information and bounded rationality. Some firms will pick good, profitable technologies, other firms will pick unsuitable, unprofitable technologies and yet other firms will not invest at all. Those firms that pick the good technologies will realize profit gains relative to other firms (as in the standard stock model). The crucial variant that the evolutionary approach adds is that realized profit is considered to be a major determinant of investment spending. Thus those firms that have picked the good technologies will now go on to invest more than other firms because they have higher profits. They will thus grow at the expense of other firms. Assuming that they invest in the same new technologies, the good technology will spread across the industry as the users of that technology grow at the expense of the non-users or users of other technologies. Thus diffusion in the industry proceeds. Clearly the cost of acquisition of the technology will play a role in all this but the crucial addition is that adoption leads to profit leads to more adoption. In this evolutionary approach therefore, the diffusion process has its own dynamic just as seen in the epidemic models.

One particular result of viewing diffusion in this evolutionary way is that it illustrates that diffusion can proceed not only by existing firms adopting new technology but by adopters growing at the expense of non-adopters. Exit from an industry of a non-adopter will lead to an increase in the proportion of firms using new technology just as would a non-adopter becoming a user. An example of such could be the spread of new technology in the UK coal mining industry. There it was more the closure of pits not using new technology rather than new investment in pits that led to increased proportions of new technology use in the industry.

The approach being discussed in this section thus far has considered the adoption of new process technologies by firms. One might ask whether the model has any applicability to households. Remember that the basis of this model is that as the number of users of a technology increases the benefits to a user compared to a non-user decline. It is not difficult to see how network externalities could impact on the utility gains from a technology for a household in this way, and these externalities are discussed later, but in the absence of such, it is difficult to see why such effects might impact on the household. The stock approach may therefore not have much applicability in this area.

3.4.4.   Intra-firm diffusion

Finally, in this section one can ask whether this approach has any applicability to intra-firm diffusion. In principle one might argue as follows. In the inter-firm model, that is across firms, as more and more firms adopt new technology so the profits from adoption decline. Within the firm, therefore, it might also be that as the firm adopts new technology more intensively the profits from further adoption also decline. Given an adoption cost this might limit the extent of use at any moment in time. As price falls the extent of intra-firm adoption will increase and so an intra-firm diffusion path might be mapped out.

Such arguments could be used to construct an intra-firm model, however the basis of that model has to differ from the inter-firm model. The inter-firm model worked mainly because as usage extends the revenue gain from adoption for a single firm decreases. There is basically an externality from the firm's adoption decision – one firm's decision to adopt reduces the revenue of other adopters and non-adopters (one may note that the epidemic model also contains an externality but of a different kind – one firm's adoption decision to adopt a new technology gives other firms information). When looking at a single firm any such revenue externalities would be internalized and show up in the calculation of the marginal revenue that results from adoption. The same reasoning as in the inter-firm model is thus not likely to work in an intra-firm model.

In fact one finds that if the cost of production with a technology is independent of the extent of use of that technology then the gross profit gain from adoption tends to be a linear or increasing function of the current extent of use of a technology, which is quite the reverse of what is required to generate an intra-firm diffusion model in this mode. To generate an intra-firm model in this way one needs to allow that either the costs of production with a particular technology depend on the extent of use of that technology or that the cost of acquiring the technology is non-linear in the amount acquired. However, neither extension is pursued here.

3.5.   The Order Model

In the stock model it is emphasized that as more firms use a new technology the profits of users and non-users decline. Thus a firm adopting a technology in time t would find that in time $t + 1$ and $t + 2$ the annual profit and annual profit gain being realized would be less than in time t. Similarly a firm that does not adopt will experience falling profits over time. However, the gross profits that a firm makes in time $\tau > t$ from the new technology are completely independent of the number of users of the technology at the date of adoption. In fact, for all points in time, as long as the technology is not improving over time, all users make the same profits and all non-users make the same profits (firms are identical apart from being users or non-users) although users and non-users make different profits.

Fudenberg and Tirole (1985) have suggested that such a property may not be completely acceptable. In fact they argue that early adoption of a technology, that is, being a first user, may generate higher profits for that user over the whole lifetime of the ownership of the new technology. Thus, instead of it being the case that all users at a point in time get the same gross returns from a technology, it might be that those users who adopt first, because they were first, get higher annual profits than those who adopt later.

The rationale for such an outcome can be on several grounds. One possibility is that early users are able to pre-empt certain inputs in fixed supply, such as the best geographical locations and/or scarce skilled labour (Ireland and Stoneman, 1985). This would imply that the profit earned included some element of rents. Alternatively it may be that early users are able to benefit from learning by doing economies that later users can never replicate. Alternatively it may be that early users are able to build up market goodwill that other firms cannot replicate. Of course it may not always be beneficial to be first, the example often quoted is that the Comet airliner, although it was the first commercial jet, never benefited from being first because unexpected problems of metal fatigue forced it out of the market and the market was won by Boeing being a fast second.

The real essence, however, of the benefit of being first is that by being first one can enjoy first mover advantages. One of the most interesting of first mover advantages is that the first mover has the ability to take actions that can affect the adoption decisions of other firms to its own benefit. The first mover may thus be able to get greater returns by influencing the adoption decisions of other firms.

A simple way to model this approach is to consider that the net present value of adopting a new technology is related to the number of other users **at the date of adoption**. The greater are the number of other users at the date of adoption the lower will be the present value of adoption. At any moment in time, therefore, given the cost of acquiring the technology, it will only be profitable for firms down to some point in the adoption order to acquire the new technology. Once that number is established, there will be no more adoption until either the technology changes (improves) or the cost of acquisition falls. As such changes occur the diffusion path will be mapped out.

In many ways this is similar to the stock and rank models with it being profitable for only a limited number of firms to adopt at a given acquisition cost. However, whereas the rank model produces this result by relying on differences across firms and the stock models rely on increased usage reducing annual profit gains, in this approach it is reductions in gains with movement down the order of adoption that generates the result.

Presenting the model in this way does capture the essence of the approach but it does not reflect the nature of the strategic game that Fudenberg and Tirole discuss. There it is the fact that early adoption by one firm can impact on the preferred adoption date of other firms that is crucial. However, by presenting it in this way one might see how the approach could also be applied to households. Whereas one might not expect households to undertake strategic competition with each other, it is sometimes argued that households will get some benefit from being 'first on the block' with a new technology. Being first yields a utility gain. If being second is less desirable, then the benefits from the technology may well depend on the household's positioning in the order of adoption. If this is so then the model could well be used to explore household diffusion.

3.6. Conclusions

In this chapter a number of different theoretical modelling frameworks used in the literature on technological diffusion have been explored. The analysis has been restricted to the demand side and stand-alone technologies, and uncertainty has not been explicitly considered. A basic distinction between the models discussed is between equilibrium and disequilibrium models. The epidemic and evolutionary approaches fall into the first category whereas the rank, stock and order models fall into the second. A basic characteristic of disequilibrium models is that diffusion in such models tends to be self-perpetuating with use of a technology today generating further use tomorrow, whereas the equilibrium models rely upon outside stimuli, and in particular reductions in the cost, or improvements in the quality, of the technology being diffused, to drive diffusion along.

The disequilibrium models emphasize how information spreading and/or success breeding success (with profits being reinvested in new technologies) generates the diffusion path. The rank model, on the other hand, emphasizes that firms are different and therefore will have different preferred adoption dates. The stock model emphasizes how the profitability of adoption is determined by the number of other users, and thus for a given cost of acquisition only some firms will find adoption profitable. The order approach emphasizes that the position in the order of adoption matters and for any given cost of acquisition only firms down to some point in that order will find adoption profitable. Whereas in the disequilibrium models diffusion is self-perpetuating, the other models emphasize that the diffusion of new technology occurs because the technology, its costs and the benefits it generates, will be changing over time. Diffusion may stop if the technology does not continue to improve or get cheaper.

The different approaches emphasize the role of different factors in the diffusion process, none of which one would wish to rule out *a priori*. Clearly it would be advantageous if an encompassing model could be generated that incorporated all the various factors discussed. (This is attempted in Karshenas and Stoneman (1993) reproduced as chapter 8.) It ought to be noted, however, that this is not a simple task because different models may actually be inconsistent with each other. Thus, for example, the rank approach assumes that the firm's own adoption and other firms' adoption does not affect the characteristics that determine the benefits of its adoption. The stock model on the other hand is built around explicitly modelling such a relationship (Götz, 1999, has produced an interesting model combining rank and stock effects). Similarly the epidemic model assumes that all potential adopters are homogeneous, while the rank model assumes quite the reverse.

The various models that have been investigated indicate that the main factors that impact upon the diffusion process are:

1   learning and information spreading
2   the cost of acquiring new technology and changes therein
3   the performance of new technology and changes therein
4   price expectations and changes therein
5   technology expectations and changes therein
6   firm characteristics and their distributions
7   discount factors and attitudes to risk
8   the extent of product differentiation and changes therein
9   the extent of first mover advantages and the economic rents to being an early adopter
10 the impact of other firm's adoption upon users and non-users profits
11 the extent to which realized profits generate new investment.

Rather than *a priori* ruling out any of these factors as determinants of diffusion it is preferable to undertake empirical testing of the various models on real world diffusion phenomena. This is done in part III of this book. Before that, however, there are a number of other factors to consider, such as the supply side, uncertainty and network effects. Thus far these have been ignored, but they are addressed in the next three chapters.

Notes

1   If $Q^*(t)$ stops falling or starts to rise over time then depending on whether the investment in the technology is reversible or not, diffusion may cease or go into reverse (although one has to be careful here in that in such a situation the profitability condition may dominate the arbitrage condition and this would require some adjustment to the acquisition condition).
2   In the marketing literature there is discussion of how firms undertake niche marketing or fill market niches. This discussion of product differentiation and diffusion is very similar in character.
3   Essentially relating to the size of the elasticity of demand.

References

Acemoglu, D. (1993) 'Labour Market Imperfections, Innovation Incentives and the Dynamics of Aggregate Innovation', presented at the RES Annual Conference, University of York, April.

Bain, A. (1964) *The Growth of Television Ownership in the UK since the War: A Lognormal Model*, Cambridge: Cambridge University Press.

Bass, F. (1969) 'A New Product Growth Model for Consumer Durables', *Management Science*, 15, 215–27.

Battisti, G. (1999) 'The Intra Firm Diffusion of New Technology', Ph.D. thesis, University of Warwick, May.

Bonus, H. (1973) 'Quasi Engel Curves, Diffusion, and the Ownership of New Consumer Durables', *Journal of Political Economy*, 81, 655–77.

Chow, G. (1967) 'Technological Change and the Demand for Computers', *American Economic Review*, 57, 1117–30.

Cohen, W. and Levinthal, D. (1989) 'Innovation and Learning: The Two Faces of R&D', *Economic Journal*, 99, 569–96.

David, P. (1969) *A Contribution to the Theory of Diffusion*, Center for Research in Economic Growth Research Memorandum, no. 71, Stanford University.

Davies, S. (1979) *The Diffusion of Process Innovations*, Cambridge: Cambridge University Press.

Fudenberg, D. and Tirole, J. (1985) 'Pre-emption and Rent Equalisation in the Adoption of New Technology', *Review of Economic Studies*, 52, 383–401.

Goodacre, A. and Tonks, I. (1995) 'Finance and Technological Change', in P. Stoneman (ed.), *Handbook of the Economics of Innovation and Technological Change*, Oxford: Basil Blackwell, 298–341.

Götz, G. (1999) 'Monopolistic Competition and the Diffusion of New Technology', *Rand Journal of Economics*, 30(4), 679–93.

Griliches, Z. (1957) 'Hybrid Corn: An Exploration in the Economics of Technological Change', *Econometrica*, 48, 501–22.

Ireland, N. (1987) *Product Differentiation and Non Price Competition*, Oxford: Basil Blackwell.

Ireland, N. and Stoneman, P. (1985) 'Order Effects, Perfect Foresight and Intertemporal Price Discrimination', *Recherche Economique de Louvain*, 51(1), 7–20.

Ireland, N. and Stoneman, P. (1986) 'Technological Diffusion, Expectations and Welfare', *Oxford Economic Papers*, June, 283–304.

Kapur, S. (1995) 'Technological Diffusion with Social Learning', *Journal of Industrial Economics*, 43(2), 173–95.

Karshenas, M. and Stoneman, P. (1992) 'A Flexible Model of Technological Diffusion Incorporating Economic Factors with an Application to the Spread of Colour Television Ownership in the UK', *Journal of Forecasting*, 11(7), 577–601.

Karshenas, M. and Stoneman, P. (1993) 'Rank, Stock, Order and Epidemic Effects in the Diffusion of New Process Technology', *Rand Journal of Economics*, 24(4), 503–28.

Mahajan, V. and Wind, Y. (1986) *Innovation Diffusion Models of New Product Acceptance*, Cambridge, MA: Ballinger.

Mansfield, E. (1968) *Industrial Research and Technological Innovation*, New York: Norton.

Metcalfe, J.S. (1995) 'The Economic Foundations of Technology Policy: Equilibrium and Evolutionary Perspectives', in P. Stoneman (ed.), *Handbook of the Economics of Innovation and Technological Change*, Oxford: Basil Blackwell, 409–512.

Quirmbach, H. (1986) 'The Diffusion of New Technology and the Market for an Innovation', *Rand Journal of Economics*, 17, 33–47.

Reinganum, J. (1981) 'Market Structure and the Diffusion of New Technology', *The Bell Journal of Economics*, 12, 618–24.

Santarelli, E. (1995) *Finance and Technological Change: Theory and Evidence*, Basingstoke: Macmillan Press.

Schumpeter, J. (1984) *The Theory of Economic Development*, Cambridge, MA: Harvard University Press.

Stoneman, P. (1989) 'Technological Diffusion and Vertical Product Differentiation', *Economic Letters*, 31, 277–80.

Stoneman, P. (1990) 'Technological Diffusion, Horizontal Product Differentiation and Adaptation Costs', *Economica*, 57, 49–62.

Stoneman, P. and Battisti, G. (2000) 'The Role of Regulation, Fiscal Incentives and Changes in Tastes in the Diffusion of Unleaded Petrol in the UK', *Oxford Economic Papers*, 52(2), 326–56.

Zettlemeyer, F. and Stoneman, P. (1993) 'Testing Alternative Models of New Product Diffusion', *Economics of Innovation and New Technology*, 2, 283–308.

Chapter four

Risk and Uncertainty

4.1. Introduction

That innovation involves risk and uncertainty has for long been recognized. When a firm or household is considering the introduction or purchase of a new technology there is uncertainty in a number of dimensions. Technological uncertainty could exist in that the potential buyer will be unclear as to the exact working performance of the technology, its potential life or the cost of maintenance. On the market side there may also be uncertainty in that the firm will not know for certain how the demand for its output will develop in the future and as such the potential profitability of adopting a new technology may be unclear; and both firms and households may be uncertain as to, for example, how cost of complementary inputs to the technology might change over time. It is thus not surprising that even from the earliest writings, risk and uncertainty have played a role in the theory of technological diffusion.

In this chapter the seminal early work of Mansfield (1968) is first discussed and then contrasted with a Bayesian learning model. This is then followed by discussion of the real options approach. A short section on financial issues in diffusion closes the chapter. The interested reader may also find the papers by Götz (2000) and Stenbacka and Tomback (1994) on stock/order models incorporating uncertainty as relevant.

4.2. The Epidemic Approach

The seminal work of Mansfield (1968) on the diffusion of new process technologies by firms is in many ways the origin of much of the later work on the economics of diffusion. The model that he presents is primarily an epidemic model and, as such, in this approach diffusion is self-propagating. The model is, however, distinguished from the earlier versions of the epidemic model by its emphasis on risk and uncertainty and reductions therein as the driving force of the diffusion process. As in the standard epidemic model existing use of the technology drives further usage, in this case by providing information that leads to reductions in uncertainty.

The story embodied in this approach can be applied either at the intra-firm or inter-firm level. Consider the intra-firm level first. Here, the firm is seen to face a technology that has an expected (constant) profitability. However, there is uncertainty attached to the use of the technology. The profit attracts the firm to the technology, the uncertainty deters adoption; but once the firm has innovated (used the technology for the first time) the firm starts to learn about the technology. As it does so, the uncertainty attached to the technology declines. This reduction in uncertainty leads to increases in use. The new higher level of use leads to further reductions in uncertainty and again higher levels of use. Over time uncertainty will reduce to zero and as it does so the level of use tends to its asymptote. The nature of the epidemic model is that the asymptote involves a fixed end level of use so that essentially the firm will end up producing all of its output using the new technology. In addition the model predicts that the rate at which the end level is approached will depend on the constant expected profitability of the technology.

In the inter-firm model the reasoning is similar. Essentially it is argued that the rate at which non-adopters become adopters is related to the expected profitability of adoption and the uncertainty attached to adoption. Use by one firm leads to reductions in uncertainty and thus use by other firms. The self-propagating nature of this mechanism drives the diffusion process to its asymptote with the speed of approach being determined by (*inter alia*) the expected profitability of adoption. As with the intra-firm model, the actual diffusion path is shown to be a logistic curve with an asymptote where all firms are users.

The essence of this approach is thus that use of a technology reduces the uncertainty involved in the technology and that reduction leads to further use. However, certain strange characteristics of this approach should be noted. The first is that throughout the diffusion process the expected profitability of the technology is not changing. In many ways this is as in the standard epidemic model where no allowance is made for the fact that technologies improve over time and become cheaper. However, in an uncertain environment this is even more of a problem. For even if the technology is not changing, one might expect that as firms learn about a technology they would change their estimates of the expected profitability. If learning is reducing uncertainty but not the expected return, then all that experience is teaching the firm is that its initial estimate of expected profitability is the correct one. The firm never learns that its estimate of the rate of return is wrong and needs changing. This also implies that there is no mechanism in this model to stop diffusion. If learning only reduces uncertainty it will always stimulate use. The firm never learns that it is incorrect or unprofitable to use the technology. Similar comments could be made if one were discussing the application of the model to household diffusion (where expected profit would be replaced by expected utility gain).

The second major criticism of the approach is less to do with the underpinnings of the model but more to do with the final outcome. As stated, the model predicts that diffusion will follow a logistic path with the speed of diffusion determined by expected profitability. This is, however, not a necessary consequence of the model. The key components of this model are uncertainty reduction driven by experience and a hypothesis that uncertainty has a negative impact on the change in the level of use whereas expected profitability has a positive impact. This hypothesis is a very general one, but is reduced by Mansfield through use of a Taylors series expansion to a very specific one that states that changes in use in a time period relative to the distance from the asymptote is linearly related to profitability and uncertainty. It is this assumption that produces the logistic curve and as such the logistic diffusion curve is imposed by assumption rather than falling out of the model naturally.

Finally one might note with this approach to diffusion that (1) in the intra-firm diffusion process the firm only learns from its own past experience whereas in the inter-firm model the firm learns from the experience of others and (2) the firm learns in a passive way. The firm never goes searching for information, it essentially only observes the experience of others or itself.

4.3.   A Mean Variance Approach

Stoneman (1980, 1981) also builds intra- and inter-firm diffusion models centring upon uncertainty reduction. The intra-firm model, which could again with appropriate redefinition be extended to the household, relies on a portfolio approach to technology choice. Essentially the firm is seen as having the possibility of using new or old technology in any preferred mix. It is thus choosing an optimum portfolio of technologies. As time proceeds the optimum portfolio might change and as it does so diffusion extends (or not, depending on what is learnt).

The portfolio choice model is the standard mean variance model frequently used in finance for modelling portfolio choice decisions. Each technology can be characterized by the expected or mean return to the use of the technology and the variance attached to those returns. A utility function is defined over the means and variances with the mean yielding positive utility and the variance negative utility. The firm maximizes utility by the appropriate choice of technology mix, trading off mean returns against variance.

There is a true mean return to each technology but that is not necessarily known to the firm at the beginning of the diffusion process and it is only as it gathers information that it learns of the true mean return. The variance for each technology is made up of two parts, the true variance determined by the nature of the world and the variance resulting from lack of knowledge (i.e. uncertainty). For simplicity, as the old technology has been used for some time, it is assumed that the mean and variance for that technology are known and fixed. For the new technology, however, the firm learns from experience and it is this learning that drives the diffusion process.

The learning in this model is different to that in the Mansfield model. The firm is assumed to learn from experience and updates its prior estimates of means and variances following Bayesian rules. Importantly, as experience accumulates the firm's estimate of the variance of the returns to the new technology declines towards the true or inherent variance as uncertainty is removed. This reduction in the variance (reduction in uncertainty) leads to increased use of the new technology, just as in the Mansfield model. More importantly, the learning is also allowed to affect the estimate of the mean return. If the initial estimate (or prior) of the mean return is below the true value then the learning will lead to increases in the prior over time. If the initial prior is above the true value then the learning will lead to reductions in the prior until the true value is reached. Increases in the prior will lead to greater use, reductions will lead to less use. Thus if the initial estimate of the mean return is too low, increased priors plus reduced variance will lead firms to portfolio mixes that show increasing levels of use of the new technology. If the prior estimate of the mean return is above the true value the effect of the reduced variance will be partly or wholly offset by the reduced estimates of the mean and thus diffusion may be stopped or put into reverse. This is not a possible outcome in the Mansfield model. Essentially it implies that a firm may start to use a new technology in the (uncertain) belief that it will be very profitable, however as time proceeds it learns (and learns with increasing certainty) that the technology will not be so profitable and thus will no longer wish to use it so extensively.

This intra-firm diffusion model can be turned into an inter-firm diffusion model of the rank or probit type (Stoneman, 1980). Firms are allowed to differ in their attitudes to risk (parameters of the mean variance utility function) and also in their initial priors of the means and variances attached to the new technologies. This will produce a set of differing preferred levels of use for all firms at a moment in time. By defining some arbitrary level of use by the firms (say 5 per cent of output produced on the new technology) one may classify firms as either users or non-users. As time proceeds and the learning process occurs estimates of mean and variances change for each of the firms, and changing levels of use are generated. This then generates the inter-firm diffusion curve as firms cross the threshold level of use with the least risk averse and those with the lowest priors for the variance and highest priors for the mean adopting first. Given the nature of the model, diffusion may also stop in an inter-firm sense if firms learn that they have been too optimistic on the potential returns from the technology.

In many ways this model is an improvement on that of Mansfield. It includes a specific theory of technique choice and also rigorously models the updating of priors as a Bayesian process. By doing so it enables a diffusion process to stop before all firms (or householders) are adopters. However it still has two particular failings:

1   The firms are still passive seekers of information. They do not actually undertake search. Tonks (1986) has also pointed out that, in such a framework as this, firms may actually acquire technology in order to learn from it and in the original formulation of this model that was not accounted for.
2   The model does not allow the technology to change or improve over time, although in principle this could be accommodated.

From personal experience I can also state that it is very difficult to apply empirically.

4.4.   The Real Options Approach

This section considers an alternative approach to modelling the diffusion process under uncertainty, labelled the real options approach, based on the work of, for example, Dixit and Pindyck (1994) as applied to investment decisions under uncertainty, (although as yet this label has not been extensively used in the diffusion literature). It should be noted, however, that many of the fundamentals of how this approach can be applied to diffusion modelling can be found in the earlier work of Jensen (1982, 1983).

This approach does have one important difference from the previous approach discussed that considerably affects the results. In the previous approach it was possible for the firm to modify the risk that it carried by only using the technology to a limited extent. The level of use of the new technology was a continuous variable. In the real options models this is generally assumed not to be the case. In such models the choice of the technology is usually modelled with the project as the lowest level of disaggregation. The firm (or household) has to decide whether to undertake a project or not to undertake a project. It is not possible to undertake a half or a third of a project. It is of course possible to model diffusion as the undertaking of a series of (interrelated) projects – that is, a series of purchases of individual capital goods – but as far as we are aware that has not as yet been done. Real options models thus tend to be inter-firm models, where the project is to equip the whole firm with a new technology. The firm (or household) thus uses the technology or does not use the technology; there is no question of it partially using the technology. For real options approaches to be valid it is also necessary to assume that investment decisions are irreversible. If a firm adopts the new technology it cannot (at least costlessly) reverse that decision.

Relevant real options models come in two forms. Those in which information is free and those where information is costly. The bases of the models are similar. For an approach of the first type, consider a firm that is evaluating investing in a project with an uncertain return, say equipping itself with a new set of capital equipment. In the discussion of the probit model under certainty above it was argued that there were two conditions that determined whether the firm would buy the technology in time t, these being the arbitrage and profitability conditions. To avoid the complication of a falling cost of acquiring the technology over time, it is assumed here that the cost of buying the technology is known and constant for all t. In such a case the profitability condition is both necessary and sufficient under certainty to determine dates of adoption. This condition states that the firm will acquire the technology at the first date that the gross present value of the future returns, $V(t)$, discounted at rate r is greater than the cost of buying the technology $P(t)$. Thus the firm will be the owner of the technology in time t if $V(t) \geq P(t)$. The real options approach makes one aware, however, that this simple formulation does not apply when the world is uncertain.

The basic reason why the simple present value comparison is no longer relevant is that the firm considering investment at time t faces a multiple choice situation rather than a two way choice (i.e. that between buying and not buying). To illustrate, assume that there are only two time periods: periods 1 and 2 or, alternatively, today and tomorrow. The cost of acquiring the technology in each period is P which is known with certainty. Assume that in the absence of the investment the payoff to the firm will be zero in period 1 and zero in period 2 also known with certainty. The gross benefit from the action in period 1 is known with certainty as x_1. Uncertainty is introduced in that in period 1 the firm does not know what the payoff will be in period 2. It is, however, known that it can take either of two values: $x_2 + \varepsilon$ or $x_2 - \varepsilon$ with respective probabilities q and $(1 - q)$ and assume that these payoffs are independent of the period in which the firm actually makes its investment decision. This simple uncertainty means that at time period 1 the expected value of x_2, $E(x_2)$ is $x_2 + \varepsilon(2q - 1)$. Allow for the sake of the argument that $x_2 + \varepsilon - P > 0 > x_2 - \varepsilon - P$ thereby ensuring that a firm that has not invested in time period 1 will prefer in period 2 to not adopt rather than to adopt in the face of an unfavourable payoff and prefer adoption to non-adoption in the face of a favourable payoff. Also assume initially that, costlessly, the true value of the second period payoff, that is, the true state of the world in period 2 will be revealed at the beginning of period 2. Define r as the riskless interest rate/discount rate.

If one were to follow the standard net present value rule, or alternatively the equivalent of the adoption rule assumed in the probit model without uncertainty above, the firm would be considered to invest in period 1 if the expected present value of such an investment were positive and if not, to invest in period 2 if the present value of adoption in period 2 were positive. The first period adoption rule would thus be to adopt if

$$EV = x_1 + (x_2 + \varepsilon(2q - 1))/(1 + r) - P > 0 \qquad (4.1)$$

In fact, a firm considering this investment project actually faces four possible courses of action in period 1:

(a)   to invest in period 1
(b)   to not invest in period 1 but to commit itself to invest in period 2
(c)   to not invest in period 1 and to commit itself to not invest in period 2
(d)   to not invest in period 1 and to delay the investment decision to period 2 when it will invest if the gross payoff is $x_2 + \varepsilon$ but not invest if the payoff is $x_2 - \varepsilon$.

Of these the standard present value rule is only considering whether it is profitable to follow strategy (a). One should not only consider whether it is profitable to follow strategy (a) but also whether it is more profitable to follow any of the other strategies.
    The payoffs from, that is, the expected present values of, the four strategies are:

$$EV(a) = x_1 + x_2/(1 + r) + \varepsilon(2q - 1)/(1 + r) - P \qquad (4.2)$$

$$EV(b) = x_2/(1 + r) + \varepsilon(2q - 1)/(1 + r) - P/(1 + r) \qquad (4.3)$$

$$EV(c) = 0 \qquad (4.4)$$

$$EV(d) = q(x_2 + \varepsilon - P)/(1 + r) \qquad (4.5)$$

Consider first the relative payoffs to strategy (b) – that is, commit in period 1 to invest in period 2 and strategy (d) – to decide in period 1 to make the decision in period 2. It is clear that

$$EV(d) - EV(b) = (1 - q)(x_2 - \varepsilon - P) \qquad (4.6)$$

Considering the relative payoffs to strategies (c) and (d) – to not buy in period 1 and commit to not buy in period 2 compared to not buying in period 1 and deciding in period 2 whether to buy – it is clear that

$$EV(d) - EV(c) = q(x_2 + \varepsilon - P)/(1 + r) \qquad (4.7)$$

and thus given that $x_2 + \varepsilon - P > 0 > x_2 - \varepsilon - P$ the payoff to strategy (d) always dominates that to strategies (b) and (c). Essentially this means that if the firm is not buying the technology in period 1 it should not commit in period 1 to any particular decision in period 2. There are always benefits to delaying the decision to period 2 relative to committing in period 1 to a period 2 decision. Essentially the rationale is that a first period commitment to a second period decision means that one has either closed off the option to buy if the state of the world is good in period 2 or not buy if the state of the world is bad in period 2.

The two dominant strategies left to the firm are thus (a) and (d) – to either acquire the technology in period 1 or to delay the decision until period 2 and buy if the state of the world is good and not buy if the state of the world is bad. For the firm to buy the technology in period 1 – that is, follow strategy (a) – it is necessary that strategy (a) is profitable and also that strategy (a) is more profitable than strategy (d) – it is thus necessary that two conditions are met: (1) that $EV(a) > 0$ and (2) that $EV(a) > EV(d)$.

Comparing the returns to strategy (d) and strategy (a) one can write that

$$EV(a) - EV(d) = x_1 + (1 - q)(x_2 - \varepsilon - P)/(1 + r) \tag{4.8}$$

where $x_2 - \varepsilon - P < 0$. Thus strategy (a) only dominates strategy (d) when the first period payoff x_1 is large relative to the second period payoff x_2 and/or when the probability of the unfavourable outcome $(1 - q)$ is small. When the probability of an unfavourable outcome is large or when the second period returns are large relative to first period returns the firm should prefer to wait before adoption.

What this approach is indicating is that one reason for firms not adopting a new technology as soon as it appears is that future returns are uncertain and as such the firm may prefer to wait until the uncertainty is resolved before committing to the new technology.

In this discussion matters have been made simple by allowing that the returns x_1 and x_2 are independent of when the technology is adopted. One could modify this assumption on the lines of the order model discussed above. Thus, for example, it may be advantageous for the firm to adopt early rather than late because of the strategic competitive advantages that this commitment generates. However, that does not invalidate the main underlying story being told here.

Matters have also been made simple by considering that all the firm has to do is to wait until period 2 and it will then known what the payoff will be in the second period. In other words, there is passive information acquisition. It is possible to vary this assumption and to get some extra insight.

Let it be the case again that there are only two periods. Allow that in neither period is it known with certainty what the payoff will be from adoption but the payoff is the same in both periods. The cost of adoption in either period is P. Let it be that if the project is a success the firm will get a payoff of $x + \varepsilon$ per period whereas if the project is a failure the payoff will be $x - \varepsilon$ per period. Allow also that at a point in time t the firm believes that the probability of success is $q(t)$ and the probability of failure $1 - q(t)$. Allow also that the firm can undertake search activity and that the impact of such search will be to change the estimates of q for time $t + 1$, that is, through search the firm will get a more certain estimate of the true probability of success and failure. In the absence of search activity $q(t)$ remains constant. Let the cost of search in any time period be fixed at $S > 0$.

A firm considering adoption in time period 1 thus has three dominant strategies available:

1 To adopt in period 1.
2 To not adopt in period 1 and to not undertake search; in this case the firm will never adopt.
3 To not adopt in period 1 but to undertake search and then reconsider adoption in period 2.

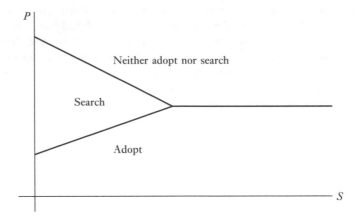

Figure 4.1   Search, real options and technology adoption

In Diederen *et al.* (1995) this framework is analysed and a diagrammatic representation of the firm's first period choices presented. This is reproduced as figure 4.1. The axes are the cost of search S and the cost of acquiring the technology P and two curves are plotted. The top curve indicates combinations of P and S for which the firm is indifferent between searching and not searching. The bottom curve shows combinations of P and S for which the firm is indifferent between searching and adopting in period 1. The reason why the two curves eventually converge is that above a certain cost of search, search can never be worthwhile. Above the top curve the firm will choose strategy 2, that is, not adopt and not search; between the top and bottom curves the firm will choose strategy 3, that is, not adopt in period 1 but search; and below the bottom curve the firm will choose strategy 1, that is, adopt in period 1. We thus see that in the presence of uncertainty when costly search can occur, the real options approach indicates that whether the firm decides to adopt in the first period depends on the cost of searching. The position of the actual curves in figure 4.1 depends upon parameters (e.g. initial beliefs on q) that may well be firm specific and as such the position of the above curves may well be firm specific. Potentially, this enables the construction of a diffusion model of a probit type.

As yet, all that has been shown is that in the presence of uncertainty, the extent of that uncertainty will affect the preferred date of adoption, but this does not yet generate a diffusion model showing how the number of firms adopting a technology will change over time. That is in fact quite difficult to do in a two-period framework, for although two periods is a useful expository simplification it is really desirable to model a multi-period story. Once way to do this is to consider that time can always be modelled as today and tomorrow. The above framework is then used to determine whether the firm will buy today. In the next period, tomorrow becomes today and again decisions are considered in the first period of a two-period world. The diffusion analysis is then the result of considering a whole series of linked date pairs. Even this is difficult, however, for it requires some model consistency between the priors in the first period tomorrow and the results of the search today.

To construct a real options diffusion model another real options framework, which is built more directly on the work of Dixit and Pindyck (1994), is analysed. Of necessity this presentation is more mathematical than previously, even though the model is considerably simplified through assumption.

Let the firm (or household) face an uncertain investment possibility, with revenue flows of $R(t)$ per period and investment cost in time t of $P(t)$. Let

$$dR(t)/R(t) = \alpha_R dt + \tau_R dz_R \qquad (4.9)$$

and

$$dP(t)/P(t) = \alpha_P dt + \tau_P dz_P \qquad (4.10)$$

where dz is the increment of a standard Weiner process. Here the α's show average growth of a variable over time and the τ's show the variance or uncertainty attached to a variable. Assume that P and R are independent of each other and also independent of the number of users of the technology and the date of adoption (i.e. no stock or order effects). This is thus basically a probit type model. Defining r as the riskless rate of interest, then following Dixit and Pindyck (1994, pp. 207–11) the firm will invest in the technology in time t rather than wait iff

$$R(t)/P(t) > \beta(r - \alpha_P)/(\beta - 1) \equiv \Omega(t) \qquad (4.11)$$

where β is the larger root of the quadratic equation

$$0.5(\tau_R^2 + \tau_P^2) \cdot \beta \cdot (\beta - 1) + (\alpha_R - \alpha_P) \cdot \beta - (r - \alpha_P) = 0 \qquad (4.12)$$

and $\Omega(t)$ may be described as the hurdle or threshold rate of return beyond which the firm will adopt in time t and below which it will not. For generality it is allowed to be time dependent, for example the interest rate may differ across time periods. It can be seen that (if $\alpha - \alpha_R > 0$, $r - \alpha_P > 0$ implying $\beta > 1$) that Ω: is decreasing in α_P and thus the faster is the cost of acquisition expected to grow the lower is the hurdle rate; and increasing in both τ_R and τ_P and thus the higher is the uncertainty attached to both revenue and costs of acquisition the greater is the hurdle rate. We are unable to sign derivatives with respect to α_R and r.

To move to a diffusion model, allow that the potential buyers of the technology differ from each other. Let N be potential market size (assumed constant for simplicity) with individual buyers being labelled as i, thus $i = 1 \ldots N$, and assume that buyers only ever buy one unit of the technology. An individual buyer i (who has not already invested in the technology prior to time t), therefore, will buy in time t iff (4.13) holds.

$$R_i(t)/P_i(t) > \Omega_i(t) \qquad (4.13)$$

It is reasonable to consider that the cost of acquisition is the same for all i and thus $P(t)$ is the same for all i. However $R(t)$ and $\Omega(t)$ may well differ across potential buyers. For example, firms or households may be different and thus get different returns from the technology in a period and also the α's and τ's may well differ across buyers. Rather than model these differences in detail it is instead assumed that

$$\text{Log } R_i(t) = \log R^*(t) + e_{1i} \tag{4.14}$$

and

$$\text{Log } \Omega_i(t) = \text{Log } \Omega^*(t) + e_{2i} \tag{4.15}$$

where starred terms are the averages across the population and the e terms reflect differences between individuals (an approach derived from the diffusion model developed by Deaton and Muellbauer, 1980). The investment condition may now be written as that firm i will invest in time t iff (4.16) holds.

$$\log R^*(t) - \log P(t) - \log \Omega^*(t) + (e_{1i} - e_{2i}) > 0 \tag{4.16}$$

Assuming that the differences between potential buyers can be modelled by allowing that $(e_{1i} - e_{2i})$ is distributed across the population according to the distribution $V(\cdot)$ (which is · what makes this a probit model) one may then derive the probability that firm i, chosen at random from the population, will own the technology in time t, $Pr_i(t)$, (following procedures laid down in Deaton and Muellbauer (1980) as (4.17)

$$Pr_i(t) = 1 - V(\log \Omega^*(t) + \log P(t) - \log R^*(t)) \tag{4.17}$$

where $V_1 > 0$, $V_2 < 0$ and $V_3 > 0$ and which after substitution of the constituent parts for $\Omega^*(t)$ may be rewritten as (4.18)

$$Pr_i(t) = \mathcal{J}(R^*(t), P(t), r(t), \alpha_R^*, \alpha_P^*, \tau_R^*, \tau_P^*) \tag{4.18}$$

where starred variables reflect averages across the population and where $\mathcal{J}_1 > 0$, $\mathcal{J}_2 < 0$, $\mathcal{J}_5 > 0$, $\mathcal{J}_6 < 0$, $\mathcal{J}_7 < 0$. Note that $Pr_i(t)$ thus expressed is independent of i, and we thus write it as $Pr(t)$.

With N as the potential number of adopters and defining $M(t)$ as the number of users in time t, in the absence of depreciation or any scrapping, the number of users or stock of technology in use in time t is given by

$$M(t) = Pr(t) \cdot N(t) \tag{4.19}$$

or

$$M(t) - M(t - 1) = Pr(t)N(t) - M(t - 1) \tag{4.20}$$

which is a reasonably standard diffusion curve formulation.

As can be seen above $Pr(t)$ is a function of $R^*(t)$, $P(t)$, $r(t)$, α_R^*, α_P^*, τ_R^*, and τ_P^* indicating that speed of diffusion will be positively related to revenue in time t to be earned from adoption in time t and the mean rate of growth of the cost of acquisition, and negatively related to the cost of acquisition in time t, and the variance or uncertainty attached to costs of acquisitions and revenues. In short this is as might be expected from earlier models except that now there is a clear prediction for given $P(t)$ and $R^*(t)$ that uncertainty will slow diffusion (and given that the uncertainty applies to both acquisition costs and revenues, it is uncertainty *per se* that really matters, not the fact that revenue might fall or that the costs of acquisition might increase).

4.5. Finance Issues

Recognizing the risky and uncertain nature of investments in new technology brings into focus issues relating to the finance of innovation. Unfortunately very little work has actually been undertaken on finance and diffusion although in the previous chapter some reference was made to the general literature on finance and technological change. There has been more work undertaken on finance and R&D, and this work is well summarized in Goodacre and Tonks (1995). However, the same issues that apply to R&D also apply to the adoption of new technology (although perhaps to differing degrees). The issues that Goodacre and Tonks emphasize are that the risky nature of the investment required creates difficulties in assessing the potential of the investment and for obtaining financing for the investment. This implies that there will be less investment than in a 'safe' project. Although it may be possible for the firm to shift risk via the capital market, it may well be that because of information asymmetries and moral hazard such risk shifting may not operate completely effectively. It might even be that the capital markets are overly 'short termist', an issue long discussed in the UK, and this will cause under investment in risky projects offering only long-term payoffs. Goodacre and Tonks suggest that loan markets may have better incentive and information properties than equity markets, but they note that the characteristics of the loan (whether it is offered as securitized debt or by a financial institution) will affect the ability of the lender to monitor the use of the loan.

For the diffusion of some new technologies it may well be that the availability of leasing or rental contracts is a key issue. One may note that in the airline industry, most airlines now lease rather than purchase their aircraft outright. In the early years of the development of the TV market in the UK most TV sets were rented rather than purchased outright. The availability of leasing provides a ready source of finance for the acquisition of new technology and also shifts considerable risk from the user to the lease holder. However, as the lease holder can hold many leases he/she is able to spread his/her risk and thus provide finance with a lesser overall risk element. The availability of leasing finance may be a factor in the diffusion of large risky technologies.

In the face of imperfect capital markets the government may well get involved in the financing of new technology developments. One policy directly aimed at the risk factor is Launch Aid. This is, however, more concerned with the development of new products than their adoption. One might also consider that venture capital, and also public provision of such funding, is more directed at the development of new technologies than their use.

Goodacre and Tonks (1995) ask whether there is an optimal method of finance for the firm considering investment in a risky project. They note in particular that there may be a substantial bankruptcy risk in such investments. They argue that the method of finance will include equity, corporate debt, bank loans and more complex financial instruments such as convertibles and venture capital, but they are unable to identify any optimal mix. They suggest that because of the speculative nature of such investments, financiers will want equity contracts whereas firms will be unwilling to borrow. However, the incentive and information problems will favour an issue of corporate debt. The optimal mix will reflect the relative importance of these factors.

There is still much work to be undertaken on the role of financial factors in the diffusion process. This is part of my personal research agenda. At the current time the theoretical (and empirical) literature is very thin.

4.6.   Conclusions

In this chapter the analysis of demand side diffusion models for stand-alone technologies has been extended to include risk and uncertainty. Several different approaches have been explored. The strongest results come from the real options framework where it was shown that greater uncertainty slows the diffusion of new technology. However it was also illustrated that reductions in uncertainty over time can be a driving factor in the diffusion process. In fact potential adopters may delay acquisition because uncertainty with respect to the nature of the technology or with respect to the futures of factor and product market is too great, but as uncertainty is reduced either through passive learning or through active information acquisition such potential buyers become adopters. The chapter also briefly discussed how the issue of financing the adoption of new technology is of greater importance in an uncertain world. However, it was argued that this has not been much discussed.

References

Deaton, A. and Muellbauer, J. (1980) *Economics and Consumer Behaviour*, Cambridge: Cambridge University Press.

Diederen, P., Stoneman, P. and Toivanen, O. (1995) 'Adoption of New Technology, Real Options and Search: Revenue Uncertainty', World Econometrics Society Congress, Tokyo, September 1995.

Dixit, A. and Pindyck, R. (1994) *Investment under Uncertainty*, Princeton: Princeton University Press.

Goodacre, A. and Tonks, I. (1995) 'Finance and Technological Change', in P. Stoneman (ed.), *Handbook of the Economics of Innovation and Technological Change*, Oxford: Basil Blackwell, 298–341.

Götz, G. (2000) 'Strategic Timing of Adoption of New Technologies under Uncertainty: A Note', *International Journal of Industrial Organisation*, 18, 369–79.

Jensen, R. (1982) 'Adoption and Diffusion of an Innovation of Uncertain Profitability', *Journal of Economic Theory*, 27(1), 182–93.

Jensen, R. (1983) 'Innovation Adoption and Diffusion When There Are Competing Innovations', *Journal of Economic Theory*, 29(1), 161–71.

Mansfield, E. (1968) *Industrial Research and Technological Innovation*, New York: Norton.

Stenbacka, R. and Tomback, M.M. (1994) 'Strategic Timing of Adoption of New Technologies under Uncertainty', *International Journal of Industrial Organisation*, 12, 387–411.

Stoneman, P. (1980) 'The Rate of Imitation, Learning and Profitability', *Economics Letters*, 6, 1179–83.

Stoneman, P. (1981) 'Intra-firm Diffusion, Bayesian Learning and Profitability', *Economic Journal*, 91, 375–88.

Tonks, I. (1986) 'The Demand for Information and the Diffusion of New Products', *International Journal of Industrial Organisation*, 4, 397–408.

Chapter five

Multiple Technologies, Complementary Inputs, Network Externalities and General Purpose Technologies

5.1. Introduction

Thus far only the diffusion of stand-alone technologies has been considered. This chapter addresses a number of issues that arise when account is taken of the fact that new technologies are generally not adopted in isolation from other technologies (either new or existing) or that joint inputs are generally required for an innovation to produce output (e.g. raw materials and labour inputs). Such discussions lead naturally into the consideration of networks and standards and also into the discussion of general purpose technologies. It is with a discussion of the latter that the chapter closes.

5.2. Multiple Technologies

The full benefit of using a new technology might only be obtained when that technology is installed alongside another new technology. Thus, for example, one hears of CAD/CAM (computer-aided design/computer-aided manufacture). It is generally accepted that both CAD and CAM can yield benefits to the firm if introduced on their own but the introduction of both would yield benefits greater than the sum of the benefits to introducing either alone. A similar example would be that the benefits to introducing an IT system without changing the organization of the company or introducing an organizational innovation without changing the IT system are much less than jointly introducing a new IT system alongside managerial or organizational innovation. When two technologies are so related they can be labelled complements. On a similar line it may be that the return to introducing a new technology may be greater if another older technology is already in place, for example, the return to a computerized warehouse may be greater if a computerized stock control system is already in place. Of course technologies may not necessarily be complements. Some technologies may be total or partial substitutes – for example, a computer numerically controlled (CNC) machine tool may be a complete substitute for a non-CNC machine tool in that once CNC is introduced the older machine is obsolete. More interesting, however, is the case of partial substitutes, where one technology only partially replaces another. An example might be mobile phones and fixed phones. The geographical coverage of the former may be less than for the latter but the former is mobile and thus there are advantages of having both. Multi-technology diffusion models have been analysed by Stoneman and Kwon (1994), Stoneman and Toivanen (1997) and Colombo and Mosconi (1995).

Following Stoneman (2000), consider two technologies A and B (and although the discussion is in terms of the potential adopter being a firm the story may be adapted to households by appropriate redefinition of profit as utility) of which firms require only one unit of each to fully equip their production processes (i.e. no intra-firm diffusion process). Allow that if owned alone the two technologies would yield profit gains to the firm per annum of g_A and g_B respectively (assuming g_A and g_B greater than zero). However, if the firm has both technologies A and B the profit gain (relative to having neither) will be $g_A + g_B + v$. Define the technologies A and B as:

1 complements if: $v > 0$ and thus $g_A + g_B + v > g_A + g_B$
2 total substitutes if: $v < 0$ and thus $g_A + g_B + v < g_A + g_B$, but also $g_A + g_B + v \leq g_A$, $g_A + g_B + v \leq g_B$ i.e. $g_B + v \leq 0$, $g_A + v \leq 0$
3 partial substitutes if: $v < 0$, and thus $g_A + g_B + v < g_A + g_B$ but also $g_A + g_B + v > g_A$, $g_A + g_B + v > g_B$ i.e. $g_B + v > 0$, $g_A + v > 0$

Let $P_A(t)$ and $P_B(t)$ be the costs of acquiring technologies A and B in time t. Assume for simplicity that firms are myopic and expect these prices to hold in perpetuity. Assume that the interest rate/discount rate is r, also taken to be a constant in perpetuity. Assume also that there is no resale market for used technologies although they have an infinite physical life.

At any moment in time there may be four types of firms: (a) those that have previously installed neither technology; (b) those that have previously installed A; (c) those that have previously installed B; and (d) those that have previously installed both. Clearly firms in category (d) will not be aiming to buy A or B in time t.

Consider a firm that has previously installed technology B. That firm's demand for technology A in time t will be determined by the profit gain from adoption relative to the cost of adoption. The net present value of that payoff is given by $V_{AS} = (g_A + v)/r - P(t)$, and the firm will buy the new technology in time t iff $g_A + v > rP_A(t)$, where in all such expressions the first subscript represents the starting configuration, the second the ending configuration. The subscript S implies both A and B and the subscript 0 implies neither A nor B. Clearly, *ceteris paribus*, the larger is v the greater is the probability that the firm will buy technology A. Thus if A and B are complements or partial substitutes the firm, having previously installed technology B, is more likely to buy technology A in time t.

Similarly a firm that has previously bought technology A will buy technology B in time t iff $V_{BS} > 0$, that is, iff $(g_B + v)/r > rP_B(t)$ and thus the greater is v the greater is the chance the firm will buy technology B in time t. Thus if A and B are complements or partial substitutes the firm, having previously installed technology A, is more likely to buy technology B in time t.

A firm that has previously bought neither technology before time t has four choices. To buy A, to buy B, to buy both A and B or to buy neither. The net present value payoffs to these four choices are

$$V_{0A} = g_A/r - P_A(t)$$

$$V_{0B} = g_B/r - P_B(t)$$

$$V_{0S} = (g_A + g_B + v)/r - P_A(t) - P_B(t)$$

$$V_{00} = 0$$

The firm will choose the adoption strategy that yields the maximum payoff. From the payoffs it is clear that as v increases the firm is more likely to buy both A and B, but as v declines it is more likely to buy only A or B.

On the basis of the above, for complementary technologies ($v > 0$), the following observations may be made:

1   The technology choice decision of the firm in time t is dependent upon its previous technological investments. Thus for example, if (P_A, P_B) are such that $P_A > (g_A + v)/r$ and $g_B/r < P_B < (g_B + v)/r$ then a firm that has previously installed technology A will find it profitable to now install technology B whereas a firm that has not previously installed technology A will not find it profitable to install technology A (or B). The lesson is clear, when there are complementarities between technologies, the previous technological state may impact on today's preferred technology choice.

2   With complementary technologies the demand for one technology will be negatively related to the price of the other technology. Thus, for example, if it is allowed that $g_B/r < P_B < (g_B + v)/r, g_A/r < P_A < (g_A + v)/r$ and one compares when P_B is less than and greater than $(g_A + g_B + v)/r - P_A$, then as P_B increases a firm that has not previously installed either technology will move from a position in which it is most profitable to buy both to a position where it is most profitable to buy neither. Thus the demand for A will decline as the price of B increases.

3   As the degree of complementarity increases (v gets larger) so the higher are the 'threshold' prices, P_A and P_B, at which a firm that has neither technology will buy both and also the higher are the prices at which a firm that already has one of the technologies will buy the other.

When $v = 0$ and there are no complementarities the demand for the two technologies is completely independent. This case is of little extra interest and thus is not explored further here. Of more interest is the case where $v < 0$, that is, the case of substitutes. Two types of substitutes have been defined: total substitutes if $v < 0$ and $g_B + v \leq 0$, $g_A + v \leq 0$; and partial substitutes where $v < 0$, and $g_B + v > 0$, $g_A + v > 0$. It is the second of these that is most interesting. Thus assume that $v < 0$, but $g_A + v > 0$, $g_B + v > 0$ and that $g_A + g_B + v > 0$.

This case is discussed in detail in Stoneman (2000). Once again the technology choice of the firm is dependent upon its previous technological state. It is also the case that the demand for one technology is dependent upon the price of the other, but now positively. Thus, for example, there are states when a firm that has previously installed neither technology will find it most profitable to install technology B, that is, 0,B is the optimal strategy in time t but as P_B increases the optimal strategy changes to either 0,0 or 0,A. In the latter case an increase in the price of technology B has increased the demand for technology A. It may also be seen that the higher is the absolute value of v so the lower are the 'threshold' prices, P_A and P_B, at which a firm that has neither technology will buy both and also the lower are the threshold prices at which a firm that already has one of the technologies will buy the other.

The partial substitute case is of interest for another reason however. As has been argued previously, diffusion may well be driven by reductions in the cost of acquisition of new technology. As P_A and P_B fall so use of A and B extend. In a multi-technology world, however, the use of A may well be related to the price of B and vice versa. It is shown in Stoneman (2000) that path dependency or non-ergodicity can result (showing that history matters). Where the economy will be today is influenced by where it has been in the past. One may note that this result only arises in the model where the two technologies are substitutes. In a world where P_A and P_B are not increasing over time, if A and B are complementary technologies there is no such path dependency.

To generate an inter-firm diffusion model on the basis of these principles is not difficult. The simplest approach is to allow that g_A, g_B and perhaps v differ across firms. Thus at any point in time threshold prices for the acquisition of A, or B or both differ across firms. One may then proceed in the way of a probit model with reductions in P_A and/or P_B generating diffusion paths for technologies A and B, with it clearly being the case that the diffusion paths for each technology are also dependent upon the prices of the other technology. Such an approach can be found in, for example, Stoneman and Kwon (1994).

5.3. Joint Inputs

In the previous section a world where two complementary technologies existed was considered. This section returns to the idea of a stand-alone technology but considers that to use the new technology one needs to acquire complementary inputs. Examples that are relevant might be:

1   Hi Fi systems where one needs CDs or tapes to produce the service flow.
2   Computer systems where one needs software as well as hardware.
3   Most production systems where raw material or intermediate input flows are required and/or where labour is required.

It should immediately be obvious that the profit or utility flow that will be generated by the technology will at least partly be related to the quantity of the joint input purchased or used. Also the greater is the cost of the joint input the greater will be the cost of generating the service flow. The net benefit of the technology will thus depend upon the price of the complementary inputs and as such these prices may be expected to affect the take up or adoption of the new technology. Gandal *et al.* (2000) explore the interaction between hardware and software prices in the determination of the diffusion of CD players. Most interestingly, however, they also address how the 'amount' of software available affected the diffusion of CD players.

If this were all there were to say about joint inputs the issue would not be particularly interesting. However, there is more to discuss. When there is a joint input, it could be that the price of the joint input falls over time and as this happens the attractiveness of the technology increases. To some degree at least the rate at which the price of the joint input falls will determine the speed of diffusion. What is really interesting, however, is that such a mechanism provides a means by which diffusion can be self-propagating as in the epidemic model. It could be, therefore, that use of a new technology by some means leads to reductions in the cost of a joint input. That reduction then stimulates further use and this leads to further diffusion.

Some examples of such a mechanism at work might be:

1 Acemoglu (1993) argues that the availability of skilled labour may act as a drag upon the use of new technologies. However if there is a mechanism by which labour learns 'on the job' as a new technology is used, as usage extends a greater number of workers will become trained. The trained personnel may leave the original using firm and create the ability for other firms to use the technology, or reduce the cost for other firms of using that technology.
2 As the ownership of hardware for joint hardware/software technologies increases, the market for software increases. This could lead to more software being made available and or software becoming cheaper and this will encourage further investment in both hardware and software (see, for example, Stoneman 1991). Thus, for example, the number of films available in DVD format will increase as the number of owners of DVD machines increases. As the number of films available increases so the attractiveness of DVD will increase.
3 As the extent of use of a new technology increases this may encourage the development of a number of specialist support markets. Thus, for example, as the ownership of cars increased so the garage or motor service trade developed. This may not only assist the further diffusion of the new technology but may also provide other means of using a new technology. At the early stages it may be that ownership is the only route. However, as markets develop and mature, outsourcing may well be more feasible. So, for instance, instead of purchasing computers one may purchase computer services.
4 Just as specialist support markets develop, other specialist markets may develop as diffusion proceeds. In particular finance markets for particular technologies may develop. An example would be the way in which, as the world market for air travel has increased and as the diffusion of air travel has advanced, so leasing as a means of financing aircraft acquisition has developed to replace outright purchase.

In many ways such happenings may be labelled as learning by doing, learning by using or even more generally network externalities. Network externalities have become important in the diffusion (and other literatures) in the last decade and are now generally recognized as an important economic phenomenon (the relevant literature includes, David and Greenstein, 1990; Arthur, 1989; Belleflamme, 1998; Choi and Thum, 1998; Saloner and Shepard, 1995; Katz and Shapiro, 1986). At the most general level, technologies with network externalities are technologies such that the benefits from ownership are increasing with the number of owners of the technology. At the simplest level this may be because the technologies are similar to say phones or fax machines, where the more users there are, the more connections can be made and thus the greater are the benefits to be gained from ownership. On the other hand, network externalities may arise through the sorts of mechanisms that we have exemplified in points 1–4 immediately above. The effects are the same.

The impact of network externalities is that the benefits to ownership of a technology increase with the number of other users. This may be directly contrasted to the arguments presented in the stock model in chapter 3 where it was considered that the benefits from ownership may decline with the number of other users. The forces are counteracting. In the stock model it was argued that at any moment in time the number of users was limited because the addition of more users would drive the benefits below the cost of acquisition. In the presence of network externalities that reasoning clearly does not apply. Also in the stock model when a firm considered adoption it had to take account of how further use by other firms in the future would reduce its own gross benefits of adoption. In the presence of network externalities further use by other firms in the future would actually lead to increased returns in the future. It is, however, possible that the arguments of the order model will still apply in the presence of network externalities (i.e. there are first mover advantages that encourage early adoption).

In the probit model considered above, two conditions were specified that had to be met by the firm in determining its optimal adoption date. A profitability criterion and an arbitrage criterion. The first guaranteed that at the date of adoption that adoption was profitable. The second determined that the adoption was most profitable at the date of adoption. However, the second order conditions on the arbitrage criterion may be violated for technologies with network externalities as the benefits of adoption may be increasing over time. This model would thus have to be used with considerable care in the presence of potential network externalities.

5.4.   Standards and Compatibility

The previous section discussed technologies with joint inputs that may illustrate network externalities. The argument was that as the technology was more extensively used the benefits to adoption increased. It has been recognized in the literature that in many cases when new technologies appear on the market they appear in different forms. This was previously discussed under the product differentiation label. However, when the technologies also exhibit network externalities then the issue becomes of greater relevance. Consider the following examples:

*   When video recorders first appeared on the market there were three basic types, VHS, BETA and Video 2000. This is a technology that showed network externalities in that the greater the number of users of a format the greater the supply of software (films) for that format. However the software was not compatible across the formats.
*   In the personal computer markets the two main formats are IBM clones or PCs and Apple machines. Full benefit of the computer only comes when software is available. However, to a large degree PC software cannot be run on Apple machines and vice versa.

These examples illustrate that network externalities may be format (or model) specific. The purchaser of a new technology may thus only get the full benefits from that technology if other buyers choose the same format. If a buyer chooses a format that others do not choose then his/her benefits from adoption may well be much less. This creates uncertainty that could well affect the adoption decision. Relevant questions are: (1) whether such incompatibilities will be removed over time through 'standardization'; (2) if they are removed can one predict which format will be dominant; and (3) what are the full implications for the nature of the diffusion process of the general technology?

The basis of the models that are analysed in this area are that there are two competing formats of a technology, say A and B. The benefits to an individual or firm from purchasing format A and format B are $\alpha + \delta_A x_A$ and $\beta + \delta_B x_B$ respectively where α and β are the inherent benefits of each format (and may differ across potential buyers) and x_A and x_B are the number of users of technology A and B respectively. As benefits increase with the number of users ($\delta_A > 0, \delta_B > 0$) there are network externalities, but the network externalities are specific to the owners of that specific format.

In such a framework, Brian Arthur (1989) has shown that, if one allows that potential buyers of the technology fall into two groups, some with an inherent preference for variant A and some with an inherent preference for variant B of the technology and these buyers arrive at the market in a random order, then as long as the network externalities are positive, (1) eventually one format will become dominant and be the industry standard; (2) the dominant standard is not necessarily the best in that, with the other standard dominant, total benefits may have been higher; (3) one cannot predict in advance which standard will become dominant. In fact the determination of the dominant format depends to some degree at least on chance and thus history matters – that is, there is path dependency. If there is a run of arrivals at the early stage who inherently prefer technology B then technology B is likely to build up network externalities encouraging even those who inherently prefer A to choose B. Alternatively if there is an early run of buyers who prefer A then A might become dominant. As arrivals to the market are random one cannot predict the eventual outcome.

Further developments of the Brian Arthur framework that allow buyers to be more forward looking and also allow firms to manipulate the market through the sponsorship of particular technologies have also been modelled but the basic principles are still present in the models (see, for example, Katz and Shapiro, 1985). Of more interest here is the approach of Choi (1997) that addresses such issues in a diffusion model.

In her approach Choi looks at the interaction between informational externalities (as per the epidemic model, see also Kapur, 1995) and network externalities. She considers irreversible investments in a technology that is available in two formats, A and B. The net benefits for an individual choosing technology A(B) are $\alpha(\beta) + \upsilon n$ where n is the number of people choosing the same format. Prior to first investment in a format the benefits or payoffs to that format, α and β, are not known with certainty, but once used by one potential adopter the true value of the payoff is known. Prior to first use α and β are assumed independently distributed and have continuous and positive density on support $(0, \infty)$.

For the sake of argument put aside the network externalities for a moment. The first buyer of the new technology must choose one format. Let this be technology A. The purchase will reveal to all the true returns to technology A. The second buyer will then also have to choose between A and B. The comparison is a simple one. If $E(\beta)$ is the expected value of the net benefits of B the second buyer will choose format B if $E(\beta) > \alpha$ and technology A if the reverse is true. If the second buyer chooses technology A then the true value of the benefit of technology B will not be revealed. The third buyer will thus have no more information than the second. But as the third buyer is the same as the second he/she will also choose A and the true value of the benefit of B will never be revealed. All buyers will choose A. If, on the other hand, the second buyer chooses B, then the true benefit to B will be revealed and all future buyers may see whether $\alpha > \beta$ or $\alpha < \beta$ and make the correct technology choice in future periods. One may see that the market will only reveal the true benefits of both technologies if the first two users make different technology choices.

When network externalities are introduced into the story, however, there is an extra force to take into account. If the first user chooses technology A then the second user will know the inherent return to that technology. The choice facing this second user is A or B. If B is chosen and B is found to be superior to A, the true returns to B are then known (and greater than to A) and all future adopters will choose B. Having chosen B the second adopter will thus get the greatest possible payoff with positive network externalities. However, if B is chosen and B is revealed to be inferior, all future adopters will know this and will then choose A. The returns to A will then increase as network effects kick in. The firm that chooses B will thus suffer much lower relative returns than just $\alpha - \beta$ because the returns to A will be $\alpha + \upsilon n$ and the returns to B just β. In making the decision on whether to buy A or B the second buyer will thus try to avoid being stranded with an inferior technology.

Choi interprets this argument as that technology A may be an industry's current standard practice. Technology B is a new practice that could be introduced. The uncertainty about the new technology combined with the information externality that a firm's use of the technology would generate would lead a firm to have excess inertia in deciding whether to use the new. One might note that this is a very different story to how information externalities drive diffusion in epidemic models. There the emphasis is on the fact that information externalities encourage further use. Here, that is not disputed, it is just the fact that as the information externality may place the firm providing the information at a relative disadvantage, it will be reluctant to undertake the investment that would generate the externality.

Further developing the model Choi shows that the effects being considered will create an inefficient delay in the adoption of technology. She calls such effects 'Penguin effects' whereby each user is reluctant to move first as long as there is a possibility that their choice might make them a technological orphan.

The insight thus provided in this discussion is that in general, the existence of alternative incompatible formats of a technology appearing on the market simultaneously, especially in the presence of network externalities and with uncertainties as to the actual benefits of the different formats, can lead buyers in a market to delay adoption while the standards are established through the behaviour of others. It may even be that if all wait for others to act then the diffusion will never start (which may lead to some interesting policy suggestions – to both governments and suppliers). It is, however, quite possible that the final standard established may not be the best format. Moreover once a standard has been established, there may well be considerable inertia in moving to any new improved standard that has appeared. The latter effects may well reduce the final or asymptotic use of the technology.

5.5.   General Purpose Technologies

General purpose technologies (GPT) is a term that is being applied to technologies that are characterized first by their pervasiveness, in that they are used as inputs by a wide and ever expanding range of sectors in the economy and secondly, as they diffuse they foster complementary investments and technical change in user sectors bringing about sustained and pervasive productivity gains. Examples quoted are steam engines, electricity and microelectronics. It has been argued (see for example, David, 1991; Bresnahan and Trajtenberg, 1995; and Helpman and Trajtenberg, 1994) that such technologies may play a major role in economic growth.

In many ways the appearance of a new GPT on the scene is very similar to the appearance of a new technological trajectory as discussed in the more evolutionary based literature. The new GPT or trajectory represents a drastic break with the foundations of previous technologies and a whole new direction of technological development.

Helpman and Trajtenberg (1996) discuss the diffusion of such GPTs. The basic principles of their discussion is that in an early stage a new GPT requires the development of complementary inputs that would allow the GPT to be used and offer greater productivity than the previous GPT. During this development phase the economy is investing resources in developing technology but as the technology is not yet available for use is not receiving any payoff benefits. At some stage the number of complementary inputs is large enough to enable the GPT to be more productive than the old technology. The benefits then start to flow. In many ways this is very similar to the concept of diffusion included in Hicks (1973), where an initial investment stage always precedes the generation of benefits from a new technology. However, once the new GPT is in use further development of the GPT takes place that reinforces its productivity effect.

Helpman and Trajtenberg consider a GPT that can be used in a number of different product sectors in the economy. For each sector they predict that there will be an initial phase of development of complementary inputs followed by use of the GPT followed then by further development. They consider the factors that will determine the order of use of the GPT by the different sectors and thus inter-sectoral diffusion. They argue that the key factors that will determine the order of use are:

1 The potential productivity gain that the new GPT will yield relative to the previous GPT which in turn may depend upon the extent to which complementary inputs for the old GPT have been developed.
2 The cost of developing complementary inputs for the new GPT.
3 The demand for the products of the sector from which a return on investment can be generated.

These are exactly the factors that one might consider relevant on the basis of discussions above. However, one might also think that with GPTs there may well be considerable inter-sectoral knowledge flows and interdependencies. Complementary inputs generated for one sector can be used in another, experiences may flow across sectors and the total of sectoral demands may generate economies of scale and scope that a single sector may not generate. There may also be significant cross-country effects if one thinks in terms of the world rather than just a domestic economy.

GPTs obviously represent the macro end of the technology diffusion debate. It is also clear that full insight into the development and use of GPTs (and also less major technologies) incorporates the supply side (the industries supplying the technologies embodying the new technologies and also the complementary inputs that go with them). This is the purview of the next chapter.

5.6. Conclusions

This chapter has extended beyond the analysis of stand-alone technologies to consider the diffusion of interrelated technologies, technologies with joint inputs, standards and compatability, and also general purpose technologies. The analysis has indicated that in such more complex environments the menu of factors that will impinge upon the diffusion process is greater. Thus, for example, it has been indicated that the acquisition costs of complementary technologies, the prices of joint inputs, uncertainty as to dominant standards and information externalities could all affect the diffusion process. It has also been shown how in the diffusion process there may be non-ergodicity and that history may well matter. It has also been illustrated how through such factors one may have diffusion paths that are self-propagating. The final part of the chapter addressed general purpose technologies which in many ways one might expect to show all the characteristics of these more complex relationships. In the next chapter supply side issues are discussed.

References

Acemoglu, D. (1993) 'Labour Market Imperfections, Innovation Incentives and the Dynamics of Aggregate Innovation', presented at the RES Annual Conference, University of York, April.

Arthur, W.B. (1989) 'Competing Technologies, Increasing Returns and Lock in by Historical Events', *Economic Journal*, 99, 116–31.

Belleflamme, P. (1998) 'Adoption of Network Technologies in Oligopolies', *International Journal of Industrial Organisation*, 16(4), 415–44.

Bresnahan, T. and Trajtenberg, M. (1995) 'General Purpose Technologies – Engines of Growth?', *Journal of Econometrics*, 65(1), 83–108.

Choi, J.P. (1997) 'Herd Behavior, the Penguin Effect and the Suppression of Informational Diffusion: An Analysis of Informational Externalities and Payoff Interdependency', *Rand Journal of Economics*, 28(3), 407–25.

Choi, J.P. and Thum, M. (1998) 'Market Structure and the Timing of Technology Adoption with Network Externalities', *European Economic Review*, 42(2), 225–44.

Colombo, M. and Mosconi, R. (1995) 'Complementarity and Cumulative Learning Effects in the Early Diffusion of Multiple Technologies', *Journal of Industrial Economics*, 43, 13–48.

David, P.A. (1991) 'Computer and Dynamo: The Modern Productivity Paradox in a Not Too Distant Mirror', in *Technology and Productivity: The Challenge for Economic Policy*, Paris: OECD.

David, P. and Greenstein, S. (1990) 'The Economics of Compatability Standards: An Introduction to Recent Research', *Economics of Innovation and New Technology*, 1, 3–42.

Gandal, N., Kende, M. and Rob, R. (2000) 'The Dynamics of Technological Adoption in Hardware/ Software Systems: The Case of CD Players', *Rand Journal of Economics*, 31(1), 43–61.

Helpman, E. and Trajtenberg, M. (1994) 'A Time to Sow and a Time to Reap: Growth Based on General Purpose Technologies', NBER Working Paper No. 4584.

Helpman, E. and Trajtenberg, M. (1996) 'Diffusion of General Purpose Technologies', NBER Working Paper No. 5773.

Hicks, Sir J.R. (1973) *Capital and Time*, London: Oxford University Press.

Kapur, S. (1995) 'Technological Diffusion with Social Learning', *Journal of Industrial Economics*, 43(2), 173–95.

Katz, M.L. and Shapiro, C. (1985) 'Network Externalities, Competition and Compatability', *American Economic Review*, 75(3), 424–40.

Katz, M.L. and Shapiro, C. (1986) 'Technology Adoption in the Presence of Network Externalities', *Journal of Political Economy*, 94, 824–42.

Saloner, G. and Shepard, A. (1995) 'Adoption of Technologies with Network Effects: An Empirical Examination of the Adoption of Automatic Teller Machines', *Rand Journal of Economics*, 26(3), 479–501.

Stoneman, P. (1991) 'Copying Capabilities and Intertemporal Competition between Joint Input Technologies: CD vs DAT', *Economics of Innovation and New Technology*, 1(3), 233–42.

Stoneman, P. (2000) 'Path Dependency and Reswitching in a Model of Multi Technology Adoption', presented at a Festchrift in honor of Paul David, Center for Economic Policy Research, Stanford University, June.

Stoneman, P. and Kwon, M.J. (1994) 'The Diffusion of Multiple Process Technologies', *Economic Journal*, 104, 420–31.

Stoneman, P. and Toivanen, O. (1997) 'The Diffusion of Multiple Technologies: An Empirical Study', *Economics of Innovation and New Technology*, 5(1), 1–18.

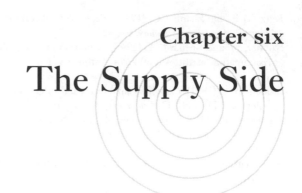

Chapter six
The Supply Side

6.1. Introduction

The previous three chapters have concentrated on the analysis of diffusion as a demand-side phenomenon. In this analysis, it was argued, for example, that the cost of acquiring new technology and changes therein, the performance of the technology and changes therein and information and changes therein will all impact on households' or firms' decisions as to whether and/or when to adopt newer technologies. However, these factors were taken as determined exogenously to the diffusion process itself. Although much of the diffusion literature continues to proceed in this way, in doing so one is restricting the analysis and as such the understanding of the process.

On a general level it is reasonable to argue that prices, performance and information, for example, are, to some degree at least, determined endogenously to the diffusion process through the interaction of supply and demand (see Stoneman and Ireland, 1983). If, for example, one considers a sector that supplies capital goods that embody new technology, then if that sector is monopolized one might expect the prices of the goods supplied to be higher than if the sector is perfectly competitive. As prices will impact on the diffusion path, the interaction of supply and demand would predict higher levels of use in a competitive environment than in a monopoly environment. A full explanation of the pattern of diffusion would thus encompass some details on the nature of the supplying sector. In this chapter the supply sector and the interaction of supply and demand are considered.

For the supplying sector, goods that embody new technology will be product innovations rather than process innovations. Thus the analysis of the supply sector is really the analysis of product innovation. The issues that need to be addressed in the analysis then encompass:

1 How will suppliers price new products embodying new technology and in particular what pattern of intertemporal price trajectories can one expect?
2 As potential suppliers of information through, for example advertising, how will supplier behaviour impact on the diffusion path?
3 How will supplier behaviour with regard to product differentiation develop and what will be the impact on the diffusion path?

4 How will suppliers' behaviour impact on the rate of appearance, improvement and technological obsolescence of new technologies?
5 How might one expect the structure (in terms of the number and size of firms) of the supplying industry to change over time and with what impact on the diffusion path?

Each of these issues is addressed in turn below, in the order in which they have been presented.

6.2. Intertemporal Pricing of New Technologies

Consider a new technology embodied in a stand-alone capital good and for the sake of exposition consider the potential buyers to be firms. Following Ireland and Stoneman (1986), reproduced as chapter 13 below, allow that the firms belong to an industry of N firms, all firms have perfect information on the performance of the technology but are heterogeneous in that different firms obtain different gross benefits from its use. The annual return is considered to be a constant and independent of the number of other users. Firms may be defined along a continuum x in order of the gross returns obtained from use of the technology. There is no uncertainty. Allow that the technology can be acquired by the purchase of one unit of the new capital good at a price in time t of $P(t)$. Following procedures laid out in chapter 3 as per the probit or rank model of diffusion one may then specify an intertemporal demand curve for the technology based upon the profitability and arbitrage conditions.

Let $g(x)$ be the return from the acquisition of the new technology to the xth ranked firm in the benefit order. As it will turn out that firms buy the technology in the benefit order and firms only ever buy one unit of the technology, one may then immediately state that the gross user benefit that will be derived from the xth unit of the technology sold will also be $g(x)$.

From the profitability condition, the xth ranked firm will be a user of the new technology in time t iff

$$g(x)/r \geq P(t) \tag{6.1}$$

and from the arbitrage condition iff

$$g(x)/r \geq P(t) - DP^e(t)/r \tag{6.2}$$

where $DP^e(t)$ is the expected change in the price of the technology between t and $t + 1$. As stated above, if firms are myopic ($DP^e(t) = 0$), then the profitability condition dominates the arbitrage condition. As an alternative, one can consider perfect foresight which implies that $DP^e(t)$ equals the actual change in price, $DP(t)$. As in this framework $DP(t)$ is always less than or equal to zero, the arbitrage condition will then dominate and define the intertemporal demand curve for the new technology. Both cases are separately considered here. In this it is assumed that at any point in time the above two conditions hold as equalities (thus ruling out corner solutions). It is also useful in this analysis to consider the flow version of the myopia condition rather than as stated above. Differentiating with respect to t, the profitability condition yields the myopia demand curve

$$-DP(t) + rP(t) = g(x(t)) - g_x Q(t)/r \qquad (6.3)$$

where $Q = dx/dt$ the quantity supplied in time t (given that as the number of adopters equals the number of units sold, the change in the number of adopters in time t also equals the amount supplied in time t).

In previous analysis it was essentially argued that as $P(t)$ falls over time so usage would extend (or diffusion proceed). However, the price change was considered exogenous. By adding the supply side we can make this change endogenous.

There are many different ways of modelling supply/demand interaction (see for an alternative, Ireland and Stoneman, 1985) and particularly how the unit cost of production of capital goods embodying the new technology, $c(t)$, changes over time. Here it is assumed that unit production costs fall over time exogenously. In other work (e.g. David and Olsen, 1986) learning by doing has been allowed and in this case costs fall with cumulative output. The different assumptions yield different results. Here, however, assume that $c(t)$ falls over time until some point in time t^*, after which costs start to rise again. The problem that faces the supplying firm is, in the face of costs falling over time and demand as given by either the myopia of foresight demand curves, what is the optimal (value maximizing) intertemporal pricing policy.

In Ireland and Stoneman (1986) it is shown that the optimal pricing policy depends on (1) whether buyers are myopic or have perfect foresight and (2) the number of competing suppliers. As a benchmark case, consider where buyers are myopic and there is a monopoly supplier. It can then be shown that the supplying firm will sell the new technology until time t^*, the date when costs stop falling, and for all $t < t^*$, it will set prices such that

$$rc(t) - Dc(t) = g(x(t)) \qquad (6.4)$$

At t^*, $Dc(t) = 0$ thus $rc(t^*) = g(x(t^*))$. Given that under myopia

$$g(x(t))/r = P(t) \qquad (6.5)$$

the time profile of prices is given by

$$P(t) = c(t) - Dc(t)/r \qquad (6.6)$$

with

$$P(t^*) = c(t^*) \qquad (6.7)$$

The price of purchasing the new technology is thus endogenized. The key condition is that $rc(t) - Dc(t) = g(x(t))$, which may be interpreted as that diffusion occurs such that the present value of the flow of benefits to the marginal adopter is equal to the rate of change of the present value of production costs. This is an intertemporal version of the standard monopolist pricing condition that marginal revenue equals marginal cost. In figure 6.1 $rc(t)$ and $rc(t) - Dc(t)$ are plotted against time and $g(x)$ against x. As time proceeds we move down the $rc(t) - Dc(t)$ curve and as $g(x)$ is brought into equality with $rc(t) - Dc(t)$, $x(t)$ increases, mapping out the diffusion path. This occurs until date t^* is reached when the diffusion

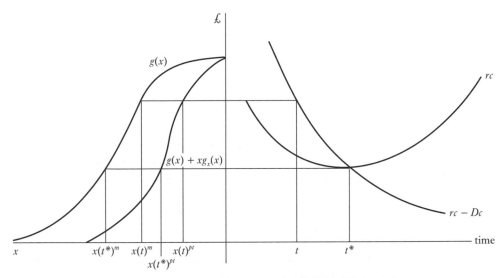

Figure 6.1 Supply–demand interaction and the diffusion path

ceases. It should be noted that under monopoly with myopic buyers $g(x(t))/r = P(t)$. That is, each buyer is paying a price that equals the present value of the gross benefits from the technology. The monopolist's revenue is thus equal to the gross present value obtained by all buyers. In essence the monopolist is perfectly price discriminating (intertemporally). The monopolist prices in order to have output in each period that will maximize the present value of the difference between revenue and the costs of production. The difference between the revenue and the costs is not only profits, but is also the social surplus, or welfare, generated by the use of the new technology. By maximizing profits under perfect intertemporal price discrimination the monopolist is thus also maximizing welfare. Under myopia and monopoly, therefore, the diffusion path being mapped out is the welfare optimal diffusion path as long as distribution issues are not considered relevant. Along this path the monopolist is appropriating all the social surplus of the innovation as profit.

   If the assumption of myopia on the part of buyers is relaxed then buyers will be expecting the price falls that actually occur. This expectation will lead them to delay adoption. The monopoly supplier will need to take account of this in his/her pricing. In fact the seller will no longer be able to perfectly price discriminate. Discrimination requires that the monopolist sells to a high benefit adopter at a high price today and a low benefit adopter at a low price tomorrow. If the high benefit adopter knows this, he/she will have an incentive to wait until tomorrow, buying at the lower price, and thus the supplier cannot appropriate all his/her gross benefit. In fact, the supplier mitigates this problem by having a slower rate of price reduction than under myopia, but this only mitigates the problem, it does not solve it. Ireland and Stoneman (1986) show that with perfect foresight the monopolist will price such that

$$g(x(t)) + x(t)g_x = rc(t) - Dc(t) \qquad (6.8)$$

until t^* where

$$g(x(t^*)) + x(t^*)g_x = rc(t^*) \tag{6.9}$$

This implies that the price profile over time is given by

$$P(t) = (DP(t) - x(t)g_x)/r + c(t) - Dc(t)/r \tag{6.10}$$

which differs from the price under myopia by $(DP(t) - x(t)g_x)/r$.

In figure 6.1 $g(x(t)) + x(t)g_x$ is plotted and the diffusion path mapped out for the case of perfect foresight. It may immediately be seen that

1   For all t, the extent of diffusion is less under perfect foresight than under myopia.
2   The end level of use is less under foresight than myopia.
3   The diffusion ends at the same date under foresight and myopia.
4   As the diffusion path under myopia was welfare optimal, the diffusion path under perfect foresight is too slow from a welfare point of view.
5   As under myopia the monopolist was able to appropriate all the surplus and now cannot do so, under foresight the profits of the monopolist are lower.

A monopolist does not have to consider the behaviour of rivals. When there are other suppliers, however, the monopolist does have to take their behaviour into account. In particular, the structure of this model is that the monopolist faces a market of fixed size (there is a given number of potential buyers each of whom will only ever buy one unit). The monopolist then prices in such a way to generate adoption dates that maximize his/her profits. When there are rivals, however, each supplier has to be aware that a sale by a rival is a sale lost forever to the firm itself. In setting prices therefore an oligopoly supplier may prefer to set prices below those that the monopolist would set rather than lose a customer in perpetuity. This is known as a common pool problem (see Dasgupta, 1987). The market is of a fixed size, and in general the more suppliers there are in the market the more will those suppliers try to make a sale before rivals make a sale and take the customer out of the market. A common result in common pool cases is that a monopolist would exploit the market at a welfare optimal rate. If there is more than one supplier then the market will be exploited at a rate that is faster than optimal (Dasgupta and Stiglitz, 1980). That is what is also found here.

The extreme case of many suppliers is perfect competition. In the case of perfect competition one may expect that the new technology will be priced at marginal cost. Thus at each point in time we will have that $P(t) = c(t)$. Under perfect foresight the diffusion path is then characterized by

$$g(x) = rP(t) - DP(t) = rc(t) - Dc(t) \tag{6.11}$$

and

$$g(x(t^*)) = rc(t^*) \tag{6.12}$$

which is exactly the same as the path under myopia with a monopoly supplier. By comparison with the path under perfect foresight and monopoly it can then be concluded that:

1 Under perfect competition the diffusion path involves higher levels of use than under monopoly for a common expectations regime.
2 The diffusion path under perfect foresight and perfect competition is the same as under monopoly and myopia, which is also the welfare optimal diffusion path.
3 Under perfect competition and myopia the diffusion path will be faster than under monopoly and myopia and thus too fast from a welfare point of view.

It should be noted, however, that although the diffusion paths under monopoly with myopia and under perfect competition with perfect foresight are the same (and is the welfare optimal path), the distribution of the benefits are quite different. Under monopoly the supplying firm gets all the benefits. Under perfect competition and perfect foresight the users of the technology get all the benefits. This will be considered further below.

The lessons of this analysis for the study of diffusion paths can be listed:

1 Analysis restricted to the demand side alone treats as exogenous factors that may well be endogenous and as such presents an incomplete picture.
2 Changes in the costs of supplying (producing) the goods that embody new technology is a major driving force on the downward movement of prices for that technology and thus a major factor driving the diffusion process.
3 The structure of the industry that supplies the new technology has an important impact on intertemporal pricing of the technology and thus the diffusion path, as well as on the distribution of the benefits gained from use of new technology.
4 The expectations held by buyers impact both directly and indirectly (through optimal pricing) on the diffusion path and also on the distribution of the benefits from new technology.
5 The consideration of both demand and supply factors enables the definition of the welfare optimal diffusion path and also some prediction of when it may be expected to be followed.

These are useful results. However, they have been derived from a rather stylized model and several issues have not been addressed. For example, from where do the reductions in the costs of supply come? They may in fact result from the diffusion of technologies developed elsewhere. Is it reasonable to assume that the market structure of the supplying industry is given and fixed? It may in fact change over time as the diffusion proceeds. Is it reasonable to allow, as above, that the nature of the technology remains the same over the whole diffusion path and, if not, from where will improvements come? Might it even be that the technology becomes obsolescent as diffusion proceeds? Finally it has been assumed that firms have full information on the technology. Is this reasonable? These issues are discussed further below.

6.3.   Information Provision and Pricing

In the previous section it was argued that diffusion proceeds as suppliers reduce the cost of acquiring technology. These reductions are in turn driven by reductions in production cost.

Essentially as production costs fall, price falls and as price falls users getting lower and lower gross benefits from the use of the new technology adopt. If/when costs of production stop falling, prices stop falling and diffusion stops. In other words it is the price reductions generated on the supply side that drive diffusion.

In this section we present some reasons why instead of prices falling over time for a new technology it may be that it is optimal (profit maximizing) for suppliers to set prices low initially and increase them later, and as such diffusion will be seen with prices rising over time. The key to this result is information spreading (see Glaister, 1974). For an analysis of information spreading amongst both buyers and suppliers, see Vettas (1998).

As has been seen in the discussion of demand side models in chapter 3, issues relating to information have played a significant role in the modelling of diffusion. The most enduring story is the epidemic one where one firm's use of a technology creates an externality in that use provides information to non-users who in turn may then become users. This, as has been seen, provides a self-propagating diffusion process.

Consider firms that supply new technology in such an environment. Initially think of there being only one supplier, a monopolist. When the supplier sells a unit of the new technology he/she will reap two benefits. The first is the revenue from the sale. The second is the extra information that is supplied to the market through the learning externality. A sale today will therefore increase the demand for his/her product tomorrow. However the size of the externality will decline as more potential buyers of the technology become informed. The greater are the number of informed potential adopters the fewer are left to be informed and thus the smaller will be the impact of the learning externality upon future demand for the product. For the supplier, therefore, in determining the price to be charged for a product incorporating the new technology, two factors have to be taken into account on the revenue side, the first is the actual revenue generated by the sale in the period and the second is the increase in revenue in the future that the sale will generate, but the second factor is declining over time.

Given the learning externality it may therefore be in a monopolist supplier's interest to price the product low in the early years in order to increase demand for later years. This incentive may be strong enough to have a price for the new technology that starts low and then increases as the learning externality declines in importance. Basically we may think of a situation in which the cost of supplying the technology is $c(t)$ and declining with time. In the early years the monopolist may price below $c(t)$ in order to generate a stock of owners who will provide information externalities. As time proceeds, usage extends and demand increases, and price may be increased to exceed $c(t)$ so that profits are generated, enabling the present value of the profit stream to be maximized. By pricing low in the early years the monopolist is (1) generating an earlier revenue stream, the increase in the revenue stream being dependent on the size of the externality and this is more desirable the greater is the discount rate, but (2) undertaking production at higher costs ($c(t)$ is falling over time) and this is less desirable the faster costs are falling. The actual price profile will thus depend on the relative size of these two forces. It should be noted that in chapter 2 it was shown that most of the empirical evidence seems to suggest that the prices of new products actually fall over time.

It might also be noted that in general the existence of an externality will tend to lead to welfare sub-optimality. Thus, as early adopters of a new technology cannot internalize all the social benefit of their adoption behaviour (the benefit of learning goes to the learners and may actually harm the firm providing the information), they will have adoption incentives that are too low from a welfare point of view and thus will tend to adopt too late. However, when the supply side is added, through pricing, the monopolist supplier is able to internalize the externality. The diffusion path generated by the monopolist pricing policy is thus likely, to some extent, to correct the welfare sub–optimality generated by the externality on the demand side.

Pricing is not the only tool that the supplier may use to encourage early use of a technology. There is also direct information provision, through, for example, advertising. The firm may advertise its new technology and by so doing increase the information available to potential buyers. Allied with a 'learning from others' mechanism one might see information on the technology developing in such a way that the firm's advertising stimulates use, that then leads to further spreading of information through social contact. In such an environment, in line with the argument on pricing, it might be expected that a profit maximizing firm will advertise more extensively in the early years of the product's life when the extra learning benefits will be large, and advertise less in later years when there are fewer potential buyers and fewer potential learners. It must of course be realized, however, that the firm does not want to stimulate early demand too much if the cost of production is falling over time.

When there is more than one supplier the story may be somewhat different. The discussion here is restricted to the case where there is no product differentiation and thus the products embodying the new technology are the same whoever supplies them. If there is more than one supplier then if the firm either expends money on advertising the technology, or sets prices low in order to stimulate future demand for the technology, then at least some of the impact of the advertising or the increased future demand will spill over to rival suppliers. The firm will no longer be able to fully appropriate the benefits of its actions. In such circumstances the incentives to advertise or to stimulate demand through low prices, are lower than under monopoly and as such the amount of advertising undertaken or the extent to which price is set low in the early years will be reduced. (Although it might be noted that advertising may have two effects, to increase the demand for the product in general and to increase demand for the firm's own product, but with the absence of any product differentiation the second of these has been ruled out.) It may thus be argued that as the number of suppliers increases less information is likely to be provided by each firm (and by the market as a whole) and also there will be less tendency to price the technology low in the early years. In fact as the market moves towards perfect competition one might expect marginal cost pricing and zero advertising.

One might also note that the case of information externalities is mirrored by a world in which the suppliers of new technology experience learning by doing in their production costs. In such a situation a supplier would have lower production costs the greater the number of units of the capital good embodying the new technology he/she had supplied to date. In line with the case of information externalities, such learning would tend to encourage suppliers to price low at the start of the diffusion process in order to generate the learning economies (David and Olsen, 1986).

6.4. Product Differentiation

In chapter 3 the impact of product differentiation on the take-up of new technology was discussed. In essence it was argued that if users have different tastes then product differentiation

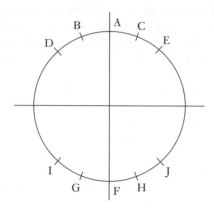

Figure 6.2   Horizontal product differentiation

would lead to a situation where the products supplied would more closely match buyers' tastes and this would encourage earlier usage and higher reservation prices. Clearly, however, the extent of product differentiation is determined by the supply side of the market (see Stoneman, 1989, 1990).

Consider initially that the supplier of the new technology is a monopolist. Assume that, as in the conceptual example discussed in chapter 3, the buyers (all of whom only ever buy one unit) have different preferences and these preferences are distributed round a unit circle (as if the buyers were located around a lake). Conceptually the scenario is as in figure 3.3, reproduced as figure 6.2. If the monopolist supplies one product variant say A, then the number of potential buyers will depend on how well that product matches their preferences and the price being charged. Let the price in time t be such that the buyers in the arc BC find purchase desirable. In time $t + 1$ the supplier (if costs are falling) will lower the price and ownership will extend to the extra consumers in the arcs BD and CE. Over time the supplier could continue to reduce prices and in doing so buyers further and further distant from A would purchase the technology.

Alternatively the supplier could make another product variant available, say of characteristics F. Assume that this variant has the same production costs as the original product. Pricing this new variant at the same price as the original variant the supplier would double his/her revenue in each time period compared to the situation in which there is only one product variant (the supplier would be selling to buyers located around F at a higher price and an earlier date). With two product variants on the market the supplier, for a given price trajectory, would sell to the whole market in half the time and have twice the revenue in each year until that point. The total (undiscounted) revenue over the whole diffusion path would also be twice that on the path with only one product variant. The advantages to the supplier of offering two product variants is that revenue is increased and it is generated at an earlier date (which with positive discounting is desirable). However, if the costs of production are falling this implies that the market is supplied at higher, rather than lower, cost. In addition one might consider that there are fixed costs to each product variant and thus the more variants that there are the higher are the firm's fixed costs. The actual number of product variants to be offered by the monopolist will depend on the interaction of these costs and benefits.

If the supplier is a monopolist, then in determining the number of product variants on offer, the firm internalizes the impact of an extra product variant on the profit of existing variants. When the supply industry is not monopolized the impact of one firm's extra variant on other firms' profit streams are not internalized. There will thus be a tendency for structures with more suppliers to offer more product variants. Again there is a common pool problem. When the common pool problem was analysed before it was shown how in the presence of a number of suppliers each would try to price so as to avoid a potential purchaser being removed form the market by a rival's action. Here the issue would be that in a common pool competing suppliers would tend to offer more product variants, in fact a number of product variants that would tend to lead to diffusion that is too fast from the welfare point of view.

The principles discussed here largely refer to horizontal product differentiation. One could also address vertical product differentiation but the points are made (see Stoneman, 1990). There are, however, a couple of follow-on issues.

If there is product differentiation in the market then the conclusions reached with respect to advertising in a world with many suppliers and no product differentiation would have to be modified. With product differentiation if a firm advertises then it may expect to some degree at least that it will be able to internalize the returns to that advertising expenditure. Thus with product differentiation, even if the number of suppliers gets large, firms may well still find it desirable to advertise and as such speed up the adoption process.

Finally there is the issue of standards and compatibility. The issue of product differentiation and standards are similar. When standards were discussed in the previous chapter this essentially concerned different product variants. The twist was, however, that in that chapter the complication of network externalities was added. The analysis of standards is essentially the analysis of product differentiated markets with each product showing product specific externalities. In many ways this is similar to having product differentiation and advertising. If there are product specific network externalities how is this likely to affect the diffusion path through supplier behaviour? If there is only one supplier, whether that supplier will offer more than one product variant will depend on the relative sizes of fixed costs and the relative benefits from selling earlier and producing later. When there is more than one supplier each with their own product variant attached to which are network externalities, one is likely to see sponsorship behaviour whereby firms will price low and advertise their product variant in the early years in order to become the dominant standard and to get the benefits therefrom. The literature would suggest that in a world of competing standards there would be insufficient standardization (see, for example, Katz and Shapiro, 1985; Farrell and Saloner, 1985).

6.5.   Product Improvement

In the second section of this chapter a model in which a given technology is supplied by one or more firms into the market was analysed. It was assumed that the cost of producing this technology was falling and as a result it was predicted that the cost of acquiring the technology would fall and thus diffusion proceed.

It was shown in chapter 2 that, generally, not only does the cost of new technology fall but also the quality tends to improve as the technology matures. The rate of improvement of the technology will impact on the diffusion path. In this section the supply side factors that may impinge on the determination of the rate of quality improvement are considered.

It is reasonable to argue that if the performance of a new technology is to improve over time then this improvement will, to some degree at least, and perhaps to a large degree, be the result of expenditures on research and development (although learning and other similar factors could also play a role). Thus the issue that needs to be addressed is how will such R&D be determined and with what impact on the performance of the technology and thus on the diffusion path? In essence the issue is what factors will determine the rate of product innovation?

There is an enormous literature in economics on R&D and its determination and this is not really the place to address this literature in its entirety (or anything like its entirety). This literature raises issues that have already appeared elsewhere, such as patent races and their common pool nature, externalities, attitudes to risk and other market failures, the implications of which in a general sense should be clear from what has been discussed above. Thus, rather than going into the detail of the literature, instead a number of hypotheses, suppositions and statements that would seem to be reasonable in the light of the literature are offered.

1   Expenditure on the improvement of the technology will be undertaken if the net private pay off from such expenditures is positive. Thus it might be argued, for example, that a monopolist supplier of new technology will improve that technology if there will be a positive return on the required R&D spend.

2   Technological improvements to a technology could impact on the suppliers' revenues by raising the price that can be charged for that technology and/or increasing the number of potential buyers and bringing forward their purchase dates. However, if technological improvements are foreseen then the prospect of such improvements could lead acquirers to delay purchase dates.

3   There may be an improvements schedule that maximizes the return to the firm's R&D spend. This schedule would be a trade off between improvements bringing forward purchase dates, and thus revenue, and costs being higher for production at early dates. In the presence of learning externalities the forces would tend to favour earlier improvements rather than later improvements.

4   Competition between suppliers of a new technology could impact on the incentive to improve in two ways. First, in the face of competition, if there are appropriability problems (other firms can easily copy) there may be little incentive for the firm to improve the technology as it will not be able to fully appropriate the revenue benefits of its R&D spend. However, secondly, under competition, the returns to technology improvement may be greater because the firm can take market share from other firms (rather than a monopolist who will only be attacking his/her own market). This incentive may lead to higher R&D. However, if the common pool issue is important, the competitive market may over invest in technology improvement from a welfare point of view.

5   Patents may play a significant role in the product improvement process. If advances can be patented they can be better protected and thus may minimize appropriability problems. However, it is known that patents may lead to patent races and thus over investment in technological improvement.

6   Technological improvement may raise the possibility of technological obsolescence, especially if the improvements impact on standards or there are network externalities such that old technologies will no longer be supported (e.g. CD players replacing vinyl disc players). The prospect of such obsolescence may reduce the desire of buyers to invest in the new technology on the one hand, but may increase the size of the market because of the need for replacement on the other.

In essence the supplying firms will improve the technology at a rate and at a time that will generate the greatest increases in net present value. That rate will be determined by the nature of the demand side in the diffusion process (e.g. learning or no learning, network externalities or not, and so on), and the improvements in the technology will be endogenous to the diffusion process.

On the other hand, the incentive for a buyer of a new technology is the difference in profits between use of a new technology and an old technology. It is quite feasible that the appearance of a new technology could lead suppliers of old technologies to improve their products. A well-documented case was the improvements in wooden shipbuilding in the face of the development of iron ships (Harley, 1973).

Of course, in addition to its product improvement effects, R&D may also be undertaken by suppliers to reduce their costs of production. This would make $c(t)$ in the model in section 6.2 above an endogenous variable. This creates further endogeneity but the issues to which it gives rise are no different than those already addressed.

Finally, in this section, it was argued above that the welfare optimal diffusion path in the model analysed would arise when either buyers are myopic and there is a monopoly supplier or when buyers have perfect foresight and there is perfect competition in the supplying industry. It was also noted, however, that in the former scenario the suppliers received all the benefits of the technology as profits whereas in the latter scenario the suppliers' profits were zero. If it is accepted that it is the profits to be realized that provide the incentive to improve new technology it should also be accepted that expected profits are the incentive to develop the original technology in the first place. This implies that if there are going to be large numbers of suppliers there will be little incentive for any one to develop the technology. Only if the developer can believe that he/she will enjoy some monopoly power is there an incentive to develop the technology (see Stoneman and Ireland, 1984).

It is often argued that patents provide such monopoly power; however, it is also argued that society has to pay a cost for such an incentive in that monopoly power limits the use of the technology. It was shown above that if the buyers are myopic then this is not so. An all-powerful patent system that granted a monopoly to the inventor would, with myopic buyers, also lead to the welfare optimal diffusion path. If buyers have some foresight, however, there will be too slow a rate of diffusion and there will be some monopoly loss from the patent system.

6.6.   Developing Market Structures

When market structures in the supplying industry were discussed above it was considered that such structures are either monopolies, oligopolies or perfectly competitive and in particular not changing over time. In the real world, as shown in chapter 2, the structure of industries supplying new products often undergo many changes. The number of firms in the industry may change, the size composition of firms may change, and entry and exit may occur. Given that some products that are studied in the diffusion literature show diffusion profiles lasting 50 years or more, many such changes may arise while diffusion proceeds.

For larger innovations it may be that the study of the supply side of the diffusion process is a study of the establishment and development of a whole industry. Thus, for example, the study of computerization may require a study of the development of the computer industry since 1945. The study of the car industry likewise. During their lifetime, industries will be experiencing major changes and such changes may well impact on the diffusion curve.

There are two extreme characterizations of industry development. In the first, typified perhaps by the motor car industry, (see, for example, Utterback, 1993), the industry initially has low entry barriers because of low capital and knowledge requirements. There is also little knowledge protection. Many firms enter the young industry and produce at a small scale using mainly labour. There is considerable product differentiation, especially horizontal differentiation. There is considerable entry and exit from the industry. As time proceeds products become standardized on a dominant design and more capital intensive modes of production are developed. These methods are potentially more productive and exhibit increasing returns to scale. Size starts to become an advantage and also entry barriers are raised. The number of firms in the industry reduces through exits and mergers with the larger firms having distinct cost advantages. Competition through price rather than quality becomes more important. Smaller firms are squeezed into niche markets. As the number of firms starts to reduce and the possibilities of further scale economies becomes less, firms will start to compete more in terms of quality and differentiation. This means higher product development and R&D costs which may further raise entry barriers. In the absence of other major exogenous impacts, for example regulation or changes in basic technology, the industry will settle down as a stable oligopoly.

The second extreme characterization is almost the reverse of the first. Here, think of an industry that starts with a single firm. This firm has some specific advantage, say for example, strong patents, and as a result entry barriers are high. However, over time the advantage is reduced, for example patents have a limited life, and as barriers are reduced other firms enter the industry. The structure thus moves from monopoly to oligopoly rather than from many firms to oligopoly as in the previous case. A possible example of such an industry could be xerography. In the early stages of the diffusion process the monopolist could intertemporally price discriminate and also develop new versions of the technology appropriating all the benefits from such improvements. However, if it is foreseen that entry will occur as the patents expire, the firm may try to sell the technology prior to new entry in order to maximize its value through such sales or through the entry barriers that such a strategy might generate. The prospect of entry may thus lead to faster adoption. As more firms enter competition increases, which may impact on both pricing and the rate of technology improvement. With more suppliers one might well expect that the technology users would retain more of the surplus. Once initial entry barriers have been removed and oligopoly is in place, whether the industry then moves towards more or less competition would depend on issues such as scale economies and future barriers to entry and exit.

These two extreme characterizations of supply industry development indicate that with different development paths in the supply industry the resultant diffusion process may also well be different. Moreover, if the supply industry is changing over time the most important drivers of the diffusion process may be different at different times. At one point in time diffusion may be driven by price reductions and other times by quality improvement. Different development paths may generate different orderings of such drivers over time. Even more relevant, it may be that the development of the industry is in some way at least connected to the development of the demand side. If the product has significant network externalities for example, the existence of such externalities may well represent a significant entry barrier and as such impact on the industry structure on the supply side. The development of the supply sector may therefore be endogenous to the whole diffusion process. The relevant literature that considers the co-evaluation of technologies and industry structures includes Carroll and Hannan (1995), Klepper (1996) and Klepper and Simons (1997).

Finally, thus far no mention has been made of foreign trade. It is not necessarily the case (or even most common) that the new technologies are produced in the home economy. The new technology may come from overseas. It may also be that a home producer of new technology may be supplying a world market rather than just a home market. In such an environment, the demand dynamics of the home market may represent only a small part of the demand dynamics of the whole market available to the producer. If this is so then the development of product pricing and quality will more reflect the world market than the home market. This will mean (1) that diffusion of technologies across different world markets may well be connected via a supply link and (2) a whole host of other factors may be seen to play a role in technology diffusion such as exchange rates, import duties and regulatory controls on high tech exports. In fact, when a world rather than domestic perspective is taken, it could be that the study of diffusion could extend to the study of industry location. If firms are geographically mobile it may be that a new technology user or producer would have a different optimal location than with the old technology and the diffusion process is allied with a shifting location of industry.

6.7.   Conclusions

In this chapter a number of issues relating to the supply of products embodying new technology have been addressed. It has been argued that through supply and demand interaction the prices charged for new technology, the degree of product differentiation and the quality, and improvement therein, of that technology can be considered endogenous to the model. The addition of the supply side has also enabled the characterization of the welfare optimal diffusion path.

It was shown that the market structure of the supplying industry is an important determinant of the diffusion process but it was also suggested that such market structure may be endogenous to the diffusion process. In the limit, taking a world view, the location of industry may also be endogenous. In addition to market structure it has been shown how buyers' expectations, learning on the demand side, network externalities and supply side cost changes may all interact in generating the time path of prices and qualities that are the drivers in the diffusion process. At the bare minimum this indicates that analysis restricted to the demand side alone only tells part of the diffusion story.

References

Carroll, G. and Hannan, M. (1995) *Organisations in Industry*, London: Oxford University Press.

Dasgupta, P. (1987) 'The Economic Theory of Technology Policy: An Introduction', in P. Dasgupta and P. Stoneman (eds.) *Economic Policy and Technological Performance*, Cambridge: CEPR/Cambridge University Press.

Dasgupta, P. and Stiglitz, J. (1980) 'Uncertainty, Industrial Structure and the Speed of R&D', *Bell Journal of Economics*, 11, 1–28.

David, P.A. and Olsen, T. (1986) 'Equilibrium Dynamics of Diffusion when Incremental Technological Innovations are Foreseen', *Richerche Economiche*, 40, 738–70.

Farrell, J. and Saloner, G. (1985) 'Standardisation, Compatability and Innovation', *Rand Journal of Economics*, 16(1), 70–83.

Glaister, S. (1974) 'Advertising Policy and Returns to Scale in Markets where Information is Passed Between Individuals', *Economica*, 41, 139–56.

Harley, C.K. (1973) 'On the Persistence of Old Techniques: The Case of North American Wooden Shipbuilding', *Journal of Economic History*, 33, 372–98.

Ireland, N.J. and Stoneman, P. (1985) 'Order Effects, Perfect Foresight and Intertemporal Price Discrimination', *Recherche Economique de Louvain*, 51(1), 7–20.

Ireland, N.J. and Stoneman, P. (1986) 'Technological Diffusion, Expectations and Welfare', *Oxford Economic Papers*, 283–304.

Katz, M.L. and Shapiro, C. (1985) 'Network Externalities, Competition and Compatability', *American Economic Review*, 75(3), 424–40.

Klepper, S. (1996) 'Entry, Exit, Growth and Innovation over the Product Life Cycle', *American Economic Review*, 86(3), 562–83.

Klepper, S. and Simons, K. (1997) 'Technological Extinctions of Industrial Firms: An Inquiry into their Nature and Causes', *Industrial and Corporate Change*, 6(2), 379–460.

Stoneman, P. (1989) 'Technological Diffusion and Vertical Product Differentiation', *Economic Letters*, 31, 277–80.

Stoneman, P. (1990) 'Technological Diffusion, Horizontal Product Differentiation and Adaptation Costs', *Economica*, 57, 49–62.

Stoneman, P. and Ireland, N.J. (1983) 'The Role of Supply Factors in the Diffusion of New Process Technology', *Economic Journal*, RES/AUTE Conference Supplement, March, 66–78.

Stoneman, P. and Ireland, N.J. (1984) 'Innovation and Diffusion: The Implications of An Integrated Approach', *Warwick Economic Research Papers*, No. 254, University of Warwick, Coventry.

Utterback, J. (1993) *Mastering the Dynamics of Innovation*, Cambridge, MA: HBS Press.

Vettas, N. (1998) 'Demand and Supply in New Markets: Diffusion with Bilateral Learning', *Rand Journal of Economics*, 29(1), 215–33.

Part III

Empirical Analysis of
the Diffusion of
New Technology

Chapter seven
Empirical Analysis: An Overview

7.1. Introduction

In chapter 2 above some detail on observed empirical patterns in the diffusion process was presented. This was then followed by a series of chapters exploring different theoretical approaches to the analysis of diffusion phenomena. In this part of the book theory and observation are brought together. The approach taken here is unashamedly econometric. Although there are less formal approaches to empirical analysis they are not pursued here. Econometric analysis has two main objectives. The first is to explore whether realized patterns – that is, the data – are consistent with theoretical propositions. As such the approach tests the theory. The second objective is to indicate the relative importance of the different factors that theory suggests are important in the diffusion process. Primarily this is achieved by considering the size of estimated parameters and especially the elasticity of the extent of technology usage with respect to the independent variables. The follow on to the empirical work is policy. If the responsiveness of technology usage to independent stimuli can be estimated then the potential effectiveness of policy instruments can be judged. Policy is considered in part IV of the book.

The chapter proceeds with an initial discussion of data types and data sources. This is followed by a discussion of several relevant general econometric issues. A short survey of existing results follows and then finally the next three chapters are introduced.

7.2. Data Types and Data Sources

There are three main types of data available for the empirical analysis of diffusion. Time series data, cross section data and panel data. Time series data provide for a given observation unit (say a firm, an industry or an economy), information on the level of use of the technology over a series of time periods, and, if one is fortunate, some ancillary information on possible explanatory variables. In the limit such data might just cover, say, the proportion of the population owning/using a new technology in each time period and time itself. Commonly, however, one would have more information than this. Such data are particularly restrictive and may not enable one to estimate models of the probit type where user heterogeneity is of importance but may be sufficient to estimate epidemic type models. In fact many of the estimates of epidemic type models do little more than relate extent of use to time; however, this does lead one to consider that such estimates may be more in the way of data summary devices rather than true tests of the epidemic model.

The second data type is cross section. Here for a single point in time one would have observations on the level of use of a technology by different units in the sample (especially firms or households) and commonly some ancillary data on the characteristics of the sample units. Such data have the advantage of allowing heterogeneity to be considered but because of their snapshot nature provide little opportunity to explore the time profile of the diffusion process across sample units. Thus, although one may have data on the extent of use in time t, with such data one is generally unable to say (a) whether usage is increasing or decreasing over time; (b) for how long the sample unit has been an owner or user; or (c) whether the characteristics of the sample unit are different in time t to previously.

The third data type is panel data. Panel data are a time series of cross sections, thus providing information both on usage at different points in time by different sample units and also characteristics information for different points in time on each of the sample units. Such data are to be preferred to the other two types because of its richness, but, not surprisingly, is rarely available.

Data availability is always an issue for the empirical analysis of diffusion phenomena. Data on the use of new technologies is rarely available from official sources and diffusion data tend not be collected regularly by national statistical offices. Time series data can often be found in privately funded studies of markets for particular products, and sometimes import statistics, being detailed, may enable the researcher to isolate measures of use of particular technologies. Cross section data can sometimes be found in publicly funded surveys of household behaviour (for example, in the UK, the Household Expenditure Survey) or workplaces (e.g. in the UK, the Workplace Employment Relations Survey), unfortunately, as the samples used in these surveys often change over time, they will not necessarily provide the preferred panel data sets.

Most diffusion data come from one-off surveys. Given that the surveys are one off, the data collected often differ across surveys, and, as the samples surveyed are often quite different, it is rare to have panel data from such surveys. Some, however, do provide panel data (see, for example, Alderman *et al.*, 1988). Such surveys of, for example, the use of technologies by firms will tend to ask whether the firm uses particular technologies, at which date the technologies were first installed, the size, profitability, and industry of the firm etc. Rarely will questions be asked as to the extent of use of the technology in the firm but where this is done one can also approach intra-firm diffusion issues. Questions may even be asked relating to the realized benefits from the technology, the barriers to adoption and other useful supplementary information.

7.3. Some General Econometric Issues

The empirical analysis of diffusion phenomena is now almost five decades old. In that period econometric techniques have advanced considerably as has the availability of computing power that enable the latest techniques to be applied. Many of the earlier diffusion studies would no longer be considered as acceptable as a result of such advances. Some of the main relevant issues are given below.

7.3.1. From theory to the estimating equation

Although it is now not as generally recommended as it once used to be, I am a great believer in that the estimating equation should be specifically derived from an underlying theoretical model. Recent approaches to time series econometrics have argued for the estimation of less constrained relationships, but as part of the reason for undertaking the econometric analysis is to validate theory, it is advantageous if the estimating equation is linked closely to the theory being tested. Although, of course, the best that the empirical analysis can do is to confirm that the data is consistent with the theory. It can never be shown that the theory is correct, only that it is not incorrect. In generating the estimating equation most time series analysis uses theory to predict the determinants of the proportion of the sample using a technology in a time period. This proportion is then usually taken as the dependent variable. Recent work on panel data has taken a more probabilistic approach. Theory is used to predict the probability that a sample unit (firm or household) that has not adopted the technology previously will adopt in time t, that is the hazard rate of adoption in time t. The resulting hazard function is then estimated using maximum likelihood methods.

7.3.2. Comparison of models

The most common approach in the diffusion literature is to apply a single model (say an epidemic model) to a single diffusion example (say the diffusion of CNCs). Occasionally alternative models will be used on the same data set to explore their differing statistical performance. This is to be preferred. Applying single models does not give any insight into the relative validity of different approaches. In fact, as different modelling approaches suggest different explanatory regressors, the application of a single model may not provide a full picture. Preferred to either approach, however, would be the construction of one encompassing model that nested all the different diffusion models. The estimation of such an overarching model should enable particular insights into which diffusion approach has greater empirical validity than others. As stated in chapter 3 the construction of an overarching model has its problems. It is thus rare for such an approach to be taken. The one clear example in the literature is Karshenas and Stoneman (1993), which is reproduced as chapter 8 below.

In judging the relative performance of one or more models standard procedures would involve the use of goodness of fit indicators and other diagnostic statistics (e.g. the t ratios of individual regressors). Good practice would also suggest that where possible the out-of-sample forecasting performance of the model should be explored using, for example, J-tests. Although this may reduce the data available for the basic estimation, it is a valuable tool for judging model performance.

7.3.3.   General to specific

In an ideal world the theoretical specification of a model would predict both the functional form of any relationship to be estimated and also the variables and the definitions of the variables to be included as regressors. Rarely, however, is the world ideal. In particular the theory may indicate many potential regressors without providing a clear means for choosing between them. In addition an encompassing model that nests alternative models may well include a number of regressors relating to frameworks that are not going to be supported empirically. In such circumstances the recommended methodology is to proceed from the general to the specific – that is, a model is initially specified with a large number of regressors included, and then if required, more parsimonious forms of the relationship estimated with regressors being removed according to some rule (e.g. remove variables in the order of their contribution to the explanatory power of the regression until all remaining variables are significant at the requisite statistical level). This is known as the general to specific procedure. In many cases of course there will be no need for the parsimonious representation. The general model may of itself give sufficient indication of required answers.

7.3.4.   Sample selection bias

Most diffusion data come from surveying, for example, samples of firms existing at a moment in time either with respect to their current use of new technology or their past history of the use of new technologies. It is quite feasible, however, that those firms that use new technologies are more likely to survive or that firms that adopted early are more likely to survive. If such effects exist then the sample used for the analysis will not be random, it will in fact over-represent firms that have adopted relative to those that have not adopted. There is some indication in the literature that the extent of such sample selection biases may not be large (see for example Karshenas and Stoneman, 1993), however one cannot always assume this to be the case. Good econometric practice would suggest use of, for example, the Heckman (1979) two-stage estimating procedure. In this procedure, for cross section data, a first stage estimation is undertaken that predicts the probability of a particular firm being included in the sample, from which one may calculate the inverse Mills ratio. This ratio is then included as a separate regressor in a second stage estimation of the diffusion relationship. Alternatively one might build front end 'sample selection' models relating to reasons for non-response to questionnaires. There are problems with all such approaches applied to panels for as yet such sample selection corrections are not fully developed for such data.

7.3.5.   Simultaneity

A less extreme form of the sample selection problem is the simultaneity problem. It is quite possible that some of the explanatory regressors are not independent of the dependent variable. Thus, for example, in the stock theory of diffusion, firm size may be dependent on use of the technology and as such firm size will not be an independent variable. Good practice would involve some initial analysis of the data (see also further below), using perhaps, Granger causality tests, of leads and lags in the data. This should yield some insights into both appropriate lags and also whether simultaneous equation estimation techniques need to be used.

7.3.6.   Time series econometrics

Almost by definition the empirical analysis of diffusion is concerned with time, and using time series or panel data this is obvious. The way that applied time series econometrics is done in practice has changed dramatically in the last 15 years. This is reflected in both the estimation methodology and the tests that are used with the growing requirement for unit root tests to be employed and also the increasing adoption of co-integration analysis. To a large extent this revolution has not yet impacted much on the diffusion literature, although it should. Much of the existing literature was written before this revolution took place, but only rarely have recent studies taken the implications on board. The paper by Stoneman and Battisti (2000), reproduced as chapter 15, is one example where the techniques have been applied.

There is still considerable controversy in econometrics as to the appropriate way to approach the modelling of long-run relationships such as the diffusion curve. The various views are well put by Granger (1997), Pesaran (1997) and Harvey (1997). Taking the Granger view, good practice requires prior analysis of data series to attempt to determine the features of each individual series in order to be sure that the main features of the dependent variables are represented somewhere amongst the independent variables. Often this comes down to unit root tests. One is trying to avoid situations in which (1) apparent regression between variables is spurious because all variables are trended on account of a third factor and (2) attempts are made to explain one variable with a certain time pattern by other variables with unrelated time patterns. Diffusion analysis can, however, present particular problems when applying the latest techniques. In particular the diffusion curve is often predicted to be non-linear. This causes problems as many of the appropriate tests such as Dickey-Fuller, assume linear trends.

This is not the place to attempt to expostulate the details of currently perceived good time series econometric practice. There are numerous econometric textbooks to which one can turn for that. The main point is that it is no longer acceptable to take two time series of data and apply some form of regression analysis without first exploring the properties of the data series and then constructing the model for estimation appropriately (say a first difference model or an error correction model).

7.3.7.   Panel data econometrics

The methods and means for analysing panel data have also improved enormously over the last 15 years. Again this is not the place to go into econometric detail. Pesaran and Smith (1995) is a useful source of information, but again there are good standard texts available to the interested reader. One particular point is, however, worth making. Diffusion analysis often involves the inclusion of a lagged dependent variable in the estimating equation. In such situations, the currently preferred estimation method is GMM (generalized method of moments) although there is still considerable argument as to the appropriate lag structures to be applied to the instrumental variables used in this approach.

7.3.8.   Functional forms

Sometimes one is fortunate in that economic theory will predict the functional form of the estimating equation. A particular example is that epidemic theory usually predicts a logistic diffusion curve. In other cases, however, the functional form is not precisely specified and the functional form has to be determined empirically. Even when the functional form is predicted by the theory this does not resolve the problem of what approach to take to estimation. Consider the case of the logistic curve. This was presented in chapter 2 as (7.1) below:

$$P_i(t) = P_i^*/(1 + \exp(-\eta_i - \phi_i \cdot t)) \tag{7.1}$$

There are two main approaches that could be used to estimate this relationship. As equation (7.1) is inherently non-linear it could be estimated using non-linear least squares with P_i^*, η_i and ϕ_i as parameters. A basic problem with using non-linear least squares is, however, that the sophistication of the techniques available for this purpose is much less than for linear relationships. The more usual approach is thus to transform (7.1) into a relationship that looks linear. In fact (7.1) can be written as

$$\log((P_i^* - Pi(t))/Pi(t)) = -\eta_i - \phi_i \cdot t \tag{7.2}$$

the right-hand side of which is linear. The linear relationship is then estimated. However the apparent linearity is a myth for P_i^* is a parameter the value of which is not known. Unless some value is assumed for this parameter (which is the common practice) then one still has a non-linear relationship. Of course, whichever of these two approaches is used, it is still necessary to pre-test the time series properties of the (possibly transformed) variables.

In estimating models of this kind it is also often assumed that either P_i^* and/or ϕ_i are themselves dependent on other variables such as profitability. This has led to another split in approaches to estimation. In one approach P_i^* and/or ϕ_i are estimated for different samples and then in a subsequent second stage estimation the resulting predicted values are regressed on a set of explanatory variables (in which case one should use weighted regression where the weights are the errors from the first stage). In an alternative approach one substitutes for P_i^* and/or ϕ_i in (7.1) or (7.2) and then estimates the relationship in one step. The choice of approach often comes down to whether the functional form arising from the second approach is linear or not.

7.3.9.   Error specification

Commonly the procedure followed is to generate the estimating equation perhaps through a transformation and then to add an error term after any transformation, assuming that the error term meets the standard requirements of zero mean and constant variance. If tests on the ordinary least squares estimates indicate heteroscedasticity or autocorrelation in the error term then alternative estimating procedures are used. More appropriately one should consider why there is an error term in the fundamental equation (e.g. equation 7.1) and the form that this should take. The transformation of (7.1) into (7.2) would also lead to a transformed error term with different statistical properties to that in the fundamental equation. This transformation should indicate the appropriate estimation techniques.

7.4.   A Brief Overview of Empirical Research

This section reviews some of the empirical results arising from past diffusion studies. No attempt is made to be comprehensive. There are in fact already a number of surveys in the public domain to which the reader can turn for fuller details (e.g. Karshenas and Stoneman, 1995; Baptista, 1999; and Sarkar, 1998). Moreover a Web search of, for example, the EconLit database (under technology adoption, innovation adoption or technology diffusion) will yield many example of papers covering the diffusion of technology x in country y.

The first issue that one would like the literature to answer is, of the various competing theories, which yields the 'best' explanation of diffusion phenomena. Unfortunately there is not much of an answer to this question. As stated above, most of the literature applies single models to single examples and very rarely is model performance compared. Thus in general one is unable to say that the rank approach works better than the stock approach or that the epidemic model better explains diffusion than an order model. There is much literature that shows that model A or model B can be successfully applied to a particular example but not that model A is better than model B in explaining this example. It is thus not possible at the current time to say with any authority that diffusion, for example, results from differences between firms, information spreading, risk reduction, cost acquisition reduction, or network effects. It is definitely not possible to say that, for examples with certain characteristics model A works better than model B whereas with other examples model B works better than model A. There is still much to be done here.

In addition a large proportion of the empirical work on diffusion uses the epidemic approach. There are many more such studies than any other kind, although rank based or probit models are becoming more popular especially in the analysis of panel data sets (see, for example, Hannan and McDowell, 1984). Order and stock models have been little applied empirically, whereas the application of uncertainty based models (except of the Mansfield, 1968, epidemic kind) has largely been restricted to the study of diffusion in developing countries of agricultural technologies (for an application to a developed economy see, for example, Fischer and Arnold, 1996).

Further gaps in the empirical literature are also obvious. To the best of my knowledge: (1) there is no empirical work exploring the impact of product differentiation on the diffusion process; (2) there is little or no empirical work that looks at diffusion as the result of supply and demand interaction, with nearly all empirical work concentrating on diffusion as a demand phenomenon with some limited work on the supply side alone; (3) only a limited literature (e.g. Stoneman and Kwon, 1994; Stoneman and Toivanen, 1997; and Colombo and Mosconi, 1995) addresses multi-technology issues; (4) apart from uncertainty driven models, risk is rarely included as an explanatory variable in diffusion studies (although see Toivanen *et al.*, 1999); and (5) network effects have rarely been explored (although see Saloner and Shepard, 1995; and Koski, 1999).

Given the nature of the literature, however, the various estimates indicate the main factors impacting on the diffusion process to be:

1   The expected profitability or benefit from adoption. From the earliest work of Mansfield (1968) and Griliches (1957) through the work of Davies (1979) it has been emphasized and confirmed that the greater the benefit of technology adoption the faster will technology be adopted and the greater will be the final level of use.
2   Firm characteristics. Papers by, for example, David (1969), Romeo (1977), Rose and Joskow (1990), Pennings and Harianto (1992) and Thomas (1999) all find that firm size impacts positively on technology adoption. However Oster (1982) finds negative effects. Other characteristics found relevant are market structure of the using industry (Hannan and McDowell, 1984; Romeo, 1977), skills, knowledge or R&D intensity (e.g. Pennings and Harianto, 1992), wage rates, and industry characteristics such as the growth of demand or general industry dummies (e.g. Karshenas and Stoneman, 1993). There is also some evidence that owner-controlled firms diffuse faster than manager-controlled firms (Koski, 1998), but Karshenas and Stoneman (1993) find no impact of corporate status on the diffusion process. Dunne (1994) looks at plants and finds that plant age has little impact on diffusion but plant size has a positive impact.
3   The cost of adopting new technology. Acquisition costs have been shown to be important (e.g. Karshenas and Stoneman, 1993; Stoneman and Kwon, 1996), and expectations of changes in such costs may also play a role, although these have been less studied (Karshenas and Stoneman, 1993).
4   Government involvement. Government intervention in the diffusion process rarely seems to speed diffusion and government-owned enterprises rarely move faster than privately owned (Hannan and McDowell, 1984; Oster and Quigley, 1977; Rose and Joskow, 1990).
5   Trade cycle. There may be trade cycle related effects (Romeo, 1977; and Davies, 1979).

7.5.   An Introduction to the Following Three Chapters

The next three chapters in this book are reproduced from Karshenas and Stoneman (1993), Stoneman and Kwon (1994) and Zettelmeyer and Stoneman (1993). Each paper exemplifies the empirical analysis of diffusion phenomena. The first concentrates on computer numerically controlled (CNC) machine tools in the UK engineering industry, the second looks at the diffusion of several technologies in the same industry and the third looks at camcorders and CD players in the UK and cars in West Germany. The papers thus cover both new producer and household technologies.

These particular papers have been chosen for several reasons.

1   The papers illustrate the use of econometric analysis for the study of diffusion phenomena, largely using best practice methods.
2   The first two papers illustrate how an encompassing model can be constructed that nests a variety of alternative modelling approaches to diffusion and from the parameter

estimates one may judge which approach is most relevant to the case under consideration. This has rarely been done in the literature.

3 The third paper illustrates a different method of model comparison whereby a series of
   different models (in this case all of the epidemic variety) are applied to a common data
   set and model performance can be compared. Again this is uncommon in the literature.
4 The second paper illustrates the importance of multi-technology effects on the diffusion
   process which again is not common.
5 The papers, especially the first and second, illustrate how the theoretical principles
   discussed in previous chapters may be incorporated in formal modelling and also how an
   estimating equation can be generated.
6 Jointly the papers show the different approaches to model specification that apply to
   time series and panel data and how such models may be estimated.

The papers are in general less accessible than the contents of this book so far. That will
always be the case when, as required by academic publication, analytical and econometric
rigour are pursued. Having said this, however, although the papers are rigorous in their
formal modelling and use of econometric techniques (for example as regards sample attrition or selection bias, simultaneity, etc.) they still have failings. For example, they do not
include any supply side modelling. The papers are also thin on issues concerning risk and
uncertainty. The independent regressors included in the papers are also limited by data
availability and the sets of regressors used are not necessarily complete – for example,
product differentiation is never discussed nor are issues relating to finance.

The papers illustrate a number of findings. The first, in terms of model comparison,
is that across the three papers there is considerable support for both epidemic and rank
approaches to the modelling of diffusion, but the support for stock and order models is
much weaker. In terms of epidemic models, it is found that the simple model does not
work particularly well and that there is good reason (1) to believe that economic factors
play much more of a role than the simple model suggests and (2) that any assumption of
a homogeneous population is difficult to sustain. It also found (in the second paper) that
multi-technology effects are of some significance.

The main factors found to affect the rate at which new technologies are adopted are: the
time that the technology has been on the market (as per the epidemic model); firm characteristics and in particular, firm size and the rate of growth of industry output (rank effects);
the (quality adjusted) cost of acquiring new technology; expected changes in the cost of
acquisition; complementarities between technologies and thus the cost and use of related
technologies; and with less empirical support, the number of users to date (through either
stock or order effects). The work on epidemic models also illustrates that the end level of
use will depend upon the cost of acquisition and economic variables such as disposable
income or GDP and interest rates.

The work in the three papers presented has been supplemented by other published work.
The third paper is paralleled by Karshenas and Stoneman (1992) which proposes the
epidemic model compared to other models in Zettelmeyer and Stoneman (1993) and applies
the model to the spread of colour television ownership in the UK. The second paper on
multi-technology diffusion was followed by another paper on the same topic taking a
slightly different approach (Stoneman and Toivanen, 1997). In addition a similar topic is
addressed in Stoneman and Kwon (1996), reproduced as chapter 17 below. In this case the

importance of multi-technology effects, and epidemic, rank stock and order approaches are explored by inverting the diffusion model and exploring how technology adoption affects firm profitability. The argument is that if, as the non-epidemic models suggest, expected profitability gains drive diffusion then one might expect diffusion to impact on realized profitability. Finally, Stoneman and Battisti (2000), reproduced as chapter 15, is also relevant. This paper has two main characteristics. The first is that the recommended, pre-estimation analysis of time series data is actually undertaken and the logical conclusions of the results of that analysis pursued. Secondly, in that paper, a probit model is used to generate the logistic diffusion curve generally associated with epidemic models. This illustrates that logistic diffusion does not necessarily require an epidemic foundation.

References

Alderman, N., Davies, S. and Thwaites, A. (1988) *Patterns of Innovation Diffusion*, Technical Report, Centre for Urban and Regional Development Studies, University of Newcastle upon Tyne.

Baptista, R. (1999) 'The Diffusion of Process Innovations: A Selective Review', *International Journal of the Economics of Business*, 6(1), 107–30.

Colombo, M. and Mosconi, R. (1995) 'Complementarity and Cumulative Learning Effects in the Early Diffusion of Multiple Technologies', *Journal of Industrial Economics*, 43, 13–48.

David, P. (1969) *A Contribution to the Theory of Diffusion*, Center for Research in Economic Growth Research Memorandum, No. 71, Stanford University.

Davies, S. (1979) *The Diffusion of Process Innovations*, Cambridge: Cambridge University Press.

Dunne, T. (1994) 'Plant Age and Technology Use in US Manufacturing Industries', *Rand Journal of Economics*, 25(3), 488–99.

Fischer, A.J. and Arnold, A.J. (1996) 'Information and the Speed of Innovation Adoption', *American Journal of Agricultural Economics*, 78(4), 1073–81.

Granger, C.W.J. (1997) 'On Modelling the Long Run in Applied Economics', *Economic Journal*, 107(440), 169–77.

Griliches, Z. (1957) 'Hybrid Corn: An Exploration in the Economics of Technological Change', *Econometrica*, 48, 501–22.

Hannan, T. and McDowell, J. (1984) 'The Determinants of Technology Adoption: The Case of the Banking Firm', *Rand Journal of Economics*, 15, 328–35.

Harvey, A. (1979) 'Trends Cycles and Autoregressions', *Economic Journal*, 107(440), 192–201.

Heckman, J. (1979) 'Sample Selection Bias as a Specification Error', *Econometrica*, 47, 153–61.

Karshenas, M. and Stoneman, P. (1992) 'A Flexible Model of Technological Diffusion Incorporating Economic Factors with an Application to the Spread of Colour Television Ownership in the UK', *Journal of Forecasting*, 11, 577–601.

Karshenas, M. and Stoneman, P. (1993) 'Rank, Stock, Order and Epidemic Effects in the Diffusion of New Process Technology', *Rand Journal of Economics*, 24(4), 503–28.

Karshenas, M. and Stoneman, P. (1995) 'Technological Diffusion', in P. Stoneman (ed.), *The Handbook of the Economics of Innovation and Technological Change*, Oxford: Basil Blackwell, 265–97.

Koski, H.A. (1998) *Economic Analysis of the Adoption of Technologies with Network Externalities*, PhD dissertation, Department of Economics, University of Oulu, Finland.

Koski, H.A. (1999) 'The Installed Base Effect: Some Empirical Evidence from the Microcomputer Market', *Economics of Innovation and New Technology*, 8(4), 273–310.

Mansfield, E. (1968) *Industrial Research and Technological Innovation*, New York: Norton.

Oster, S. (1982) 'The Diffusion of Innovations among Steel Firms: The Basic Oxygen Furnace', *Bell Journal of Economics*, 13, 45–56.

Oster, S. and Quigley, J. (1977) 'Regulation and the Diffusion of Innovation: Some Evidence from Building Codes', *Bell Journal of Economics*, 8, 361–77.

Pennings, J. and Harianto, F. (1992) 'The Diffusion of Technological Innovation in the Commercial Banking Industry', *Strategic Management Journal*, 13, 29–46.

Pesaran, M.H. (1997) 'The Role of Economic Theory in Modelling the Long Run', *Economic Journal*, 107(440), 170–91.

Pesaran, M.H. and Smith, R.P. (1995) 'Estimating Long Run Relationships from Dynamic Heterogeneous Panels', *Journal of Econometrics*, 68, 79–113.

Romeo, A. (1977) 'The Rate of Imitation of a Capital Embodied Process Innovation', *Economica*, 44, 63–9.

Rose, N. and Joskow, P. (1990) 'The Diffusion of New Technologies: Evidence from the Electric Utility Industry', *Rand Journal of Economics*, 21, 354–73.

Saloner, G. and Shepard, A. (1995) 'Adoption of Technologies with Network Effects: An Empirical Examination of the Adoption of Automatic Teller Machines', *Rand Journal of Economics*, 26(3), 479–501.

Sarkar, J. (1998) 'Technological Diffusion: Alternative Theories and Historical Evidence', *Journal of Economic Surveys*, 12(2), 131–76.

Stoneman, P. and Battisti, G. (2000) 'The Role of Regulation, Fiscal Incentives and Changes in Tastes in the Diffusion of Unleaded Petrol in the UK', *Oxford Economic Papers*, April, 52(2), 326–56.

Stoneman, P. and Kwon, M.J. (1994) 'The Diffusion of Multiple Process Technologies', *Economic Journal*, 104, 420–31.

Stoneman, P. and Kwon, M.J. (1996) 'Technology Adoption and Firm Profitability', *Economic Journal*, 106, 952–62.

Stoneman, P. and Toivanen, O. (1997) 'The Diffusion of Multiple Technologies: An Empirical Study', *Economics of Innovation and New Technology*, 5, 1–17.

Thomas, L.A. (1999) 'Adoption Order of New Technologies in Evolving Markets', *Journal of Economic Behaviour and Organisations*, April, 453–82.

Toivanen, O., Stoneman, P. and Diederen, P. (1999) 'Uncertainty, Macroeconomic Volatility and Investment in New Technology', in C. Driver, and P. Temple (eds), *Investment Growth and Employment*, London: Routledge.

Zettelmeyer, F. and Stoneman, P. (1993) 'Testing Alternative Models of New Product Diffusion', *Economics of Innovation and New Technology*, 2, 283–308.

Chapter eight

Rank, Stock, Order and Epidemic Effects in the Diffusion of New Process Technologies: An Empirical Model

Co-written with Massoud Karshenas

8.1. Introduction

The literature on technological diffusion, i.e., the process by which the use of new technology spreads, has grown apace in recent years (for surveys see Stoneman, 1983, 1986, and 1987). A number of significant theoretical advances have been made in this literature, but it is still fair to state that the majority of the empirical work on this topic has not yet caught up with the theory. It is also noticeable that even the most recent empirical articles in the field (see, for example, Rose and Joskow, 1990) tend to shy away from explicit links with recent theoretical developments. As a result, there is very little empirical support for recent theoretical advances, and thus scant guidance as to the appropriate ways in which to approach the analysis of real-world diffusion phenomena. In order to gain some insight into the extent to which various suggested theoretical frameworks have some empirical validity, in this article we attempt to construct an empirical model of the diffusion process that is tied closely to theory and then proceed to apply the model to data on the spread of computer numerically controlled machine tools (CNC) in the UK. The work of Bresnahan and David (1986) is a forerunner in a similar vein.

Early work on the diffusion of new technology tended to concentrate upon epidemic theories of diffusion which, in their crude form, considered that potential adopters would acquire new technology upon receipt of information relating to its existence. Some refinement of this approach (see, for example, Mansfield, 1968) has improved the conceptual basis

Reprinted from the *Rand Journal of Economics*, 24(4), 503–28, 1993, with kind permission of the *Rand Journal*.

of such models, but the reliance on awareness and information spreading remains. This approach has been particularly relevant in empirical work (see, for example, Mansfield, 1989). In contrast, a major aspect of recent theoretical developments has been the increasing emphasis placed on the explicit treatment of a firm's (or consumer's) decision to adopt, with very little, if any, account being taken of information spreading or other epidemic-type forces.

The essential prediction of a theory of diffusion is that potential adopters of a new technology should have different (preferred) adoption dates, or, synonymously, that at any given date only some of the potential adopters will wish to be (or are sufficiently informed to be) actual users. In the recent theoretical literature, three different mechanisms have been suggested that will yield such an outcome.

1   *Rank effects.* These effects result from the assumption that potential adopters of a technology have different inherent characteristics (such as firm size) and as a result obtain different (gross) returns from the use of new technology. These different returns then generate different preferred adoption dates. The model is operationalized by ranking potential adopters in terms of their returns from adoption (from highest to lowest), thereby generating a benefit distribution across these potential adopters. An acquisition rule relating benefits to the cost of acquisition (and, depending on expectations assumptions, changes therein) enables the derivation of a distribution of reservation acquisition costs from the benefit distribution. Firms adopt the new technology as acquisition costs fall below reservation acquisition costs. Acquisition costs are assumed to fall over time. As acquisition costs fall, the cumulative benefit distribution is mapped out as a diffusion path, with the firms achieving high returns adopting early and the firms achieving low returns adopting late. Such models, generally known as probit models, are exemplified by the work of David (1969), Davies (1979), and Ireland and Stoneman (1986).

2   *Stock effects.* These effects result from the assumption that the benefit to the marginal adopter from acquisition decreases as the number of previous adopters increases. The model is made operational by then arguing that for any given cost of acquisition there will be a number of adopters beyond which adoption is not profitable. This number is assumed to actually adopt at that cost of acquisition. It is further assumed that the cost of acquisition falls over time and, as it does so, further adoptions take place, with a diffusion path being generated. In such models the impact of past adoptions on the return to the marginal adopter results from endogenizing the output decisions of firms. As firms acquire new technology, their production costs fall. This leads to changes in the output of firms and the industry, thereby affecting industry prices and the profitability of further adoption. This approach is often labeled 'game-theoretic,' after the use of the term by Reinganum (1981), although Quirmbach (1986) in his extension of that work shows that the results do not necessarily rely upon firms' behavior being strategic.

3   *Order effects.* These effects result from the assumption that the return to a firm from adopting new technology depends upon its position in the order of adoption, with high-order adopters achieving a greater return than low-order adopters. The model is made operational by arguing that the firm's adoption decision will take into account how waiting and thus moving down the adoption order will affect its profits. For any given cost of acquisition it will be profitable only for firms down to some point in the order of adoption to actually adopt. That is assumed to be the number that actually adopt. The cost of acquisition

is assumed to fall over time, and as it does so the number of adopters increases. This maps out the diffusion path.

The order effect can be rationalized on a number of grounds. On a general level it can be argued that early adopters can, for example, obtain prime geographic sites or preempt the pool of skilled labor. Such a rationalization is the basis of the model in Ireland and Stoneman (1985). A more game-theoretic or strategic approach is to be found in the model of Fudenberg and Tirole (1985). This is built upon the observation that, in the stock–effects model, earlier adopters get the greatest returns and thus there will be a race to be high in the order of adoption. In this model, first-mover advantages exist whereby the decisions of high-order adopters can affect the adoption dates of low-order adopters.

These three effects – the rank, stock, and order effects – summarize the basis upon which recent theoretical advances in diffusion analysis have been built. There is, however, one further theoretical advance that should be mentioned. In David and Olsen (1986) and a series of articles by Stoneman and Ireland (exemplified by Stoneman and Ireland, 1983), it has been argued that although the majority of the theoretical and empirical literature concentrates on the demand side alone, observed diffusion paths are the result of an interaction between both demand-side and supply-side forces. Thus, for example, in the brief sketches of the rank, stock, and order effect models above, it was assumed in each case that the cost of acquiring new technology fell over time. A complete model would attempt to relate these reductions in acquisition costs to supply-side factors. In this article we keep this point in mind and address it where relevant, but it is not addressed in its entirety. It is fortunate, however, that in the particular empirical example addressed in the article we do not consider the problem to be of great importance (largely because the technology being studied was, to a considerable degree, imported from overseas suppliers).

In Section 2 we build a decision-theoretic model that simultaneously incorporates the three effects discussed above and is also extended to incorporate epidemic effects. The prime objective of doing so is eventually to obtain a model that may be used to assess empirically which, if any, of the rank, stock, order, and epidemic effects play a role in an example of a real-world diffusion process. In the first two parts of section 8.2 the modelling of the decision to adopt is conditional upon awareness. In the third part of section 8.2 we introduce the epidemic effect to reflect awareness factors, thereby generating the model that incorporates all four of the basic approaches to diffusion analysis. The resulting model is applied to data on the diffusion of CNC in the UK, with the data and the implications of the sample design for the specification of the estimating model discussed in section 8.3 and estimation and results discussed in section 8.4. The main conclusions of the article are reviewed in section 8.5.

8.2.   An Empirical Model

The empirical approach taken here is based upon a hazard rate formulation that derives from the work of Hannan and McDowell (1987). Defining $X(t)$ as a vector of relevant explanatory variables, they assume that $h_i(t)$, the hazard rate, or the conditional probability that firm i adopts a given new technology in time t (given that it has not adopted by $\{t-1\}$), is given by

$$h_i(t) = \exp\{\mathbf{X}'(t)\boldsymbol{\beta}\}, \tag{8.1}$$

where $\boldsymbol{\beta}$ is a vector of coefficients. Hannan and McDowell 'use as a guide, the presumption that an innovation will appear more attractive to a potential adopter the greater the positive differential between expected profits with and without the innovation and the less the uncertainty or risk associated with the innovation,' and as a result they include the following as the main components of $\mathbf{X}$: the wage rate, market growth, concentration, firm size, time, and usage to date. Our approach is similar to that of Hannan and McDowell in that we model the adoption duration; however, our model is theoretically explicit rather than based upon a presumption, and as a result, we have cause to change the list of relevant explanatory variables. We also assume a more general functional form for the hazard rate. However, in our approach we do not explicitly consider risk and uncertainty. Only to the extent to which this can be considered as implicitly part of the epidemic effect is it incorporated at all. A theoretical model explicitly incorporating risk can be found in Stoneman (1980).

8.2.1. A deterministic model

Assume a new technology that firm i in industry j may acquire by purchase of a new capital good at price $P(t)$ in time t. Also, initially, assume that all firms are aware of this new technology. Define $g_{ij}(\tau)$ as the (gross) profit obtained by a firm in period τ from use of the new technology. Further assume that these per-period profits are determined by the rank, stock, and order effects outlined above. Specifically, define $\mathbf{C}_i$ as a vector of firm characteristics and $K_j(t)$ as the number of firms in industry j that have already adopted the technology by time t. For expositional purposes, enabling a clearer distinction between stock and order effects, also define $S_j(t) = K_j(t)$. We then specify that for the ith firm in industry j adopting a new technology at time t, its benefit in time τ will be

$$g_{ij}(\tau) = g(\mathbf{C}_i, S_j(t), K_j(\tau)), \quad \tau \geq t, \quad g_2 < 0, \quad g_3 < 0. \tag{8.2}$$

To clarify, in equation (8.2), $S_j(t)$ reflects order effects, with the benefits from adoption in each period of use being dependent upon the number of previous adopters *at the date of adoption*. The stock effects are reflected in the $K_j(\tau)$ term, with the return in each period of use being dependent upon the number of other users *at that date*. The representation of the rank effects does not need explanation.

Defining r as the discount rate/interest rate and assuming no depreciation (and dropping j subscripts where their existence is obvious), we may write the present value of the increase in gross profits arising from adoption at time $t(G_i(t))$ as

$$G_i(t) = \int_t^\infty g(\mathbf{C}_i, S(t), K(\tau))\exp\{-r(\tau - t)\}d\tau. \tag{8.3}$$

The acquisition decision, or the choice of an optimal t, t^*, will be determined by two conditions (of which Hannan and McDowell seem to only consider the first): the profitability condition and the arbitrage condition. The first we may interpret as that acquisition must yield positive profits; the second condition requires that the net benefit from acquisition is not increasing over time. Defining $Z_i(t)$ as the net present value of acquisition at time t, for acquisition to be profitable at time t it is necessary that

$$Z_i(t) = -P(t) + G_i(t) \geq 0, \tag{8.4}$$

where $P(t)$ is the cost of acquiring the technology in time t.

For it not to be more profitable to wait before acquisition, it is necessary that

$$y_i(t) \equiv \frac{d(Z_i(t) \cdot \exp\{-rt\})}{dt} \leq 0, \tag{8.5}$$

where $Z_i(t)$ is discounted to ensure a common time basis of evaluation. Assuming profit-maximizing behavior by the firm, although the profitability condition determines the set of potential adopters, it is the arbitrage condition that actually governs optimal adoption time, t^*, for each potential adopter. We may then specify that the optimal adoption date for firm i, t_i^*, is given by

$$y_i(t_i^*) \leq 0, \tag{8.6}$$

where the inequality sign allows for the possibility of corner solutions, e.g., when it is optimal to adopt the technology immediately on the first date of its introduction.

To prove the existence of an optimum value for $Z_i(t)$ at some $t < \infty$, we first note the conditions under which $Z_i(t)$ is bounded. Assuming an upper bound $\bar{g}$ for per-period benefits $g(\cdot)$, and a lower bound for the price of technology $\underline{P}$, it is clear from equations (8.3) and (8.4) that $Z_i(t) \leq -\underline{P} + \int_t^\infty \bar{g} \exp\{-r(\tau - t)\}d\tau \leq -\underline{P} + \bar{g}/r$ and $Z_i(t)$ is bounded from above. One may then show that if each member i of the population is a potential adopter, there exists an optimum time, $t_i^* < \infty$, where net benefits of adoption are maximized. Noting that for a firm to be a potential adopter there must exist a price $P_t \geq \underline{P}$ where net benefits of adoption $(Z_i(t))$ are nonnegative, the limit of $Z_i(t)$ as time goes to infinity is given by $\lim_{t\to\infty} Z_i(t) = \lim_{t\to\infty} [-\underline{P} + \int_t^\infty \bar{g} \exp\{-r(\tau - t)\}d\tau] = -\underline{P} < 0$. However, since it is assumed that each firm is a potential adopter, i.e., $Z_i(t) \geq 0$ for all i, it follows that $Z_i(t)$ must achieve its maximum at some $t < \infty$. This also means that for a potential adopter the arbitrage condition dominates the profitability condition, and thus in what follows we need only consider the arbitrage condition.

Using lowercase letters for derivatives with respect to time, define $s(t)$ and $p(t)$ respectively as the expected changes in the number of users and the price of technology in the small time interval $\{t, t + dt\}$. Using (8.3) and (8.4) and differentiating $e^{-rt} \cdot Z_i(t)$ with respect to t yields the expression for $y_i(t)$ as follows:

$$y_i(t) = rP(t) - p(t) + \int_t^\infty g_2(\mathbf{C}_i, S(t), K(\tau))s(t)\exp\{-r(\tau - t)\}d\tau$$

$$- g(\mathbf{C}_i, S(t), K(t)). \tag{8.7}$$

Equation (8.7) states that the benefit from waiting for a time interval before acquisition equals the interest saved $(rP(t))$, plus any expected reduction in the cost of acquisition

$(-p(t))$, minus the net present value of the changes in benefits resulting from a move down the order of adoption for all $\tau \geq t$ (the integral term), and minus the benefits forgone from not having the new technology for the time interval.[1]

One might note at this stage that given complete myopia, where $p(t) = s(t) = 0$ and $K(\tau) = K(t)$ for all $\tau > t$, the condition $y_i(t) = 0$ yields a t_i^* that would be the same as that implied by $Z_i(t) = 0$, and thus under myopia the arbitrage and the profitability conditions coincide.

To simplify matters, it is plausible to make the assumption that the marginal benefit changes resulting from moving down the order of adopters at time t are independent of the level of future stock of adopters $K(\tau)$ for $\tau > t$. This can be obtained, for example, if the benefit function is of the form $g(\mathbf{C}_i, S(t), K(\tau)) = g^1(\mathbf{C}_i, S(t)) + g^2(\mathbf{C}_i, K(\tau))$. Under this assumption equation (8.7) can be simplified to

$$y_i(t) = rP(t) - p(t) + g_2(\mathbf{C}_i, S(t), K(t))s(t)/r - g(\mathbf{C}_i, S(t), K(t)). \tag{8.8}$$

8.2.2.   A stochastic model

Under the assumption of perfect foresight, equations (8.6) and (8.8) above give the exact date of adoption t_i for firm i. The model as specified above, however, abstracts from various real-life factors that, though they may be known with certainty to the individual adopters, cannot be incorporated into the model. These factors are introduced into the model through a stochastic error term ε. Assuming that the distribution of ε remains invariant across the firms over time, the adoption condition as specified in equation (8.6) now becomes

$$y_i(t) + \varepsilon \leq 0. \tag{8.9}$$

Assuming ε is distributed independent of y with a distribution function $V(\varepsilon)$, the probability of adoption in the small time interval $\{t, t + dt\}$ for a firm that has not adopted the technology by time t, i.e., $h(t)$ the hazard rate, becomes

$$h_i(t) = \text{Prob}\{y_i(t) + \varepsilon \leq 0\} = V(-y_i(t)). \tag{8.10}$$

From (8.8), $y_i(t)$ is a positive function of $r(t)P(t)$, $S(t)$, and $K(t)$, through the first and last terms; it is also a function of $\mathbf{C}_i$ with sign to be determined.[2] The second and third terms in (8.8) imply also that $y_i(t)$ is negatively related to the expected change in the cost of acquisition $p(t)$ and, given $g_2 < 0$, is negatively related to the expected change in the number of users of new technology $s(t)$. Given that V is a decreasing function in y, and removing the artificial distinction between $K(t)$ and $S(t)$ that was only imposed for expositional purposes, one may then write (8.10) as

$$h_i(t) = \mathcal{J}(r(t)P(t), K(t), \mathbf{C}_i, p(t), k(t)/r(t)), \tag{8.11}$$

where $\mathcal{J}_1 < 0, \mathcal{J}_2 < 0, \mathcal{J}_3 \gtreqless 0, \mathcal{J}_4 > 0$, and $\mathcal{J}_5 > 0$. It should be noted, as is clearly evident from equation (8.8), that $g_2(\cdot)$ is a variable function of $\mathbf{C}_i$ and $K(t)$. This signifies the fact that marginal changes in benefits resulting from moving down the order of adoption depend on such factors as characteristics of the firm, market conditions, and level of adoptions to date. These effects can be allowed for, assuming a linear functional form for $g_2(\cdot)$, by introducing cross-product variables between $k(t)$ on the one hand and C_i and $K(t)$ on the other. The hazard function incorporating these cross-product terms then becomes

$$h_i(t) = \mathcal{J}\{r(t)P(t),\ K(t),\ C_i,\ p(t),\ (a_0 + a_1 C_i + a_2 K(t))k(t)/r(t)\}. \tag{8.12}$$

Hypotheses regarding the existence of order effects can then be tested by considering the joint significance of coefficients a_0, a_1, and a_2 in (8.12).

8.2.3.   Epidemic and learning effects

In the absence of a specific functional form, at least for the $g(\cdot)$ function, we cannot be precise as to the functional form of $\mathcal{J}(\cdot)$ in equation (8.12). A common approach in the econometric literature has been to introduce the explanatory variables in the hazard function in exponential form, which has the advantage of ensuring a positive hazard without the need to impose any further restrictions on the parameters of the model. More specifically, a common practice has been to adopt some version of the general class of proportional hazard functions suggested by Cox (1972), where the explanatory variables act multiplicatively on the hazard rate (or additively on log hazard). Here too, we assume a proportional hazard form but allow the data to determine the appropriateness of this assumption at the empirical stage.

However, economic theory may impose some restrictions on the baseline hazard and on the other parameters of interest in the model. The general form of the proportional hazard function is

$$h(t \mid X,\ \beta) = h_0(t)\exp\{X'\beta\}, \tag{8.13}$$

where X is a vector of explanatory variables incorporating all the variables discussed under rank, stock, and order effects above, β is a vector of parameters, and $h_0(t)$ is the baseline hazard. If the variables included under the rank, stock, and order effects provide an adequate explanation of the diffusion process, the baseline hazard $h_0(t)$ would be expected to remain constant over time. This leads to the exponential hazard function – as estimated, for example, by Hannan and McDowell (1987) – of the following form:

$$h(t \mid X,\ \beta) = \exp\{X'\beta\}, \tag{8.14}$$

where h_0, the baseline hazard, is absorbed in the constant term in the vector X. An alternative formulation is to specify a model with a time-dependent baseline hazard. In fact, the incorporation of epidemic effects into the model does suggest that the baseline hazard ought to be considered time dependent.

Thus far, epidemic effects have been ignored in the modelling. However, the important role they have played in the past literature suggests that they ought to be incorporated. Epidemic effects relate to endogenous learning as a process of self-propagation of information about a new technology that grows with the spread of that technology. Such endogenous learning effects can be introduced by specifying the hazard function as

$$h(t \mid \mathbf{X}, \boldsymbol{\beta}, \boldsymbol{\Theta}) = h_0(t)\exp\{\mathbf{X}'\boldsymbol{\beta}\}\Phi(t; \boldsymbol{\Theta}),\tag{8.15}$$

where Φ incorporates the endogenous learning effects and $\boldsymbol{\Theta}$ is a vector of parameters. There have been different parameterizations of the function Φ in the literature (see, for example, Karshenas and Stoneman, 1992 and the references quoted there). We argue below that the behavior of Φ remains invariant under a wide range of specifications; however, the simplest and most commonly used form is based on the logistic function, and it is thus on this one that we concentrate.

The behavioral justification for the use of the logistic in characterizing the endogenous learning effects in the diffusion process is often made by analogy to the spread of epidemics as discussed in biological sciences. Consider a community with a number N of persons susceptible to a new infection, a number S of already infected people, and a constant rate of infection Θ_1 (where Θ_1 is the probability of contracting the infection after a contact is made). Under the assumption of a homogeneously mixing population, it is plausible to assume that the probability for a susceptible person to meet an infected person and contract the disease in a small time interval dt is $\Theta_1(S/N)dt$. In a population of $(N - S)$ susceptibles, the average number of infections in a small time interval dt would therefore be

$$dS = \Theta_1(S/N)(N - S)dt.\tag{8.16}$$

Integrating this equation gives the simple logistic curve for the spread of the epidemic as a single-valued function of time:

$$S = N/(1 + \exp\{-\Theta_0 - \Theta_1 t\}),\tag{8.17}$$

where Θ_0 is the constant of integration. The analogy often made between the spread of epidemics and the diffusion of a new technology is usually based on one of the following: (i) the learning processes involved in the use of new technology and its transmission through human contact, with the 'infection' being information; (ii) pressure of social emulation and competition; or (iii) reductions in uncertainty resulting from extensions of use.

Simple manipulation of equations (8.16) and (8.17) yields the epidemic hazard function, i.e., the conditional probability for a firm that has not adopted the technology by time t to 'get informed' about the technology and adopt in the small interval $\{t, t + dt\}$:

$$\Phi(t; \boldsymbol{\Theta}) = (dS/dt)/(N - S) = (\Theta_1 \exp\{\Theta_0 + \Theta_1 t\})/(1 + \exp\{\Theta_0 + \Theta_1 t\}).\tag{8.18}$$

It follows that

$$d\Phi/dt = \Theta_1^2 \exp\{\Theta_0 + \Theta_1 t\}/(1 + \exp\{\Theta_0 + \Theta_1 t\})^2,\tag{8.19}$$

which is greater than zero. In other words, epidemic diffusion as characterized by the simple logistic growth curve implies a hazard rate that increases with the elapsed duration.

This result can be shown to hold under a variety of functional forms put forward in the epidemic-based literature.[3] As there is not a unique parametric specification of the epidemic effect, we proceed by assuming a nonparametric epidemic hazard with the proviso that $d\Phi/dt > 0$, i.e., that the hazard rate should be increasing. Equation (8.15) can therefore be written as

$$h(t \mid \mathbf{X}, \boldsymbol{\beta}) = h_0(t)\exp\{\mathbf{X}'\boldsymbol{\beta}\}\Phi(t). \tag{8.20}$$

Equation (8.20) is a general model that now incorporates the epidemic effect as well as the rank, stock, and order effects. However, as is immediately apparent from (8.20), it is not possible to separately identify the baseline hazard from the epidemic hazard in this equation. Thus the epidemic hazard is absorbed into the baseline hazard, and in the empirical work the time dependence of the baseline hazard is tested. Specifically, the estimated model is of the form

$$h(t \mid \mathbf{X}, \boldsymbol{\beta}) = h_0(t)\exp\{\mathbf{X}'\boldsymbol{\beta}\}, \tag{8.21}$$

where $\mathbf{X}$ incorporates $rP(t)$, $K(t)$, $\mathbf{C}_i$, $p(t)$, $k(t)$, and the cross-product terms in (8.12). Strictly speaking, in the pure game-theoretic and probit models, after full account is taken of the relevant explanatory variables in the model, the baseline hazard should remain constant. In fact, if anything, the omission of some of the explanatory variables due to lack of data or information is expected to lead to a negative bias in the time dependence of the estimated baseline hazard (for an example of a proof, see Heckman and Singer, 1984). Thus if the estimates suggest a positive duration dependence, then this is indicative of the existence of epidemic effects in the diffusion process.

In seminar presentations of earlier versions of this article it was pointed out that in epidemic models the endogenous learning effects are often represented via the use of the existing stock of adopters ($K(t)$) as an explanatory variable. In the model constructed here, $K(t)$ enters the estimating equation via the stock and order effects. It is of course possible that estimates of the coefficient on $K(t)$ will reflect endogenous learning. One should note, however, that endogenous learning would suggest that $K(t)$ carries a sign opposite to what would be predicted from the stock and order effects. This particular point and the general comment are further addressed in the estimation section below.

8.2.4.   Parameter restrictions

In the section below we proceed to estimate equation (8.21). The following restrictions on the coefficients of the model are suggested by the theory in this section. The coefficient, including cross-product terms, on $k(t)$ (reflecting $g_2(\cdot)$) is indicative of the order effect. In the presence of an order effect this coefficient should be significantly greater than zero. The coefficient on $K(t)$ reflects both the stock and order effects. If both exist, then the coefficient on $K(t)$ should be significantly less than zero. The coefficients on the elements of $\mathbf{C}_i$ are indicative of the rank effect, and in the presence of such an effect the coefficients should be significantly different from zero. The baseline hazard reflects epidemic forces, and in the presence of epidemic effects the baseline hazard should show a positive duration dependence.

Thus: (i) if the coefficient on $k(t)$ is significantly greater than zero and the coefficient on $K(t)$ is significantly less than zero, then the hypothesis that there are both stock and order effects cannot be rejected; (ii) if the coefficient on $k(t)$ is not significantly greater than zero but the coefficient on $K(t)$ is significantly less than zero, then the hypothesis of there being an order effect can be rejected but the hypothesis that there is a stock effect cannot be rejected; and (iii) if the coefficient on $k(t)$ is significantly greater than zero but the coefficient on $K(t)$ is not significantly less than zero, then the hypothesis of there being a stock effect cannot be accepted but the hypothesis that there is an order effect cannot be rejected. This latter situation would provide weak support for the order hypothesis. In addition, if the baseline hazard shows a positive time dependence, then the hypothesis of an epidemic effect cannot be rejected; if the expectation terms $p(t)$ and $k(t)$ carry significant positive coefficients, then the hypothesis that acquisition decisions are not myopic (Hannan and McDowell, 1984, 1987 implicitly assume myopic behavior) cannot be rejected; and finally, if the elements of C_i carry significant coefficients, then the hypothesis of rank effects cannot be rejected.

8.2.5.   Firm characteristics and rank effects

The variables included in the rank effect have thus far been implicitly referred to as the vector C_i. It is necessary to be more specific about these variables before moving to estimation. There are of course numerous firm-specific factors influencing the adoption decision, some of which may not be even observable or quantifiable. The factors that will be considered below are those which, in the literature, are believed to exert a systematic influence on the adoption decision – the unsystematic random factors being absorbed in the residual, that is, the baseline hazard.

This dataset is on the basis of establishments, and in this article each establishment is treated as an individual firm (subject to the comments on the *STATUS* variable below). The factors related to the rank effect that have been included in the model are the following:

SIZE OF THE FIRM (*SIZE*).   This is the variable most frequently used in probit-type models. The common justification for its inclusion is that many new technologies show positive scale effects, which make adoption more profitable for larger firms and thus larger firms adopt early. It can also be argued that size can be taken as an indicator of the differences in relative risks faced by different-sized firms in adopting the new technology (although, as stated above, risk and uncertainty have not explicitly been considered). This would again suggest that larger firms adopt early. On the other hand, it can be argued that, for example, larger firms may be less flexible in their managerial and labor relations, which could impede adoption. The existing empirical evidence, however, indicates a positive relation between size and the speed of adoption (see, for example, Davies, 1979; and Alderman, Davies, and Thwaites, 1988), and the expectation is that *SIZE* will carry a positive coefficient.

Because the model incorporates stock effects as well as rank effects, and in the stock-effect model firm size is endogenous and determined by adoption dates, a problem does arise from including firm size as an exogenous explanatory variable. In principle, this could be accommodated by treating *SIZE* as a time-varying endogenous covariate. At the estimation stage one could then model *SIZE* in terms of adoption time, $K(t)$, and other exogenous variables, and consistent estimates of the coefficients of interest of the model could then be made by using a two-stage estimation method (as discussed, for example, in Lee, 1981). This is not possible, however, because the data source only provides information on the size of the firm at a point in time. Given the availability of data, the approach taken is to allow for the scale (rank) effects by using the point estimate of firm size, proxied by the number of employees, as an exogenous variable, and to allow the stock effects to be implicitly introduced through the effect of $K(t)$ on the hazard rate.

GROWTH OF OUTPUT (GY) AND DATE OF ESTABLISHMENT ($EDATE$). The theory above was not very explicit as to exactly what is measured by g_{ij}. It has been defined above as the per-period benefit from adoption of new technology, but little attention has been devoted to further explanation. At the most general level, g_{ij} refers to the differences in the profits that arise from use of the new technology relative to use of the old technology. Define π as the quasi-rents per period on the new technology and π^* as the quasi-rents on the old technology, then $g_{ij} = \pi - \pi^*$. The analysis above has concentrated implicitly on the decision of a firm considering the replacement of an existing stock of old technology by new technology. Such a firm under an assumption of myopia (to simplify matters for this discussion) will effect such a replacement in time t if $\pi - \pi^* \geq rP(t)$. However, not all potential adopters of new technology will be replacing old technology. If the new technology is to be used for expanding capacity, or if the previous technology is physically obsolescent, or if the firm is new, a different adoption rule will apply. Under myopic expectations the new technology will be acquired if $\pi - rP(t) \geq \pi^* - rP(t)^*$, where $P(t)^*$ is the price of the old technology in time t.

It is thus clear from the two adoption decision criteria that new firms, or firms with worn-out equipment, or firms expanding capacity are, *ceteris paribus*, more likely to adopt new technology than other firms. We attempt to cater for this in the empirical work by introducing variables reflecting output growth rates (GY) and the date of establishment of the firm ($EDATE$) as relevant explanatory variables. We expect both variables to carry positive coefficients.

In addition, one might argue that these two variables should carry positive coefficients because (i) financial constraints on firms may well be eased in periods of rapid market expansion, and (ii) new firms may not be encumbered by the organizational restructuring that the adoption of new technology often entails.

The available data on GY is limited, and we were not able to obtain estimates for GY for each firm in our sample for every period. We have thus proceeded by placing each firm in either the electrical or nonelectrical sector, and for each time period we have measured GY by the growth rate of the sector to which it belongs.

RESEARCH AND DEVELOPMENT EXPENDITURE ($R\&D$). This variable is included as an indicator of a firm's ability to process information about the latest technologies arriving in the market. It is also argued by Cohen and Levinthal (1989) that firms undertaking research and development are able to reduce the risks associated with the adoption of a new technology. It could be interpreted as representing the exogeous learning process (as opposed to the endogenous, epidemic process). The sign of the coefficient associated with this variable is expected to be positive.

There is an operational problem associated with the inclusion of the $R\&D$ variable. As pointed out by a referee, prior work on R&D shows that unnormalized R&D effort is closely and proportionately related to firm size. This may lead to problems of multicollinearity. Therefore, in the estimation below we explore the impact of including both $SIZE$ and $R\&D$ on our estimates of the coefficient on $R\&D$.[4]

The variable is proxied by an estimate of the number of full-time employees in the R&D department of the establishment. It takes the value of zero when the firm has no R&D department.

CORPORATE STATUS OF THE ESTABLISHMENT (*STATUS*).   This is a dummy variable that indicates whether the establishment is an independent unit or part of a larger corporate unit. The expected effect of this variable on the speed of adoption is ambiguous. On the one hand, independent units may be better positioned with regard to speed of implementation once the decision to adopt is taken. On the other hand, establishments that are part of a larger corporation may be better informed and bear less risk in adopting a new technology.

CONCENTRATION RATIO (*CRATIO*).   The establishments in the sample belong to nine different industries. (The industry classification is discussed further in appendix 8B.) *CRATIO* is a measure of the market structure of the industry to which the firm belongs. In the theoretical literature, the effect of market power on the diffusion path is ambiguous. In part of the literature, greater market power in the user industry is said to lead to faster diffusion of process technologies (Reinganum, 1981), the reason being that the cost reductions resulting from the adoption of the new technology lead to greater profit increments in more concentrated user industries, hence the incentives to adopt are greater. Quirmbach (1986), on the other hand, sets up a model where collusive action between a small number of users in a more concentrated industry retards the pace of diffusion. This results from cooperative behavior amongst users aimed at protecting profit flows from existing equipment. Theory, then, does not provide much guide as to the expected sign for this variable. The variable is measured as the share of the five largest firms in total industry output.[5]

8.3.   The Data and Sampling Distribution of the Model

To estimate the above model, the ideal would be a dataset with complete life histories of the population of potential adopters, as well as the characteristics of a well-defined new technology over a sufficiently long period beginning with the appearance of the technology in the market. Such ideal datasets are seldom available, and in particular, disaggregated data on the adoption of new technologies are scarce. The data used here originate from a technology adoption survey, conducted by the University of Newcastle's Centre for Urban and Regional Development Studies (CURDS), which meets most of the requirements.[6] In this section we give a brief description of the data and investigate the likely implications of the sample design for the specification of the estimating equation.

The CURDS survey was conducted in 1981 and covered all identified establishments in UK manufacturing within nine Minimum List Headings in engineering and metalworking industries.[7] The questionnaire asked about the adoption date of a number of new technologies for the period up to and including 1980; of these technologies, computerized numerically controlled machine tools (CNC) was selected for the present study. The survey also provides information on all establishment-specific variables included in the model. Data on the price of technology and on industry-specific variables have been compiled from other sources.[8] The first recorded adoption of CNC in the UK engineering industry was in 1968, which is taken as the base year for measuring the duration of adoption. After purging the dataset of the establishments that reported incomplete information or, because of the nature of their activities, were unlikely to be potential adopters,[9] there remained 1,056 observations in the dataset that were used in the estimation of the model.

Before proceeding to the estimation stage, we must address two issues. The first relates to the fact that the data refer to the establishment as the unit of adoption, while most of the theory of diffusion is addressed to the firm as the decision-making unit. In using these data for estimation, therefore, we are implicitly assuming that the decision to adopt is an establishment-level decision. Empirical evidence suggests that this may not be an unreasonable assumption, especially for small technological changes such as the adoption of CNC.[10] We have nevertheless included a dummy variable in the estimating model that captures possible differences in the hazard rates between the independent establishments and those with corporate affiliation.

The second issue relates to the possible effect of sample design on the sampling distribution of the model. As noted above, the CURDS survey records the adoption time of the 'stock' of establishments existing in 1980, and thus there may exist a selection bias due to sample attrition. In other words, the establishments that close down or exit during the period 1968–1980 have zero probability of being selected by the sampling procedure. In constructing the likelihood function for estimation, therefore, it would be necessary to allow for the fact that the sample is conditional on survival of the establishment beyond 1980. For the sampling plan to be ignorable, the probability of exit should be independent of the adoption time; otherwise the sampling plan is not ignorable and, in constructing the sample likelihood, different observations have to be weighted according to the selection probabilities in order to counteract the bias introduced by sample attrition. We show in appendix 8A that the hypothesis of state dependence of exit probabilities can be rejected, and thus in constructing the likelihood function for estimation, the sampling plan is ignorable.

8.4.   Estimation and Results

The hazard function $h(t; \mathbf{X}, \boldsymbol{\beta})$ specified in equation (8.21) uniquely determines the density function $f(t; \mathbf{X}, \boldsymbol{\beta})$ and the distribution function $F(t; \mathbf{X}, \boldsymbol{\beta})$ for adoption time by each individual establishment. Time is measured from the date of first recorded adoption of CNC in each industry for the plants that were established before that date, and from the date of establishment for the plants that entered after the date of first industry adoption. Allowing the variable t to represent the time of adoption for establishments that adopted the technology before 1981 and the time of censoring for nonadopters, the likelihood function for the model's parameters of interest is

$$L(\boldsymbol{\beta}) = \prod_{1,n} f(t; \mathbf{X}, \boldsymbol{\beta})^{\sigma}(1 - F(t; \mathbf{X}, \boldsymbol{\beta}))^{1-\sigma}, \tag{8.22}$$

where σ is an indicator variable that takes the value of one for adopters and zero for establishments that had not yet adopted the technology by the time of the survey.[11]

One may estimate the model as specified in equation (8.21) assuming a nonparametric baseline hazard. However, since we are interested in testing the time dependence of the baseline hazard, and also since the computational costs of estimating the nonparametric model were found to be prohibitive,[12] it was decided that it was more appropriate to estimate a parametric version of the model. The sensitivity of the results to specific parameterizations of the baseline hazard, as well as to the proportional hazard assumption, is further examined below. Time dependence of the baseline hazard was first tested by estimating a proportional hazard model assuming a Weibull distribution of adoption time, which takes the form $h(t; \mathbf{X}(t), \boldsymbol{\beta}, \alpha) = \alpha t^{(\alpha-1)} \exp\{\beta_0 + \mathbf{X}'(t)\boldsymbol{\beta}\}$, where the time subscript on $\mathbf{X}$ is indicative of the fact that some of the explanatory variables are time dependent. With $\alpha = 1$, this model is transformed to a model with constant hazard, i.e., one with exponential distribution of adoption time. With $\alpha > 1$, the model suggests positive duration dependence of adoption time which, as we discussed above, is indicative of the existence of epidemic effects.

Various elements of the vector $\mathbf{X}(t)$, such as adoption-precedence variables K and k, output growth, and concentration ratio, are industry specific. It is plausible to assume that the epidemic effects as captured by the baseline hazard would also be industry specific. Even if there is *a priori* reason to suggest the contrary, still it is desirable to be able to test this proposition in a general model with industry-specific epidemic effects. We therefore estimate the following more general Weibull model with industry-specific baseline hazard:

$$h_j(t; \mathbf{X}(t), \boldsymbol{\beta}, \alpha) = \alpha_j t^{(\alpha_j-1)} \exp\{\beta_{0j} + \mathbf{X}'(t)\boldsymbol{\beta}\}, \tag{8.23}$$

where subscript j indicates industrial specificity of the baseline hazard or epidemic effects. Clearly, the model with homogeneous baseline hazard is a special case of this model, with $\alpha_j = \alpha_k$ and $\beta_{0j} = \beta_{0k}$ for all j and k.

The model was estimated for both the exponential and Weibull hazard specifications in continuous time, where the integral of the time-varying explanatory variables was evaluated by a Simpson approximation.[13] The list of explanatory variables included in the model is presented in table 8.1. Six of the variables (with t subscripts[14]) are time varying and four of them are industry specific (namely, K_t, k_t, GY_t and $CRATIO$). Industry-specific variables are distinguished between nine MLH groups, as discussed in appendix 8B.[15,16]

The inclusion of such variables as the price of the technology P_t and the number of adopters K_t as explanatory variables raises the question of possible endogeneity bias. Price of new technology normally falls with an increase in the number of adopters, and the diffusion path is traced out as a result of the interaction between supply and demand. Although we recognize the importance of the supply-side factors in the diffusion process, it is unlikely that the endogeneity bias resulting from ignoring supply-side factors would be important in the present case. This is so partly because here we model first adoptions by individual plants, but more importantly because the major part of the supply of CNC in the UK during the period under study consisted of imports. The price level P_t and its expected change p_t are therefore set equal to their actual values. Since P_t is monotonically decreasing over the observation period, the use of other expectation-formation assumptions may not substantially change the results – especially given that expected price change is a time-varying covariate, the entire path of which affects parameter estimates.

Table 8.1   Definitions of explanatory variables

P_t	=	Price of new technology at time t.
p_t	=	Expected change of the price of new technology measured by $(P_{t+1} - P_t)$.
K_t	=	Cumulative number of owners of the technology up to and including time t.
k_t	=	Expected change in the cumulative number of adopters in the interval $\{t, t+1\}$, measured by $(K_{t+1} - K_t)$.
SIZE	=	Size of the establishment, measured by total number of employees.
GY_t	=	Expected growth of industry output measured by $(\log(O_{t+1}/O_t))$, where O_t is real industry output. The data only allowed a distinction to be made between electrical engineering and other engineering industries.
STATUS	=	The corporate status of the establishment; a dummy variable taking the value of zero for independent establishments and one for others.
R&D	=	Intensity of R&D activity of the establishment as measured by the number of full-time employees in the R&D department. It takes the value of zero for establishments without an R&D department.
EDATE	=	Date of establishment of new entrants measured from the appearance of the new technology; takes the value of zero for those established before the appearance of the technology in the market, and a value ranging between 68 to 80 for other establishments.
CRATIO	=	Concentration ratio in the industry (three-digit SIC) to which the establishment belongs. Measured by the percentage share of gross output belonging to the five largest firms in the industry.
r_t	=	Discount rate, measured by yield on Treasury Bills expressed as annual interest rates.

As regards the adoption-precedence variables K_t and k_t, however, the endogeniety bias may be more important, especially since the number of adopters has been calculated at a disaggregated industry level. Stochastic shocks that affect the decision to adopt by one firm in a particular industry may also exert a significant influence on the total number of adopters in the industry as a whole. Consistent estimates of the parameters of the model can nevertheless be obtained by using a two-stage estimation procedure as discussed by Lee (1981) and Murphy and Topel (1985). In the first stage we estimate time-series models of the total number of adopters in each industry, based on industry-level adoption data.[17] We then substitute the predicted values of K_t from these time-series models in the main model, which is estimated by the maximum-likelihood method. The expectation term k_t at the second stage is calculated as the first difference of the predicted K_t values.

The maximum-likelihood estimates of the parameters of the exponential and Weibull models with industry-specific baseline hazards are shown in table 8.2. Since one of the aims of the model is to test the importance of epidemic effects, in estimating the model we dropped adopters in the first period in each industry from the sample, which reduced the sample size from 1,056 to 1,041.[18] As can be seen, the likelihood ratio test for industry-specific baseline hazard rejects the hypothesis of aggregate epidemic effects in favor of industry-specific epidemic effects. We shall therefore discuss the results only for the heterogeneous or industry-specific baseline hazard case.

The parameter vector β remains remarkably stable in moving from the exponential to the Weibull model, though the likelihood ratio test for the significance of epidemic effects rejects the exponential model in favor of the Weibull model. The coefficient α_j in the Weibull model is significantly greater than one in the case of four industries, suggesting

Table 8.2 Maximum likelihood estimates of the exponential and Weibull models

Coefficient	Variable	Exponential model	Weibull model
α_1	TIME	–	1.8443 (0.6086)
α_2	TIME	–	1.0274 (0.7049)
α_3	TIME	–	1.6791 (0.6210)
α_4	TIME	–	2.8534 (0.6612)**
α_5	TIME	–	2.1120 (0.7682)
α_6	TIME	–	2.1774 (0.5765)*
α_7	TIME	–	3.7242 (2.2146)
α_8	TIME	–	3.3413 (0.8347)**
α_9	TIME	–	1.8581 (0.4745)*
β_{01}	CONSTANT	−4.5205 (1.0719)**	−5.1788 (1.4948)**
β_{02}	CONSTANT	−5.1291 (1.1092)**	−3.8722 (1.5439)*
β_{03}	CONSTANT	−3.1888 (1.0461)**	−3.3933 (1.2256)**
β_{04}	CONSTANT	−4.3820 (1.0931)**	−6.0950 (1.4714)**
β_{05}	CONSTANT	−3.7481 (1.0962)**	−5.1931 (1.8167)**
β_{06}	CONSTANT	−7.8031 (1.3428)**	−8.8598 (1.4446)**
β_{07}	CONSTANT	−2.7395 (1.0612)**	−7.7088 (4.5282)
β_{08}	CONSTANT	−2.9994 (1.0524)**	−4.7861 (1.4895)**
β_{09}	CONSTANT	−3.3459 (1.2935)**	−4.3003 (1.5332)**
β_1	K_t	0.2053 (0.0208)**	0.1793 (0.0286)**
β_2	k_t/r_t	0.7030 (0.1602)**	0.6204 (0.1922)**
β_3	SIZE	0.0620 (0.0198)**	0.0637 (0.0244)**
β_4	GY_t	0.3233 (0.0843)**	0.3433 (0.0832)**
β_5	r_tP_t	−0.0092 (0.0037)*	−0.0099 (0.0049)*
β_6	p_t	0.0306 (0.0150)*	0.0324 (0.0144)*
β_7	R&D	−0.0003 (0.0054)	−0.0013 (0.0059)
β_8	EDATE	−0.0071 (0.0082)	−0.0055 (0.0084)
β_9	STATUS	0.5475 (0.4874)	0.5849 (0.5043)
β_{10}	CRATIO	0.0105 (0.0178)	0.0088 (0.0177)

Cross-product terms

Coefficient	Variable	Exponential model	Weibull model
β_{11}	$K_t \cdot [k_t/r_t]$	−0.1998 (0.0562)**	−0.1954 (0.0476)**
β_{12}	$SIZE \cdot [k_t/r_t]$	0.0010 (0.0562)	−0.0094 (0.0614)
β_{13}	$GY_t \cdot [k_t/r_t]$	0.8025 (0.2356)**	0.7538 (0.2420)**
β_{14}	$R\&D \cdot [k_t/r_t]$	−0.0051 (0.0142)	−0.0031 (0.0147)
β_{15}	$EDATE \cdot [k_t/r_t]$	0.0077 (0.0156)	0.0078 (0.0156)
β_{16}	$STATUS \cdot [k_t/r_t]$	−0.5543 (0.9668)	−0.6043 (0.9584)
β_{17}	$CRATIO \cdot [k_t/r_t]$	−0.0060 (0.0302)	−0.0034 (0.0322)
Log-likelihood		−631.1	−613.7
Number of observations		1041	1041

Likelihood ratio test for industry-specific
baseline hazard: ($\alpha_1 = \alpha_2 = \alpha_3 \ldots = \alpha_9$
and $\beta_{01} = \beta_{02} = \beta_{03} \ldots = \beta_{09}$)   153.2 ($\chi^2_{0.99}(8) = 20.1$)   179.6 ($\chi^2_{0.99}(16) = 32.0$)

Likelihood ratio test for the significance of
epidemic effects: ($\alpha_1 = \alpha_2 = \alpha_3 \ldots = \alpha_9 = 1$)   34.8 ($\chi^2_{0.99}(9) = 21.7$)

Likelihood ratio test for the existence of
order effects:
($\beta_2 = \beta_{11} = \beta_{12} = \beta_{13} = \beta_{14} = \beta_{15} = \beta_{16} = \beta_{17} = 0$)   180.0 ($\chi^2_{0.99}(8) = 20.1$)   89.4 ($\chi^2_{0.99}(8) = 20.1$)

Figures in parentheses refer to the asymptotic standard error of coefficient estimates.
* Significant at the 0.05 level (in the case of α's significantly greater than 1 at the 0.05 level).
** Significant at the 0.01 level (in the case of α's significantly greater than 1 at the 0.01 level).

Table 8.3   Maximum likelihood estimates of restricted Weibull models

Coefficient	Variable	Restricted stock model	Myopic model
α_1	TIME	6.4841 (0.6363)**	3.8600 (0.5820)**
α_2	TIME	5.6992 (0.6796)**	2.9040 (0.5621)**
α_3	TIME	2.7558 (0.5917)**	2.4616 (0.5784)**
α_4	TIME	7.7780 (0.6265)**	2.3189 (0.5620)**
α_5	TIME	4.4050 (0.6909)**	4.0625 (0.7220)**
α_6	TIME	4.2438 (0.5402)**	3.9826 (0.4599)**
α_7	TIME	5.7297 (2.1467)*	5.2477 (2.1398)*
α_8	TIME	5.1026 (0.7983)**	4.7004 (0.7531)**
α_9	TIME	4.0345 (0.4396)**	3.4622 (0.4041)**
β_{01}	CONSTANT	−12.644 (1.5048)**	−5.3295 (1.3561)**
β_{02}	CONSTANT	−9.5162 (1.4736)**	−2.6646 (1.1172)*
β_{03}	CONSTANT	−3.8904 (1.2602)**	−0.4615 (0.8865)
β_{04}	CONSTANT	−11.557 (1.3944)**	−1.7170 (1.0636)
β_{05}	CONSTANT	−8.9197 (1.6882)**	−5.0400 (1.4906)**
β_{06}	CONSTANT	−10.957 (1.3850)**	−6.5924 (1.1030)**
β_{07}	CONSTANT	−10.960 (4.5919)**	−6.7496 (4.6841)
β_{08}	CONSTANT	−5.0243 (1.4264)**	−1.9382 (0.8360)*
β_{09}	CONSTANT	−7.8532 (1.4517)**	−3.5031 (1.1257)**
β_1	K_t	–	0.0566 (0.0120)**
β_2	k_t/r_t	0.2651 (0.1638)	–
β_3	SIZE	0.0552 (0.0288)*	0.0526 (0.0131)**
β_4	GY_t	0.4475 (0.0731)**	0.5135 (0.0339)**
β_5	$r_t P_t$	0.0001 (0.0051)	−0.0226 (0.0039)**
β_6	p_t	0.0274 (0.0129)*	–
β_7	R&D	−0.0024 (0.0057)	−0.0056 (0.0026)*
β_8	EDATE	−0.0022 (0.0083)	−0.0003 (0.0039)
β_9	STATUS	0.7271 (0.5680)	0.3127 (0.2269)
β_{10}	CRATIO	0.0157 (0.0147)	0.0082 (0.0109)
Cross-product terms			
β_{11}	$K_t \cdot [k_t/r_t]$	−0.0794 (0.0239)**	–
β_{12}	$SIZE \cdot [k_t/r_t]$	0.0142 (0.0686)	–
β_{13}	$GY_t \cdot [k_t/r_t]$	0.3253 (0.2219)	–
β_{14}	$R\&D \cdot [k_t/r_t]$	−0.0018 (0.0132)	–
β_{15}	$EDATE \cdot [k_t/r_t]$	0.0065 (0.0156)	–
β_{16}	$STATUS \cdot [k_t/r_t]$	−0.8731 (1.1605)	–
β_{17}	$CRATIO \cdot [k_t/r_t]$	−0.0069 (0.0291)	–
Log-likelihood		−656.9	−665.5
Number of observations		1041	1041

Likelihood ratio test for zero stock effect:
($\beta_1 = 0$)   86.4 ($\chi^2_{0.99}(1) = 6.63$)

Likelihood ratio test for the myopic model:
($\beta_2 = \beta_6 = \beta_{11} = \beta_{12} = \beta_{13} = \beta_{14} = \beta_{15} = \beta_{16} = \beta_{17} = 0$)   103.6 ($\chi^2_{0.99}(9) = 21.7$)

Figures in parentheses refer to the asymptotic standard error of coefficient estimates.
* Significant at the 0.05 level (in the case of α's significantly greater than 1 at the 0.05 level).
** Significant at the 0.01 level (in the case of α's significantly greater than 1 at the 0.01 level).

positive duration dependence of adoption probabilities. But this does not necessarily imply that the remaining five industries do not exhibit epidemic effects in technology diffusion. As discussed below, epidemic effects in the case of the latter industries seem to have been captured by a positive stock effect.

A notable aspect of the results is that the coefficient on K_t, though statistically significant, has the opposite sign to that predicted by the order-effects and stock-effects models. This does not, however, necessarily indicate the absence of stock effects in diffusion. As we noted earlier, it is difficult to distinguish empirically between the negative effect of adoption precedence assumed by stock and order models and its positive epidemic effects. By allowing a time-varying baseline hazard to capture some of the epidemic effects, we attempted to make the negative stock effects empirically more visible. But the evidence suggests that even if such negative stock effects exist, they are by far outweighed by the positive effects of adoption precedence suggested by epidemic theories. To highlight the difficulty in separating the stock effect from the epidemic effect, we reestimated the Weibull model by restricting the coefficient of K_t to equal zero. The results are given in table 8.3 under the column 'restricted stock model.' As can be seen, the omission of K_t from the Weibull model leads to a sharp increase in the estimated α_j coefficients, with the coefficients becoming significantly greater than one for all industries. The original Weibull model nevertheless remains the preferred model, both on the basis of the likelihood ratio test of zero stock effect reported in table 8.3, and by having the correct signs (e.g., the sign of the price coefficient in the restricted model is wrong).

Order effects are reflected in the coefficient of k_t inclusive of the interaction terms (i.e., $g_2(\cdot) = a_0 + a_1 C_i + a_2 K_t$ as in equations (8.8) and (8.12)). As the likelihood ratio test for the existence of order effects shows, there is evidence of significant influence of k_t on the diffusion process (table 8.2). It should be noted that with the inclusion of the interaction terms, the sign of the order-effect coefficient varies between establishments and over time. Evaluated for the Weibull model, and at values prevailing at the adoption time/censoring time for the time-varying covariates, this coefficient turned out to be negative in the case of 1,037 out of 1,041 establishments, with a mean value of -5.65. In other words, as in the case of stock effect, the order-effect coefficient seems to be significant but with the wrong sign.

Size of establishment, which has traditionally played an important role in the probit-type or rank-oriented models, has a significant and positive effect on adoption probability, in conformity with the *a priori* predictions of theory and with other empirical studies. Rose and Joskow (1990) have argued that the positive correlation between firm size and adoption probability often found in empirical studies may be spurious because of a lack of distinction between adoption decisions and new-investment decisions in what they call naive diffusion models. More frequent new investments by large firms relative to small firms may thus create the impression of decreasing adoption duration with size, which is picked up in the 'naive' models as the size effect. They attempt to correct for this by using a double-censored model that utilizes information on the frequency and timing of new investments in the case of power generating plants. In the case of small technological changes, such as the first adoption of a CNC machine being considered here, this criticism may not be very relevant. Nevertheless, as explained in the previous section, we have tried to allow for this by including the date-of-establishment variable (*EDATE*) and the output-growth variable (*GY*) in the model. The date of establishment has no significant effect on adoption probability, implying that, allowing for all other firm characteristics, new firms do not appear to have a higher adoption probability than old firms. Output growth, on the other hand, has a positive and significant coefficient, suggesting that periods of market expansion correspond to faster rates of new technology adoption.

The coefficient of the technology-price variable is also significant and has the correct sign. The highly significant and positive coefficient of the expected-change-in-price variable (p_t), which is also in conformity with the predictions of theory, suggests that the myopic-type models, as used for example by Hannan and McDowell (1987), may be seriously misspecified. To investigate this further, the results for the Weibull model can be compared with those of the myopic model. As mentioned in section 8.2, the adoption decision in myopic-type models is based on the profitability condition rather than the arbitrage condition. The myopic model is thus a special case of the model developed here, which will be attained if all the coefficients of the expectation terms (i.e., p_t, k_t, and the cross-product terms) are restricted to be zero. The coefficient estimates of the myopic model are shown in table 8.3, where it can also be seen that the likelihood ratio statistic rejects the myopic model in favor of the model with expectation terms. While the coefficient estimates for variables such as $SIZE$, K_t, P_t, and GY_t remain significant and carry the correct sign, the myopic model shows significant coefficient estimates for $R\&D$ with signs contrary to *a priori* expectations and exhibits strong positive time dependence of the baseline hazard, compared to the original model.

From table 8.2, the rest of the establishment-specific characteristics such as $R\&D$, corporate $STATUS$, and date of establishment of the plant ($EDATE$) do not seem to exert a significant influence on the speed of adoption. This may be due to multicollinearity between these variables and other explanatory variables in the model. In particular, size of the establishment is expected to be positively correlated with R&D expenditure, and as a result it may act as a proxy for the latter in the model, picking up most of the R&D influences. To test this proposition, we dropped the $SIZE$ variable and reestimated the model, but the $R\&D$ coefficient, as well as those of $EDATE$ and $STATUS$, still remained insignificant.

The variable $CRATIO$ (concentration ratio) in the model is meant to capture the effect of market structure on the speed of adoption. According to the empirical results, the concentration ratio appears to have no significant effect on the probability of adoption (table 8.2). This may of course be partly due to the fact that the five-firm concentration ratio measure may not provide an adequate representation of market power within the industries concerned.

In terms of the rank, stock, order, and epidemic effects, it appears that the pattern of CNC adoption in the UK indicates the existence of rank and epidemic effects but provides little support for the stock and order effects. Although the above results have been obtained under specific parametric assumptions about the baseline hazard, the similarity of the parameter β estimates for the exponential and Weibull models appears to suggest that the results are robust in relation to the specific underlying baseline hazard assumptions. To further check this proposition, we reestimated the model assuming a log-logistic baseline hazard. The log-logistic baseline hazard is of the form $h_0 = (\beta_0 \alpha (\beta_0 t)^{(\alpha-1)})/(1 + (\beta_0 t)^\alpha)$, which is decreasing for $\alpha < 1$, and for $\alpha > 1$ is first increasing and then decreasing, achieving its unique maximum at $t = (\alpha - 1)^{1/\alpha}/\beta_0$.

The log-logistic model was estimated in two forms. The first was the proportional hazard form

$$h_j = [(\beta_{0j}\alpha_j(\beta_{0j}t)^{(\alpha_j-1)})/(1 + (\beta_{0j}t)^{\alpha_j})]\exp\{\mathbf{X}'(t)\boldsymbol{\beta}\}, \tag{8.24}$$

where, as in the case of the earlier models, the independent variables act multiplicatively on the hazard rate. Secondly, to check the sensitivity of the results to the proportional hazard assumption, we estimated a nonproportional hazard log-logistic model of the form

$$h_j = [\exp\{\beta_{0j} + \mathbf{X}'(t)\boldsymbol{\beta}\}\,\alpha_j t^{(\alpha_j-1)}]/(1 + \exp\{\beta_{0j} + \mathbf{X}'(t)\boldsymbol{\beta}\}t^{\alpha_j}). \tag{8.25}$$

The subscript j in both models, as before, indicates the industry-specific baseline hazard or epidemic effect. The estimation results for both the proportional and nonproportional hazard models are shown in table 8.4.

The estimated $\boldsymbol{\beta}$ coefficients for the proportional hazard log-logistic model are remarkably close to those of the Weibull model.[19] With the exception of industries 5 and 9, however, the α coefficients are not significantly greater than one. The coefficient on K_i is positive and significant, and dropping this variable made the α coefficients significantly greater than one.[20] Thus, as in the case of the Weibull model, there seems to exist a strong epidemic or positive stock effect. The strong resemblance between the coefficient estimates of the three proportional hazard models estimated, namely exponential, Weibull, and log-logistic, supports the findings of other empirical studies that within the class of proportional hazard models the assumed form of the baseline hazard does not significantly affect the parameter estimates.[21]

A more important test of the sensitivity of the results of the Weibull model is to compare these results with those of the nonproportional hazard model. As can be seen from table 8.4, the results from the nonproportional hazard model by and large support the conclusions reached on the basis of the proportional hazard Weibull model. With the exception of the variable *SIZE*, the estimated $\boldsymbol{\beta}$ coefficients in terms of sign and statistical significance closely follow those of the Weibull model.[22] While the coefficient of *SIZE* seems to be no longer significant, the interaction between *SIZE* and the order effect is now positive and significant. This may be due to multicollinearity resulting from the functional form in which the explanatory variables are entered into the model. To check this, we dropped the interaction term regarding *SIZE* and reestimated the model. The result was that the coefficient of *SIZE* became positive and highly significant, thus supporting the hypothesis of positive correlation between size and adoption probability.[23]

The nonproportional hazard model also seems to lend strong support to the existence of epidemic effects. The estimated α coefficients in the majority of industries, with the exception of industries 4 and 7, are significantly greater than one. This, combined with a positive and highly significant coefficient estimate for K_{it}, indicates a positive correlation between adoption precedence and the speed of diffusion. Considering that measurement errors and omitted explanatory variables are likely to have caused a downward bias in the estimated time dependence of the baseline hazard, these results lend strong support to the existence of epidemic effects in the diffusion process. Furthermore, with the estimated values for α_j and β_{0j} coefficients, the baseline hazards in most industries attain their maximum well into the future, which in effect implies monotonically increasing hazard rates in accordance with the Weibull model assumptions.

Table 8.4 Maximum likelihood estimates of the log-logistic model

Coefficient		Proportional hazard model	Nonproportional hazard model
α_1	TIME	1.5951 (0.5297)	3.6522 (0.7415)**
α_2	TIME	1.3586 (0.6278)	6.3748 (1.1117)**
α_3	TIME	0.5292 (0.6810)	3.5351 (0.9428)**
α_4	TIME	1.4688 (0.6619)	0.9184 (0.5410)
α_5	TIME	2.4021 (0.6761)*	7.9925 (0.8573)**
α_6	TIME	1.7059 (0.7861)	4.0825 (1.2083)**
α_7	TIME	1.8578 (0.5415)	0.6876 (0.4106)
α_8	TIME	3.7076 (2.3505)	5.1178 (2.7865)*
α_9	TIME	3.1925 (0.9344)**	8.6437 (1.4662)**
β_{01}	CONSTANT	0.0471 (0.0512)	−6.1293 (3.0681)
β_{02}	CONSTANT	0.0217 (0.0251)	−12.978 (2.6979)**
β_{03}	CONSTANT	0.0025 (0.0101)	−9.4341 (2.5255)**
β_{04}	CONSTANT	0.0611 (0.0648)	−0.3693 (2.1748)
β_{05}	CONSTANT	0.0517 (0.0325)	−14.964 (2.2167)**
β_{06}	CONSTANT	0.0392 (0.0352)	−8.2442 (3.0179)**
β_{07}	CONSTANT	0.0048 (0.0066)	−8.5848 (2.5547)**
β_{08}	CONSTANT	0.0771 (0.0317)**	−9.6934 (6.4819)
β_{09}	CONSTANT	0.1332 (0.0637)*	−12.945 (2.7466)**
β_1	K_t	0.1900 (0.0275)**	0.3503 (0.0601)**
β_2	k_t/r_t	0.6876 (0.1818)**	1.6160 (0.4031)**
β_3	$SIZE$	0.0639 (0.0242)**	−0.0219 (0.0890)
β_4	GY_t	0.3320 (0.0768)**	0.7051 (0.1629)**
β_5	$r_t P_t$	−0.0070 (0.0048)	−0.0238 (0.0103)*
β_6	p_t	0.0349 (0.0147)**	0.0673 (0.0274)*
β_7	$R\&D$	−0.0004 (0.0060)	−0.0122 (0.0194)
β_8	$EDATE$	−0.0063 (0.0085)	−0.0001 (0.0150)
β_9	$STATUS$	0.6052 (0.5142)	0.8805 (1.1274)
β_{10}	$CRATIO$	0.0125 (0.0177)	0.0117 (0.0336)
Cross-product terms			
β_{11}	$K_t \cdot [k_t/r_t]$	−0.2033 (0.0460)**	−0.5065 (0.1152)**
β_{12}	$SIZE \cdot [k_t/r_t]$	0.0062 (0.0627)	0.6536 (0.2694)*
β_{13}	$GY_t \cdot [k_t/r_t]$	0.8059 (0.2285)**	1.7417 (0.4818)
β_{14}	$R\&D \cdot [k_t/r_t]$	−0.0044 (0.0152)	−0.0693 (0.0579)
β_{15}	$EDATE \cdot [k_t/r_t]$	0.0075 (0.0157)	−0.0067 (0.0349)
β_{16}	$STATUS \cdot [k_t/r_t]$	−0.6339 (0.9846)	−1.2112 (2.6653)
β_{17}	$CRATIO \cdot [k_t/r_t]$	−0.0073 (0.0323)	−0.0212 (0.0856)
Log-likelihood		−610.3	−572.1
Number of observations		1041	1041

Figures in parentheses refer to the asymptotic standard error of coefficient estimates.
* Significant at the 0.05 level (in the case of α's significantly greater than 1 at the 0.05 level).
** Significant at the 0.01 level (in the case of α's significantly greater than 1 at the 0.01 level).

8.5.   Concluding Remarks

Almost without exception, the existing empirical diffusion literature proceeds by the estimation of single, preselected diffusion models, and model selection has never played a major role in this literature. This also means that the relative performance of different diffusion models in explaining real-world diffusion phenomena has rarely been compared. In this article we have set up a general empirical model of the process of technological diffusion that simultaneously incorporates rank, stock, order, and epidemic effects. These four effects represent the main theoretical streams in the existing literature. This model provides an effective method for analyzing diffusion phenomena that overcomes problems of model preselection and also enables a comparison of relative model performance.

The new model was applied to the data on the diffusion of CNC machine tools in the UK engineering industry for the period 1968–1980. It was found that while the rank and endogenous learning effects, as discussed respectively in the probit-type and epidemic-type models, seemed to play an important role in the diffusion process, there was little support for the stock and order effects as discussed in game-theoretic models. Although this finding is a negative one, it is important in that it goes some (modest) distance in undercutting the more recent theoretical work on diffusion.

The apparent failure of the stock and order effects may be due to the nature of CNC technology. Such effects require that the new technology have significant impacts on a firm's costs and thus output, and it is possible that CNC is not sufficiently drastic to have such impacts. In the study reported upon here, no impact on sample attrition from the adoption of CNC was found, and this may provide support for the view that this technology is not sufficiently drastic to illustrate stock and order effects. Further research currently being initiated is exploring these issues by considering the impact of the adoption of technology on firm performance. Prior to any results from this new work, the implication of the work reported here is that if stock and order effects have real-world relevance, it is limited at best to very major innovations.

Apart from the comparison of models, the article also reports results that may be of interest in themselves. It was found that growth of output in the user industry had a significant positive impact on the diffusion speed, whereas user industry concentration did not seem to have a significant influence on the speed of diffusion. Firm size had a significant positive impact on the firm's date of adoption, but the R&D spending of the firm, its corporate status, and its date of establishment did not appear as significant. These results confirm existing findings in the literature. It was further found that static or myopic models of diffusion that concentrate on the single-period profitability of adoption may suffer from serious misspecification error. The finding that expectations have a significant role to play in the diffusion process is new and confirms theoretical predictions.

Empirical research on the diffusion of new technologies has in the past been severely handicapped by lack of data. The relatively high cost of compiling panel data on complete life histories of individual adopters may have been a prohibitive factor. However, as has been shown, sampling the stock of adopters at a point in time can be adequate. In particular, the problem of sample attrition in the case of small technological changes may be ignorable. Even for major innovations, sampling at two points of time can produce the necessary information for correcting the possible selection bias arising from sample attrition. The availability of datasets, similar to the one used here, on other new process technologies is essential for extending this type of research. We are exploring our dataset further in several directions, one of which is to more adequately address supply-side factors. We also look forward to further research by others in the field that will carry on the process of linking more closely the empirical and theoretical research on this important issue.

Appendix 8A

THE EFFECT OF SAMPLE ATTRITION ON THE SAMPLING DISTRIBUTION OF THE MODEL

The possible life histories of establishments over the observation period, 1968–1980, are depicted in figure 8A.1. Time is measured along the horizontal axis. The solid lines represent establishments that have not yet adopted the technology, and the dotted lines represent establishments after adoption. The figure shows six establishment types, A1 to A6, classified according to their adoption behavior and entry and exit times during the 1968–1980 period. Establishment type A1 exists before the appearance of the new technology (1968) and survives beyond 1980 without adopting the technology. A2 has the same life history as A1, with the difference that it adopts the technology at calendar time D1. Plant type A3 enters at time D2, after the appearance of the technology, and survives beyond 1980 without adopting, A4 enters at time D3, adopts the technology at time D4 (which may equal D3), and survives beyond 1980. Establishment types A5 (adopter) and A6 (nonadopter) exit at dates X1 and X2 respectively, and are therefore excluded from the sample observed in 1980.

In an unbiased sample for the population as a whole, the contributions of establishments A1 to A4 to the likelihood function are uniquely determined on the basis of the hazard function discussed above. Let $f(t)$ and $F(t)$ be respectively the density and distribution functions corresponding to the

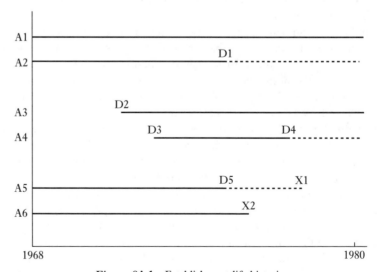

Figure 8A.1   Establishment life histories

population hazard function $h(t)$, where t (time of adoption or time of censoring for nonadopters) is measured from the base year 1968, or from the entry date for new entries during the 1968–1980 period.[24] Clearly, in an unbiased sample the contribution of establishments such as A2 and A4 (adopters) to the likelihood function is $f(t)$, and that of A1 or A3 (nonadopters) is $[1 - F(t)]$. The systematic exclusion of establishments such as A5 and A6, however, may introduce a selection bias in the sampling distribution of the model. To account for this, the likelihood function must be made conditional on survival of the establishments beyond 1980, i.e., the time of the survey. The probability of adoption at time t, conditional on the exit time x being greater than x^* ($x^* = \min\{12, (\text{entry date} - 1980)\}$), could be written as

$$f(t \mid x > x^*) = \frac{f(t)\int_{x^*}^{\infty} g(x \mid t)dx}{\int_{x^*}^{\infty}\int_0^{\infty} g(x \mid t)f(t)dtdx},$$

where $g(x \mid t)$ is the conditional density of exit time given the adoption time. Clearly, for the sampling plan to be ignorable the probability density of exit time should be independent of that of adoption time. In that case, the right-hand side of the above equation becomes equal to $f(t)$ and the sample likelihood equals the population likelihood. If this condition is not satisfied, then the sampling plan is not ignorable, and different observations have to be weighted according to the selection probabilities in order to counteract the bias introduced by sample attrition (see, e.g., Hoem, 1985).

Sampling from the stock at one point in time does not generate the information necessary to test the state dependence of the exit rate of establishments. However, there also exists a follow-up survey of the original sample of establishments, conducted by CURDS in 1986, which can be used to make inferences about the state dependence of the exit rates during the 1981–1986 period. Though this follow-up survey is not as complete as the original survey in terms of questionnaire details, it does provide a complete list of the establishments that were closed down during the intervening period. In this appendix we have used this information to test the hypothesis of state dependence of the exit probabilities.

We have stratified the original sample according to adoption date and calculated the conditional frequencies of exit during the 1981–1986 period for each adoption time interval. These are reported in table 8A.1. As can be seen, there seems to be no systematic variation in exit frequencies across adoption times. To test this proposition statistically, we set up a probability model of the exit times. If we assume that exit time follows an exponential distribution, its hazard rate conditional on the adoption time can be written as $h(x \mid t, \lambda) = \exp\{\lambda_0 + \lambda_1 t\}$, where t and x are the adoption and exit times as defined above. If $\Omega(x)$ is the distribution function of the exit time, then the probability of exit between times x_1 and x_2 given survival up to x_1 is $[(\Omega(x_2) - \Omega(x_1))/(1 - \Omega(x_1))]$, and the probability of survival beyond x_2 given survival up to x_1 is $[(1 - \Omega(x_2))/(1 - \Omega(x_1))]$. If we take x_1 and x_2 to represent exit times corresponding to 1981 and 1986 respectively, the likelihood function for the exit probabilities of the sample of 267 establishments that adopted the technology before 1981 and survived beyond 1980 can be written as

$$L = \prod_{n=1,267} [1 - \exp\{-(x_2 - x_1)\exp(\lambda_0 + \lambda_1 t)\}]^{\delta}[\exp\{-(x_2 - x_1)\exp(\lambda_0 + \lambda_1 t)\}]^{(1-\delta)},$$

where δ is an indicator variable taking the value of one for establishments that exit during 1981–1986 and the value of zero for the censored observations, i.e., those that survive beyond 1986. The maximum likelihood estimates of λ_0 and λ_1 are reported in table 8A.2. Since λ_1 is not significantly different from zero, we may reject the hypothesis of state dependence of exit time and thus regard the sample design as ignorable for estimation purposes.

Table 8A.1   Relative frequency of exits conditional on adoption time, 1981–1986

Adoption time (in years, 1968 = 0)	0–2	3–4	5–6	7–8	9–10	11–12	12<	All
Number of adopters	6	11	16	55	72	107	789	1056
Number of exits	2	3	3	9	17	17	228	279
Exit frequency	0.33	0.27	0.19	0.16	0.24	0.16	0.29	0.26

Table 8A.2   Maximum likelihood estimates of the parameters of the conditional exit model

λ_0	−2.84 (−5.86)
λ_1	−0.055 (−1.06)
Log-likelihood	−129.7
Number of observations	267
Likelihood ratio test for the significance of adoption time variable	1.0 $(\chi^2_{0.90}(1) = 2.7)$

Figures in parentheses refer to the ratios of estimated coefficients to their asymptotic standard error.

Appendix 8B

INDUSTRIAL CLASSIFICATION OF CNC ADOPTERS

The nine industry groups distinguished in the estimation above are defined in table 8B.1. In industry 1 we have combined three MLH groups, each of which consisted only of a very small number of establishments. The rest of the industries consist of MLH groups (1968 SIC) distinguished in the original survey (see Alderman, Davies, and Thwaites, 1988). Table 8B.2 provides data on the date of first adoption and cumulative number of adopters for each industry. As can be seen, industries vary noticeably with regard to both the first adoption date and percentage cumulative adoptions. The maximum length of time between first adoption dates is seven years, relating to industries 2 and 9. Industry 2 has the highest (44.8 per cent) and industry 6 the lowest (8.7 per cent) rate of adoptions.

Table 8B.1   Sectoral definition of industries

Industry index	Minimum list heading	
1	331, 336, 349	Agricultural Machinery, Contractors' Plant and Machinery, Other Mechanical Engineering
2	332	Metalworking Machine Tools
3	333	Pumps, Valves, and Compressors
4	337	Mechanical Handling Equipment
5	339	General Mechanical Engineering
6	341	Industrial Plant and Machinery
7	361	Electrical Machinery
8	390	Engineers' Small Tools and Gauges
9	Subcontractors	

Table 8B.2 Cumulative CNC adoptions by industry

Industry index	First year of adoption	Total number of adopters (1980)	Total number of firms	Percentage adopters
1	1971	21	91	23.1
2	1968	47	105	44.8
3	1971	44	103	42.7
4	1974	16	74	21.6
5	1972	61	221	27.6
6	1970	17	196	8.7
7	1973	22	106	20.7
8	1970	16	95	16.8
9	1975	28	65	43.1
Total	1968	272	1056	25.7

Table 8B.3 Estimation results for the time series model of cumulative adopters

Industry index	a_0	a_1	R^2	Durbin's h-statistic
1	1.25	1.11	0.94	−0.4686
	(0.87)	(0.09)		
2	1.92	1.28	0.96	0.9387
	(1.33)	(0.07)		
3	2.25	1.19	0.97	−0.6335
	(1.31)	(0.06)		
4	2.04	1.03	0.97	−0.1631
	(0.63)	(0.07)		
5	4.03	1.14	0.96	1.5216
	(2.21)	(0.08)		
6	0.17	1.39	0.97	−0.4550
	(0.51)	(0.07)		
7	1.12	1.27	0.95	−0.1555
	(1.08)	(0.11)		
8	0.42	1.34	0.97	0.8393
	(0.45)	(0.07)		
9	3.85	1.03	0.92	1.3340
	(1.96)	(0.13)		

Figures in parentheses refer to the standard errors of coefficient estimates.

To implement the two-stage estimation procedure explained in the text, the cumulative number of adopters in each industry is used in estimating time-series models of the type $K_t = a_0 + a_1 K_{t-1} + u_t$. Predicted values from these auxiliary time-series models are employed in the two-stage estimation procedure. The OLS estimation results for the nine industries are shown in table 8B.3. It can be shown that under very general conditions this two-stage procedure yields consistent estimates of the parameters of the model (see, e.g., Lee, 1981; and Murphy and Topel, 1985). The means and standard deviations of the variables included in the model are shown in table 8B.4, for the overall sample.

Table 8B.4   Mean and standard deviation of the variables

Variable	Units	Mean[a]	Standard deviation[a]
Constant	–	1.00	0
K_t	(units)	28.59	17.90
k_t/r_t	(units)	5.05	2.46
SIZE	(100 employees)	2.20	4.14
GY_t	(% growth rate)	−4.87	2.81
$r_t P_t$	(1975 = 100.0)	175.01	26.79
p_t	$(P_{t+1} − P_t)$	−10.95	4.89
R&D	(employees)	5.26	18.24
EDATE	(date, 1968–1980 or 0)	18.62	31.35
STATUS	(dummy variable)	0.56	0.49
Cross-product terms[b]			
$K_t \times k_t/r_t$		16.87	15.96
$SIZE \times k_t/r_t$		1.09	2.14
$GY_t \times k_t/r_t$		−2.27	1.64
$R&D \times k_t/r_t$		2.82	11.17
$EDATE \times k_t/r_t$		9.49	18.24
$STATUS \times k_t/r_t$		0.29	0.32
Number of observations		1041[c]	
Number of adoptions		252[c]	
Number of censored observations		789	

[a] For the time-varying covariates, refers to the values prevailing at the time of adoption or censoring.
[b] All cross-product terms are divided by 100.
[c] Excludes adopters in the first period in each industry.

Acknowledgements

This work is part of a project funded by the Economic and Social Research Council and the Department of Trade and Industry in the UK, some other results of which are available in Karshenas and Stoneman (1992).

Notes

1   In the derivation of equation (8.7), all conjectures as to the impact of the firm's adoption decision on the adoption decisions of other firms are included implicitly rather than explicitly, being incorporated in the expectations terms (especially $s(t)$). In the sections below we then proceed to largely assume that these expectations are formed with perfect foresight. It has been pointed out to us that this does not fully reflect the strategic nature of some of the recent contributions, in particular the model of Fudenberg and Tirole (1985). Although we do accept this to some degree, we would counter by arguing that in this article we are primarily interested in an empirical model that reflects the main currents of the literature, and unfortunately the theoretical literature gives no indication of what might be a more adequate empirical approach. We would also argue that the current formulation is consistent with the previously published work of Ireland and Stoneman

referred to above. We would not argue, however, that there is no need for further research on the issue of strategic interaction, and in fact would consider it an area of research priority.

2   In the empirical model discussed above we assumed a fixed discount rate r for ease of exposition. It is, however, straightforward to show that the same results are obtained if we substitute a time-varying discount factor for r in the model. In the estimating model, therefore, we treat $r(t)$ as a time-varying covariate. The first two terms on the right-hand side of equation (8.8) could be written as $P(t)[r(t) - p(t)/P(t)]$, where the expression within the square brackets is the familiar user-cost-of-capital formula. We have, however, preferred to incorporate $r(t)P(t)$ and $p(t)$ as separate terms in the estimating equation, as this allows a more explicit discussion of the misspecification error in myopic-type models in the subsequent sections of the article.

3   Under the general functional form $dS/dt = H(S(t))$, it can be easily seen that a sufficient condition for $d\Phi/dt > 0$ is that $dH/dS > 0$ – which is generally true with the epidemic-type diffusion curves in the literature.

4   A further issue concerns the possible linkages between endogenous and exogenous learning. Above we have modeled endogenous learning by a time-dependent baseline hazard and here represent exogenous learning by $R\&D$. It is of course possible to argue that there may be connections between these two learning processes. In the estimation we did not in fact observe any significant impact on the estimates of the baseline hazard from the inclusion of the $R\&D$ variable, and thus do not consider the issue to be an important one.

5   Although one might argue that concentration should be considered as an endogenous variable in some of these diffusion models, it is treated here as exogenous. This might be justified on the basis of the results presented in section 8.3 that the adoption of a single technology has no apparent effect on sample attrition and by implication on market structure.

6   We are grateful to Alfred Thwaites and Neil Alderman for making this data available to us. We are particularly indebted to Alderman, who has given generously of his time to extract the dataset from the original survey data.

7   The survey covered the following Minimum List Headings (based on 1968 SIC): MLH 331, MLH 332, MLH 333, MLH 336, MLH 337, MLH 339, MLH 341, MLH 361, and MLH 390. The response covered 1,127 establishments in these MLH groups together with subcontractors (65 establishments) and a number of establishments (29) in other mechanical engineering. Further detail is provided in appendix 8B.

8   Price series for CNC over the period 1968–1986 were provided by the Machine Tool Technologies Association. We are grateful to Geoff Noon for sending us this data. Industry-level data on outputs, prices, and concentration indices are based on the Census of Production.

9   We thus purged from the sample establishments that did not have any metalworking activities, which reduced the sample to 1,069. The rest of the purges were due to defective questionnaire response.

10   See, Alderman, Davies, and Thwaites (1988). Evidence from interview surveys conducted at CURDS suggests that 'although the parent company in many cases will impose investment criteria on the establishment, the decision to adopt, if these criteria can be met, will very often be left to plant level management' (p. 8).

11   It should be noted that since the date of entry varies amongst the firms, the censoring scheme is a case of random censoring as discussed, for example, by Kalbfleisch and Prentice (1980). To derive the above likelihood function it is thus implicitly assumed that entry dates are independent of the parameters of interest of the model. In that case the inclusion of the variable $EDATE$ (date of entry) as an exogenous explanatory variable would capture the possible effect of the variation in entry date on the adoption probability, as suggested by Cox and Oakes (1985).

12   Given the large number of time-varying covariates in the model, a nonparametric version of the model that also distinguished between the nine industry groups would entail some 250 variables in the model, which could not be accommodated by the computer software available to us.

13   The model was estimated using MLPACK on the Cambridge University IBM3084 computer. We would like to thank Gordon A. Hughes for making the package accessible to us, which substantially facilitated the task of estimation.

14   Subscripts are used for presentational clarity despite the convention of including t in brackets in the text above.

15   For the output-growth variable GY_t, due to lack of data we could only distinguish between electrical and nonelectrical engineering industries.

16   In the estimates presented below, the data were treated as a panel. It has been suggested that there may be advantages from estimating equation (8.23) on each of the nine industries separately. Attempts to do this were confounded, for the results converged in only three industries.

17   The model used is a first-order autoregressive model of the form $K_t = a_0 + a_1 K_{t-1} + u_t$. The results for the nine MLH groups are given in appendix 8B.

18   Note also that the inclusion of first adopters with zero adoption time makes the estimation of the Weibull model problematic, as the model involves the logarithm of time. We estimated the model including the first adopters and setting their adoption time equal to 0.5, but the results were similar to those reported below.

19   It should be noted that because of the functional form in which they are introduced into the model, the estimated β_{0j} coefficients from all other models should be exponentiated to be comparable to the proportional hazard log-logistic model.

20   For brevity the results are not reported here. The average for the estimated α coefficient was about 5, and for β_{0j} it was -13.4. At these values the maximum value for $h_0(t)$ is attained well into the future, which in effect implies a monotonically increasing baseline hazard as in the Weibull model.

21   Thus McCullagh and Nelder (1990) maintain that 'in practice it frequently makes surprisingly little difference to estimates and inferences whether we put a structure on the baseline hazard or not' (p. 421).

22   It should be noted that due to the difference in functional forms, the absolute values of coefficients in the nonproportional hazard model are not comparable to other models.

23   Restricting the coefficient of the interaction term related to $SIZE$ to equal zero gives an estimate for the coefficient of $SIZE$ equal to 0.1351 with a standard error of 0.0226, which is significant at the 1 per cent level.

24   For ease of exposition, we have dropped the explanatory variables and the related parameters of interest from the hazard function. Their inclusion would not change the above conclusions if we maintain the assumption of ancillarity of the explanatory variables and variables such as entry and exit times for the parameters of interest.

References

Alderman, N., Davies, S., and Thwaites, A. (1988) *Patterns of Innovation Diffusion*. Technical Report, Centre for Urban and Regional Development Studies, University of Newcastle upon Tyne.

Bresnahan, T.F. and David, P.A. (1986) 'The Diffusion of Automatic Teller Machines Across U.S. Banks,' Paper presented at the Conference on Innovation Diffusion, Venice, March.

Cohen, W.M. and Levinthal, D.A. (1989) 'Innovation and Learning: The Two Faces of R&D,' *Economic Journal*, 99, 569–96.

Cox, D.R. (1972) 'Regression Models and Life Tables,' *Journal of the Royal Statistical Society*, Series B, 34, 187–220.

Cox, D.R. and Snell, E.J. (1968) 'A General Definition of Residuals,' *Journal of the Royal Statistical Society*, Series B, 30, 248–75.

Cox, D.R. and Oakes, D. (1985) *Analysis of Survival Data*, London: Chapman & Hall.

David, P.A. (1969) *A Contribution to the Theory of Diffusion*, Stanford Center for Research in Economic Growth, Memorandum No. 71, Stanford University.

David, P.A. and Olsen, T.E. (1986) 'Equilibrium Dynamics of Diffusion When Incremental Technological Innovations are Foreseen,' *Ricerche Economiche*, 40, 738–70.

Davies, S. (1979) *The Diffusion of Process Innovations*, Cambridge: Cambridge University Press.

Fudenberg, D. and Tirole, J. (1985) 'Preemption and Rent Equalization in the Adoption of New Technology,' *Review of Economic Studies*, 52, 383–401.

Hannan, T.H. and McDowell, J.M. (1984) 'The Determinants of Technology Adoption: The Case of the Banking Firm,' *RAND Journal of Economics*, 15, 328–35.

Hannan, T.H. and McDowell, J.M. (1987) 'Rival Precedence and the Dynamics of Technology Adoption: An Empirical Analysis,' *Economica*, 54, 155–71.

Heckman, J.J. and Singer, B.L. (1984) 'Econometric Duration Analysis,' *Journal of Econometrics*, 24, 63–132.

Hoem, J.M. (1985) 'Weighting, Misclassification, and Other Issues in the Analysis of Survey Samples of Life Histories,' In J.J. Heckman and B. Singer (eds.), *Longitudinal Analysis of Labour Market Data*, Cambridge: Cambridge University Press.

Ireland, N. and Stoneman, P.L. (1985) 'Order Effects, Perfect Foresight and Intertemporal Price Discrimination,' *Recherches Economiques de Louvain*, 51, 7–20.

Ireland, N. and Stoneman, P.L. (1986) 'Technological Diffusion, Expectations and Walfare,' *Oxford Economic Papers*, 38, 283–304.

Kalbfleisch, J.D. and Prentice, R.I.. (1980) *The Statistical Analysis of Failure Time Data*, New York: Wiley.

Karshenas, M. and Stoneman, P.L. (1992) 'A Flexible Model of Technological Diffusion Incorporating Economic Factors with an Application to the Spread of Colour Television Ownership in the UK,' *Journal of Forecasting*, 11, 577–602.

Lawless, J.F. (1982) *Statistical Models and Methods of Lifetime Data*, New York: Wiley.

Lee, L.F. (1981) 'Simultaneous Equations Models with Discrete and Censored Variables,' In C.F. Manski and D. McFadden, (eds.), *Structural Analysis Discrete Data with Econometric Applications*, Cambridge, Mass.: MIT Press.

Mansfield, E. (1968) *Industrial Research and Technological Innovation: An Economic Analysis*, New York: Norton.

Mansfield, E. (1989) 'The Diffusion of Industrial Robots in Japan and the United States,' *Research Policy*, 18, 183–92.

McCullagh, P. and Nelder, J.A. (1990) *Generalized Linear Models*, London: Chapman and Hall.

Murphy, K.M. and Topel, R.H. (1985) 'Estimation and Inference in Two-Step Econometric Models,' *Journal of Business and Economic Statistics*, 3, 370–9.

Quirmbach, H.C. (1986) 'The Diffusion of New Technology and the Market for an Innovation,' *RAND Journal of Economics*, 17, 33–47.

Reinganum, J.F. (1981) 'Market Structure and the Diffusion of New Technology,' *Bell Journal of Economics*, 12, 618–24.

Rose, N.L. and Joskow, P.J. (1990) 'The Diffusion of New Technologies: Evidence from the Electric Utility Industry,' *RAND Journal of Economics*, 21, 354–73.

Stoneman, P.L. (1980) 'The Rate of Imitation, Learning and Profitability,' *Economics Letters*, 6, 179–83.

Stoneman, P.L. (1983) *The Economic Analysis of Technological Change*, Oxford: Oxford University Press.

Stoneman, P.L. (1986) 'Technological Diffusion: The Viewpoint of Economic Theory,' *Ricerche Economiche*, 40, 585–606.

Stoneman, P.L. (1987) *The Economic Analysis of Technology Policy*, Oxford: Oxford University Press.

Stoneman, P.L. and Ireland, N.J. (1983) 'The Role of Supply Factors in the Diffusion of New Process Technology,' *Economic Journal*, Supplement, 66–78.

Chapter nine

The Diffusion of Multiple Process Technologies

Co-written with Myung-Joong Kwon

Most of the past literature on technological diffusion has been exclusively concerned with individual technologies considered in isolation from other technologies that may at the same time be either in use or on their own diffusion path. However, one may well expect that there exist interconnections between technologies such that the diffusion of any one technology is not independent of the diffusion of another technology. The objective of this paper is to explore theoretically and empirically the implications of such interconnections for the determination of the patterns of use in the two technology case.[1]

David (1975), Ayres and Ezekoye (1991) and Pyatt (1963) have approached this topic but the work reported here is more explicitly grounded in the theory of diffusion than cither of the former two papers, whereas the latter deals with consumer technologies as opposed to producer technologies. There are also parallels between this work and the burgeoning literature on standards (see Arthur, 1989). This paper builds upon the literature relating to single technology diffusion models in order to analyse the multi technology case. The approach found in one particular paper (Karshenas and Stoneman, 1993) is used extensively throughout.

In the next section we discuss the nature of interconnections between technologies and analyse the determinants of the returns to adoption. In section 9.2 we analyse the adoption decision. The data used for estimation is detailed in section 9.3, estimation methods are discussed in section 9.4 and the empirical results are presented in section 9.5. Conclusions are stated in section 9.6.

9.1. Complementary and Substitute Technologies and the Determinants of the Return to Adoption

Technologies may be substitutes or complements in the production process. Consider two technologies, A and B, available to the firm. Define g_A as the per annum gross profit gain

Reprinted from the *Economic Journal*, 104, 420–31, 1994 with kind permission of Blackwell Publishers.

from the adoption of technology A alone and g_B as the per annum gross profit gain from the adoption of B alone. Define g_{AB} as the per annum gross profit gain (relative to the no adoption baseline) from having both A and B. We then specify that

$$g_{AB} = g_A + g_B + v, \qquad (9.1)$$

and, subject to the statements in the next paragraph, if A and B are complements in production, $v > 0$; if A and B are substitutes in production, $v < 0$.

However, from a simple model of a firm operating on an oligopolistic market, one may show that the profit gain to the firm from a given reduction in costs is the smaller the lower is the level of costs. This implies that if technologies A and B each will generate a given cost reduction, then the gain in profits from adopting both A and B will be less than the sum of the gains from adopting A alone and adopting B alone. The implication is that in the absence of complementarities in the production process, v will be negative, and for v to be positive it is necessary that the complementarities are more than sufficient to overcome this product market effect.

In Karshenas and Stoneman (1993), it is argued that a general diffusion model that incorporates epidemic, rank, stock and order effects in essence represents a summary of the existing literature on technological diffusion. In this paper we proceed in a similar way to that earlier paper by relating g_A, g_B and v to variables that reflect the rank, stock and order effects. Epidemic effects are introduced later in the paper. Following Karshenas and Stoneman (1993) we may specify that:

$$g_{iA}(t, \tau) = g_A[\mathbf{c}_i, \sigma(\tau), N_A(t), N_B(t), N_A(\tau), N_B(\tau)], \qquad (9.2)$$

where $g_{A1} \gtreqless 0, g_{A2} \geq 0, g_{A3} \leq 0, g_{A4} \leq 0, g_{A5} \leq 0, g_{A6} \leq 0$, and

$$g_{iB}(t, \tau) = g_B[\mathbf{c}_i, \sigma(\tau), N_A(t), N_B(t), N_A(\tau), N_B(\tau)], \qquad (9.3)$$

where $g_{B1} \gtreqless 0, g_{B2} \geq 0, g_{B3} \leq 0, g_{B4} \leq 0, g_{B5} \leq 0, g_{B6} \leq 0$.

In (9.2) and (9.3) $g_{iA}(t, \tau)$ is the gross profit gain in time τ to firm i from installing technology A alone in time t and $g_{iB}(t, \tau)$ is the gross profit gain in time τ to firm i from installing technology B alone in time $t(\tau \geq t)$, both of which are functions of: a vector of firm characteristics, $\mathbf{c}_i$, and the level of industry demand in time τ, $\sigma(\tau)$, jointly reflecting rank effects: the number of other users of technology A and technology B in the industry at the date of installation, $N_A(t)$ and $N_B(t)$, reflecting the order effect: and the number of users of technologies A and B in time τ, $N_A(\tau)$ and $N_B(\tau)$, reflecting the stock effect.

For the purposes of simplicity assume that there are no order effects in the determination of v and thus

$$v_i(\tau) = v[\mathbf{c}_i, \sigma(\tau), N_A(\tau), N_B(\tau)], \qquad (9.4)$$

where $v_1 \gtreqless 0, v_2 \geq 0, v_3 \leq 0, v_4 \leq 0$. In (9.4) $v_i(\tau)$ is the gain in profits to firm i in time τ over and above $(g_A + g_B)$ from having both technologies A and B installed.

9.2.   The Adoption of Multiple Technologies

9.2.1.   A deterministic model

Assume that firm i can acquire either or both of two new technologies A and B by the purchase of single units of capital goods A and B. Further assume that these capital goods are infinitely long lived and thus there is no depreciation, and that any decision to adopt a new technology is irreversible. Define $P_A(\tau)$ and $P_B(\tau)$ as the price of capital goods A and B respectively in time τ. $P_A(\tau)$ and $P_B(\tau)$ are assumed to fall over time.

The firm's adoption decision is crucially dependent upon its expectations of movements in prices over time (see Ireland and Stoneman, 1986). We assume perfect foresight. Under this assumption adoption dates are determined by arbitrage conditions requiring equality between the costs and benefits of waiting.

Define a series of variables, $y_{ij}(t)$, as the net cost to firm i in time t of waiting until $(t + dt)$ before adoption takes place. Specifically, $y_{iA}(t)$, $y_{iB}(t)$ and $y_{iS}(t)$ relate respectively to the adoption of A alone, B alone, or A and B simultaneously where firm i has not adopted A or B previously; $y_{iAB}(t)$ relates to the adoption of B for firm i when A has already been adopted; $y_{iBA}(t)$ relates to the adoption of A when B has already been adopted.

Under an assumption that the derivatives of the g and v functions are time invariant constants we may write:

$$y_{iS}(t) = rP_A(t) + rP_B(t) - p_A(t) - p_B(t) - g_{iA}(t, t) - g_{iB}(t, t)$$

$$- v_i(t) + (g_{A3} + g_{B3})n_A(t)/r + (g_{A4} + g_{B4})n_B(t)/r, \tag{9.5}$$

$$y_{iA}(t) = rP_A(t) - p_A(t) - g_{iA}(t, t) + g_{A3}n_A(t)/r + g_{A4}n_B(t)/r, \tag{9.6}$$

$$y_{iAB}(t) = rP_B(t) - p_B(t) - g_{iB}(t, t) - v_i(t) + g_{B3}n_A(t)/r + g_{B4}n_B(t)/r, \tag{9.7}$$

$$y_{iB}(t) = rP_B(t) - p_B(t) - g_{iB}(t, t) + g_{B3}n_A(t)/r + g_{B4}n_B(t)/r, \tag{9.8}$$

$$y_{iBA}(t) = rP_A(t) - p_A(t) - g_{iA}(t, t) - v_i(t) + g_{A3}n_A(t)/r + g_{A4}n_B(t)/r, \tag{9.9}$$

where $g_{iA}(t, t)$, $g_{iB}(t, t)$ and $v_i(t)$ are values of $g_{iA}(t, \tau)$, $g_{iB}(t, \tau)$ and $v_i(\tau)$ evaluated at $\tau = t$, g_{A3} and g_{B3} are derivatives with respect to the number of firms having already adopted A at t and g_{A4} and g_{B4} are derivatives with respect to the number of firms having adopted B. Lower case n and p are used to represent expected changes in the small time interval $\{t, t + dt\}$ in N and P.

We may now specify that firm i in time t, if it has not adopted technology A or B by time $t - dt$, will:

Install technology A alone in time t if: $y_{iA}(t) \leq 0$; $y_{iAB}(t) \geq 0$,

Install technology B alone in time t if: $y_{iB}(t) \leq 0$; $y_{iBA}(t) \geq 0$,

Install both A and B in time t if: $y_{iS}(t) \leq 0$; $y_{iAB}(t) \leq 0$; $y_{iBA}(t) \leq 0$.

A firm having already installed technology A by time $t - dt$ will:

Install technology B in time t if: $y_{iAB}(t) \leq 0$

and a firm having already installed technology B by time $t - dt$ will:

Install technology A in time t if: $y_{iBA}(t) \leq 0$.

The first two conditions above are reasonably self explanatory. They state that a firm will install *only* one technology if in time t it is not desirable to wait any longer before installing that technology, and having got the first in place, it is still desirable to wait before installing the second. The last two conditions are also simple and clear. The condition for the joint adoption of A and B needs a little further explanation. The explanation is made clearest under a myopia assumption when the arbitrage conditions can be interpreted as profitability conditions. There are three parts to the condition (i) $y_{iS}(t) \leq 0$; this states that it is profitable to install both technologies (ii) $y_{iAB}(t) \leq 0$; if this condition does not hold, then once A has been installed it is not profitable to install B and thus joint adoption will not occur (iii) $y_{iBA}(t) \leq 0$; if this condition does not hold, then once B has been installed it is not profitable to install A and thus joint adoption will not occur.

9.2.2. A stochastic model

The model as specified above abstracts from various real life factors which though they may be known with certainty to the individual adopters cannot be incorporated in the model. We introduce these factors, following Karshenas and Stoneman (1993), through a series of independent stochastic error terms e_j($j = A$, B, or S). It is assumed that the distributions of e_j remain invariant across the firms over time and that the e_j are distributed independent of y_j with distribution functions V_j($j = A$, B, or S).

Define a series of hazard rates $_k h_{ij}(t)$ as the probability of firm i moving to technology state j($j = A$, B, or S, both technologies) in the time interval $\{t, t + dt\}$, given technology state k($k =$ zero, A or B) at time t. From (9.6), (9.7), (9.8) and (9.9)

$$y_{iAB}(t) = y_{iB}(t) - v_i(t) \tag{9.10}$$

$$\text{and} \quad y_{iBA}(t) = y_{iA}(t) - v_i(t). \tag{9.11}$$

We may now write the adoption conditions as laid out in the final paragraph of section 9.2.1 as:

$$_0 h_{iA}(t) = \{V_A[-y_{iA}(t)]\}\{1 - V_B[-y_{iB}(t) + v_i(t)]\}, \tag{9.12}$$

$$_0 h_{iB}(t) = \{V_B[-y_{iB}(t)]\}\{1 - V_A[-y_{iA}(t) + v_i(t)]\}, \tag{9.13}$$

$$_0 h_{iS}(t) = V_S[-y_{iS}(t)]V_A[-y_{iA}(t) + v_i(t)]V_B[-y_{iB}(t) + v_i(t)], \tag{9.14}$$

$$_A h_{iS}(t) = V_B[-y_{iB}(t) + v_i(t)], \tag{9.15}$$

$$_B h_{iS}(t) = V_A[-y_{iA}(t) + v_i(t)], \tag{9.16}$$

where $V'_j \geq 0$ for all j.

From (9.12)–(9.16) it is clear that as v increases (or as one compares complementary technologies to substitute technologies) the likelihood of the adoption of a single technology is reduced and the likelihood of joint adoption is increased. It is also clear that the probability of adopting a second technology given that a first has already been adopted, *ceteris paribus*, is increased as v increases.

At this point we may introduce the epidemic effect. In diffusion analysis the epidemic effect represents a passive form of information acquisition. As time proceeds either more potential users become aware of a technology or firms in general become more aware of the characteristics of the technology, and this leads to greater use of the technology. Following the method of Karshenas and Stoneman (1993), if one defines T_A and T_B as the number of years since technologies A and B were first introduced, then one can argue that as T_A and T_B increase technologies A and B are more likely to be known about and used.

Equations (9.12)–(9.16) represent the basis of the estimating equations below. Given the simultaneity inherent in this set of equations, we suggest an approach to estimation whereby first equations (9.15) and (9.16) are estimated, and then predicted values of $_Ah_{iS}(t)$ and $_Bh_{iS}(t)$ are substituted in (9.12)–(9.14) prior to estimation of those equations. Taking account of epidemic effects and equations (9.5)–(9.11) we may write (9.15) as:

$$_Ah_{iS}(t) = H_1[rP_B(t), p_B(t), n_A(t)/r, n_B(t)/r, c_i, \sigma(t), N_A(t), N_B(t), T_B].\qquad(9.15a)$$

Estimates of (9.15a) will yield predicted values for $_Ah_{iS}(t) = E[_Ah_{iS}(t)]$.
    Similarly (9.16) may be written as (9.16a)

$$_Bh_{iS}(t) = H_2[rP_A(t), p_A(t), n_A(t)/r, n_B(t)/r, c_i, \sigma(t), N_A(t), N_B(t), T_A].\qquad(9.16a)$$

Estimates of (9.16a) will yield predicted values for $_Bh_{iS}(t) = E[_Bh_{iS}(t)]$.
    One may now write (9.12), (9.13) and (9.14) as (9.12a), (9.13a) and (9.14a)

$$_0h_{iA}(t) = \{1 - E[_Ah_{iS}(t)]\}H_3[rP_A(t), p_A(t), n_A(t)/r, n_B(t)/r,$$
$$c_i, \sigma(t), N_A(t), N_B(t), T_A]\qquad(9.12a)$$
$$_0h_{iB}(t) = \{1 - E[_Bh_{iS}(t)]\}H_4[rP_B(t), p_B(t), n_A(t)/r, n_B(t)/r,$$
$$c_i, \sigma(t), N_A(t), N_B(t), T_B]\qquad(9.13a)$$
$$_0h_{iS}(t) = \{E[_Ah_{iS}(t)]\}\{E[_Bh_{iS}(t)]\}H_5[rP_A(t), rP_B(t),$$
$$p_A(t), p_B(t), n_A(t)/r, n_B(t)/r, c_i, \sigma(t), N_A(t), N_B(t), T_A, T_B].\qquad(9.14a)$$

In H_1–H_5, *a priori* expectations are that the derivatives with respect to n_A, n_B and $\sigma(t)$ are positive and with respect to N_A and N_B negative. Derivatives with respect to the elements of c_i depend upon the variables included in c_i. In table 9.1 the expected signs of other derivatives of H_1–H_5 are detailed.

9.3. Data and Sources

The main data source upon which the empirical analysis is based is two surveys undertaken by the Centre for Urban and Regional Development Studies (CURDS) at the University of

Table 9.1 Expected signs of derivatives: equations (9.12a)–(9.16a)

	H_1	H_2	H_3	H_4	H_5
rP_A	0	−	−	0	−
p_A	0	+	+	0	+
rP_B	−	0	0	−	−
p_B	+	0	0	+	+
T_A	0	+	+	0	+
T_B	+	0	0	+	+

Newcastle upon Tyne (see Alderman *et al.* 1988). This survey of 1,127 *establishments* within nine Minimum List Headings in the UK engineering and metalworking industries provides data upon: the date of adoption of five different technologies; employment; R&D spending; year of start up; and status in terms of whether the establishment is part of a group or independent.

The empirical analysis reported upon below considers the joint adoption of Numerically Controlled (NC) machine tools and coated carbide tools (CCT) for the period from 1965. Technologically, NC machines and CCT are complements in the production process. For carbide tools the data provides information upon firms that adopted this technology in the period 1965–86. For NC however, information is not available on adoptions between 1981 and 1986 and thus the sample is censored for the period beyond 1981.

Price data for NC machines were supplied by the CSO. The import price of 'Dies' made of sintered metal carbide was used as a proxy for prices of coated carbide tools. Total industry sales was used to measure the level of demand in the industry to which the establishment belongs, with due account being taken of changes in the SIC industrial classification.

Employment is used as an indicator of the heterogeneity of establishments, other variables being insignificant in the earlier Karshenas and Stoneman (1993) analysis based upon this data set. That study also found that the distinction between firms and establishments was not an important one.

From the original set of 1,127 establishments, the usable sample covers 740 establishments. This reduction results primarily from removing those establishments for which employment data were not available (367 establishments). No evidence was found to indicate that this led to a sample selection bias.

In table 9.2 the explanatory variables are defined. Two main points should be noted. First, the $n(t)$ and $N(t)$ variables are defined at the level of the industry to which the firm belongs rather than at the level of the sample as a whole. This is in keeping with the spirit of the rank and order models. Secondly all expectations variables are defined under a perfect foresight assumption.

The firms in the sample may be divided into four main groups: (i) those firms who in the sample period adopt neither technology (356 firms); (ii) those firms who adopt only NC (75 firms); (iii) those firms who adopt only carbide tools (CCT) (172 firms) and (iv) those firms who adopt both technologies (137 firms). Group (iv) can be subdivided into: (iva) those firms who adopt the two technologies simultaneously (14 firms); (ivb) those firms who adopt NC before CCT (94 firms) and (ivc) those firms who adopt CCT before NC (29 firms).

Table 9.2 Definitions of explanatory variables

$rP_A(t)$	Price of NC machine tools at time t multiplied by the discount rate (measured by the yield on Treasury Bills)
$DP_A(t)$	Expected change in the price of NC machine tools at time t measured by $P_A(t + 1) - P_A(t)$
$rP_B(t)$	Price of coated carbide tools at time t multiplied by the discount rate (measured by the yield on Treasury Bills)
$DP_B(t)$	Expected change in the price of coated carbide tools measured by $P_B(t + 1) - P_B(t)$
$CN_{Aj}(t)$	Number of establishments in industry j owning NC machine tools at time t
$CN_{Bj}(t)$	Number of establishments in industry j owning coated carbide tools at time t
Dm	Change in demand for the industry to which establishment i belongs, measured by $\log[Q(t + 1) - Q(t)]$, where $Q(t)$ is total sales of the industry in time t
$DCN_{Aj}(t)$	Expected change in the cumulative number of NC adopters in the interval $(t, t + 1)$, (measured by $[CN_{Aj}(t + 1) - CN_{Aj}(t)]$), divided by the yield on Treasury Bills
$DCN_{Bj}(t)$	Expected change in the cumulative number of adopters of coated carbide tools in the interval $(t, t + 1)$, (measured by $[CN_{Bj}(t + 1) - CN_{Bj}(t)]$ divided by the yield on Treasury Bills
$Size$	Size of the establishment, measured by total number of employees in 1986
$CR(t)$	Concentration ratio in the industry to which the establishment belongs, measured by the percentage share of gross output of the 5 largest firms in the industry
T_A	Time measured from the year in which NC was first introduced (1957)
T_B	Time measured from the year in which coated carbide tools were first introduced (1960)

9.4. Estimation Methods

Equations (9.12a)–(9.16a) have been estimated by pooling a time series of cross sections and using probit methods. Thus for example, in estimating equation (9.12a) the sample in any time period t is all firms who have not adopted technologies A or B prior to time t. Once a firm adopts technology A, or B, or both, it drops out of the sample. A firm established after the start date of the estimation (1965) enters the sample at its date of establishment. A series of (1, 0) dependent variables (y) is created. Thus with equation (9.12a) the dependent variable in time t takes the value 1 for a firm adopting technology A alone in time t, and 0 for all other events (no adoption in time t, adoption of B alone in time t or adoption of both A and B in time t). Similar but appropriately defined dependent variables are created for equations (9.13a) and (9.16a).

We may then define the likelihood function for each of equations (9.12a)–(9.16a) as:

$$L(\beta) = \Pi\{1 - V_j[-\boldsymbol{\beta}'\mathbf{X}(t)]\}\Pi V_j[-\boldsymbol{\beta}'\mathbf{X}(t)] \quad t = 65 - 86,$$

$$y_i(t) = 0 \qquad\qquad y_i(t) = 1,$$

where V_j is the distribution function of $\mathbf{e}_j$ and $\mathbf{X}$ is a vector of explanatory variables. This formulation is equivalent to the direct estimation of an exponential hazard model (Sinha, 1993) but has the advantage, which is important with the current data set, that it enables the estimation of the hazard function with small data sets. Maximum likelihood methods were used throughout and all estimates were produced using LIMDEP 6.

Table 9.3 Maximum likelihood estimates of equations (9.12a)–(9.16a)

	H_3	H_4	H_5	H_1	H_2
$rP_A(t)$	−0.127	–	−2.23	–	−0.07
	(−3.96)		(−3.41)		(−8.14)
$DP_A(t)$	4.67	–	23.00	–	−1.19
	(1.19)		(1.14)		(−1.06)
$rP_B(t)$	–	−0.11	2.48	−0.03	–
		(−10.4)	(3.60)	(−2.91)	
$DP_B(t)$	–	−2.10	6.11	−0.09	–
		(−8.7)	(2.33)	(−0.35)	
$CN_{Aj}(t)$	−0.397	0.03	−2.30	−0.31	0.01
	(−0.89)	(3.08)	(−0.28)	(−1.72)	(1.57)
$CN_{Bj}(t)$	−1.88	−0.10	−8.98	−0.56	−0.10
	(−4.71)	(−14.01)	(−0.48)	(−3.87)	(−12.45)
$Dm(t)$	−7.006	−0.95	−7.93	−0.46	−2.13
	(−2.91)	(−1.10)	(−0.96)	(−0.49)	(−2.36)
$DCN_{Aj}(t)$	6.10	2.11	12.47	0.05	0.99
	(7.15)	(4.76)	(2.63)	(0.13)	(2.21)
$DCN_{Bj}(t)$	2.65	1.73	7.21	0.05	−0.42
	(3.03)	(7.97)	(2.12)	(0.17)	(−1.61)
$Size$	0.05	−0.09	6.32	0.05	−0.16
	(0.68)	(−3.17)	(2.57)	(1.69)	(−5.01)
$CR(t)$	−0.003	−0.01	0.04	0.002	0.008
	(−0.39)	(−4.33)	(1.00)	(0.70)	(3.04)
T_A	0.04	–	−10.02	–	0.16
	(4.39)		(−2.33)		(15.16)
T_B	–	0.14	13.88	0.11	–
		(13.61)	(2.66)	(9.50)	
Log likelihood	−356.46	−943.46	−23.24	−464.99	−541.54
No. of observations	9,917	12,247	9,917	1,478	2,885
Log likelihood ratio test (χ^2)	303.25	39.918	165.26	120.88	375.50
Significance level ( ): t-ratio	0.00	0.00	0.00	0.00	0.00

9.5. Results

Pooling the whole sample and using linear functional forms generated the results presented in table 9.3. For each equation in the table, the log likelihood ratio test rejects, at less than 0.001 significance, the hypothesis that the model is misspecified.

The estimates in column 4 relate to the function H_1, and refer to the determinants of the adoption of carbide tools by firms that have previously adopted NC machine tools. Variables that are significant and carry coefficients of the expected sign are: the price of carbide tools; the stock effects variables, $CN_{Aj}(t)$ and $CN_{Bj}(t)$ (both significant at the 10 per cent level or above); firm size (significant at the 10 per cent level); and the epidemic variable T_A. Thus the hypothesised order effects do not show up but the rank, stock and epidemic effects do gain some support. In essence the probability that a firm having adopted NC machine tools will then go on to adopt carbide tools is the greater: the lower the price of carbide tools, the fewer firms who have already adopted such tools and NC machine tools, the larger is the firm and the longer the period since carbide tools have been available.

The results in the last column, relating to H_2, refer to the adoption of NC machine tools by firms that have previously adopted carbide tools. Variables that are significant and carry coefficients of the expected sign are: $rP_A(t)$; $CN_{Bj}(t)$; $DCN_{Aj}(t)$; and T_A. These results indicate some support for the order effect and some support for the stock effect. There is also support for the epidemic effect, but rank effect variables do not work well. The results suggest that a firm that has already adopted carbide tools is more likely to adopt NC machine tools: the lower is the price of NC machine tools, the more firms that have already adopted carbide tools, the greater is the expected increase in the number of users of NC machine tools, and the longer it has been since NC was first introduced.

Substituting the predicted values from (9.15a) and (9.16a) into (9.12a)–(9.14a) and then estimating H_3, H_4 and H_5 yields the results in columns 1, 2 and 3 in table 9.3. Column 1 relates to the adoption of NC machines alone by firms that have not previously adopted either technology. Own price is significant and of the correct sign but price expectations although of the correct sign are not significant at the 5 per cent level. $CN_{Bj}(t)$ is significant and of the correct sign as are the two order effect variables. The epidemic variable is significant and of the correct sign.

Column 2 relates to the adoption of carbide tools alone by firms that have not previously adopted either technology. Again own price is significant with the correct sign, but price expectations carry the wrong sign. $CN_{Bj}(t)$, $DCN_{Aj}(t)$ and $DCN_{Bj}(t)$ carry significant coefficients of the correct sign. The concentration and size variables carry negative and significant coefficients. The epidemic effect is again of the expected sign and significant.

Column 3 relates to the simultaneous adoption of carbide tools and NC machine tools. The price of NC carries a significant coefficient of the correct sign but the coefficient of the price of carbide tools although significant is of the wrong sign. Price expectations are significant and of the correct sign. Both order effects are of the correct sign and significant. Firm size carries a significant positive sign confirming *a priori* expectations. One epidemic variable, T_B, carries the correct sign and is significant.

The results in columns 1–3 indicate that there is some evidence in favour of a stock effect but greater support for an order effect. The epidemic effect works well but the rank effect does not. The price variables generally perform as expected *a priori*, but price expectations do not.

Some further estimates have been produced but are not reported here. For example the epidemic variables were removed and the equations re-estimated to see if these variables were acting as proxies for the stock effects. There was no evidence that there was such a proxy effect. The equations above were also estimated for individual industries. The results are available from the authors on request but, in general, the results from the pooled sample were confirmed.

The above results may now be used to discuss the determinants of the various hazard rates. The results in columns 4 and 5 give direct information upon $_A h_{iS}(t)$ and $_B h_{iS}(t)$, and these have been discussed above. For $_0 h_{iA}(t)$, using (9.12a), we need to consider the results in column 1 and the results in column 4. These results suggest that $_0 h_{iA}(t)$, is determined not only by $rP_A(t)$ but also, positively, by $rP_B(t)$ and thus the probability of installing just

NC machine tools (and not also carbide tools) is the greater the higher is the price of carbide tools. This is confirmation that the consideration of multi-technology models does provide extra insight. Further, consider the impact of $CN_{Bj}(t)$ on $_0h_{iA}(t)$. This has a negative direct effect via column 1 but through column 4 there is an offsetting positive effect. Thus in general one cannot predict the sign of the effect. The order effect in column 4 is not significant and thus the positive effect through column 1 appears to be the dominant effect.

Turn then to consider $_0h_{iB}(t)$. Here we see, as with $_0h_{iA}(t)$, that through column 2 own price is significant, but through column 5 the price of NC machine tools also has the predicted positive effect. This is exactly as the theory predicts.

Finally consider $_0h_{iS}(t)$. Using (9.14a) and the results in columns 3, 4 and 5 we see that the negative coefficient on $rP_A(t)$ in column 3 is reinforced by the negative coefficient on $rP_A(t)$ in column 5, whereas the wrong sign on $rP_B(t)$ in column 3 is to some degree offset by the correct sign on $rP_B(t)$ in column 4.

Although one could go further in this discussion the point is made. When more than one technology is being diffused then there are significant cross technology effects to be taken into account in modelling the diffusion of cither technology.

Before leaving these results there is one further check of the internal consistency of the model that can be made. The estimation methods enable the calculation of values for $v(t)$ for each firm at its date of adoption of a technology. The *a priori* expectation is that for these two technologies v will be positive. Moreover, the theory above indicates that the greater is v the greater is the likelihood that firms will adopt both technologies simultaneously. We thus calculated the value for v for simultaneous adopters (the mean value was 0.40), and for those firms that adopted both technologies but either adopted NC prior to carbide tools or adopted carbide tools before NC. These latter two groups had mean values for v of 0.24 and 0.11 respectively.

Thus the prediction that greater v leads to a greater likelihood of simultaneous adoption is confirmed. In addition the theory predicts that a higher value of v will be associated with earlier adoption. The simultaneous adopters had a mean adoption date of 1973 whereas the date by which the other two groups had finally adopted both technologies were 1978 and 1976 respectively. To confirm this finding, within each of the three groups of adopting firms, we regressed the date by which both technologies were adopted on the value for v for the firm. There was significant positive coefficient on v in each case.

These results on v indicate that, to some degree at least, firms have different adoption orders because the synergistic benefits between technologies differ across firms. These in turn are the result of different firm characteristics and different industry characteristics. In the presence of such heterogeneity, one should expect firms to have different preferred adoption orders and dates.

9.6.   Conclusions

The objective of this paper has been to explore the simultaneous diffusion of two new process technologies theoretically and empirically. The theoretical framework is developed from a single technology framework used by Karshenas and Stoneman (1993) that simultaneously incorporates the main theoretical streams in the diffusion literature, namely the rank, stock, order and epidemic effects. The theory indicates that the degree of complementarity between technologies is a major factor influencing the order and the dates of adoption of technologies. It is shown that the greater is the degree of complementarity, the more likely is simultaneous adoption and the earlier are adoption dates likely to be.

In the multi technology case the adoption of any one technology will be affected not only by variables relating to itself but also by variables relating to other technologies. Thus the adoption of technology A will be influenced not only by its own price and the number of other users of technology A, but also by the price of technology B and the number of other users of technology B.

The theory was developed to yield an empirical model that was applied to the analysis of data upon the adoption of two complementary technologies, NC machine tools and coated carbide tools. The empirical results indicate that there are significant cross technology effects (via prices, installed bases and expectations of both) and thus the presence of technology $B(A)$ does affect the adoption of technology $A(B)$. The results also indicate that the predicted impacts of the degree of complementarity on the probability of simultaneous adoption and the dates of adoption are supported by the data.

Karshenas and Stoneman (1993) found in the application of their model to single technology adoption that there was little support for stock and order effects but considerable support for rank and epidemic effects. They also found that the price of a technology and price expectations had a significant effect upon adoption times. In the work reported above it is found that the role of price, price expectations (weakly) and epidemic effects can be confirmed. In contrast to the previous work there is less support for rank effects. It was also found in this study that the stock and order effects often appear as significant, carrying coefficients of the correct signs. *A priori* reasoning would suggest that these are more likely to be apparent in a multi technology framework. Thus the Karshenas and Stoneman (1993) results may be too pessimistic as to the importance of stock and order effects.

Note

1 A longer and more complete version of this paper is available as Stoneman and Kwon (1993). The work reported upon has been funded by a grant from the Economic and Social Research Council.

References

Alderman, N., Davies, S. and Thwaites, A. (1988) 'Patterns of Innovation Diffusion,' Technical Report, CURDS, University of Newcastle upon Tyne.

Arthur, B. (1989) 'Competing Technologies, Increasing Returns and Lock-in by Historical Events,' *Economic Journal*, 99, 116–31.

Ayres, R.U. and Ezekoye, I. (1991) 'Competition and Complementarity in Diffusion,' *Technological Forecasting and Social Change*, 39, 145–58.

David, P.A. (1975) 'The Landscape and the Machine: Technical Interrelatedness, Land Tenure and the Mechanization of the Harvest in Victorian Britain,' In *Technical Choice Innovation and Economic Growth* (ed. P.A. David), Cambridge: Cambridge University Press.

Ireland, N. and Stoneman, P. (1986) 'Technological Diffusion, Expectations and Welfare,' *Oxford Economic Papers*, 38, 283–304.

Karshenas, M. and Stoneman, P. (1993) 'Rank, Stock, Order and Epidemic Effects in the Diffusion of New Process Technology,' *Rand Journal of Economics* 24(4), 503–28.

Pyatt, F.G. (1963) *Priority Patterns and the Demand for Household Durable Goods*, Cambridge: Cambridge University Press.

Reinganum, J.F. (1981) 'Market Structure and the Diffusion of New Technology,' *Bell Journal of Economics*, 12, 618–24.

Sinha, R. (1993) 'Technological Discontinuity and Dynamics of Market Entry,' Working Paper, Department of Marketing, Arizona State University.

Stoneman, P. and Kwon, M.J. (1993) 'The Diffusion of Multiple Technologies,' Warwick Business School Research Papers No. 88, Warwick Business School, University of Warwick.

Chapter ten

Testing Alternative Models of New Product Diffusion

Co-written with Florian Zettelmeyer

10.1. Introduction

Over the last twenty years the analysis of technological diffusion has made a number of significant advances. However the work in the two main disciplines interested in diffusion, Marketing and Economics, has proceeded along almost separate and independent paths. In Marketing (see Mahajan, Muller and Bass, 1990), the emphasis has been placed upon variations of the epidemic diffusion model building upon the seminal contribution of Bass (1969). In Economics, although the epidemic diffusion model played a major role in the earlier literature (Griliches, 1957; Mansfield, 1968), recent research has emphasized probit models (David, 1969; Davies, 1979; Stoneman, 1981), and game theoretic models (Reinganum, 1981a, b) Fudenberg and Tirole, 1985).[1] A crucial distinction between the Economics and Marketing literatures is that the Economics literature gives a greater emphasis to the role played by economic factors in the diffusion process than is generally the case in the Marketing literature. The Economics literature tends also to be more concerned with the behavioural basis of diffusion models whereas the Marketing literature places greater emphasis upon forecasting performance.

In a recent paper Karshenas and Stoneman (1992) (hereinafter referred to as KS) attempt to move towards some greater integration of the Marketing and Economics literatures by building and testing a diffusion model which not only incorporates economic factors but which is also based firmly in the epidemic tradition of the Marketing literature. However, in modelling the epidemic, KS reconsider the behavioural basis of this tradition and propose a model that not only, in their view, more adequately represents the nature of real world learning (or epidemic) processes, but one that nests a number of other epidemic models in the literature. Estimating the more general model on data on actual diffusion phenomena enables one to judge on the basis of coefficient estimates where the more general model is to be preferred to the other epidemic models nested within it.

Reprinted from the *Economics of Innovation and New Technology*, 2, 282–308, 1993, with kind permission of Gordan and Breach Publishers.

KS (1992) estimate their model using data on the ownership of colour televisions in the UK. The performance of the general model is judged to be superior to the individual models nested within it. KS also compare their model to a number of other models suggested in the literature that are not nested within it and show again that the performance of the new model is superior.

The purpose of this paper is to extend the KS analysis by applying the new model to three other examples of diffusion phenomena. The three examples are the diffusion of camcorders in the UK, CD players in the UK and cars in West Germany. In each case the performance of the new model is compared with that of other models in the literature. There are three main reasons for undertaking this work: the first is purely to provide further evidence upon which to compare different diffusion models; the second is that the nature of the KS model is such that a crucial parameter α should vary systematically across technologies and thus evidence on the size of this parameter across technologies gives a further test of the KS model; the third is to explore more fully the reasons why the performance of the KS model is different from that of other models in the literature.

In section 10.2 of the paper the KS model and the comparison models are presented with some detail on the former. In section 10.3 the data is discussed. In section 10.4 estimation issues are addressed with the results of the estimations presented in section 10.5. In section 10.6 the results are discussed more fully with an emphasis upon the causes of the relative performance of the different models. Conclusions and suggestions for further research are contained in section 10.7.

10.2. The Models

Consider a new consumer technology that can be acquired by the purchase of a durable good and for which there are N potential adopters. Assume also that each potential adopter will only buy a maximum of one unit of the technology and that there is no replacement demand. Using the model of Bass (1969), if a stock of $S(t)$ consumers have purchased the product up to time t one can express sales in time t as:

$$\frac{dS}{dt} = \left(q + p\frac{S}{N} \right)(N - S) \tag{10.1}$$

Equation (10.1) says that the change in the stock of adopters in a small time interval dt is a fixed proportion q of those that have not adopted at time t, plus a proportion p of those who have not adopted at time t multiplied by their probability of meeting an owner of the product (S/N). One may define q as the coefficient of innovation (or the exogenous factor of influence) and p as the coefficient of imitation (or the endogenous factor of influence).

In the Bass model the relative importance of exogenous and endogenous factors in the diffusion process can be determined at the estimation stage by looking at the estimates of the p and q coefficients. However, although both exogenous and endogenous factors are included in the Bass model, KS point out that, by construction, endogenous factors play a dominant role in the Bass model and its variations and that this is an *a priori* assumption that really ought to be subject to testing (as it is in the KS model). It is worth noting that in the Bass model if $q = 0$ then there is only endogenous growth and (10.1) reverts to the simple epidemic model.

The KS model differs from the Bass model in two major respects: first KS assume that the parameter p is a function of economic variables one result of which is to allow p to vary over time; second, they argue that in the simple epidemic model and by implication in the endogenous part of the Bass model, there is an implicit assumption (among a number of others) that the population mixes homogeneously, which they consider to be unnecessarily restrictive and therefore remove. KS argue that as a consequence of this second change the *a priori* dominance of endogenous growth factors in the Bass model is also removed.

KS model non homogeneous mixing by splitting the stock of adopters S into influential adopters X and non-influential adopters Y. A proportion α of influential adopters become non-influential in every period of time. The lower α, the longer do adopters contribute to the learning process. The model can be written as:

$$\frac{dS}{dt} = p\left(q + \frac{X}{N}\right)(N - S) \tag{10.2}$$

$$\frac{dY}{dt} = \alpha(S - Y) \tag{10.3}$$

where

$$S = X + Y$$

The split of adopters into influential and non-influential adopters generates mathematical properties for the model that differ from those of the Bass model. While the Bass model will always reach the saturation level the KS model can 'get stuck' at some value well below N if no exogenous factors stimulate the diffusion.

Normalizing the total number of potential adopters N to 1 and formulating the discrete analogue, the KS model can be written as:

$$\Delta S_t = p_t(q + S_{t-1} - Y_{t-1})(1 - S_{t-1}) \tag{10.2'}$$

$$\Delta Y_t = \alpha(S_{t-1} - Y_{t-1}) \tag{10.3'}$$

where S and Y are to be interpreted as a proportion of N. KS take into account that the variance of ΔS_t may vary as the saturation level is approached and additionally rewrite (10.3') as $Y_t = \alpha S_{t-1} + (1 - \alpha)Y_{t-1}$ and then repeatedly substitute for Y in (10.3') to yield:

$$\frac{\Delta S_t}{(1 - S_{t-1})} = p_t(q + S_{t-1} - Y_{t-1}(\alpha)) \tag{10.4}$$

where

$$Y_{t-1}(\alpha) = \alpha \sum_{i=0}^{t-1} (1 - \alpha)^i S_{t-i-1}$$

In the KS model the parameter α reflects the rate of decay of an adopter as a source of information for other potential adopters. The closer is α to zero the longer is the period for which an adopter spreads information. Within the context of the model it is reasonable to argue that with very innovative technologies (e.g. CD players and camcorders) an adopter would remain a source of information for a considerable period of time whereas for less innovative well known technologies (e.g. cars) the period for which an adopter would be an influential information source would be shorter. One might thus expect differences in the value of α across technologies. One test of the KS model therefore concerns whether the estimates of α across technologies do reflect these arguments.

The Bass model is nested within the KS model and results from the KS model with $\alpha = 0$. The simple epidemic model is nested within the KS model with $\alpha = 0$ and $q = 0$. The appropriateness of the Bass, KS and simple epidemic models for explaining any particular diffusion phenomena can thus be compared directly by considering whether estimates of α and q from the KS model differ significantly from zero.

For presentational purposes it is informative to represent the Bass and the simple epidemic as models in their own right as two alternatives to the KS model. In the sections below the performance of the KS model in explaining three separate diffusion processes is compared to that of these two models and a number of others. In these alternative models economic variables are incorporated wherever possible (following KS) to ensure comparability.

The models against which the KS model is compared can be represented as follows (where parameters that are functions of economic variables carry the time subscript t).

The Bass model (10.5) is represented as modified by KS by assuming that the exogenous factor of influence q is a scaled version of the endogenous factor of influence p. Normalizing N and correcting for possible changes of the variance of ΔS_t as the saturation level is approached yields the discrete analogue, written as (10.5′)

$$\frac{dS}{dt} = \frac{1}{N} p(Nq + S)(N - S) \tag{10.5}$$

$$\frac{\Delta S_t}{(1 - S_{t-1})} = p_t(q + S_{t-1}) \tag{10.5′}$$

The discrete analogue of the simple logistic (or epidemic) model (10.6) is written as (10.6′) after normalizing N and taking account of the changes in variance as saturation is approached.

$$\frac{dS}{dt} = p\frac{S}{N}(N - S) \tag{10.6}$$

$$\frac{\Delta S_t}{(1 - S_{t-1})} = p_t S_{t-1} \tag{10.6′}$$

The Gompertz growth curve (10.7) is similar to the simple logistic model in that it only incorporates endogeneous growth factors. It cannot, however, be seen as a special case of the KS model. After normalization the discrete analogue can be written as (10.7′).

$$\frac{dS}{dt} = p\frac{S}{N}\ln\left(\frac{N}{S}\right)$$

(10.7)

$$\Delta S_t = p_t S_{t-1}\ln\left(\frac{1}{S_{t-1}}\right)$$

(10.7′)

The Harvey model differs from the other models in that there is no obvious method for incorporating economic variables. The procedure of KS is thus followed and the model is considered in its original form as proposed by Harvey (1984). The model (10.8) and its discrete analogue (10.8′) are:

$$\ln\left(\frac{dS}{dt}\right) = b_0 + b_1 \ln(S) + b_2 t$$

(10.8)

$$\ln(\Delta S_t) = b_0 + b_1 \ln(S_{t-1}) + b_2 t$$

(10.8′)

The model by Hernes (1976) is based on the simple logistic model and encompasses the latter. The endogenous growth parameter of the logistic, p, is replaced by pb^t, where t is a time trend and b's value ($\langle$, $\rangle$, = 1) determines the skewness of the curve (10.9). The discrete analogue again contains a normalized N yielding (10.9′):

$$\frac{dS}{dt} = pb^t \frac{S}{N}(N - S)$$

(10.9)

$$\Delta S_t = p_t b^t S_{t-1}(1 - S_{t-1})$$

(10.9′)

The model by Easingwood, Mahajan and Muller (1983) (denoted EMM) enhances Bass' model by raising the proportion S/N that is multiplied by the endogenous growth factor p to the power σ, where σ has to be estimated. This allows the endogenous growth factor to be of a time varying nature. KS slightly modify the model by making the exogenous growth parameter a proportion of the endogenous growth parameter (10.10). In this model it is again possible to correct for changes in variance of ΔS_t so that, after normalizing N in the discrete time version of the model, one obtains (10.10′):

$$\frac{dS}{dt} = p\left[q + \left(\frac{S}{N}\right)^\sigma\right](N - S)$$

(10.10)

$$\frac{\Delta S_t}{(1 - S_{t-1})} = p_t(q + (S_{t-1})^\sigma)$$

(10.10′)

The last model used for comparison is by Horsky (1990). It is identical to the Bass model except that the saturation level is assumed to be a function of economic variables.

Following KS the model is considered here in its original form (10.11) with economic variables introduced into only the saturation level and not into the parameter p. Normalizing N to 1 yields the discrete analogue (10.11').

$$\frac{\mathrm{d}S}{\mathrm{d}t} = (q + pS)\left(\frac{N}{1 + e^{-f(z)}} - S\right) \qquad (10.11)$$

$$\Delta S_t = (q + pS_{t-1})\left(\frac{1}{1 + e^{-f(z_1)}} - S_{t-1}\right) \qquad (10.11')$$

where z is a vector of economic variables. This model does not permit an easy correction for the changing variance of ΔS_t as the saturation level is approached.

10.3.   The Data

Three diffusion cases are analysed in this paper: the diffusion of camcorders and CD players in the UK and the diffusion of cars in West Germany.[2]

The data on camcorders and CD players consist of monthly sales data by unit and value thus also generating a series on average prices. The data on camcorders cover the period from 12/85 to 5/91 while the data on CD players cover the period from 7/85 to 5/91.[3] Two features of the data are worth pointing out: first, the starting point of both series suggests that the data capture most of the diffusion process to date; second, sales of these two products are subject to large seasonal variations.

The data on the diffusion of cars in Germany are on an annual basis and measure cars in use over the period from 1946 to 1990.[4] An especially noteworthy feature in the data is the sensibility of car sales (as measured by the change in the stock in use) with respect to the economic situation. Particularly noticeable is the impact of the oil price shocks and the 1982 recession.

The economic variables used by KS for their study of colour television ownership were the retail price of colour televisions, real disposable income and, as a proxy for credit conditions, the hire purchase deposit. For the cases studied here the hire purchase deposit variable was considered to be subject to many institutional problems and the interest rate was used as an alternative.

There is a further issue to be addressed as far as interest rates are concerned. Should the rate used be the nominal of the real rate? In tests with all three data sets nominal interest rates consistently proved to outperform real rates. In the results presented below therefore it is nominal rates that are used. Our interpretation is that the nominal rate is a proxy for the ease of borrowing.

To summarize, in the case of CD players and camcorders relevant economic variables were considered to be UK interest rates, product prices and disposable income[5] (both deflated by the Retail Price Index (RPI) on a 1986 basis). For cars, relevant economic variables were considered to be car prices, approximated by yearly manufacturer prices deflated by the consumer price index to a 1985 base (one may note that unlike the prices of many new consumer durables, the real price of cars rose over the estimation period), disposable income[6] (deflated to 1985 prices) and interest rates as measured by the rate for overdrafts up to 1000000 DM reported by the Bundesbank.

10.4.   Estimation Issues

Throughout this study ordinary least squares (OLS) and nonlinear least squares (NLS) are used. It is worth pointing out the advantages and disadvantages of these different estimation procedures. As Mahajan, Mason and Srinivasan (1986) remark, the use of OLS in Bass type models necessitates a two step estimation procedure. As a result exact standard errors for the parameters of the model cannot be obtained. Moreover, making the endogenous factor in the Bass model a function of economic variables yields nonlinearities, and thus the modified Bass type models cannot be estimated using OLS. However, the simplicity of OLS makes OLS attractive and it has been used in this paper where at all applicable.

The use of NLS in diffusion models in Marketing was proposed by Srinivasan and Mason (1986) in order to overcome the problems with Maximum Likelihood Estimation (MLE) as proposed by Schmittlein and Mahajan (1982). The latter had wanted to overcome a time interval bias arising in OLS from estimating a continuous time model with discrete data. Srinivasan and Mason pointed out that MLE only considers sampling errors and does not take into account other error sources. This may lead to overoptimistic standard errors with the use of MLE. They thus propose NLS with an additive error term that captures all types of errors. In this paper NLS is used where OLS is not applicable thus allowing the estimation of model parameters in a single step. Moreover as standard errors are available with NLS one is enabled to perform inference.

Where appropriate the economic variables are incorporated in the models detailed in the previous section by assuming that $p_t = a_0 P_{t-i}^{a_1} YD_{t-j}^{a_2} R_{t-k}^{a_3}$ where P is price of the respective product, YD personal disposable income and R the interest rate. *A priori* expectations derived from economic theory are that $a_1 < 0$, $a_2 > 0$, $a_3 < 0$. i, j and k stand for lags that will be chosen individually for each data set. The above was substituted in the discrete analogues of the models.

To enable use of OLS, the simple logistic and Hernes models were divided by $S_{t-1}(1 - S_{t-1})$ and the Gompertz curve by

$$S_{t-1} \ln\left(\frac{1}{S_{t-1}}\right)$$

with the natural logarithm (ln) of the resulting equation being taken. Choosing from several possibilities an additive white noise error term is incorporated that attributes the random element to sales (changes in the stock) rather than to the stock itself. The resulting estimating equations are:

KS:

$$\ln\left(\frac{\Delta S_t}{1 - S_{t-1}}\right) = a_0 + a_1 \ln(P_{t-i}) + a_2 \ln(YD_{t-j}) + a_3 \ln(R_{t-k}) + \ln(q + S_{t-1} - Y_{t-1}(\alpha)) + u_t$$

Bass:

$$\ln\left(\frac{\Delta S_t}{1 - S_{t-1}}\right) = a_0 + a_1 \ln(P_{t-i}) + a_2 \ln(YD_{t-j}) + a_3 \ln(R_{t-k}) + \ln(q + S_{t-1}) + u_t$$

Simple Logistic:

$$\ln\left(\frac{\Delta S_t}{S_{t-1}(1 - S_{t-1})}\right) = a_0 + a_1 \ln(P_{t-i}) + a_2 \ln(YD_{t-j}) + a_3 \ln(R_{t-k}) + u_t$$

Gompertz Growth:

$$\ln\left(\frac{\Delta S_t}{S_{t-1} \ln\left(\frac{1}{S_{t-1}}\right)}\right) = a_0 + a_1 \ln(P_{t-i}) + a_2 \ln(YD_{t-j}) + a_3 \ln(R_{t-k}) + u_t$$

Harvey:

$$\ln(\Delta S_t) = b_0 + b_1 \ln(S_{t-1}) + b_2 t + u_t$$

Hernes:

$$\ln\left(\frac{\Delta S_t}{S_{t-1}(1 - S_{t-1})}\right) = a_0 + a_1 \ln(P_{t-i}) + a_2 \ln(YD_{t-j}) + a_3 \ln(R_{t-k}) + a_4 t + u_t$$

EMM:

$$\ln\left(\frac{\Delta S_t}{1 - S_{t-1}}\right) = a_0 + a_1 \ln(P_{t-i}) + a_2 \ln(YD_{t-j}) + a_3 \ln(R_{t-k}) + \ln(q + (S_{t-1})^\sigma) + u_t$$

Horsky:

$$\ln(\Delta S_t) = \ln\left(\frac{1}{\exp(a_0 + a_1 \ln(P_{t-i}) + a_2 \ln(YD_{t-j}) + a_3 \ln(R_{t-k}))} - S_{t-1}\right)$$
$$+ \ln(q + p S_{t-1}) + u_t$$

10.5. Results

The results from estimating the different models on the three data sets are presented in tables 10.1, 10.2 and 10.3. Table 10.1 covers camcorders, table 10.2 CD players and table 10.3 cars. The first column of each table specifies the models and the estimation method, the first row specifies the explanatory variables.[7] Each entry in the left hand half of the tables then contains four elements: 'Coeff', the coefficient estimate; 'SE', the corresponding estimated standard error; the t-ratio; and 'conf. int.', the corresponding confidence interval belonging to the t-ratio. The right hand side of the tables contain additional information on the regressions and a selection of diagnostic indicators: 'T' is the number of observations used in the regression; 'LL' is the maximized value of the log-likelihood function; R2 is the coefficient of determination; R-bar2 is R2 adjusted for degrees of freedom; RSS is the

Table 10.1　Camcorders, UK: estimations 12/85–5/91

Model	Legend	Intercept	$\ln(P)_t$	$\ln(P)_{t-1}$	$\ln(YD)_{t-3}$	$\ln(R)_t$	q	σ	t	$M2t$	$M6t$	$M7t$
KS	Coeff.	−20.335	−0.702	−0.577	2.349	0.508	0.019			−0.226	0.262	0.229
a = 0.03	SE	5.82	0.30	0.31	0.54	0.11	0.01			0.05	0.05	0.05
	t-ratio	−3.50	−2.36	−1.88	4.39	4.74	2.61			−4.85	5.14	4.50
NLS	conf. int.	[1.00]	[0.98]	[0.93]	[1.00]	[0.99]				[1.00]	[1.00]	[1.00]
Bass	Coeff.	−21.491	−0.678	−0.641	2.446	0.484	0.033			−0.224	0.260	0.229
	SE	5.83	0.30	0.31	0.52	0.11	0.01			0.05	0.05	0.05
	t-ratio	−3.69	−2.24	−2.10	4.66	4.56	2.55			−4.78	5.08	4.48
NLS	conf. int.	[1.00]	[0.97]	[0.96]	[1.00]	[1.00]	[0.99]			[1.00]	[1.00]	[1.00]
Simple	Coeff.	118.861	−0.569	0.773	−12.693	1.854				−0.208	0.143	−0.006
Logistic	SE	15.45	0.75	0.73	1.35	0.28				0.12	0.14	0.14
	t-ratio	7.69	−0.76	1.06	−9.39	6.61				−1.68	1.05	−0.04
OLS	conf. int.	[1.00]	[0.55]	[0.71]	[1.00]	[1.00]				[0.90]	[0.70]	[0.03]
Simple	Coeff.	33.970	−1.097	−0.701	−2.626	0.373				−0.240	0.160	0.085
Logistic	SE	28.97	0.34	0.32	2.85	0.37				0.04	0.05	0.05
	t-ratio	1.17	−3.24	−2.17	−0.92	1.00				−6.15	3.18	1.56
CO AR(1)	conf. int.	[0.75]	[1.00]	[0.97]	[0.64]	[0.68]				[1.00]	[1.00]	[0.88]
Gompertz	Coeff.	101.133	−0.774	0.363	−10.623	1.649				−0.207	0.149	0.022
Growth	SE	12.51	0.61	0.59	1.10	0.23				0.10	0.11	0.11
	t-ratio	8.08	−1.27	0.61	−9.70	7.26				−2.06	1.36	0.20
OLS	conf. int.	[1.00]	[0.79]	[0.46]	[1.00]	[1.00]				[0.96]	[0.82]	[0.16]
Gompertz	Coeff.	39.725	−1.018	−0.642	−3.388	0.317				−0.238	0.157	0.080
Growth	SE	27.73	0.33	0.31	2.73	0.36				0.04	0.05	0.05
	t-ratio	1.43	−3.13	−2.08	−1.24	0.88				−6.18	3.16	1.49
CO AR(1)	conf. int.	[0.84]	[1.00]	[0.96]	[0.78]	[0.62]				[1.00]	[1.00]	[0.86]
Harvey	Coeff.	−12.372						−0.286	0.057	−0.184	0.228	0.194
	SE	0.64						0.07	0.00	0.07	0.08	0.08
	t-ratio	−19.41						−3.84	11.81	−2.49	2.84	2.42
OLS	conf. int.	[1.00]						[1.00]	[1.00]	[0.98]	[0.99]	[0.98]
Harvey	Coeff.	−14.069						−0.504	0.069	−0.215	0.187	0.130
	SE	2.37						0.29	0.02	0.05	0.06	0.06
	t-ratio	−5.93						−1.72	4.09	−4.58	3.24	2.25
CO AR(1)	conf. int.	[1.00]						[0.91]	[1.00]	[1.00]	[1.00]	[0.97]
Hernes	Coeff.	67.207	−1.879	−0.693	−5.298	1.506			−0.055	−0.213	0.175	0.091
	SE	12.03	0.52	0.52	1.27	0.19			0.01	0.08	0.09	0.09
	t-ratio	5.59	−3.58	−1.34	−4.17	7.87			−8.24	−2.59	1.94	1.00
OLS	conf. int.	[1.00]	[1.00]	[0.81]	[1.00]	[1.00]			[1.00]	[0.99]	[0.94]	[0.68]
Hernes	Coeff.	39.968	−1.331	−0.913	−2.665	0.674			−0.045	−0.238	0.163	0.087
	SE	20.34	0.33	0.32	2.05	0.32			0.01	0.04	0.05	0.05
	t-ratio	1.96	−4.07	−2.89	−1.30	2.11			−5.18	−6.10	3.32	1.69
CO AR(1)	conf. int.	[0.95]	[1.00]	[0.99]	[0.80]	[0.96]			[1.00]	[1.00]	[1.00]	[0.90]
EMM	Coeff.	13.748	−0.996	−0.751	−1.031	0.734	0.040	0.258		−0.217	0.216	0.167
	SE	8.71	0.29	0.28	0.83	0.12	0.13	0.18		0.04	0.05	0.05
	t-ratio	1.58	−3.47	−2.73	−1.24	6.07	0.32	1.47		−5.01	4.50	3.42
NLS	conf. int.	[0.88]	[1.00]	[0.99]	[0.78]	[1.00]	[0.25]	[0.85]		[1.00]	[1.00]	[1.00]
EMM	Coeff.	14.764	−1.024	−0.769	−1.110	0.745		0.216		−0.216	0.214	0.165
q = 0	SE	7.47	0.26	0.26	0.75	0.11		0.04		0.04	0.05	0.05
	t-ratio	1.98	−3.94	−2.92	−1.49	6.67		5.46		−5.05	4.57	3.47
OLS	conf. int.	[0.95]	[1.00]	[0.99]	[0.86]	[1.00]		[1.00]		[1.00]	[1.00]	[1.00]

M11t	M12t	T	LL	R2	R-bar2	RSS	S.E.	DW	LM12	RESET	Norm.	Heteros
0.352	0.770	63	58.5365	0.9858	0.9831	0.5752	0.1052	1.6629	1.4677	2.5323	1.0970	0.5839
0.05	0.05											
6.62	14.85											
[1.00]	[1.00]								[0.82]	[0.88]	[0.42]	[0.55]
0.349	0.766	63	58.3279	0.9857	0.9830	0.5790	0.1055	1.6376	1.4336	2.0973	1.0484	0.2069
0.05	0.05											
6.55	14.72											
[1.00]	[1.00]								[0.81]	[0.85]	[0.41]	[0.35]
0.335	0.782	63	−3.7235	0.8299	0.8010	4.1515	0.2799	0.4377	9.7356	25.0927	0.5636	8.0420
0.14	0.13											
2.239	5.81											
[0.98]	[1.00]								[1.00]	[1.00]	[0.25]	[0.99]
0.367	0.745	63	46.5169	0.9596	0.9517	0.8095	0.1260	2.4949	AR Err.	ut =	ρ ut-1	
0.05	0.05								Specification	Coeff.	0.932	
7.21	14.90									t-ratio	41.93	
[1.00]	[1.00]									con. int.	[1.00]	
0.326	0.760	63	9.5685	0.8100	0.7777	2.7224	0.2266	0.5252	7.6125	21.2898	0.6121	8.0250
0.11	0.11											
2.87	6.98											
[0.99]	[1.00]								[1.00]	[1.00]	[0.26]	[0.99]
0.362	0.741	63	48.4102	0.9359	0.9234	0.7616	0.1222	2.5327	AR Err.	ut =	ρ ut-1	
0.05	0.05								Specification	Coeff.	0.898	
7.25	15.11									t-ratio	25.31	
[1.00]	[1.00]									con. int.	[1.00]	
0.392	0.838	65	27.8542	0.9614	0.9566	1.6152	0.1683	0.8310	4.7909	3.5820	2.6491	1.9250
0.08	0.08											
4.89	10.45											
[1.00]	[1.00]								[1.00]	[0.94]	[0.73]	[0.83]
0.372	0.764	65	42.8388	0.9757	0.9722	0.9825	0.1337	1.9201	AR Err.	ut =	ρ ut-1	
0.06	0.06								Specification	Coeff.	0.611	
6.41	13.17									t-ratio	5.54	
[1.00]	[1.00]									con. int.	[1.00]	
0.271	0.667	63	22.5994	0.9262	0.9120	1.8001	0.1861	0.6416	3.2555	45.9199	4.3405	2.5726
0.09	0.09											
2.89	7.37											
[0.99]	[1.00]								[1.00]	[1.00]	[0.89]	[0.89]
0.353	0.726	63	53.4251	0.9677	0.9606	0.6478	0.1138	2.4708	AR Err.	ut =	ρ ut-1	
0.05	0.05								Specification	Coeff.	0.712	
14.61										t-ratio	9.26	
[1.00]	[1.00]									con. int.	[1.00]	
0.329	0.735	63	64.0386	0.09881	0.9855	0.4830	0.0973	1.7172	1.0191	0.2520	1.8573	2.2421
0.05	0.05											
6.63	15.18											
[1.00]	[1.00]								[0.55]	[0.38]	[0.60]	[0.86]
0.327	0.732	63	64.0036	0.9881	0.9858	0.4836	0.0964	1.7103	0.9419	0.2140	1.9009	2.3353
0.05	0.05											
6.77	15.76											
[1.00]	[1.00]								[0.48]	[0.35]	[0.61]	[0.87]

Table 10.2   CD players, UK: estimations 7/85–5/91

Model	Legend	Intercept	$\ln(P)_{t-5}$	$\ln(YD)_{t-1}$	$\ln(R)_{t-1}$	q	σ	t	$M1t$	$M11t$
KS	Coeff.	12.295	1.908	−2.589	0.254	0.00031			0.566	0.593
α = 0.01	SE	7.80	0.18	0.70	0.10	0.00012			0.05	0.05
	t-ratio	1.58	10.58	−3.68	2.55	2.59			10.94	11.51
NLS	conf. int.	[0.88]	[1.00]	[1.00]	[0.99]	[0.99]			[1.00]	[1.00]
Bass	Coeff.	13.803	2.121	−2.851	0.205	0.00026			0.571	0.587
	SE	7.64	0.18	0.69	0.10	0.00011			0.05	0.05
	t-ratio	1.81	12.06	−4.15	2.11	2.37			11.29	11.64
NLS	conf. int.	[0.92]	[1.00]	[1.00]	[0.96]	[0.98]			[1.00]	[1.00]
Simple	Coeff.	14.675	2.317	−3.072	0.338				0.563	0.583
Logistic	SE	8.05	0.17	0.72	0.09				0.05	0.05
	t-ratio	1.82	13.73	−4.27	3.81				10.56	10.96
OLS	conf. int.	[0.93]	[1.00]	[1.00]	[1.00]				[1.00]	[1.00]
Gompertz	Coeff.	2.027	1.463	−1.495	0.362				0.560	0.570
Growth	SE	7.70	0.16	0.69	0.08				0.05	0.05
	t-ratio	0.26	9.06	−2.17	4.27				10.99	11.21
OLS	conf. int.	[0.21]	[1.00]	[0.97]	[1.00]				[1.00]	[1.00]
Harvey	Coeff.	−4.509					0.527	−0.006	0.563	0.570
	SE	0.19					0.02	0.002	0.06	0.06
	t-ratio	−23.82					22.06	−3.09	9.47	9.62
OLS	conf. int.	[1.00]					[1.00]	[1.00]	[1.00]	[1.00]
Harvey	Coeff.	−4.119					0.584	−0.009	0.548	0.510
	SE	0.29					0.04	0.003	0.05	0.06
	t-ratio	−14.43					15.41	−3.34	10.32	8.87
CO AR(1)	conf. int.	[1.00]					[1.00]	[1.00]	[1.00]	[1.00]
Hernes	Coeff.	17.550	2.711	−3.569	0.191			0.07	0.566	0.582
	SE	8.23	0.32	0.79	0.13			0.005	0.05	0.05
	t-ratio	2.13	8.43	−4.50	1.42			1.43	10.69	11.03
OLS	conf. int.	[0.96]	[1.00]	[1.00]	[0.84]			[0.84]	[1.00]	[1.00]
EMM	Coeff.	4.194	1.581	−1.672	0.205	0.00016	0.821		0.563	0.575
	SE	10.67	0.46	1.15	0.10	0.00065	0.14		0.05	0.05
	t-ratio	0.39	3.45	−1.46	2.12	0.24	5.68		11.10	11.29
NLS	conf. int.	[0.30]	[1.00]	[0.85]	[0.96]	[0.19]	[1.00]		[1.00]	[1.00]
EMM	Coeff.	2.726	1.503	−1.497	0.211		0.792		0.561	0.573
q = 0	SE	8.44	0.31	0.84	0.09		0.07		0.05	0.05
	t-ratio	0.32	4.93	−1.78	2.29		11.85		11.26	11.51
OLS	conf. int.	[0.25]	[1.00]	[0.92]	[0.97]		[1.00]		[1.00]	[1.00]

M12t	T	LL	R2	R-bar2	RSS	S.E.	DW	LM12	RESET	Norm.	Heteros
1.131	67	51.9795	0.9777	0.9751	0.8313	0.1187	1.7748	0.9526	3.8856	2.3900	0.0443
0.05											
21.98											
[1.00]								[0.49]	[0.95]	[0.70]	[0.17]
1.131	67	53.4162	0.9787	0.9761	0.7964	0.1162	1.8400	1.0030	4.0174	2.2436	0.0035
0.05											
22.46											
[1.00]								[0.54]	[0.95]	[0.67]	[0.05]
1.128	67	49.2322	0.9785	0.9763	0.9023	0.1226	1.6462	0.8302	0.7478	1.4933	0.3410
0.05											
21.23											
[1.00]								[0.38]	[0.61]	[0.53]	[0.44]
1.105	67	52.2065	0.9587	0.9546	0.8257	0.1173	1.6703	0.7865	3.2494	1.8932	0.2570
0.05											
21.73											
[1.00]								[0.34]	[0.92]	[0.61]	[0.39]
1.080	75	45.2170	0.9774	0.9757	0.1315	0.1381	1.3514	1.2066	1.6391	2.0867	9.4272
0.06											
18.21											
[1.00]								[0.70]	[0.80]	[0.65]	[1.00]
1.059	75	53.6517	0.9807	0.9789	1.0163	0.1232	1.9012	AR Err.	ut =	ρ ut–1	
0.06								Specification	Coeff.	0.313	
18.34									t-ratio	2.6820	
[1.00]									con. int.	[0.99]	
1.133	67	50.3800	0.9792	0.9768	0.8719	0.1216	1.7657	1.0348	1.6688	0.8676	0.2244
0.05											
21.46											
[1.00]								[0.57]	[0.80]	[0.35]	[0.36]
1.110	67	54.3697	0.9793	0.9764	0.7740	1.8097	0.7790	5.4322	2.1747	0.4106	
0.05											
21.17											
[1.00]								[0.33]	[0.98]	[0.66]	[0.48]
1.107	67	54.3395	0.9768	0.7747	0.1146	1.7990	0.7706	3.9519	2.0826	0.5358	
0.05											
22.10											
[1.00]								[0.32]	[0.95]	[0.65]	[0.53]

Table 10.3   Cars, Germany: estimations 1946–1990

Model	Legend	Intercept	$\ln(P)_{t-1}$	$\ln(YD)_t$	$\ln(R)_{t-1}$	q	σ	t	D46-66t	D74t
KS	Coeff.	−22.950	−0.128	1.656	−0.277	0.119			0.362	−0.760
∞ = 1	SE	2.29	0.14	0.14	0.23	0.10			0.11	0.16
	t-ratio	−10.02	−0.89	11.84	−1.20	1.21			3.33	−4.83
NLS	conf. int.	[1.00]	[0.62]	[1.00]	[0.76]	[0.76]			[1.00]	[1.00]
Simple	Coeff.	6.097	0.188	−0.626	−0.249				0.277	−0.764
Logistic	SE	2.10	0.17	0.14	0.32				0.15	0.22
	t-ratio	2.90	1.12	−4.60	−0.77				1.84	−3.55
OLS	conf. int.	[0.99]	[0.73]	[1.00]	[0.55]				[0.93]	[1.00]
Simple	Coeff.	2.731	0.000	−0.332	−0.214				0.432	−0.782
Logistic	SE	2.85	0.27	0.23	0.31				0.18	−0.21
	t-ratio	0.96	0.00	−1.44	−0.68				2.24	−3.67
CO AR(1)	conf. int.	[0.66]	[0.00]	[0.84]	[0.50]				[0.97]	[1.00]
Gompertz	Coeff.	−4.219	0.215	0.081	−0.239				0.261	−0.783
Growth	SE	1.95	0.15	0.13	0.30				0.14	0.20
	t-ratio	−2.16	1.39	0.64	−0.79				1.87	−3.93
OLS	conf. int.	[0.96]	[0.83]	[0.48]	[0.57]				[0.93]	[1.00]
Gompertz	Coeff.	−7.017	0.056	0.326	−0.203				0.391	−0.788
Growth	SE	2.56	0.24	0.20	0.30				0.17	0.20
	t-ratio	−2.74	0.24	1.62	−0.69				2.31	−3.89
CO AR(1)	conf. int.	[0.99]	[0.18]	[0.89]	[0.50]				[0.97]	[1.00]
Harvey	Coeff.	−0.679					1.303	−0.062	0.663	−0.928
	SE	1.03					0.20	0.03	0.42	0.52
	t-ratio	−0.66					6.64	−2.32	1.58	−1.80
OLS	conf. int.	[0.49]					[1.00]	[0.97]	[0.88]	[0.92]
Harvey	Coeff.	−1.646					0.907	−0.043	0.333	−0.892
	SE	0 32					0.07	0.01	0.13	0.15
	t-ratio	−5.21					13.57	−5.29	2.66	−5.80
CO AR(1)	conf. int.	[1.00]					[1.00]	[1.00]	[0.99]	[1.00]
Hernes	Coeff.	−13.941	1.428	0.612	−0.082			−0.084	0.297	−0.927
	SE	10.09	−0.63	0.62	0.32			0.04	0.14	0.22
	t-ratio	−1.38	2.26	0.98	−0.26			−2.03	2.05	−4.19
OLS	conf. int.	[0.82]	[0.97]	[0.67]	[0.20]			[0.95]	[1.00]	[1.00]
Hernes	Coeff.	−12.836	1.054	0.617	−0.119			−0.069	0.409	−0.850
	SE	12.47	0.84	0.77	0.34			0.05	0.18	0.23
	t-ratio	−1.03	−1.25	0.80	−0.36			−1.30	2.29	−3.69
CO AR(1)	conf. int.	[0.69]	[0.78]	[0.57]	[0.28]			[0.80]	[0.97]	[1.00]
EMM	Coeff.	−50.593	−0.552	3.604	−0.328	−0.751			0.461	−0.843
q = 0	SE	8.43	0.15	0.63	0.21	0.26			0.10	0.14
	t-ratio	−6.00	−3.59	5.75	−1.54	2.92			4.51	−5.97
OLS	conf. int.	[1.00]	[1.00]	[1.00]	[0.87]	[0.99]			[1.00]	[1.00]

D80–83t	T	LL	R2	R-bar2	RSS	S.E.	DW	LM1	RESET	Norm.	Heteros
−0.545	41	23.1026	0.9690	0.9624	0.7778	0.1535	1.8706	0.1263	2.1434	0.2902	0.2670
0.12											
−4.72											
[1.00]								[0.28]	[0.85]	[0.14]	[0.39]
−0.614	41	8.5376	0.8993	0.8816	1.5828	0.2158	1.1542	6.6606	6.7136	0.6739	1.5790
0.16											
−3.83											
[1.00]								[0.99]	[0.99]	[0.29]	[0.78]
−0.546	41	13.8858	0.9155	0.8970	1.1697	0.1912		AR Err.	ut =	ut-1	
0.16								Specification	Coeff.	0.451	
−3.35									t-ratio	2.78	
[1.00]									con. int.	[0.99]	
−0.604	41	11.6830	0.7230	0.6741	1.3577	0.1998	1.2200	5.3261	3.0687	0.5297	1.4093
0.15											
−4.07											
[1.00]								[0.97]	[0.91]	[1.23]	[0.76]
−0.547	41	16.3495	0.7794	0.7311	1.0341	0.1798	1.9967	AR Err.	ut =	ut-1	
0.15								Specification	Coeff.	0.406	
−3.59									t-ratio	2.45	
[1.00]									con. int.	[0.98]	
−0.723	44	42.3745	0.7134	0.6757	17.6799	0.6821	1.4364	0.2427	5.3182	873.6575	17.0635
0.38											
−1.89											
[0.93]								[0.37]	[0.97]	[1.00]	[1.00]
−0.703	44	10.6190	0.9259	0.9136	1.5364	0.2066	1.5260	AR Err.	ut =	ut-1	
0.11								Specification	Coeff.	−0.043	
−6.26									t-ratio	−0.84	
[1.00]									con. int.	[0.60]	
−0.716	41	10.9419	0.9105	0.8915	1.4077	0.2065	1.2603	5.3114	0.0380	0.1761	0.9144
0.16											
−4.43											
[1.00]								[0.97]	[0.15]	[0.08]	[0.66]
−0.605	41	15.0156	0.9201	0.8995	1.1054	0.1888	1.9694	AR Err.	ut =	ut-1	
0.17								Specification	Coeff.	0.409	
−3.61									t-ratio	2.23	
[1.00]									con. int.	[0.97]	
−0.537	41	26.5521	0.9738	0.9682	0.6574	0.1411	1.9066	0.0670	0.0909	0.4978	1.0571
0.11											
−5.09											
[1.00]								[0.20]	[0.24]	[0.22]	[0.69]

residual sum of squares; and S.E. the standard error of the regression. The diagnostic indicators are: the Durbin-Watson statistic (DW); the LM test for serial correlation of l'th degree ('LM 1'); Ramsey's RESET for functional form misspecification ('RESET'); Jarque-Bera's test for normality of the residuals ('Norm.'); and a test for heteroscedasticity ('heteros'). All test statistics in the tables are supplemented with corresponding confidence intervals.[8]

KS mainly use the maximized log-likelihood value (LL) to compare the performance of different models.[9] Hendry (1983) proposes the standard error of the regression divided by the mean of the dependent variable (%SE) as a criterion for model comparison and this represent a useful additional criterion. Whereas LL is determined by the probability that a set of parameters corresponds to those generating the data within a given model, in contrast, the %SE is not conditional on the functional form and as such better suited for inter-model comparisons.[10] To operationalize %SE, equations in logs can be compared by applying Sargan's criterion.[11] If all equations being compared are in logs then any transformation of the standard error of the regression is unnecessary: the standard error (S.E.) is identical to %SE despite different left hand sides in the equations. The standard errors of all equations can thus be directly compared within the tables and provide an intuitive measure of the goodness of fit.

10.5.1.   Camcorders

Given the seasonality of camcorder sales dummy variables (M) were introduced for the months of February (low post-Christmas sales), June, July (high vacation period sales), November and December (high Christmas period sales). Given that the estimating equations are in logs these additive dummies can be seen either as variables with economic significance or as statistical correction terms.

For camcorders the saturation level N was approximated by the total number of households in the UK.[12] Preliminary analysis indicated that the lag structure best suited to the data involved prices in t and $t - 1$, disposable income in $t - 3$ and the interest rate in time t. On theoretical grounds R_t, P_t and P_{t-1} should carry negative coefficients and YD_{t-3} a positive coefficient.

The H_0 hypothesis that the residuals are normally distributed (see table 10.1: Norm.) cannot be rejected in any of the models. In the absence of other problems one can thus assume that correct inference is possible and that NLS estimates replicate MLE estimates.

The KS model performs at its best with $\alpha = 0.03$. This can be interpreted as that only a few, 3 per cent, of influential adopters in every period lose their impact on the learning process – which corresponds to what one would expect from a highly innovative and recent technology. All estimated coefficients in the KS model are significant at a 5 per cent significance level (s.l.) except the coefficient for P_{t-1} which carries a t-ratio corresponding to a 7 per cent s.l. The signs of all but the interest rate coefficient match *a priori* expectations. The diagnostic statistics do not indicate any statistical problems with the model at either a 5 per cent or even a 10 per cent s.l.

The Bass model generates results very similar to those of the KS model, which is unsurprising given that in the estimates of the KS model $\alpha = 0.03$ and the Bass model is a special case of the KS model with $\alpha = 0$. The estimated coefficients are of the same sign and of similar magnitude to those in the KS model. Similarly the diagnostic statistics do not suggest any statistical problems.

Original estimates of the simple logistic model, the Gompertz growth curve, Harvey's model and the model by Hernes all show 1st order autocorrelation. The models were thus re-estimated using the Cochrane-Orcutt iterative method assuming an AR(1) process. This improves the statistical fit of the models. However, in general, the economic variables in these models tend to be either insignificant or to carry the wrong sign (except of course for the Harvey model where economic variables are not included).

The EMM model has satisfactory diagnostic statistics. However the coefficient on income is of the wrong sign (and insignificant at the 5 per cent s.l.). In addition, the coefficient of exogenous influence q and the elasticity σ in the term $\ln(q + (S_{t-1})^\sigma)$ are both insignificant at the 5 per cent s.l. Since both q and σ are in the same term it is possible to conjecture that they describe identical features of the data. This proves right as σ becomes highly significant when q is set equal 0, although even with such a restriction the coefficient on income is still negative and not significant at a 5 per cent s.l.

The Horsky model was not estimable because of singularity problems. Parameter restrictions under NLS with $q = 0$ and afterwards $q = 0$ and $p = 1$ did not solve the problem. Only with very special restrictions could the model be estimated. However, as the resulting model differs so much from Horsky's original it was decided not to report the results.

Finally, it is worth noting that the coefficient on the interest rate is significant in nearly all the models but consistently exhibits a sign contrary to *a priori* expectations based on theory (and this, as shown below, applies to CD players as well). Possible explanations are: first, both camcorders and CD players are products targeted at higher income groups who are net savers and thus might be net gainers from high interest rates (an income effect); second, interest rates have been used by the UK Government as a policy instrument to bring down 'excessive' consumer spending, which in the data might suggest that periods of high consumer spending (lead to or generate) high interest rates implying a positive casual relationship between interest rates and product sales: and, third, interest-free credit has been increasingly used over the sample period as a marketing tool, implying that the interest rate data may not be a true reflection of the cost and/or availability of credit, and/or that higher interest rates may encourage purchase because zero interest credit terms in periods of high interest rates then represent a larger discount.

10.5.2. CD players

Seasonality is equally as important for CD players as it is for camcorders, however, for CD players dummies for November, December and January were found to be sufficient.

For CD players the saturation level N was again approximated by the total number of households in the UK. Tests with different lag structures led to the inclusion of P_{t-5}, YD_{t-1} and R_{t-1}. There appears to be no obvious intuition behind why prices should lag by five months, but one can note that the use of other lag structures led to dramatic reductions in LL and increases in %SE.

The hypothesis that the residuals are normally distributed (see table 10.2: Norm.) cannot be rejected for any model. Thus, as with camcorders, it can be inferred that, in the absence of other problems, correct inference is possible.

For all models the results are very similar: the coefficients on the economic variables are of the wrong sign, and with the exception of the coefficient on income in the EMM model and the coefficient on the interest rate in the Hernes model all of these 'wrong-signed' coefficients are significant at the 5 per cent level.

Even the diagnostic tests exhibited similar results across the models. The F-statistics from LM12 and LM tests of serial correlation of 1st, 2nd, and 3rd order are insignificant at the 5 per cent s.l. for all models except that of Harvey. Ramsey's RESET is only just rejected for the KS model, the Bass model, the EMM model with $q = 0$ and clearly rejected for the EMM unrestricted model at the 5 per cent s.l. The test for heteroscedasticity leads to the rejection of the null hypothesis at the 5 per cent s.l. only in the case of Harvey's model. Because of serial correlation the Harvey model was re-estimated using Cochrane-Orcutt AR(1).

The KS model performs best with $\alpha = 0$ in which case it reduces to the Bass model. For comparison purposes the estimates of the model are presented in table 10.2 with the smallest α tested: $\alpha = 0.01$. As with the case of camcorders a very low α is a perfectly plausible result given that CD players are relatively new and only recently accessed a mass market.

In the EMM model the elasticity σ was again not significant and setting $q = 0$ improved the models performance by reducing the F-statistic of the RESET test. The Horsky model was impossible to estimate with NLS without a complete change in the structure of the model.

Overall these results for CD players are very disappointing but further discussion of two particular points might give some indication as to why the results are poor.

First, the results consistently yield coefficient estimates on economic variables of the wrong sign. This contrasts markedly with the camcorder results. One key difference between CD players and camcorders is that CD players depend on software to yield their service flow whereas camcorders do not so depend. It is reasonable to suggest that the diffusion of CD players will depend on the number of available titles and the price of compact discs (Stoneman, 1991). Given that the models above take no account of these the poor results may not be too surprising.

Secondly, the different models have very similar values for goodness of fit criteria such as the maximized log-likelihood value and the %SE. Especially interesting is the fact that the Harvey model (after correction for autocorrelation) with LL = 53.7 performs within a negligible difference to the top performer, the EMM model (LL = 54.4). However the Harvey model does not contain a single economic variable whereas the EMM model is 'fully loaded'. This suggests that the economic variables included might be missing out on key variables that contribute to the diffusion of CD players, especially the availability and cost of software.

10.5.3. Cars

The data on cars is on annual basis and relates to the West German market. Three dummy variables proved important: a dummy for 1946–66 ('D46–66' in table 10.3) that takes into account that before 1967 interest rates were regulated by the Bundesbank; a dummy capturing the 1974 oil price shock (D74); and a dummy capturing the major recession in Germany between 1980 and 1983 (D80–83).

For cars the saturation level was approximated by the number of potential drivers in Germany.[13] The best lag structure involves P_{t-1}, R_{t-1} and YD_t. The hypothesis that the residuals are normally distributed (see table 10.3: Norm) has to be rejected for Harvey's model. Correct inference is thus possible for all other models.

The KS model performs at its best with $\alpha = 1$. This can be compared to the KS study of colour televisions where they find $\alpha = 1.2$ and conclude 'that the epidemic or endogenous growth factor was not very important in the diffusion process.'[14] These estimates of α are in stark contrast to the estimates for camcorders and CD players. However, both colour TVs and cars were both well known products during the estimation period (Colour TVs: 1968–86, Cars 1946–90) and as discussed above the values of α for such products is expected *a priori* to be large.

The sign of all the coefficient estimates in the KS model match *a priori* expectations, however, the estimated coefficients on price and the interest rate and the coefficient of exogenous influence (q) are not significant at the 5 per cent s.l. None of the diagnostic statistics suggested any statistical problems at the 5 per cent or even 10 per cent s.l.

The Bass model and the Horsky model could not be estimated because of singular matrices of regressors. The simple logistic function, the Gompertz growth curve and the model by Hernes exhibited problems of autocorrelation. Re-estimation with Cochrane-Orcutt AR(1) apparently removed first order autocorrelation but in the new estimates the coefficient of all economic variables in these models are insignificant. Moreover the coefficient on price always has the wrong sign, and with the simple logistic function the sign on income is contrary to *a priori* expectations.

Although inference in Harvey's model is speculative, re-estimation was attempted with Cochrane-Orcutt AR(1), but the results were still unsatisfactory.

The EMM model exhibits excellent results: all coefficients carry correct signs, and apart from the interest rate, are highly significant at the 5 per cent s.l. None of the diagnostic tests suggests the presence of statistical problems.

One might note that, in the case of cars, in contrast to the camcorder and CD cases, the interest rate in all models carries the expected sign but is not significant at the 5 per cent s.l.

10.6. Model Comparisons

There are a number of criteria by which the performance of different models can be compared. The first obvious criterion concerns the internal performance of the models, for example whether the estimates of coefficients are of the correct sign and statistically significant. This material has largely been covered in the previous section. A second obvious criterion is in terms of the comparative performance of models as reflected by the log likelihood value and the %SE. A third criterion is in terms of forecasting performance. In this section we concentrate upon the latter two criteria and then explore why some models work better than others.

One may note initially that despite the fact that camcorders, CD players and cars represent three very different diffusion processes, the relative performance of the different models across the three data sets is very similar.

In terms of minimizing the %SE the EMM model clearly outperforms all other models in each of the data sets. The KS model is always second in the ranking. The Bass model always performs slightly worse than the KS model. All other models performed considerably worse than these three and, consistently, it was not possible to even estimate the Horsky model.

In terms of LL the ranking of models is the same in the case of cars and camcorders as the ranking use %SE. With CD players, for reasons detailed above, the LL values for the different models are very similar.

Although the EMM model outperformed the KS model in a ranking by both LL and %SE, it is inadvisable to immediately declare the EMM model to be the 'best model'. First, there are some problems in estimating the EMM model. For cars it was necessary to assume that $q = 0$ before the model could be estimated, and for camcorders and CD players it was only possible to estimate the model by setting the initial values of parameters (prior to the use of numerical approximation methods) equal to the estimates derived from OLS estimation with $q = 0$. Secondly the fit of the model was never improved by not imposing $q = 0$. This drawback is much more than just an 'unpleasant' feature in the estimation of the model. It means that the parameter values that are consistent with the best performance of the EMM model are such as to imply that the diffusion process is entirely driven by endogenous factors, and the exogenous factors, which have played such a major role in the Marketing literature since the seminal contribution by Bass, have no role to play in the diffusion process. This is contrary to all *a priori* expectations.

The KS model, on the other hand, proved extremely robust. It could be estimated in each case and yielded coefficient estimates with signs matching *a priori* expectations more often than any other model including the EMM model. The values for %SE and LL differ little from those of the EMM model and (as with the EMM model) the KS model did not appear to violate any of the classical assumptions underlying the estimation methods. In addition the ranking of α across the different technologies matched *a priori* expections.

The EMM and KS models were both tested for structural stability and forecasting performance. For camcorders and CD players, 12, 24 and 36 month forecast periods were chosen and for cars a 9 year forecast period was selected. The tests used were Chow's first test and the Predictive failure test.[15] For these tests to be valid it is necessary that the subsample variances are equal and thus a test for equality of the variances in the subsamples was performed.[16] This test could only be made on camcorders and CD players as the forecast period for cars did not allow a separate regression to be run on the later period subsample. Only for the 24 month camcorder forecast was the hypothesis of the equality of variances rejected. Chow's first test and the Predictive Failure test can thus safely be applied to camcorders and CD players, but for the 24 month camcorder forecast period the tests are inaccurate, and for cars the tests should be treated with care. The detailed results from the regressions on the subsamples and Chow's first and Predictive Failure test are available from the authors.

The KS and the EMM model both perform well in forecasting. Only with the 24 month forecast period for Camcorders does the Predictive Failure test suggest the rejection of the hypothesis of structural stability and then it is in both the KS and EMM models. The coefficient estimates of the KS model for each product and each subsample (except for camcorders with a 36 month forecast period) have the same signs as the estimations based on whole samples. In the estimates of the EMM model there is also only one change in sign – in the estimation of CD players with a 36 month forecast period (where it might be noted the estimated coefficient on income now carries a sign matching *a priori* expectations).

Overall both the EMM and KS models can be considered as 'good' models and definitely better suited than any other model used in this comparison to describing the diffusion processes analysed here. In some ways this confirms the findings of KS when analysing the

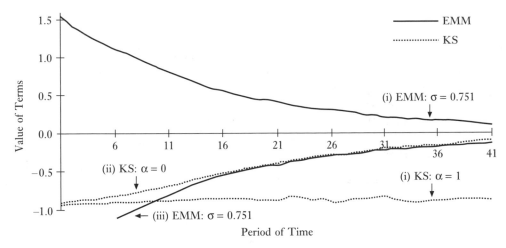

Figure 10.1   Diffusion of cars

diffusion of colour televisions. However in that work KS found the EMM model to have coefficient estimates of the wrong sign, problems of first order serial correlation and a moderate fit. This contrasts with the generally good performance of the EMM model found here. However, given the estimation problems of the EMM model, the implications of that model that exogenous forces have no role to play in the diffusion process and the superiority of the KS model in terms of coefficient estimates matching *a priori* expectations, the KS conclusion that their model is superior still merits considerable support.

This conclusion however still leaves open two questions. Why are the KS and EMM models capable of explaining diffusion better than the other models considered here, and why does the EMM model outperform the KS model in terms of goodness of fit? The answer to the first question is relatively simple. Only the EMM and KS models allow that less than the entire stock of adopters may actively contribute to the learning process.[17] The EMM model caters for this by introducing an elasticity of current sales with respect to cumulated sales. The KS model assumes that a certain percentage of adopters become non-influential in each period. The validity of this theoretically important innovation is fully confirmed by the empirics above.

The answer to why the EMM model fits the data better than the KS model is more involved, but can be approached by looking at the data generated by the two terms that distinguish one model from the other: $\ln(q + S_{t-1} - Y_{t-1}(\alpha))$ in the KS model and $\ln(q + (S_{t-1})^{\sigma})$ in the EMM model. Taking the coefficient estimates for cars from the above regressions (for the EMM model $\sigma = -0.751$ and $q = 0$ and for the KS model $\alpha = 1$ and $q = 0.119$) the two terms are plotted against time in figure 10.1, with the EMM term labelled '(i) EMM' being downwards sloping and positive and the KS term labelled '(i) KS' being negative and virtually flat.

The downward sloping curve '(i) EMM' reflects the fact that in the EMM model the elasticity of sales with respect to the existing stock is negative. The flat '(i) KS' curve with $\alpha = 1$, on the other hand, reproduces the effect of a zero elasticity. The KS model by construction does not allow for the elasticity of sales with respect to the stock to be negative.

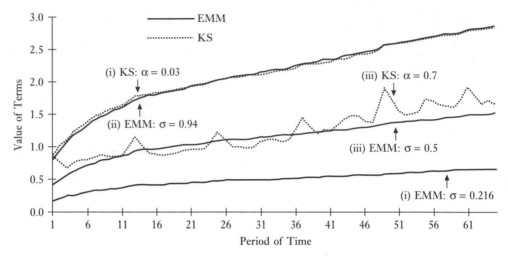

Figure 10.2   Diffusion of camcorders

Thus a major reason for the superior performance of the EMM model in terms of goodness of fit is its ability to reflect a negative elasticity. However, one might well ask whether it is reasonable on *a priori* grounds for this elasticity to be negative.

Two further curves are plotted in figure 10.1. The first, '(ii) KS' shows how the '(i) KS' term would look with $\alpha = 0$, i.e. when the KS model is reduced to the Bass model. Given that the EMM model was best in describing the data it is not surprising that the Bass model created estimation problems under NLS, for whereas '(i) EMM' is downward sloping '(ii) KS' is upward sloping.

The final curve in figure 10.1 labelled '(iii) EMM' plots '(i) EMM' with the $\sigma = +0.751$ as opposed to -0.751. The parallel to the Bass result is so close that it is clear why the Bass model works less well than the EMM model.

For the case of camcorders $\ln(q + S_{t-1} - Y_{t-1}(\alpha))$ in the KS model and $\ln(q + (S_{t-1})^{\sigma})$ in the EMM model have more similar time profiles. In figure 10.2 both '(ii) EMM' (with $\sigma = 0.216$ and $q = 0$) and '(i) KS' (with $\alpha = 0.03$ and $q = 0.019$) are plotted. Both plots are in the positive quadrant and positively sloped.

One may note in this case that the term in the EMM model may be approximated by the term in the KS model (and vice versa) by selecting appropriate values of α and σ: '(ii) EMM' shows how close the EMM term approximates the KS term by setting $\sigma = 0.94$.

It is clear, however that '(i) KS' and '(i) EMM' have significantly different values for the camcorder example. One possible reason for this can best be explained by considering the curve labelled '(iii) KS' for which we set $\alpha = 0.7$ (a relatively high value). A very similar curve can be generated from the EMM model with $\sigma = 0.5$ (plotted as '(iii) EMM)'. However whereas the KS term is very spiky the EMM term is smooth. This difference is easy to explain. In the KS model if a large quantity Y_{t-1} of the stock of adopters up to the beginning of period $t - 1$ is subtracted from all adopters at the end of period $t - 1$ (S_{t-1}), the new adopters (= sales) during period $t - 1$ will have a great impact on $\ln(q + S_{t-1} - Y_{t-1}(\alpha))$. Given the strong seasonal pattern of camcorder sales the spikiness emerges. In contrast, in the EMM model it is always the entire stock of adopters that matters, and even a strong seasonal sales pattern does not affect the entire stock sufficiently to produce spikiness.

If α is high the KS model implicitly assumes that learning is to a large extent dependent on only one period's sales. This implies that endogenous growth will be much higher in January, i.e. after the Christmas peak than one month later. With respect to the data this could mean that the decay coefficient α in the KS model was being seriously underestimated: as can be seen in figure 10.2, higher values of α lower the value of the KS term and bring it closer to the EMM term. Considering that the EMM term generates a better fit such a higher value for α should improve the performance of the KS model. However, a higher α would also increase the spikiness of the KS term. One may argue that the estimation procedures generate too low a value for α because of a trade off between these two effects, i.e. the 'lowness' and 'smoothness' of the curve. It should be noted that the greater is α the more dependent is 'learning' on recent as opposed to past sales and a high value of α does probably not capture the true nature of 'learning'. Learning seems a far more persistent process that should be less immediately dependent on recent adopters.

Given the generally poor results obtained for the case of CD players that data set has not been explored further in this context. However, from the evidence relating to cars and camcorders it is clear that if the KS model were modified (i) to allow a negative elasticity of sales with respect to the stock and (ii) to have a learning process with a reduced sensitivity to shocks, then the performance of that model in terms of goodness of fit could well be improved.

10.7.   Conclusions

This paper reports the results of a comparison of the performance of eight different diffusion models applied to data on the diffusion of CD players and camcorders in the UK and cars in West Germany. The central model to which others are compared is one recently proposed and tested by Karshenas and Stoneman (1992). Wherever possible economic variables such as product price, disposable income and interest rates were taken into account in the various models.

The results consistently indicate the empirical superiority of the models by Easingwood, Mahajan and Muller and Karshenas and Stoneman. The reason for superiority of the KS and EMM models relative to the others is their assumption that less than the entire stock of adopters may actively contribute to the learning process.

The EMM model suffers from a drawback in that it works best, empirically, when it is effectively assumed that exogenous factors do not influence diffusion. In contrast, the KS model is empirically more robust although inferior in terms of fit to the EMM model. The KS model also more consistently generated coefficient estimates with signs matching *a priori* expectations. The differences in estimated values for α across technologies in the KS model also matched *a priori* expectations. The results indicate that for less familiar technologies the rate at which adopters become non influential in the learning process is slower than for more familiar technologies. The results also indicate that product price has a negative effect and disposable income a positive effect on the diffusion process.

An analysis of the functional differences between the KS and the EMM models, based on the actual data, suggested that the better fit of the EMM model was due to (i) its capability to assume a negative elasticity of sales with respect to the current stock and (ii) the sensitivity to shocks of the learning process in the KS model.

On balance, one can argue that the evidence in this paper supports the findings of Karshenas and Stoneman that the KS model is superior to other epidemic models used in the literature. Even so, the KS model still suffers from a number of limitations. In particular the model assumes a constant saturation level, a constant coefficient of decay and an infinite product life. It is also assumed that the exogenous factor q is of the same functional form as the endogenous growth factor p. However, perhaps of more importance is that the KS model, in line with all the other models tested here, does not have a supply side incorporated into the model.

Attempts have been made to overcome some of these limitations, with the results suggesting, however, that the limitations are more important in theory than in practice. Replacement purchases were modelled along the lines of Kamakura and Balasubramanian (1987); different functional forms for α were tried; and advertising effects were also included. The empirical results suggested that only this latter enhancement of the KS and other models was empirically important.

In these extensions it was not possible to include a supply side and that must be a major item on any future research agenda, whether it be the agenda of Marketing or Economics. Future research could also usefully concentrate on further testing of extensions to the KS model that overcome its theoretical limitations.

In Economics the potential of epidemic diffusion models has probably been underestimated. On the other hand, econometrically well founded studies (of which we believe this is an example) remain rare in Marketing. Given that, both theoretically and empirically, the analysis of epidemic diffusion models still offers considerable research challenges, this appears to be an ideal area for more interdisciplinary collaboration.

Acknowledgements

The authors wish to thank Michael Jung and Jurgen Schrader of McKinsey and Company Inc. for their help with data sourcing, Christopher Walther, a referee, and an editor for comments on an earlier draft, and Jeromin Zettelmeyer for encouragement and support. All errors that may remain are the sole responsibility of the authors.

Notes

1   Stoneman (1983) and (1987) presents a comprehensive survey of this literature.
2   This data has been made available to the authors on confidential terms by McKinsey & Company, Inc.
3   The original data is 4-weekly. Monthly intervals were calculated by weighting the data points according to the days that fell into the respective month. The data is not based on 4-weekly sample surveys but on 4-weekly reports of retailers serving approximately 95 per cent of the market for white and brown goods in the UK.
4   This series is sourced from the 'Kraftfahrtbundesamt' in Flensburg/Germany.
5   'Selected retail banks: base rates' as published by the Bank of England were used as interest rates. Each date of change is published such that a weighted average for each month could be calculated. Personal disposable income is sourced from the Central Statistical Office and is only published on a quarterly basis. The best results could be achieved by linear interpolation of the quarterly data to monthly data.

6   Both from the Statistisches Bundesamt. Manufacturer prices as published by the Statistisches Bundesamt are a weighted average of product prices throughout the respective industry.

7   For Harvey's model the estimates for the parameter 'b$_1$' are listed under the column heading 'σ'.

8   We use the approximate F-version of the tests except for the normality test as the small sample properties are superior to the χ^2 versions. For Jarque-Bera's test see Jarque and Bera (1980) and Bera and Jarque (1981). The table lists the χ^2 version with 2 degrees of freedom. The heteroscedasticity test is based on $H_0: \alpha = 0$ in the auxiliary regression $\hat{\mu}_t^2 = \text{constant} + \alpha \hat{y}_t^2$.

9   As KS remark, the LLs in the different models have to be rescaled as the dependent variables are not the same in all models. They continue by saying: 'However, as it happens the Jacobean of the transformation in each case turns out to be exactly the same. This is due to the fact that the dependent variables are all in log forms and the denominators are all composed of lagged dependent variables. As a result, the Jacobean only depends on the numerators which turn out to be the same in all models'.

10 This advantage of %SE can of course also be claimed by $\bar{R}^2$ only it loses the intuitiveness of R^2 for its values are no longer confined to values between 0 and 1. Further it is difficult to compare models in differences using $\bar{R}^2$.

11 See Sargan (1964).

12 This number was calculated by using the population figure of 'Population Projections 1987–2027' and dividing it by the average number of persons in a household as determined by the 'General Household Survey'. The resulting number was $N = 23185500$ households.

13 This value was approximated by the number of 15 to 64 year olds reported in the World Bank Development Report 1990. The number is $N = 42664800$.

14 See KS (1992).

15 For both tests see Chow (1960).

16 H_0: 'Variances of the subsamples are equal' with the F statistic computed by $F = \sigma_i^2/\sigma_j^2$ (with $N_i - k$ and $N_j - k$ degrees of freedom) and $\sigma_i^2 > \sigma_j^2$. N_i and N_j are the number of observation in the respective subsamples and k is the number of regressors.

17 Strictly speaking this also applies to the Harvey model. However, as it was not possible to explicitly incorporate economic variables in that model, it is not possible to make a direct comparison with the KS and EMM models.

References

Bain, A.D. (1962) The Growth of Television Ownership in the United Kingdom, *International Economic Review*, **3**, 145–57.

Bass, F.M. (1969) A New Product Growth Model For Customer Durables, *Management Science*, **15**, 215–27.

Bera, A.K. and Jarque, C.M. (1981) An Efficient Large Sample Test for Normality of Observation and Regression Residuals, Australian National University Working Paper in Econometrics, No. 90, Canberra.

Chow, G.C. (1960) Tests of Equality Between Subsets of Coefficients in Two Linear Regression Models, *Econometrica*, 1960, 591–605.

David, P.A. (1969) A Contribution to the Theory of Diffusion, Stanford Centre for Research in Economic Growth, *Memorandum no. 71*, Stanford University.

Davies, S. (1979) *The Diffusion of Process Innovation*, Cambridge: Cambridge University Press.

Easingwood, C., Mahajan, V. and Muller, E. (1983) A Nonuniform Influence Innovation Diffusion Model of New Product Acceptance, *Technological Forecasting and Social Changes*, **22**, 199–213.

Fudenberg, D. and Tirole, J. (1985) Preemption and Rent Equalization in the Adoption of New Technology, *Review of Economic Studies*, **52**, 383–401.

Griliches, Z. (1957) Hybrid Corn: An Exploration in the Economics of Technological Change, *Econometrica*, **48**, 501–22.

Harvey, A.C. (1984) Time Series Forecasting Based on the Logistic Curve, *Journal of Operational Research Society*, **35**, 641–46.

Hendry, D.F. (1983) Econometric Modelling: The 'Consumption Function' in Retrospect, *Scottish Journal of Political Economy*, **30**, 193–220.

Hernes, G. (1976) Diffusion and Growth – The Non-Homogeneous Case, *Scandinavian Journal of Economics*, **78**, 427–36.

Horsky, D. (1990) A Diffusion Model Incorporating Product Benefits, Price, Income and Information, *Marketing Science*, **9**(4), 342–65.

Ireland, N. and Stoneman, P. (1986) Technology Diffusion, Expectations and Welfare, *Oxford Economic Papers*, **38**, 283–304.

Jain, D.C. and Rao, R.C. (1990) Effect of Price on the Demand for Durables: Modeling, Estimation and Findings, *Journal of Business & Economic Statistics*, **8**(2), 163–70.

Jarque, C.M. and Bera, A.K. (1980) Efficient Tests for Normality, Hetorscedasticity and Serial Independence of Regression Residuals, *Economic Letters*, **6**, 225–29.

Kamakura, W.A. and Balasubramanian, S.K. (1987) Long-term Forecasting with Innovation Diffusion Models: The Impact of Replacement Purchases, *Journal of Forecasting*, **6**, 1–19.

Karshenas, M. and Stoneman, P. (1992) A Flexible Model of Technological Diffusion Incorporating Economic Factors with an Application to the Spread of Colour Television Ownership in the UK, *Journal of Forecasting*, **11**(7), 577–601.

Mahajan, V., Mason, C.H. and Srinivasan, V. (1986) An Evaluation of Estimation Procedures for New Product Diffusion Models, in *Innovation Diffusion Models of New Product Acceptance*, V. Mahajan and Y. Wind (eds.), Cambridge, MA: Ballinger Publishing Company.

Mahajan, V., Muller, E. and Bass, F.M. (1990) New Product Diffusion Models in Marketing: A Review and Directions for Research, *Journal of Marketing*, **54**, 1–26.

Mansfield, E. (1968) *Industrial Research and Technological Innovation*, New York: W.W. Norton.

Reinganum, J.F. (1981a) Market Structure and the Diffusion of New Technology, *Bell Journal of Economics*, **12**, 618–24.

Reinganum, J.F. (1981b) Dynamic Games of Innovations, *Journal of Economic Theory*, **25**, 21–41.

Sargan, J.D. (1964) Wages and Prices in the UK: A Study in Econometric Methodology, in *Econometric Analysis for National Economic Planning*, B.E. Hart, G. Mills, J.K. Whitaker (eds.), London: Butterworth.

Schmittlein, D.C. and Mahajan, V. (1982) Maximum Likelihood Estimation for an Innovation Diffusion Model of New Product Acceptance, *Marketing Science*, **1**, 57–78.

Srinivasan, V. and Mason, C.H. (1986) Nonlinear Least Squares Estimation of New Product Diffusion Models, *Marketing Science*, **5**, 169–78.

Stoneman, P. (1981) Intra Firm Diffusion, Bayesian Learning and Profitability, *Economic Journal*, **91**, 375–88.

Stoneman, P. (1983) *The Economic Analysis of Technological Change*, Oxford: Oxford University Press.

Stoneman, P. (1987) *The Economic Analysis of Technology Policy*, Oxford: Oxford University Press.

Stoneman, P. (1991) Copying Capabilities and Intertemporal Competition Between Joint Input Technologies, *Economics of Innovation and New Technology*, **1**(3), 233–42.

Stoneman, P. and David, P.A. (1986) Information Provisions vs. Adoption Subsidies as Instruments of Technology Policy, *Economic Journal*, RES/AUTE Conference Supplement, pp. 142–50.

Williams, R.A. (1972) Growth in Ownership of Consumer Durables in the United Kingdom, *Economica*, 61–9.

Part IV
Diffusion Policy

Chapter eleven
Diffusion Policy: An Introduction

This fourth part of the book addresses issues relating to policy and in particular government policy. The primary interest is in why and how the government might intervene in the diffusion process. The main concern is with developed economies. The same issue addressed in a developing economy framework may well cover a number of extra issues. The relevant concept of government can be local or regional, national or supra national (such as the European Commission). In different countries the relative importance of the three defined tiers differ; however, the basic principles of analysis should be the same at each level.

There is only a limited literature upon diffusion policy. Recently Geroski (2000) has addressed the issue, and there is a useful group of three papers in an Economic Journal Policy Forum in 1994 (Greenaway, 1994; Metcalfe, 1994; Stoneman and Diederen, 1994). The second of these takes an explicit evolutionary-based approach which can also be found in Metcalfe (1995), and can be contrasted with the more neoclassical approach of Stoneman and Diederen (1994). Discussions of the practice of diffusion policy, *inter alia*, can be found in Diederen *et al.* (1999), Soete and Arundel (1993) and OECD (1998, chapter 8) but here we play down such 'institutional' issues.

The policy debate concerns three main issues – rationale, instruments and impact – that is, why should the government intervene, how should it intervene and what has been the impact of previous interventions. The next chapter reproduces Stoneman and Diederen (1994) which provides an overview of all three issues placing the discussion of diffusion policy in its wider institutional and academic context. This paper is, however, non-technical and as such does not illustrate to any degree how policy issues can be modelled and addressed. In chapters 12 and 13 two further papers are thus reproduced that do illustrate the formality of policy modelling. The first (Ireland and Stoneman, 1986) is included for two main reasons. The first is because of the obvious policy implications of the work contained therein. This paper is one of the first that actually addressed diffusion policy from the point of view of defining a welfare optimal diffusion path and then considering policy as justified on the grounds of deviations from that path. Prior to such analysis much policy debate was largely based upon the premise that faster is always better and this paper helps to show the weakness of such an approach. The second reason for including the paper is that it provides an example of positive as opposed to normative analysis that combines supply and demand factors in the analysis of diffusion and it is thus a useful reference point for material covered in chapter 6.

The paper reproduced as chapter 13 (originally published as Stoneman and David, 1986) is included for three reasons. The first is because it addresses the two main classes of policy instruments – information and subsidies – and illustrates how they interact and, perhaps more importantly, how supplier behaviour can wholly or partly negate the intent of policy intervention. Secondly, it is included because it considers both the supply and demand side. Thirdly, it is included because, as stated above, it is desirable to attempt to integrate different approaches to diffusion analysis in encompassing models. This paper integrates the epidemic approach with the probit approach.

There is in fact only a very limited literature that has undertaken any analysis of the impact of policy instruments upon the diffusion process. Within the government departments that use such policies there are often internal evaluation exercises. Rarely, however, are these made public and even more rarely do they meet the requirements of best academic practice. The last paper included in this section (originally published as Stoneman and Battisti, 2000) is an example of how the impact of policy instruments can be studied. The paper concerns the effectiveness of fiscal subsidies and regulation in the encouragement of the use of unleaded petrol in the UK. Sister papers applying to a UK/Italian comparison and a pan-European comparison can be found as Stoneman and Battisti (1998) and Battisti and Stoneman (1998). There are two other reasons for including this paper. The first is that the methodology follows guidelines on current best econometric practice in undertaking pre-estimation analysis of the main data series and as a result an error correction model is estimated (which is probably unique in the field). Secondly, the paper considers diffusion of non-durable consumer technologies, which is rare, and in doing so adapts a diffusion model suggested by Deaton and Muellbauer (1980) that has not otherwise been applied empirically. In doing so it illustrates how a logistic diffusion curve can be derived from a probit model as opposed to the more standard epidemic model.

Jointly the papers provide an overview, illustrate the different approaches to diffusion policy modelling and also generate a number of results with varying empirical support. It is quite reasonable to argue, however, that there is still much to be done in this field. This is particularly so as regards empirical verification of the impacts of policy. Our knowledge in that area is really quite thin, although this is just the time when policy makers are beginning to switch their interest from the generation of technology to the use of technology, and thus just the time when knowledge is of most value.

References

Battisti, G. and Stoneman, P. (1998) 'The Diffusion of Unleaded Petrol: An Anglo Italian Comparison', *Labour*, 12(2), 255–78.

Deaton, A. and Muellbauer, J. (1980) *Economics and Consumer Behaviour*, Cambridge: Cambridge University Press.

Diederen, P., Stoneman, P., Toivanen, O. and Wolters, A. (1999) *Innovation and Research Policies: An International Comparative Analysis*, Cheltenham: Edward Elgar.

Geroski, P. (2000) 'Models of Technology Diffusion', *Research Policy*, 29, 603–25.

Greenaway, D. (1994) 'The Diffusion of New Technology, Editorial Note', *Economic Journal*, 104, 916–17.

Ireland, N.J. and Stoneman, P. (1986) 'Technological Diffusion, Expectations and Welfare', *Oxford Economic Papers*, 38, 283–304.

Metcalfe, J.S. (1994) 'Evolutionary Economics and Technology Policy', *Economic Journal*, 104, 931–44.

Metcalfe, J.S. (1995) 'The Economic Foundations of Technology Policy: Equilibrium and Evolutionary Perspectives', in P. Stoneman (ed.), *Handbook of the Economics of Innovation and Technological Change*, Oxford: Blackwell, 409–512.

OECD (1998) *Technology, Productivity and Job Creation, Best Policy Practices*, Paris: OECD.

Soete, L. and Arundel, A. (1993) *An Integrated Approach to European Innovation and Technology Diffusion Policy*, Brussels: Commission of the European Communities.

Stoneman, P. and Battisti, G. (1998) 'Fiscal Incentives to Consumer Innovation: The Use of Unleaded Petrol in Europe', *Research Policy*, 27, 187–213.

Stoneman, P. and Battisti, G. (2000) 'The Role of Regulation, Fiscal Incentives and Changes in Tastes in the Diffusion of Unleaded Petrol in the UK', *Oxford Economic Papers*, 52, 326–56.

Stoneman, P. and David, P. (1986) 'Adoption Subsidies vs. Information Provision as Instruments of Technology Policy', *Economic Journal*, Conference Supplement, March, 142–50.

Stoneman, P. and Diederen, P. (1994) 'Technology Diffusion and Public Policy', *Economic Journal*, 104, 918–30.

Chapter twelve

Technology Diffusion and Public Policy

Co-written with Paul Diederen

12.1. Introduction

A useful typology of technological change is provided by the Schumpeterian trilogy: invention (the generation of new ideas), innovation (the development of those ideas through to the first marketing or use of a technology) and diffusion (the spread of new technology across its potential market). Until recently, policy schemes in most OECD countries have tended to focus predominantly on the invention and innovation, or science and R&D, end of this technology spectrum (see e.g. Limpens *et al.*, 1992). Although it is generally realised that it is the process of diffusion, or use of technology that creates productive potential and competitiveness, policy initiatives have largely bypassed opportunities to improve the diffusion process. If this may seem misplaced emphasis, it does in fact reflect the state of the academic literature which is wide ranging and extensive as it relates to policies on R&D, but small and fragmented as regards policies on diffusion.

Currently a gradual reorientation of policy direction toward diffusion seems to be taking place. The US and UK governments, for example, have recently proposed major technology policy initiatives that, despite differences in emphasis, both stress the importance of creating an infrastructure conducive to a rapid spread of awareness and knowledge of innovations. We argue that, although sensible in themselves, such policies may be too limited in scope and that a broader policy stance may be needed.

This paper has two main objectives. The first is to provide an overview of why policy intervention in the diffusion process may be desirable and what form it might take. This discussion is rather long, since to the best of our knowledge there is no published systematic synthesis of the diffusion policy literature (though see Stoneman, 1987 for an earlier attempt). The second aim is to look at actual diffusion policies and their impacts.

To make the task manageable we are restricting this paper to a discussion of the diffusion of new process technologies. Although similar issues apply to new consumer technologies these are not explicitly addressed. We also consider diffusion policy only within the context of a given institutional and macroeconomic environment. Although it may well be that the

Reprinted from the *Economic Journal*, 104, 918–30, 1994 by kind permission of Blackwell Publishers.

supply of skilled manpower, the nature of the capital market, animal spirits and entrepreneurship, fiscal and monetary policies will all impact upon the diffusion path, improvements in these areas will also impact upon a whole host of other aspects of the economy's performance. To use a plea for diffusion policy as a rationale for changes in such areas would be equivalent to the tail wagging the dog, and thus they fall outside the remit of this paper.

12.2.   The Theory of Diffusion Policy

The diffusion process is characterised by increases over time in both the number of firms using or owning a technology (inter firm diffusion) and more intensive use of the technology by the firm (intra firm diffusion). Technological diffusion takes time, with the period from the date of first use of a technology to the date of use, or ownership, of a technology by (say) 90 per cent of potential users possibly extending from five to fifty years (Mansfield, 1968).

The time path of ownership and use of a new technology will be the result of the interaction of supply and demand factors. Demand will be related to the intertemporal pattern of the costs of acquiring that technology. Supply will depend upon the costs of capital goods producers and their intertemporal pricing strategy. Any case for diffusion policy should therefore be built on an account of the peculiar aspects of the functioning of the markets for new technologies and their intertemporal patterns of change.

The benchmark according to which we should judge the need for and the effectiveness of diffusion policies is the welfare optimal diffusion path. On this path the rate of adoption maximises the net present value of the intertemporal stream of social costs and benefits. If the development path of a technology were predetermined and fixed, the optimal path of diffusion would be that path on which at any point in time the social benefit to be gained from the adoption of the technology by the marginal user in time t (as opposed to earlier or later) will equal the marginal social cost of producing the capital goods that embody that technology in time t. However, while the diffusion process is proceeding there is often a feedback from the profits generated during the earlier parts of the diffusion process into research and development, thereby generating both improvements in the production processes for the capital goods that embody the technology and in the technology itself. Partly as a result of these improvements, new technologies tend to become cheaper, at least in a quality adjusted sense, as diffusion proceeds. Taking this feedback loop into account considerably complicates the specification of the welfare optimal diffusion path benchmark.

The definition of a welfare optimal diffusion path implies that there may be situations when diffusion is too fast as well as occasions when diffusion is too slow. The idea of too fast a rate of diffusion for an economy often causes some consternation amongst policy makers for whom the principle that new technology should be introduced as quickly as possible is almost a statement of faith (usually on the grounds that use of new technology will increase competitiveness). However, in the absence of significant differences between private and social costs and benefits, a rate of diffusion that is too fast could result in firms adopting a technology before it has become profitable to do so or adopting a less well developed or higher priced technology today at the expense of adopting a more developed or cheaper technology in the future. If technologies are adopted before they become profitable then this will not improve competitiveness, and if adoption of today's technology delays adoption of tomorrow's technology, current competitiveness is being bought at the expense of future competitiveness (cf. Solow, 1963).

The welfare optimal diffusion path as defined above is optimal in the sense of Pareto. It may be argued that optimality defined in this sense is too weak and that it is important to take other criteria, in particular pertaining to the distribution of adoption benefits, into account when judging the optimality of a diffusion path. First, the market by itself may not provide a satisfactory distribution between present and future benefits, necessitating environmental policy and a stimulus for a speedier diffusion of sustainable technologies. Second, the market may not yield a geographically satisfactory distribution of benefits, suggesting support to technology diffusion on a regional basis. Third, the market may not yield a socially satisfactory distribution of benefits across industries or social classes, calling for industry specific support or government intervention in the direction of technological change (cf. Soete and Arundel, 1993). In general, different criteria yield different optimal diffusion paths and there is a trade-off between attainment of different distributional objectives. The significance to be attached to these objectives is a matter of political choice rather than economic analysis and therefore distributional criteria fall outside the scope of our brief.

Having defined an optimal diffusion path we need to explore why the actual diffusion path may differ from the optimal. In general terms the cause for sub-optimality is market failure. There are a number of sources of market failure endemic to the diffusion process, many of which echo issues that are also found in the R&D policy literature. The most obvious and most common source of market failure is the lack of enforceable property rights. As is well known, in the absence of property rights the market for an innovation might not even come into existence. Thus in a sense the most important diffusion policy must be patent protection, which enables the market for the innovation to exist by guaranteeing benefits to the creator of the innovation. This being covered in a literature of its own we shall not elaborate on patent policies here (see e.g. Kaufer, 1989); however, an aspect of the issue is discussed in the section on market structure below. Assuming the market for a specific new technology to exist, we deal with three main sources of market failures, imperfect information, market power and externalities, and consider each of these in turn.

12.2.1.   Imperfect information

Imperfect information is endemic to the process of technological change: in a fundamental way technology is information and markets for information are notorious for being imperfect (Arrow, 1962). The efficiency of a market for a new technology is, more than other markets, constrained by both information asymmetries and deficiencies. It should thus come as no surprise that in the face of imperfect information there should be welfare sub-optimality.

Typically, the available information on a given innovation changes over the course of the diffusion process. The literature considers three basic mechanisms by which information increases: (i) potential adopters acquire passively knowledge from the (costless) observation of the experience of actual adopters (cf. epidemic theory (e.g. Mansfield, 1968)), (ii) potential adopters acquire passively information from the promotional and other information spreading activities of capital goods suppliers (Glaister, 1974) and (iii) potential adopters undertake active search for information (Jensen, 1982, 1988). All three mechanisms are likely to give rise to market failure. For example, if late adopters learn from the experience of early adopters, then there is an externality deriving from the adoption of technology by early users. If firms recognise that they cannot fully appropriate the benefits of their expenses on adoption, they are likely to underinvest relative to the optimal rate. On the other hand if firms undertake active search there is the potential for unnecessary replication of search. With capital goods suppliers providing information one faces the same welfare issues as addressed by the literature on advertising (e.g. Dixit and Norman, 1978). To the extent that suppliers promote their own brands rather than the technology in general there is likely to be an oversupply of advertising. This will have the effect of bringing forward the use of technology relative to the welfare optimal path.

Information may be imperfect in the sense that the existence and the current character-istics of an innovation are not general knowledge; it may also be imperfect in the sense that expectations about the future technological improvement or the future acquisition cost of the innovation may be inaccurate. The optimal date of adoption of new technology for a firm will depend upon a profitability condition (whether it is profitable to adopt a techno-logy in time t) and upon an arbitrage condition (whether it is more profitable to wait until a later date before adoption). If the cost of acquisition is falling or the technology is improving over time the arbitrage condition subsumes the profitability condition (Ireland and Stoneman, 1986). The optimal date of adoption for the firm will be that date where the opportunity cost of waiting, the profit foregone from not having the technology, starts to fall short of the benefit of waiting, the possibility to acquire at a later date an improved technology at a cheaper price. If expectations with respect to the technological improvements or price reductions are too pessimistic, then adoption will take place too early from a welfare point of view, and vice versa.

Clearly, in the face of imperfect information, policy intervention in terms of information provision is desirable up to the point where the marginal social benefit of information provision is equal to the marginal social cost of that intervention. There is a very wide range of information related policies that may be, and often have been, used, e.g. demonstration projects and advertising campaigns, publicly funded technology monitoring exercises that inform industry of recent technology advances, public subsidy of consulting activities, public encouragement and subsidy of Science Parks and Technopolis concepts.

Information policies are generally favoured for, it might be argued, a better informed economy will be a better functioning economy. It is important to note, however, that information provision will not necessarily speed up diffusion. Assuming that agents are generally risk averse, more information will on average lead to earlier adoption. However, more information may also retard diffusion via its impact upon technological expectations. For example, a technology monitoring exercise may make adopters more aware of techno-logical advances still to come which may lead to a postponement of adoption in the expecta-tion of a better future technology.

Moreover, one must look carefully at whether such policies will actually work. The suppliers of capital goods that embody the new technology will, in a non perfectly competit-ive market, spread information and advertise themselves. The public provision of informa-tion will tend to crowd out the private provision (see Stoneman and David, 1986). However, the more the supply industry tends to a perfectly competitive structure, the less private provision there will be (Gibbons, 1989) and thus the less probability there is of public provision leading to a reduction in private provision. Also, if potential adopters are under-taking active search, a policy initiative involving public information provision will feed back upon this search effort, and it is the net effect that must be considered in the evaluation of policies.

Supplying information to the market is only one option in countering market failure originating from imperfect information. Such market failure could also be dealt with by shifting the burden of the risk which results from imperfect information (at least as far as it cannot be insured against) towards the public sector. Policies to shift risk are frequently discussed relating to R&D, but rarely examined in terms of their impact upon technological diffusion. Policies similar to the UK Aerospace Launch Aid programme could in principle be used to stimulate diffusion with the government acting as a risk carrier. The usual problem with such policies, i.e. the problems of moral hazard, would exist in the case of diffusion policies as in the case of other policies.

A third policy option for government is to reduce uncertainty by 'creating' information. This would happen, for example, if the government imposes a technical standard on the market. It is generally the case that, in their early stages of development, new technologies appear in many variations that are often not cross compatible. Over time (possibly as the number of suppliers in the market is reduced) an industry standard will be established. However, there is no guarantee that the standard that the free market establishes will be optimal (see Arthur, 1988, 1989; David, 1985), nor that the timing of its establishment will be optimal. During the period before a standard is established, potential adopters face the risk of opting for the wrong standard. The uncertainty can have a crippling effect on diffusion.

There is a reasonably long history of governments being involved in standard setting. David (1987) argues that, in standard setting, government intervention would be most cost effective at the start of the diffusion process but that is exactly when government is least informed and thus is most liable to make mistakes. Moreover, the selection of a standard by government may be politically embarrassing, possibly creating 'angry orphans' who have invested in a standard that is not chosen.

12.2.2.   Market structure

Both the market structure of the supplying industry and of the using industry may generate market failure. If the supply industry is perfectly competitive but the number of potential users is finite then common pool problems may arise (Ireland and Stoneman, 1986). One may think of the potential buyers of a new technology as representing a pool of limited size, and that a sale made by one supplier is a sale lost (in perpetuity) by another supplier. This will lead sellers to attempt sales before rivals and, as is well known, such common pool problems generate diffusion paths that are too fast from a welfare point of view. In essence, the sellers are interested in who sells to a user whereas society is interested only in whether the user acquires and not from whom.

More often the supplying industry is concentrated. In essence we may think of the producers of capital goods that embody new technology as determining an intertemporal price path for the technology subject to the time path of the costs of production and the intertemporal demand pattern. If the supplier is a monopolist that monopolist will attempt to price discriminate intertemporally. The extent to which this can be successful depends upon the (price and technology) expectations of buyers (see Ireland and Stoneman, 1986). If buyers hold myopic expectations the monopolist can perfectly intertemporally price discriminate and thus through his actions will maximise the sum of consumer and producer surplus and generate the welfare optimal diffusion path. If buyers do not hold myopic expectations then they will be expecting prices to change (fall) over time and this will limit the extent to which the monopolist can perfectly intertemporally discriminate. In fact non-myopic expectations will delay the adoption of technology and as a result produce a diffusion path that is too slow from a welfare point of view.

The two factors, market structure of the supply industry and expectations on the using side may act in opposite directions. Myopic expectations tend to speed up the diffusion path, monopoly structures tend to slow down the diffusion path. Different combinations of expectations regimes and supply side market power may generate a welfare optimal diffusion path (cf. Ireland and Stoneman, 1986), but obviously with radically different profit distributions. Under perfect competition the suppliers make zero (abnormal) profits, whereas under monopoly the supplier makes monopoly profits.

The market structure of the using industry will also affect the incentives to adopt a new technology. However the diffusion literature has little to add over and above that found in the R&D literature which looks at the incentives to firms to undertake R&D given that those incentives arise from the introduction of the new technology that the R&D generates. The R&D literature is inconclusive as to whether concentrated structures generate the greater incentive. Some argue that more competition produces greater incentives to innovate (Arrow, 1962), some that monopoly power is a necessary condition for innovativeness (Schumpeterian theory, see e.g. Kamien and Schwartz, 1982) and some that the truth is in the middle (Scherer, 1980). Important assumptions explaining the differences in results pertain to the likelihood of technology spill-overs and to capital availability. Empirical evidence on the issue is conflicting (Cohen and Levin, 1989). From a welfare point of view the literature is equally inconclusive on whether private incentives are greater or less than is socially desirable and there are thus few conclusions that one can draw.

Overall, there is no clear prediction in the literature as to which market structure will generate an optimal diffusion path. The 'best' structure will depend upon other factors such as expectations formation processes, imperfect information and so on. One cannot thus make simple predictions as to how monopoly and mergers policy, or subsidies to users, can be manipulated to improve economic welfare through its impact on the diffusion path. It is, however, often argued that the patent system, which is principally designed to yield a return to the inventor's innovative efforts, generates a welfare cost in that the monopoly created by the patent slows the diffusion path. The literature and our discussion above support the view that monopoly supply will slow the diffusion path. However, as stated above, in some circumstances the diffusion path is too fast and thus the impact of the patent system may in fact be welfare improving through its impact on the diffusion path as well as through the stimulus that it gives to the R&D process.

12.2.3. Externalities

If the adoption of a technology by one firm impacts upon the profits of all other firms, where these external impacts are not being accounted for in the single firm's decision to adopt, then there are negative externalities to adoption. Adoption of technology by one firm may impact negatively on profits of competitors and on their gain in profit from adoption if early adoption leads to preemption, i.e. there are first mover advantages of some sort to adoption. Under such conditions adopters high in the adoption order receive greater returns than firms lower in the order of adoption (see Fudenberg and Tirole, 1985). Such a framework obviously leads to modelling the diffusion process as a race, and as such will have similar welfare effects to those discussed in the literature on patent races: the diffusion speed is likely to be higher than optimal from a welfare point of view. Two types of policy are usually advocated to deal with negative externalities: taxing the origin of the externality and creating or changing ownership rights to internalise the externality. To the best of our knowledge, neither of these lines of approach have been explored in this context.

Besides and sometimes in addition to negative externalities, a firm's adoption of an innovation may also give rise to positive externalities. These may be of two kinds. On the one hand, adoption can generate information flows which may spill over to the rest of the industry. Above we noted that this is one way in which available information increases along the diffusion path. On the other hand, technologies may have network characteristics that give rise to positive externalities. In this situation the benefits from adoption increase with the number of users. Obvious examples are telephones and fax machines, where the gain from ownership of the technology depends upon the number of other users connected to the network. However, many modern production technologies require skilled labour, software or a service network to operate efficiently, or require standardised inputs and produce standardised outputs, and as such the number of technologies with network traits may be vast and increasing, and positive network externalities may be much more prominent than often recognised. If a network technology comes into existence that it would be desirable for society to diffuse on a wide scale, it is quite possible that, left to the market, the diffusion process will not start, or takes off too slowly, because first users would not find it profitable to install the technology given the size (and their expectations of size) of the network at the date of the decision to install (Katz and Shapiro, 1985, 1986).

Appropriate policy would involve support for early adopters and may take the form of subsidies (or tax benefits) or the provision of network infrastructure (e.g. Minitel in France). For some technologies government procurement may be a proper instrument to help a technology take off, or early setting of standards (e.g. high definition television). Direct support may be given as subsidies to producers or to users of a new technology. The effectiveness of subsidies to users will depend on the extent to which subsidies will cause producers of the new technology to change the prices they charge (Stoneman and David, 1986). Producers' price setting may counteract the intent of the policy. However, if the subsidy feeds into higher profits for producers this may lead to further technological development and thereby stimulate further diffusion.

The effectiveness of subsidy policy will depend on the time profile of the subsidy. If potential buyers do not have myopic expectations the imposition of a subsidy will change their expectation of the intertemporal price profile. If the subsidy is to exist for a limited period this may well bring forward adoption of the technology by firms. If the subsidy is to last in perpetuity the intertemporal price pattern may be little affected and thus the subsidy will have only a limited impact on the diffusion path. If a subsidy is expected to appear at some future date this will lead to delayed adoption today.

In addition there are strategic issues involved in expectations of policy interventions. The return to early adopters of a technology is related to the rate at which other potential users adopt that technology, as later users reduce the return to early adopters. Therefore expectations of a subsidy, or any other policy incentive that will increase the number of users, will reduce the expected return to early users. This in turn may discourage early adopters. Thus any policy is bound to have a complex impact upon the diffusion path. Directly the policy may stimulate use, but indirectly, by reducing the incentives for firms to adopt because of the greater (expected) number of other users, part (or all) of the direct impact may be offset by indirect responses.

12.2.4. Diffusion in a wider perspective

Thus far we have implicitly taken technology adoption to be identical to acquisition of a (capital) good in which new technology is embodied. We have based our case for diffusion policy on an analysis of market failure in markets for embodied innovations. However, technologies are not always embodied and do not always diffuse by means of trade (Arrow, 1993). There is a growing stream of literature that recognises that often the diffusion of new technology is not purely a matter of buying capital equipment off the shelf. Often the decision to adopt a certain technology is only one element of a coherent strategy and the problem of technology diffusion is therefore wider than the issues surrounding the market for a single innovation.

In many cases technology has to be adapted to individual firms' requirements (Gold, 1981). Especially in its early years of development, technology is often purpose designed and built. In addition, firms need to expand resources adapting their organisation, upgrading their knowledge base, training their labour force and restructuring their work methods to suit the new technology. Any new technology that a firm introduces has to fit in with other practices in the same part and in other parts of the firm. In particular, a new technology may be a substitute or a complement to techniques currently in use. Therefore the adoption decisions concerning different technologies at different moments in time are bound to be interdependent (see Stoneman and Kwon, 1994 for empirical evidence supporting this assertion).

A wider concept of technology adoption is also at the basis of the recent literature on the relationship of a firm's capacity to engage in R&D and its likelihood to adopt an innovation (Cohen and Levinthal, 1989). R&D generates the knowledge required internally for the monitoring, evaluation and adaptation of new technologies as they become available from outside sources. The literature on learning by doing and on learning by using stresses similar issues: the efficiency and profitability of an innovation is developed over time, both by suppliers and in the using firm, but at a resource cost. Acquisition of a capital good embodying an innovation is thus only a first step in a learning process meant to generate information, extend knowledge and develop skills.

An account of diffusion that centres on such a broader perspective is also emerging from evolutionary theory. This theory starts from the assertion that at any point in time firms are heterogeneous in their knowledge base, in their capabilities to take informed decisions and in their abilities to operate specific technologies. Consequently, they use different technologies, attain different levels of efficiency, and as a result generate different rates of profit. Firms expand by reinvesting profits in the technologies in which they have developed expertise. Therefore those using the most profitable technologies grow fastest. As successful firms expand and product prices fall, firms with inferior technologies see their profit margins squeezed and disappear from the market. A diffusion path results as the inefficient are weeded out and the efficient come to dominate the industry. Thus non-simultaneous adoption from an evolutionary viewpoint is not primarily a process driven by the market for an innovation, but arises as firms' growth rates differ, which is a consequence of heterogeneity of internal developments within firms (see Metcalfe, 1988, 1995; Silverberg *et al.*, 1988).

The importance of this broader perspective on diffusion (a systems approach, in the words of Soete and Arundel (1993)) is that the determinants of the speed of diffusion, and thus the answer to whether diffusion is too fast or too slow, are to be found, not only on the market for the innovation itself, but also in markets for related technologies, in the internal structure of the firm itself, in its current technology, in the flexibility of its organisation and in its capability to learn. However, the implications of taking this wider view on the issues of diffusion policy are not straightforward. First, as adoption decisions on different techno-logies are interdependent, the argument for government intervention, based on an analysis of the market for a single innovation, may need to be extended to include a complex of markets. Second, if diffusion and R&D are interrelated processes, then this indicates that R&D policies may well impact upon diffusion paths by stimulating a firm's learning and monitoring capacities. Third, if a firm's knowledge base is a key element in its ability to adopt an innovation and to do so at the optimal moment, then all policies affecting this knowledge base, ranging from labour market regulations to educational policies, impinge on diffusion.

12.3. The Practice of Diffusion Policy

Given that there is a serious theoretical case for diffusion policy, it is surprising to find that in fact there are very few policy initiatives in developed countries aimed at tuning the speed of innovation diffusion (patent laws apart). What schemes there are largely counter prob-lems of imperfect information and are directed at small and medium size enterprises. All such schemes are assumed (and designed) to increase the speed of technology diffusion. In many countries regional innovation centres have been set up giving mainly consultancy support to small and medium sized enterprises (e.g. the Advanced Information Technology Programme and the Regional Office Technology Transfer Programme in the United King-dom and the Centres Regionaux d'Innovation et de Transfert de Technologie in France). Some initiatives have been launched by the European Union, e.g. the SPRINT programme. There have been programmes to facilitate the adoption of specific techniques (e.g. the CIM initiative in Germany). There have been attempts to cluster firms in particular spatial locations in order to encourage the interchange of knowledge and ideas (business parks or technology parks), and there are attempts to stimulate formation of networks (like Research and Technology Organisations and (proposed) Faraday Institutes in the United Kingdom) and to link science and technology more closely (cf. UK Government White Paper on Science and Technology, 1993). The latter is expected to induce technologists to increase the use of scientific advances (although a technological expectations effect may delay use), but also to lead science to generate technologies that are more 'applicable'. It is not clear, however, that the incentive structure for science will necessarily ensure this outcome (see Dasgupta, 1987; Dasgupta and David, 1993), the scientific incentive structure being more closely tied to publications than generating competitiveness.

However, although there are few policy initiatives (and these are usually of relatively minor size in budget terms) aimed specifically at changing the speed of technology diffusion, diffusion of many innovations is strongly affected by public policy. There is a whole range of 'diffusion policies in disguise' that have other objectives but have a major impact on diffusion. Three examples will suffice to illustrate our point. First, after the virtual shake out of the UK motor industry in the early eighties, UK policy on direct foreign investment from Japan was intended to create employment in the United Kingdom in Japanese owned car manufacturing enterprises. The presence of Japanese car manufacturing plants in the United Kingdom has given an enormous impetus to technology diffusion in the indigenous motor firms, to the extent that in ten years they have managed to regain their competitive edge on the European market (see Mair, 1994). Second, European agricultural policy, intended to guarantee income levels of European farmers, has given such an impetus to technology diffusion in agriculture that the sector produces surpluses that cannot be disposed of on world markets. Thirdly, for all kinds of reasons governments in many countries tend to intervene heavily in the budgets administered to the health care system. This has tended to stimulate rapid diffusion of health technologies in hospitals (e.g. Eastaugh, 1990; Wilensky, 1990). Obviously, many other policies have a major impact on innovation diffusion, like R&D policies, industrial policies, policies on education, on infrastructure and public transport, on employment and industrial relations, on tariffs, on accounting rules (depreciation) and on environmental protection, but a full discussion of these is beyond the scope of this paper.

For an evaluation of diffusion policy one would wish to judge whether the costs incurred by government in pursuing the policy are greater or less than the welfare increases generated by the policy. There have been no evaluations of actual diffusion policies in such terms. The DTI in the United Kingdom, for example, legitimates its diffusion policy with reference to market failure but evaluates its diffusion programmes predominantly in terms of the efficiency of their management, the accuracy of their targeting, the appropriateness of their tool mix and the appreciation of the recipients of information (see DTI, 1987, 1992, 1993). More importantly, however, the 'disguised diffusion policies' alluded to above, which have influenced the speed and also the extent of diffusion of certain innovations merely as a side effect, are never evaluated in terms of the efficiency of the diffusion path. So it could happen that the rapid diffusion of car manufacturing technology in the UK motor industry came as a pleasant but unexpected surprise, that the costly technical overcapacity in European farming came as an unforeseen long lasting burden, and that certain health technologies have been too widely diffused, contributing to growing concerns over the rising costs and overall efficiency of health care provision.

12.4.   Conclusion

In this paper we argued that on the basis of market failure a good case can be made for public policy aimed at tuning the speed of diffusion. Market failure may arise from imperfect information, as a consequence of market structure or because there are externalities to adoption. Moreover, sub-optimality may also originate from other sources. It is important to take account of the fact that the adoption of any specific technology is only one element in a firm's strategy to increase its competitiveness. The decision to adopt one innovation is therefore linked to other technology adoptions, to R&D efforts, to learning and skill management and to other strategic choices.

We discussed a range of possible diffusion policies but have noted that although there are good reasons for having such policies, there are few explicit diffusion policies in existence (although there are many other policies that effect diffusion), and those that do exist have rarely been properly evaluated.

It is our view that diffusion policy merits as much emphasis as R&D policy (if not more), but that diffusion policy should not proceed upon a presumption that faster is always better nor that only an information providing policy is required. The tapestry of the economic and social environment within which technological change takes place is rich and varied and it is necessary that any policy adequately reflects the diversity and heterogeneity of markets, environments, and objectives.

References

Arrow, K.J. (1962) 'Economic welfare and the allocation of resources to invention.' In *The Rate and Direction of Inventive Activity* (ed. R.R. Nelson). New York: Princeton University Press.

Arrow, K.J. (1993) 'The production and distribution of knowledge.' In *The Economics of Growth and Technical Change; Technologies, Nations, Agents* (ed. G. Silverberg and L. Soete). Cheltenham: Edward Elgar.

Arthur, W.B. (1988) 'Competing technologies.' In *Technical Change and Economic Theory* (ed. G. Dosi, C. Freeman, R. Nelson, G. Silverberg and L. Soete). London: Pinter Publishers.

Arthur, W.B. (1989) 'Competing technologies, increasing returns, and lock-in by historical events.' *Economic Journal*, 99, 116–31.

Cabinet Office (1993) *Realising our Potential, A Strategy for Science, Engineering and Technology*. London: HMSO.

Cohen, W.M. and Levin, R.C. (1989) 'Empirical studies of innovation and market structure.' In *Handbook of Industrial Organization* (ed. R. Schmalensee and R.D. Willig). Amsterdam: North Holland.

Cohen, W.M. and Levinthal, D.A. (1989) 'Innovation and learning: the two faces of R&D.' *Economic Journal*, 99, 569–96.

Dasgupta, P. (1987) 'The economic theory of technology policy: an introduction.' In *Economic Policy and Technological Performance* (ed. P. Dasgupta and P. Stoneman). Cambridge: Cambridge University Press.

Dasgupta, P. and David, P. (1993) *Toward a New Economics of Science*. Stanford University: Center for Economic Policy Research, mimeo, May.

David, P.A. (1985) 'Clio and the economics of QWERTY.' *American Economic Review*, 75, 332–7.

David, P.A. (1987) 'Some new standards for the economics of standardization in the information age.' In *Economic Policy and Technological Performance* (ed. P. Dasgupta and P. Stoneman). Cambridge: Cambridge University Press.

Department of Trade and Industry (1987) *An Evaluation of the Manufacturing Advisory Service*. Assessment Paper no. 1, London.

Department of Trade and Industry (1992) *A Review of the Technology Transfer and Awareness Mechanisms used by the DTI*. Assessment Paper no. 18, London.

Department of Trade and Industry (1993) *An Evaluation of the Regional Office Technology Transfer Programme*. Assessment Paper no. 21, London.

Dixit, A. and Norman, G. (1978) 'Advertising and welfare.' *Bell Journal of Economics*, 9, 1–17.

Eastaugh, S.R. (1990) 'Financing the correct rate of growth of medical technology.' *Quarterly Review of Economics and Business*, 30, 54–60.

Fudenberg, D. and Tirole, J. (1985) 'Pre-emption and rent equalization in the adoption of new technology.' *Review of Economic Studies*, 52, 383–401.

Gibbons, A.M. (1989) 'The diffusion of new consumer durables and the role of advertising.' University of Warwick, Ph.D. Thesis.

Glaister, S. (1974) 'Advertising policy and returns to scale in markets where information is passed between individuals.' *Economica*, 41, 139–56.

Gold, B. (1981) 'Technological diffusion in industry: research needs and shortcomings.' *The Journal of Industrial Economics*, 29, 247–69.

Ireland, N. and Stoneman, P. (1986) 'Technological diffusion, expectations and welfare.' *Oxford Economic Papers*, 38, 283–304.

Jensen, R. (1982) 'Adoption and diffusion of an innovation of uncertain profitability.' *Journal of Economic Theory*, 27, 182–93.

Jensen, R. (1988) 'Information cost and innovation adoption policies.' *Management Science*, 34, 230–9.

Kamien, M.I. and Schwartz, N.L. (1982) *Market Structure and Innovation*. Cambridge: Cambridge University Press.

Katz, M.L. and Shapiro, C. (1985) 'Network externalities, competition, and compatibility.' *American Economic Review*, 75(3), 424–40.

Katz, M.L. and Shapiro, C. (1986) 'Technology adoption in the presence of network externalities.' *Journal of Political Economy*, 94, 822–41.

Kaufer, E. (1989) *The Economics of the Patent System*. London: Harwood Academic Press.

Limpens, I., Verspagen, B. and Beelen, E. (1992) *Technology Policy in Eight European Countries: A Comparison*. Report. Maastricht: MERIT.

Mair, A. (1994) *Honda's Global Local Corporation*. Basingstoke: Macmillan, and New York: St Martins.

Mansfield, E. (1968) *Industrial Research and Technological Innovation*. New York: Norton.

Metcalfe, J.S. (1988) 'The diffusion of innovations: an interpretative survey.' In *Technical Change and Economic Theory* (ed. G. Dosi, C. Freeman, R. Nelson, G. Silverberg and L. Soete). London: Pinter Publishers.

Metcalfe, J.S. (1995) 'The economic foundations of technological policy: equilibrium and evolutionary perspectives.' In *Handbook of the Economics of Innovation and Technical Change* (ed. P. Stoneman). Oxford: Blackwell.

Rogers, E.M. (1983) *Diffusion of Innovations*. New York: Free Press.

Scherer, F.M. (1980) *Industrial Market Structure and Economic Performance*. Chicago: Rand McNally.

Silverberg, G. (1991) 'Adoption and diffusion of technology as a collective evolutionary process.' In *Diffusion of Technologies and Social Behaviour* (ed. N. Nakicenovic and A. Grübler). Berlin: IIASA and Springer Verlag.

Silverberg, G., Dosi, G. and Orsenigo, L. (1988) 'Innovation, diversity and diffusion: a self-organisation model.' *Economic Journal*, 98, 1032–54.

Soete, L. and Arundel, A. (1993) *An Integrated Approach to European Innovation and Technology Diffusion Policy*. Brussels: Commission of the European Communities.

Solow, R.M. (1963) *Capital Theory and the Rate of Return*. Amsterdam: North Holland.

Stoneman, P. and David, P.A. (1986) 'Adoption subsidies vs. information provision as instruments of technology policy.' *Economic Journal*, 96, Supplement (March), 142–51.

Stoneman, P. (1987) *The Economic Analysis of Technology Policy*. Oxford: Oxford University Press.

Stoneman, P. and Kwon, M.J. (1994) 'The diffusion of multiple process technologies.' *Economic Journal*, 104, 420–31.

Wilensky, G.R. (1990) 'Technology as culprit and benefactor.' *Quarterly Review of Economics and Business*, 30, 45–53.

Chapter thirteen
Technological Diffusion, Expectations and Welfare

Co-written with N. Ireland

13.1. Introduction

The analysis of the process by which new technology spreads across an economy is still in its infancy. Despite a growing interest in the subject there remain many unanswered questions. This paper is concerned with two of these questions. The first concerns the role of expectations in the diffusion process, and the second, the 'optimal' rate of take up of a new technology.

Rosenberg (1976) has discussed the role of expectations in technological diffusion at some length. In essence we may think of there being two variables on which expectations may be formed: price and technology. Rosenberg's argument is that for a given current price and technology, the lower is the expected future price or the more improvements are expected in technology in the future, the greater is the likelihood that a potential adopter of the new technology will delay adoption. Thus expectations will affect the diffusion path. As examples, one may consider the purchase of a calculator three or four years ago or a personal computer today. One's predictions on future changes in price and technology definitely seem to impinge on the decision whether to buy or to wait.

Our first task is to investigate these propositions of Rosenberg. They require further investigation because:

a) the above arguments take current price as given. We need therefore to explore the impact of expectations on current prices before any definitive statements on their effect can be made. This requires an investigation of the whole time profile of prices over the diffusion rather than taking a snapshot of any one particular point on the diffusion path.

b) Rosenberg's arguments suggest that diffusion is delayed by expectations of price falls or technology improvements. It does not tell us anything of the end point of the diffusion process in the sense of whether the introduction of expectations will lead to more or less use as the limit of the process is reached, or whether the limit of the process occurs earlier or later in time.

To investigate such issues we have to be more formal than Rosenberg. In an earlier paper (Stoneman and Ireland, 1983)[1] it was argued that a demand-oriented diffusion model

Reprinted from *Oxford Economic Papers*, 38, 283–304, 1986, by kind permission of Oxford University Press.

(e.g. that generated by David, 1969 and Davies, 1979) is insufficient by itself to fully determine the diffusion path (even with specific expectations formation functions included) until the time profile of prices can be specified. We thus proceed by jointly modelling a supply sector with a demand side consisting of buyers with appropriate adoption rules; the interaction of supply and demand generating a time profile of prices.

The new technology is assumed to be embodied in a new product manufactured by the supplying industry. If the new product is a new consumer good then the potential buyers are households and we label this case product innovation. If the new product is a producer good the potential buyers are firms and we label this case process innovation. In our modelling of the demand side below the product/process distinction is not an important one. The model we build could apply to either, although as we shall see, there are certain characteristics that may favour a product innovation interpretation.

On the expectations side we have two variables on which buyers and sellers can form expectations; technology and price. On technology we may consider two dimensions; the first is the potential improvement in the quality of the product the diffusion of which is being analysed; the second is the potential appearance of a completely new product causing obsolescence. We explicitly consider the latter but only implicitly include the former to the extent that prices can be defined as quality adjusted. The prospect of obsolescence is incorporated by allowing potential purchasers and suppliers to hold subjective probabilities on the date of obsolescence of the technology under consideration. Variations in the 'hazard rate' thus incorporated in the model are used to represent variations in the expectation of future technological changes.

On the price side we incorporate within the adoption choice rule explicit price expectation formation hypotheses. These are all of a genre whereby prices are forecast for period $t + 1$ based on information available at time t. The several approaches investigated include myopia, perfect foresight, adaptive expectations, and Goodwin (or μ) expectations. To demonstrate the differences in results due to expectations formation hypotheses, we concentrate on the first two approaches but we also discuss specific points relating to the diffusion process under other expectations regimes. This analysis is pursued in section 13.3.

Although, as we shall show, expectations play an important role in determining the diffusion path, the whole area of the diffusion of new technology, both when expectations are considered or ignored, also raises a number of welfare and policy questions. Thus in section 13.4 we present an initial attempt to approach some policy issues concerning the optimal diffusion path and subsidisation of the use of new technology. In section 13.5 we investigate further the issues under discussion by relaxing an earlier assumption that for process innovation the size of the user industry is exogenous. This allows parallels to be drawn between our work and the seminal Arrow (1962) paper on the incentives to R&D. Also, the welfare analysis of section 13.4 is extended to incorporate the welfare effects of induced changes in the size of the using industry. Section 13.6 summarises our conclusions.

13.2. Demand

13.2.1. The expected return from acquisition

We consider a new product that can be viewed as either a producer or consumer good. In the latter case, the potential buyers are households, in the former case firms. In either case we consider that if a potential buyer purchases the product he or she will only buy one unit. (Although this is a rather restrictive assumption, in the case of process innovations it is in the tradition of similar work on such models by e.g. David, 1969, and in the case of product innovations may not be too inappropriate, e.g. video recorders). We will assume that the number of potential buyers is fixed at N, although we will explore the possibilities of relaxing this assumption in section 13.5. We further assume no depreciation prior to obsolescence and thus that buyers receive a constant flow of services from the new technology from the time of purchase until the technology is rendered obsolescent, when the flow is reduced to zero. The assumption of a constant flow of services may be more appropriate to the case of a consumer good than a producer good, for the return to a particular firm may reduce as other firms adopt the technology. However, this possibility is approached in section 13.5, and we also discuss it further in a separate paper (Ireland and Stoneman, 1985). David and Olsen (1984) also consider this possibility.

We will index buyers in decreasing order of the size of their service flow and assume a sufficiently large number of potential buyers for this index to be represented as continuous. Thus the buyer with index x obtains a constant flow of services or benefit of value $g(x)$ per period until obsolescence. The ordering of buyers then implies that $g_x < 0$.

Previous work in this tradition has tended to derive the $g(x)$ function from considering the characteristics across which users differ. For example, if the benefits of new technology are related to firm size, then from the firm size distribution one obtains a distribution of benefits, the inverse of the cumulative distribution of which is the $g(x)$ function. It has always been taken that the characteristic distribution is continuous and sufficiently dense to yield a $g(x)$ function in which x can be considered a continuous variable. We are just following the tradition, without making explicit the characteristics that matter.

The assumption of a continuum of buyers is obviously reasonable for the case of the diffusion of a new consumer product, but it may somewhat restrict the general applicability of our model to process innovations. We will return a little later to consider the additional problems which may arise from the case where N is not large, and thus where x may not be continuous.

Given that the benefit to the xth indexed user from buying is thus $g(x)$ for each period prior to obsolescence, we further assume (1) that after the date of obsolescence, the benefits reduce to zero and (2) that buyers hold expectations on the date of obsolescence, each agent (buyer or seller) holding the same expectations. Specifically the date of obsolescence is considered as a random variable. Let $s(t)$ be agents' subjective probability that obsolescence will occur by time t. Assume that $s(t)$ follows the differential equation

$$Ds(t) = h(1 - s(t)) \tag{13.1}$$

where D is the differential operator with respect to time, and h is the probability that obsolescence will occur in the interval $\{t, t + dt\}$ given that obsolescence has not occurred at t. We assume h (termed a hazard rate in reliability theory, see Barlow and Proschan, 1965) is constant over time. The solution to (13.1) given that $S(0) = 0$ is

$$1 - s(t) = e^{-ht} \tag{13.2}$$

Defining $r = r' + h$, where r' is the certainty discount rate and r is the discount rate adjusted for the hazard of obsolescence, we may write that the expected profit for the xth indexed user from buying in time t, given that obsolescence has not occurred by t, is

$$E(\pi(t, x)) = -p(t) + \int_t^\infty g(x)e^{-r(\tau-t)}\,d\tau$$

$$= -p(t) + \frac{g(x)}{r} \tag{13.3}$$

where $p(t)$ is the price of the new good in time t.

It is clear that a necessary condition for the xth indexed buyer to purchase the technology in time t given risk neutrality is that (13.3) is non-negative. This condition, however, will not generally be sufficient.

13.2.2.   The role of price expectations

We now further assume that the purchase decision cannot be reversed. The potential purchaser must thus decide, even if (13.3) is non-negative, whether it is worth waiting to a later period in order to obtain greater profits from ownership. If, without loss of generality, we consider the present time as zero, and define

$$E(\Pi(x)) = \left\{ -p(t) + \frac{g(x)}{r} \right\} e^{-rt} \tag{13.4}$$

then the additional condition for a risk-neutral buyer with index x to adopt in time t is that (13.4) is expected to not increase with time. Thus we have two conditions to be satisfied for adoption in time t:

$$-p(t) + \frac{g(x)}{r} \geq 0 \quad \text{(profitability condition)} \tag{13.5(i)}$$

$$-D\hat{p}(t) + rp(t) - g(x) \leq 0 \quad \text{(arbitrage condition)} \tag{13.5(ii)}$$

Condition 13.5(ii) includes the term $D\hat{p}(t)$. This is a continuous time representation of the buyers' expectation of the change in price (equivalent in discrete time to the price expected to hold in period $t + 1$, minus the price holding in time t). Throughout the paper we use such continuous time approximations to discrete time expectations models to simplify the analysis. We may thus in the case of process innovation, interpret 13.5(i) and 13.5(ii) as implying that acquisition will occur in time t by the xth ranked buyer if the technology is profitable and if profitability is not expected to increase (in the sense that it is believed that the purchase price will fall by less than the flow of benefits $(g(x) - rp(t))$.[2] Note that it is immediate from 13.5(i) and 13.5(ii) that buyers will adopt in the order of this index. It is also clear, given buyers purchase only one unit, that the rank of the marginal buyer in time t, $x(t)$, will also represent the cumulative output (stock) of new products at time t, which will also equal the number of adopters at time t.

Given 13.5(i) and 13.5(ii) we may now proceed to define the different expectations models. We will concentrate on two models, and leave comments on others until after developing these.

(1) Myopia. Under myopic assumptions the currently observed price is expected to hold forever, in which case $D\hat{p}(t) = 0$. If $D\hat{p}(t) = 0$, then 13.5(i) and 13.5(ii) are identical and thus the xth indexed buyer will purchase the technology at the first t when $rp(t) = g(x)$.

(2) Perfect foresight. If we assume that the complete price path is announced by the sellers of the new technology *ab initio* and no deviations are permitted[3] we can credit the buyers of the new technology with perfect foresight and thus assume $D\hat{p}(t) = Dp(t)$. In this case given, as we will argue in the next section, $D(p(t)) < 0$, 13.5(ii) holding as an equality implies 13.5(i) satisfied but not vice versa. Thus 13.5(ii) as an equality defines the dynamic demand for the technology.

From 13.5(i) and 13.5(ii) we may derive a generalised dynamic demand function (13.6)

$$-Dp + rp = \alpha g_x Q + \beta g(x) \qquad (13.6)$$

where $Q = Dx$ is the current rate of industry sales. Under myopia, 13.5(i) is binding so that $p = g(x)/r$ and (13.6) has the parameters, $\alpha = -1/r$, $\beta = 1$, yielding (13.7m). Under perfect foresight 13.5(ii) is binding so (13.6) has the parameters $\alpha = 0$, $\beta = 1$ yielding (13.7pf)

$$-Dp + rp = g(x) - g_x Q/r \qquad (13.7m)$$

$$-Dp + rp = g(x) \qquad (13.7pf)$$

The generalised dynamic demand function (13.6) thus incorporates (13.7m) and (13.7pf) as special cases, and as we shall see below will also incorporate other expectations regimes as special cases.

13.3.   The Diffusion of Technology

13.3.1.   The supplying industry

We will assume that the supplying industry is composed of n quantity-setting, identical firms, each maximising its expected profit given the behaviour of the other $(n - 1)$ firms. Assuming that product obsolescence renders future profits zero, expected profit of a typical seller is simply

$$E(\Pi s) = \int_0^\infty (p(t) - c(t))q(t)\mathrm{e}^{-rt}\, \mathrm{d}t \qquad (13.8)$$

where $r = r' + h$ as defined before, $q(t)$ is the output of the firm in time t and $c(t)$ is unit cost. We assume that, while production takes place, unit cost falls until some time, $\hat{t}$, after which it increases i.e. $Dc(t) \lessgtr 0$ as $t \lessgtr \hat{t}$. The reduction prior to $\hat{t}$ may be considered a simple reflection of learning by doing, and the limit to this learning and its subsequent reversal may be considered to reflect increasing costs (as the age of design increases) relative to a general index of products. Of course obsolescence may occur before $\hat{t}$ is reached.

The supplying firms will produce, providing earlier obsolescence does not occur, until some time t_1, after which production will cease, and no further purchases can be made. The terminal condition that will hold at t_1, is that for the marginal (last) buyer 13.5(i) is zero. If the latter's index is x_1 then

$$p(t_1) = g(x_1)/r \qquad (13.9)$$

On the assumption that the supplying firms are profit maximisers, each producer will maximise (13.8). The integral in (13.8) can now be curtailed to limits between 0 and t_1 and then integrated by parts to obtain

$$E(\Pi_s) = (p(t_1) - c(t_1))(x_1 - y_1)\,\mathrm{e}^{-rt_1} + \int_0^{t_1} (-Dp + rp + Dc - rc)(x - y)\mathrm{e}^{-rt}\mathrm{d}t \qquad (13.10)$$

In (13.10) time arguments have been dropped where their existence is obvious, and y is defined as the sales until time t of all other suppliers i.e. $yn = (n - 1)x$ given the assumption of symmetry. It is now assumed that the supplying firms have complete knowledge of buyers' behaviour. An open loop equilibrium then occurs when each supplier maximises (13.10) by the choice of its own output path, given (13.6), (13.9) and the output trajectory of other suppliers.

The derivation of the optimal supply trajectories and associated paths for price and output obtained from (13.6), (13.9) and (13.10) is delegated to appendix 13. The optimal path may involve some initial jump in sales to the optimal initial level (this is also discussed in appendix 13), after which the two trajectories for myopia and perfect foresight can be characterised by

$$\text{Myopia: } g(x) = rc - Dc + \frac{n-1}{n} \cdot Q \cdot g_x/r \qquad (13.11\text{m})$$

$$g(x_1) = rc(t_1) \qquad (13.12\text{m})$$

$$\text{Perfect Foresight: } g(x) = rc - Dc - g_x x/n \qquad (13.11\text{pf})$$

$$g(x_1) = rc(t_1) - g_{x_1} x_1/n \qquad (13.12\text{pf})$$

Equation (13.11) characterises the diffusion path for $t < t_1$ and equation (13.12) defines a terminal surface.

13.3.2.   Diffusion under monopolised supply conditions

First, consider the optimal paths when there is a single supplier ($n = 1$). In fig. 13.1, we plot in the right hand diagram two curves, the first being rc, the second $rc - Dc$. Given $Dc(\hat{t}) = 0$, the curves intersect at $\hat{t}$. Given also that $Dc(t) \lessgtr 0$ as $t \lessgtr \hat{t}$, rc has a minimum at $\hat{t}$.

From (13.11m) and (13.12m) with $n = 1$ we see that under myopia the optimal x trajectory is such that $g(x)\mathrm{e}^{-rt} = (rc - Dc)\mathrm{e}^{-rt} = D\{c\mathrm{e}^{-rt}\}$, so that diffusion occurs such that the present value of the flow of benefits to the marginal buyer is equal to the rate of change of the present value of production cost. Thus $g(x(t))$ follows the $rc - Dc$ curve as we have shown in fig. 13.1 until $\hat{t}$ when no further sales occur. Under perfect foresight it is not $g(x(t))$ which

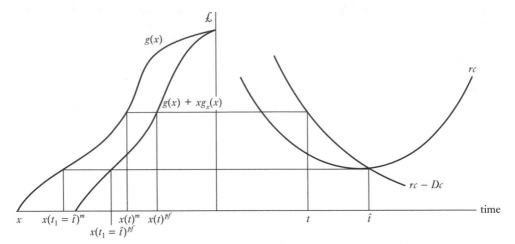

Figure 13.1   The diffusion paths

follows this path but $g(x) + g_x x$. As $g_x < 0$, the value of x for any t will be lower than that under myopia (again see fig. 13.1). The $g(x(t))$ path under perfect foresight will thus lie above $rc - Dc$ in fig. 13.1, but sales will again terminate at $\hat{t}$.

Note that under myopia, if initially $g(0) < rc - Dc$ then no sales will take place until costs have reduced sufficiently that this inequality no longer holds. If initially $g(0) > rc - Dc$ then sufficient sales will occur in the first instance to again bring $g(x)$ into equality with $rc - Dc$. The nature of this instantaneous 'jump' in x is discussed in appendix 13; under myopia there is perfect price discrimination among all customers served in this 'instant'. However, under perfect foresight any jump in x necessary to equate $g(x) + g_x x$ with $rc - Dc$ at $t = 0$ involves a single price and no such price discrimination.

We can state our major result as:

> *Proposition* 1: With a monopoly supplier diffusion terminates at $\hat{t}$ under both myopia and perfect foresight expectations if prior obsolescence has not occurred, but ownership or use of the new product will be less at all times under perfect foresight.

We may provide a rationale for Proposition 1 as follows. The diffusion itself is not instantaneous because the supplier gains from initially decreasing costs of production. However, the positive discount rate implies that the producer will not wait forever. Thus the diffusion itself is a balance of these two counteracting forces. Ownership is always greater under myopia than perfect foresight because any given rate of decrease of price gives rise to 'arbitrage' behaviour by buyers with perfect foresight: this slows down the rate of diffusion, for the supplier can only mitigate the effect of perfect foresight behaviour by reducing the rate of price decrease; he cannot reverse the effect.

Given that the inclusion of perfect foresight on future prices reduces the level of ownership of the new technology at all times, it is of interest to investigate the impact of changes in technological expectations concerning product obsolescence. Expectations of earlier obsolescence are represented in our model as an increase in the hazard rate embodied in r.

If r increases then both rc and $rc - Dc$, as shown in fig. 13.1, shift upwards, and $\hat{t}$ does not change. However, under both myopia and perfect foresight $x(t)$ for $t \leq \hat{t}$, i.e. the usage of the technology, is reduced. We may state this as:

> *Proposition* 2: Under both myopia and perfect foresight, a higher expectation of obsolescence reduces usage along the diffusion path, which however still terminates at $\hat{t}$, unless prior obsolescence has occurred.

13.3.3. *Diffusion under oligopolistic supply conditions*

Turn now to consider an oligopolistic supply industry ($n > 1$). The first point to make is that as $n \to \infty$ (13.11pf) and (13.12pf) tend to (13.11m) and (13.12m) with $n = 1$. I.e. the perfect foresight path for a large number of producers approaches the myopia path with a single supplier. The logic of this result is that, as n increases, the supplying industry becomes nearer to being competitive. Then all profit from the adoption of the new technology goes to the users, who choose a rate of take-up to maximise total rents – thus emulating the choice of the single monopoly supplier with myopic buyers.

For $2 \leq n \leq \infty$ on the perfect foresight path, (13.11pf) and (13.12pf) indicate that at t_1, $Dc = 0$ and thus $t_1 = \hat{t}$. Thus the terminal date is unaffected by n, and is still $\hat{t}$. From (13.12pf) a sufficient condition for $x(t)$, $t \leq \hat{t}$ to increase with n is that $d(xg(x))/dx > 0$, and $d^2(xg(x))/dx^2 < 0$. This condition is analogous to that of positive but declining marginal revenue in a static market and we will assume that it holds. Then a greater number of suppliers implies increased usage for all t due to the lower price trajectory of the more competitive environment and we can state:

> *Proposition* 3: Multiple suppliers and buyers' perfect foresight yields an open loop equilibrium with sales until $\hat{t}$ and higher sales at any point in time the greater the number of suppliers. As the number of suppliers becomes infinite the perfect foresight path approaches the path under myopia with one supplier.

Under myopia with multiple suppliers, we have from (13.11m) that for all $t < t_1$, $rc - Dc = g(x) - (n-1)Q g_x/rn$, whereas with a single supplier $rc - Dc = g(x)$. Given $g_x < 0$, x will be greater for all $t < t_1$ with a greater number of suppliers. One solution to (13.11m) and (13.12m) has $Dc = 0$ and $Q = 0$ at t_1, which implies $t_1 = \hat{t}$. Although other solutions to (13.11m) and (13.12m) which involve $Dc < 0$ and $Q > 0$ at t_1 (and thus $t_1 < \hat{t}$) are possible, we cannot consider any t_1 thus generated as a valid terminal point since such a solution would not constitute an open loop equilibrium. The reason for this is that any one firm would then take other firms' productions to end at t_1 and would conjecture additional profits for itself by remaining in production at t_1 and waiting for cost savings to generate further profitable sales. As all firms would have similar conjectures, an open loop equilibrium can only be characterised by production continuing until $\hat{t}$ after which no further cost reductions are possible. We can thus state:

> *Proposition* 4: Multiple suppliers and buyers' myopia yield an open loop equilibrium where accumulated sales are greater at any time before $\hat{t}$ than in the case of a single supplier.

To extend our discussion of the impact of an increase in the risk of obsolescence to the case where $n > 1$, we may observe that in this case if r is greater then x will be lower at each point in time under both myopia and perfect foresight, so Proposition 2 continues to hold under oligopolistic supply conditions.

13.3.4.   The possibility of sigmoid diffusion

One of the key results in the diffusion literature (see Stoneman, 1983) is that the time path of use is commonly but not always observed to be sigmoid. It is thus interesting to see whether the model discussed here will produce a sigmoid path. Consider the simplest case with myopia and $n = 1$. Then from (13.11m) we obtain

$$DQ = \frac{rD^2c - D^3c - g_{xx}Q^2}{g_x} \tag{13.13}$$

For a sigmoid path we require $Dx = Q > 0$ and $D^2x = DQ$ changing sign from positive to negative as x increases. From (13.13) the latter condition depends on factors such as g_{xx} and D^3c which we have not needed to specify for our model. Thus we should conclude that sigmoid diffusion is possible but not certain in our model. Also, even if it is the case that D^2x is of the form to change sign as required, it is possible that obsolescence which occurs at a random point in time, may take place prior to this event.

13.3.5.   Diffusion under different price expectation regimes

We have now investigated in some detail the two extremes of price expectations: myopia and perfect foresight. However, other formulations of expectations do merit consideration, and it is to examples of these that we now turn.

1   Adaptive expectations. We define adaptive expectations such that

$$Dp^e = k(p(t) - p^e(t)) \quad 0 < k < 1 \tag{13.14}$$

where $p^e(t)$ is the expectation of price in time t formed at time $t - 1$. The formulation thus assumes that the forecast is continually adjusted by a proportion of the error in the forecast. From (13.14) it is trivial to show that if $p^e(t) \geq p(t)$ then $p^e(t) \geq p^e(t + 1) \geq p(t)$, and thus $D\hat{p}(t) \simeq p^e_{t+1} - p_t > 0$. It is also trivial to show that if $p(t) \leq p(t - 1)$ for all t, then $p^e(t) \geq p(t)$ for all t and thus $D\hat{p}(t) \geq 0$ for all t. If $D\hat{p}(t) \geq 0$ for all t then the arbitrage condition 13.5(ii) will always be satisfied and 13.5(i) must be the binding constraint on acquisition. In effect, at each point in time, if price falls continuously, buyers will be surprised to find a fall in price, and will continue to predict an increase in price. Thus the current price always appears to be a 'bottom' price. If we suppose that initially the period zero price is announced one period ahead so that the error $p(t) - p^e(t) = 0$ for $t = 0$, then in period zero condition 13.5(i) will determine acquisition. From 13.5(i) we can predict that price will fall over time, which following our argument above implies that 13.5(ii) will never be binding and diffusion will follow the myopia path. One may generalise this result to state that under adaptive expectations if the initial forecast of prices is correct or too high then the acquisition path will be the same as the path under myopia and price expectations play no role in determining the diffusion path (although expectations concerning obsolescence will play the same role as discussed under myopia).

2   μ expectations. Here we assume that $D\hat{p}(t)$ is such that there is a tendency to consistently over (or under) estimate the change in the present value of prices. Specifically $D\hat{p}(t)$ solves

$$-D\hat{p} + rp = \mu(-Dp + rp); \quad \mu > 0 \tag{13.15}$$

If $\mu = 1$ this collapses to the perfect foresight case. If $\mu < 1$, there is consistent under-estimation, if $\mu > 1$ then consistent over-estimation.

If $D\hat{p} < 0$, 13.5(ii) holding as an equality will imply that 13.5(i) is satisfied and thus 13.5(ii) will determine the demand for the technology, and the diffusion process will be similar to the perfect foresight case. If $\mu \geq 1$ then $Dp < 0$ is sufficient for this. However, if $\mu < 1$ then from (13.15) $D\hat{p} < 0$ is not assured even though current price is actually falling. Let $\bar{\mu} < 1$ be the smallest μ such that $D\hat{p} < 0$ all t. If $\mu < \bar{\mu} < 1$, then the possibility arises that satisfying 13.5(ii) as an equality does not satisfy 13.5(i). In this case it is possible that the diffusion path has a mixed character. Part of the path has buyers' preferences modelled as under myopia, and part similar to perfect foresight expectations. We have not attempted to model this specifically. The main point of interest raised is that even with price expectations included in the model, these expectations may only have an impact on the diffusion path for a part of the whole diffusion period.

13.3.6.   The number of buyers

Our analysis so far has concerned the case where N is sufficiently large and the distribution of buyers sufficiently dense that a continuum of buyers could be postulated. Complementary with this assumption was that suppliers set quantities rather than prices and received the market price according to the dynamic demand function (13.6). A number of problems arise if the fundamental assumption of large N is not tenable. First, sales cannot be considered as continuous; there would be intervals of time during which no sales would occur, and competition over the timing of sales would lead to uninteresting equilibria or no equilibrium at all. Secondly, precise equilibria in any market may fail to exist if quantities are limited to integers. Thirdly, quantity setting behaviour becomes unrealistic relative to price setting behaviour when sales are few and far between while the latter encounters problems of Bertrand equilibria.

The continuous marketing character of our model is dependent on the large number of buyers assumption. If N is very small then the connectedness of each sale may be slight unless output capacities, product differentiation and price adjustment costs are added. In order to avoid these additional complications we prefer to maintain the assumption of large N and quantity-setting suppliers. However, in the sections that follow, particularly section 13.5, we will be increasingly concerned with the diffusion of new processes rather than new consumer products, and thus with sales to a population of firms rather than households. As we maintain the assumption of large N we would not therefore claim any general validity for what follows. Nevertheless there will be occasions when the technology is of sufficiently widespread application that N is large enough for our model to be relevant. An alternative justification for proceeding might be that a firm can be considered as having a (possibly) large number of applications for the new product. The technology is not then acquired by the purchase of a single product but by the sequential purchase of (possibly large) numbers of the product, allowing an intra-firm diffusion. The firm then contributes a number of points on the index of buyers (is a repeating buyer), each application is associated with a specific benefit $g(x)$, and multiple sales per firm counteracts the small number of firms. However, in general, problems outlined above for when N is small have no simple solution and should be recognised as limiting the applicability of our analysis.

13.4.   Welfare and Regulation

The model we have been describing is characterised by costs of production in the supplying industry which reduce over time and by impatience on the part of both suppliers and buyers, represented by a positive discount rate. For the kinds of expectation formulations we have considered we wish now to enquire into the relationship of the implied diffusion paths to a simple characterisation of a socially optimal diffusion. Then a natural extension is to consider how intervention into the market may improve welfare and the form such intervention may take.

   We can postulate that social welfare arising from the new product is equal to the sum of benefits of buyers minus the sum of costs of production in the supplying industry. We assume here that, if the new product is a producer good, there is no induced change in the structure or performance of the buying industry which affects consumers of the products of that industry. We will return to these questions in the next section. Thus social welfare is

$$W = \int_0^{t_1} (g(x)/r - c)Q\,e^{-rt}\,dt \qquad (13.16)$$

where $Dx = Q = nq$ from symmetry. It is readily apparent from 13.5(i) and (13.8) that the maximisation of welfare is exactly the same problem as that faced by a monopolist supplier with myopic buyers; the xth-ranked buyer paying a price of $g(x)/r$ at time t, and $Q = q$ as $n = 1$. Thus either directly or following the procedure used in appendix 13, we can state that the socially optimal diffusion path can be represented by:

$$g(x) = rc - Dc \qquad (13.11°)$$

$$g(x_1) = rc(t_1) \qquad (13.12°)$$

We may thus state

   Proposition 5(a): The welfare optimal diffusion path is the same path as that produced with a single supplier with buyers' myopia.

That the diffusion path which maximises welfare is the same as that pursued by a monopolist faced with myopic buyers is easily explained. The monopolist obtains all the consumer surplus for himself by perfectly discriminating among all the buyers: each buyer will pay exactly the value to him of the new technology, and the monopolist's profits are thus equivalent to W defined by (13.16). The situation of a monopolist faced with myopic buyers is, however, just one of a number of structures we have considered, and it is appropriate to review the relationship of the diffusion path in other cases to the welfare optimum defined by (13.11°) and (13.12°). At the same time we will investigate what kind of specific tax/subsidy policy would improve welfare.

Assume first that the supplying industry is a monopoly but that dynamic inefficiency in creating welfare arises due to buyers' expectations. In the case of perfect foresight, an appropriate policy would be to have a decreasing specific subsidy $v(t)$, paid to the producer of the new technology, such that

$$rv(\hat{t}) = -g_x(x_1)x_1 > 0$$

and

$$Dv(\hat{t}) = 0$$

Such a subsidy would result in counteracting the $g_x x_1/n$ term in equations (13.11pf) and (13.12pf). Similar intervention is desirable in the case of μ-expectations, when the subsidy would decrease faster (slower) if $\mu > 1$ ($\mu < 1$).

Buyers' myopia is not sufficient to yield socially optimal diffusion. If the supplying industry is characterised by a symmetric oligopoly and buyers are myopic, the oligopolists will tend to compete for profits by selling more; thus the competition prevents perfect discrimination and leads to too fast a diffusion from a welfare point of view.

The correct regulatory response to prevent this too fast diffusion is to place a decreasing specific tax on the production of the technology. The tax becomes zero, but is still decreasing, at $\hat{t}$. The result is that the effect of $n > 1$ is counteracted. Then the diffusion will be less than before in the early stages and price will be held above marginal cost for longer.

The need for subsidy in the cases of non-myopic expectations is less the greater the number of supplying firms. Thus for $n > 1$, the subsidy profiles will be such that a smaller specific subsidy is paid at each moment in time. Indeed the perfect foresight path has the property that as $n \to \infty$ so the diffusion path tends to the welfare optimum. This is ensured by standard welfare theorems but we state it as.

Proposition 5(b): If buyers have perfect foresight the open loop equilibrium generates a diffusion path as $n \to \infty$ that is the welfare optimal path.

We should note, however, that although perfect foresight with $n \to \infty$ and myopia with $n = 1$, can both yield the welfare optimal path, the distribution of the welfare gains is very different under the two regimes. Under the former the suppliers get no profits, under the latter the suppliers appropriate all the surplus. If the profits are treated as an incentive to technological innovation and invention the two regimes may have very different welfare implications. (See Stoneman and Ireland, 1984.)

The implications of our discussion are thus that the regulation of diffusion is crucially dependent on identifying the buyers' expectation regime; particularly in distinguishing whether or not buyers are myopic. For example, if the number of firms in the supply industry is few but greater than one, a declining but always positive subsidy is the pre-scribed policy if buyers have perfect foresight, whereas a declining tax ending at zero is prescribed if buyers are myopic.

13.5.   Industry Size, Market Structure and the Return to R&D

13.5.1.   Endogenous market size

The issues with which we are concerned in this section are relevant only to the case of process innovation. We will thus talk of the buyers as firms or plants. The prime issue with which we shall deal is that of the endogeneity of market size in the buying industry. To this point we have considered that buyers are individual firms or plants and that the number of plants does not change with the advent or diffusion of the technology. One can provide a number of justifications for this assumption, e.g. there are oligopoly barriers to entry, or the buyers come from a number of different industries and make up a small part of any one industry, or indeed because the new technology makes only a small change to overall profitability (because a number of production processes are involved or because most of the increased profitability potential is expropriated by the supplier of the new technology). However it seems worthwhile to relax the assumption which we do here. When we do relax this assumption we will also have to consider a world where the benefits from the use of the technology $g(x)$ may be dependent on the number of other users of the technology. Again relaxing an assumption from above.

Consider now that the number of firms and plants in the user industry is endogenous to the model, so that there is a derived demand for 'plants' given by the demand for the plants' product(s). We will consider two situations. In the first, each plant acts as an independent economic agent and we call this case a competitive industry. In the second all plants are controlled by a monopolist, no entry is possible, and the monopolist acts to maximise (joint) profits. We might consider this situation to be the intra-firm diffusion case discussed at the end of section 13.3. We call this monopoly. In both cases we will limit our analysis to the single supplier ($n = 1$) model.

Let N represent the (large) number of plants in the user industry and let each plant have a fixed production capacity (of 1). This assumption is made to simplify the analysis by producing an exact correspondence between industry output and plants in use. A by-product of the assumption is that industry output only expands as the number of plants expands. This in turn implies that when diffusion involves an increase in the number of plants the benefits obtained by each user depends on the number of other users.

Prior to the appearance of the new technology let production cost per unit per period be b_0 per plant, and let the industry face a downward sloping demand curve AR with associated marginal revenue curve, MR, as in fig. 13.2. The competitive industry, prior to innovation, will thus have that number of plants that equalises price and marginal cost (N_0^c); the

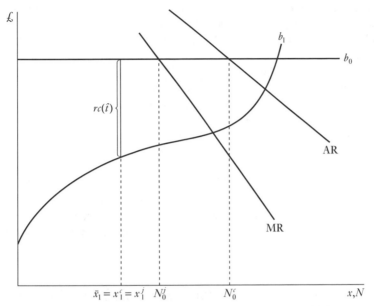

Figure 13.2   Myopia, market structure and the extent of diffusion

monopoly industry that which equalises marginal revenue and marginal cost (N_0^j:j for joint profit maximisation).

Allow now that the new technology will shift production costs from b_0 to b_1 where b_1 is as characterised in fig. 13.2. The important point to note about b_1 is that we have allowed the costs to vary across plants, thus some plants benefit more from the new technology than others; a distribution of benefits being crucial to our justification of the demand side of the diffusion process. In the present circumstances the justification for the shape of b_1 might rest on, for example, differences in entrepreneurial ability, or geographic location or even on shortages of factor inputs (such as skilled labour appropriate to the new technology) so that input prices rise as usage extends. Along b_1, plants are ranked by the amount of cost reduction to be obtained.

To analyse the impact of the introduction of the new technology we only detail the myopic expectations case. We have investigated perfect foresight but the results are no different in a qualitative sense and are thus not reported. Our analysis considers first the case where the post-diffusion number of users (x_1) is less than the pre-diffusion number of plants, N_0, and then we consider the case where an expansion in the number of plants is indicated.

13.5.2.   Replacing existing technology

If $x_1 < N_0$, then the benefit per period to a plant with index x from adopting the new technology, $g(x)$, equals $b_0 - b_1(x)$. Under myopic behaviour our analysis above indicates that diffusion will proceed to the point where $g(x_1) = rc(\hat{\imath})$ following a path characterised by $g(x) = rc - Dc$. To determine the post diffusion number of users of the new process we may note that (1) under competition, for $x_1 < N_0^c$, $g(x) = b_0 - b_1(x)$, and thus diffusion will proceed to the point where $rc(\hat{t}) = g(x_1) = b_0 - b_1(x_1)$. It is clear that if $rc(\hat{t}) > b_0 - b_1(N_0^c)$, then $x_1^c < N_0^c$. (2) Under monopoly, if $x_1 < N_0^j$, then $g(x) = b_0 - b_1(x)$ and diffusion will proceed to the point where $rc(\hat{t}) = g(x_1) = b_0 - b_1(x_1)$. It is clear that $x_1^j < N_0^j$ if $rc(\hat{t}) > b_0 - b_1(N_0^j)$. When the post diffusion number of users of new technology is less than the original number of plants, the remaining plants continue in existence but use old technology.

The main point to note about this case is that if in a monopolised industry the post diffusion number of users x_1^j is less than the original number of plants, N_0^j, then the number of users in a competitive industry x_1^c would equal x_1^j (fig. 13.2 is drawn to illustrate this case). The difference between the two industries post diffusion would be in the number of old technology plants.

The important result arising from this is that if $rc(\hat{t}) > b_0 - b_1(N_0^j)$, then $x_1^j = x_1^c$ and the number of buyers of the new technology is unaffected by the market structure of the buying industry; the supplier's profits are similarly unaffected and independent of market structure. We may note that if we assume $b_1(x) = \bar{b}_1$, some constant, then these results could not be generated.

13.5.3.   Expansion induced within a competitive industry

The case under consideration here involves the situation where with competition the post diffusion number of plants is greater than in the original situation (N_0^c). As the number of plants increases above N_0^c, market price for the industry's products will fall below b_0, with the industry moving down its average revenue (AR) curve. This produces the case where the user's benefit is a function of the number of users.

Under myopia it seems reasonable to argue that buyers are as myopic on the demand side as on capital good prices and thus make their acquisition decisions on the assumption that the perceived benefit at the date of adoption will last forever (in the absence of obsolescence). Then one can still model the diffusion by $g(x_1) = rc(\hat{t})$ and $g(x) = rc - Dc$. We further assume (a) that no new plants are added until all the existing plants have been replaced by new type plants and (b) that new plants are added in ascending order of production costs. We may then consider that for all existing plants the benefits from buying the new technology are $g(x) = b_0 - b_1(x)$, and for new plants the benefits from entering the industry are $g(x) = AR(x) - b_1(x)$. The post diffusion number of plants, which for clarification we will label N_1^c rather than x_1^c, will be given where $rc(\hat{t}) = AR(N_1^c) - b_1(N_1^c)$, as illustrated in fig. 13.3.

One should note, however, that the assumption of myopia on the demand side enables the supplier to appropriate greater rents from the users than are actually realised. It is also interesting that even if $b_1(x) = \bar{b}_1$, some constant, then it is now possible to have a time intensive diffusion process, for the downward sloping $AR(x)$ function can yield $g_x(x) < 0$. This result holds whenever $N_1 > N_0$.

13.5.4.   Expansion induced within a monopoly

We must now consider a monopolised industry that is expanding so $N_1^j > N_0^j$. No problems really arise in the analysis until $N_1^j > N_0^c$ for beyond that point the price received for output

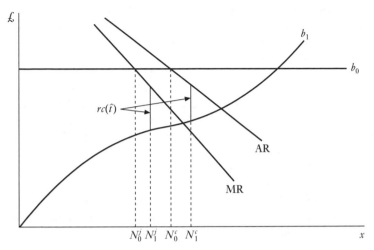

Figure 13.3   Diffusion, myopia and market structure

is less than b_0 and the benefit to the firm from earlier replacements of old plants are not invariant to the number of new plants added. Let us then ignore such a possibility and consider only $N_1^j < N_0^c$. Then for plants of index $x \leq N_0^j$, $g(x) = b_0 - b_1(x)$ and for plants of index x such that $N_0^c > x > N_0^j$, $g(x) = \mathrm{MR}(x) - b_1(x)$. Thus under myopia, if $N_1^j > N_0^j$, then the terminal diffusion level solves $\mathrm{MR}(N_1^j) - b_1(N_1^j) = rc(\hat{\imath})$. It should be clear that if $N_1^j > N_0^j$, then $N_1^j < N_1^c$ and the profit to the supplier is greater if he faces a competitive rather than a monopolistic industry (recalling that under myopia the single supplier appropriates, at least, the total users' rents). In fig. 13.3 we show the levels of N_1^j under competition and monopoly when expansion is occurring.

13.5.5.   Implications for R&D and welfare

We can draw two implications from this analysis. The first concerns incentives to research and development, the second concerns the extent of diffusion and the consequent welfare implications.

Arrow (1962) argued that the incentives to R&D are greater under competition than monopoly using a model in which a developed new process is sold to either a competitive or a monopolistic industry. Although this result has been much discussed our analysis here throws some further light on the issue. Arrow has a basic assumption that $b_1(x)$ is some constant $\bar{b}_1$. We have argued above that only if the new technology requires expansion of the industry will this assumption generate a time-intensive diffusion process, otherwise $g(x)$ is the same for every x and the model is inapplicable. If one removes the assumption that $b_1(x)$ is the same for all x, then we have shown that if the post-diffusion number of new-type plants in the monopolised industry is less than the initial total number of plants ($rc(\hat{\imath}) > b_0 - b_1(N_0^j)$ under myopia) then the supplier's profits, and thus the incentives to R&D are invariant to market structure. If $x_1^j > N_0^j$, the competitive industry will yield a greater incentive. We may thus argue that 'small' innovations yield invariant incentives whereas 'large' innovations yield more if sold to a competitive industry.

On the welfare side we argued above that a single supplier facing myopic buyers would produce a welfare optimum. We may now expand on this statement for as we have seen, if the number of firms using the new technology is endogenous, the take-up rate, even under myopia, may vary with the organisation of the using industry. In fact, if expansion in the number of plants is induced by the diffusion of the new innovation then the diffusion could still be optimal if the buying industry is competitive with myopic expectations. This is because each plant evaluates its worth in terms of its revenue $(AR(x))$ and so the firm's private $g(x)$ will also reflect the social value flow from adoption. We should note, however, that it would also be necessary, if the welfare optimum is to be achieved, that the firms' private valuations take account of the future effects of supply expansion. If the buying industry is a monopoly, however, the marginal plant evaluates its worth in terms of the addition to joint revenue $(MR(x))$ and the firm's $g(x)$ function is less than the social valuation, leading to too little diffusion. Thus if expansion in the using industry is induced, myopia and a monopoly supplier is not sufficient to ensure welfare-maximising diffusion. A competitive using industry is also necessary.

13.6.   Conclusions

In this paper we have modelled the time profile of the take up of a new technology allowing that each user (or potential user) purchases only one unit of the new technology. The benefit to be obtained from the adoption of the technology by the user depends upon his or her own characteristic(s), the date of acquisition and the price paid for the technology at that date. We argue that the date of acquisition will depend upon (a) the observed current price for the technology, (b) movements in prices expected to occur in the future and (c) expectations of obsolescence. By combining the derived demand function for the technology with a model of the supplying sector we generate an equilibrium time path for the usage of the new technology and are also able to characterise the end point of the diffusion process.

We have shown that the way in which buyers form their expectations concerning future prices can be crucial factors in determining the profile and extent of diffusion. However, we have also shown that certain types of expectations formation behaviour imply only *non-binding* constraints on the diffusion process (for either some or all of the diffusion period) and thus the type of expectations formation included is just as important as the inclusion of expectations *per se*.

Rosenberg's hypotheses regarding the impact of expectations on the diffusion path are to some extent confirmed. In particular, if expectations are always correct (perfect foresight) the level of usage is lower relative to the myopic path at all points in time. However, we have also shown that if the industry supplying the technology is competitive with a large number of suppliers, the slower diffusion implied by perfect foresight is the optimal path i.e. faster diffusion is not necessarily desirable. Rosenberg's hypotheses on the effect of earlier obsolescence also appear to be confirmed.

On the other hand, we have also generated examples where Rosenberg's intuition is incomplete or misleading. We have argued that adaptive expectations behaviour (under certain conditions) will not affect the diffusion path, and that μ expectations behaviour (for $(\mu < \bar{\mu} < 1)$ may similarly be irrelevant. We have also shown that under μ expectations, if $\bar{\mu} < \mu < 1$, then the level of usage will be greater than that under perfect foresight for all t prior to the terminal point. We can perhaps best state that Rosenberg's arguments are correct if the expectations are correct.

In addition to the insights into the diffusion path we have been able to throw some light on the incentives to R&D: the incentive from selling to a competitive as opposed to a monopoly industry is only greater if the technological change is large and will cause an expansion of the industry. In addition we have been able to illustrate that the commonly observed sigmoid curve can be predicted from our model if further assumptions are imposed.

Finally, we have been able to relate the equilibrium diffusion path to that which would maximise social welfare. A welfare–optimal diffusion path will result under myopic expectations if there is one supplier, the using sector is competitively organised and users' valuations take account of future effects of supply expansion. However, if the number of suppliers increases, or expectations behaviour becomes binding, or the using industry structure becomes monopolistic (with large technological advances), a deviation from the optimal path occurs. However, the welfare reducing effects of expectations behaviour (if these expectations imply perfect foresight) can be offset by having a competitive supplying industry. We considered policy requirements to correct deviations from the welfare-optimal diffusion paths. For example, if there was more than one supplier, an appropriate regulatory tool would be a declining specific tax if buyers were myopic and a declining specific subsidy if buyers had perfect foresight. Thus buyers' expectations are a crucial factor in any regulatory policy.

There are three main qualifications to our analysis. First, a number of simplifying assumptions have been made in order to produce a tractable model, and therefore we cannot claim general theorems, only tentative propositions. Second, our treatment of welfare implies either neutrality with respect to income distribution between buyers and suppliers or the existence of non–distortionary (in a dynamic as well as static sense) redistributive policy instruments. Thirdly, we have in most cases taken the number of supplying firms n as exogenous. An alternative possibility is that n is endogenous, responding to the magnitude of the profit stream. This is a function of buyers' expectations, and so it may be necessary to compare diffusion paths across expectation regimes with different n.

Appendix 13

The mathematical problem that we are concerned with in this paper can be expressed in the form

$$\max_{\langle q \rangle, t_1} Z = G(x_1, t_1) + \int_0^{t_1} \{h(x, t) + k(x, t)Q\} dt \tag{A13.1}$$

subject to

$$Dx = Q = q + (n - 1)\bar{q}(t)$$

$$q \geq 0 \tag{A13.2}$$

We allow the possibility of an initial 'jump' in the state variable x attained by an instantaneous unbounded Q by considering time 0^+, arbitrarily near 0, and rewriting (A13.1) as

$$Z = G(x_1, t_1) + \int_0^{0^+} \{h(x, t) + k(x, t)Q\}\,dt + \int_{0^+}^{t_1} \{h(x, t) + k(x, t)Q\}\,dt$$

Now the first integral of $h(x, t) \to 0$ as $0^+ \to 0$, and we can then also write

$$\int_0^{0^+} k(x, t)Q\,dt = \int_0^{x(0^+)} k(x, 0)\,dx = K(x(0^+))$$

Thus Z can be expressed as

$$Z = G(x_1, t_1) + K(x(0^+)) + \int_{0^+}^{t_1} \{h(x, t) + (x, t)q\}\,dt \tag{A13.3}$$

Write the Hamiltonian of this problem:

$$H = h(x, t) + k(x, t)Q + \lambda Q \tag{A13.4}$$

First-order conditions are (A13.2) together with:

$$H_x = h_x + k_x Q = -D\lambda \tag{A13.5}$$

$$H_q = k(x, t) + \lambda \le 0 \quad \text{and} \quad q = 0 \quad \text{or} \quad k(x, t) + \lambda = 0 \tag{A13.6}$$

$$h(x_1, t_1) + G_t(x_1, t_1) = 0 \quad \text{(optimal endpoint } t_1) \tag{A13.7}$$

$$G_x(x_1, t_1) = \lambda(t_1) \quad \text{(transversality condition)} \tag{A13.8}$$

$$k(x(0^+), 0) \le -\lambda(0^+) \quad \text{and} \quad x(0^+) = 0 \quad \text{or} \quad k(x(0'), 0) = -\lambda(0^+)$$
$$\text{(optimal initial jump condition)} \tag{A13.9}$$

Now $q = \bar{q}$ (from symmetry), so that while sales are positive and finite we have from (A13.5) and (A13.6), using (A13.2),

$$h_x(x, t) = k_t(x, t) \tag{A13.10}$$

An initial adjustment phase may take place involving zero output until $k(0, t) + \lambda(t)$ becomes equal to zero (from being negative) or an instantaneous jump in output at time zero until $k(x, 0) + \lambda(0)$ becomes zero (from positive). After this (A13.10) will hold until the diffusion process is complete providing H is strictly concave in x. At t_1, we have (A13.6) as an equality and (A13.8) so that

$$G_x(x_1, t_1) = -k(x_1, t_1) \tag{A13.11}$$

Note that (A13.7) is redundant as it is implied by the integration by parts procedure used to obtain (A13.1). Thus there is no terminal adjustment phase. (A13.10) and (A13.11) fully characterise the diffusion path after any initial adjustment.

Now we may apply our analysis to our specific models by identifying the $G(\cdot)$, $h(\cdot)$ and $k(\cdot)$ functions. Equations of type (13.11) are derived from (A13.10), and of type (13.12) from (A13.11).

Notes

1   The earlier paper was limited to a consideration of what we will later term 'myopic expectations'. A perfect foresight model of intertemporal price discrimination is presented in Stokey (1979).
2   We will ignore the general second-order condition on 13.5(ii) as this involves the term $D^2\hat{p}(t)$. We could return to specific second-order conditions for particular expectation regimes, but note that $D^2\hat{p}(t)$ involves the comparison of the *current* (t-period) expectation of price in period $t + 1$ and $t + 2$, and thus includes information that is not used elsewhere in our analysis. Given this, we will simply assume that the second-order condition holds where necessary.
3   If deviations from suppliers' announced plans can occur, then these announced plans would almost certainly be time inconsistent. An analysis of time inconsistency in a model with a much simpler dynamic specification is given in Ireland and Stoneman (1985).

References

Arrow, K. (1962) 'Economic Welfare and the Allocation of Resources for Invention', in R.R. Nelson (ed.), *The Rate and Direction of Inventive Activity*, Princeton University Press.
Barlow, R.E. and Proschan, F. (1965) *Mathematical Theory of Reliability*, John Wiley & Sons, New York.
David, P.A. (1969) 'A Contribution to the Theory of Diffusion', Stanford Centre for Research in Economic Growth, Memorandum, No. 71.
David, P.A. and Olsen, T.E. (1984) 'Anticipated Automation: a Rational Expectations Model of Technological Diffusion', paper presented to the Warwick Summer Workshop on the Economics of Technological Change, July.
Davies, S. (1979) *The Diffusion of Process Innovations*, Cambridge University Press.
Ireland, N.J. and Stoneman, P. (1985) 'Order Effects, Perfect Foresight and Intertemporal Price Discrimination', *Recherches Economiques de Louvain*, 51, 7–20.
Rosenberg, N. (1976) 'On Technological Expectations', *Economic Journal*, 86, 523–35.
Stokey, N.L. (1979) 'Intertemporal Price Discrimination', *Quarterly Journal of Economics*, 93, 355–71.
Stoneman, P. (1983) *The Economic Analysis of Technological Change*, Oxford University Press, Oxford.
Stoneman, P. and Ireland, N.J. (1983) 'The Role of Supply Factors in the Diffusion of New Process Technology', *Economic Journal*, Conference Supplement, 65–77.
Stoneman, P. and Ireland, N.J. (1984) 'An Integrated Approach to the Economics of Technological Change', paper presented to the Warwick Summer Workshop on the Economics of Technological Change, July.

Chapter fourteen

Adoption Subsidies vs Information Provision as Instruments of Technology Policy

Co-written with Paul A. David

Our main concern in this paper[1] is to focus analytical attention on government policies which aim to influence the diffusion of technological innovations into actual use. This subject has been relatively neglected in recent discussions of technology policy which increasingly have centred on the first two parts of the Schumpeterian trilogy – invention and innovation. Yet it would be difficult to exaggerate the significance of diffusion in the contexts which presently give rise to an interest in technology policy. What determines improvements in productivity and product quality, thereby enhancing economic welfare and the competitiveness of firms and industries, is not the rate of development of new technologies but the speed and extent of their application in commercial operations. However feasible the designs for new products and processes may be from an engineering standpoint, it is the prospects for diffusion which ultimately imparts economic value to this form of new knowledge. We have discussed elsewhere (Ireland and Stoneman, 1984; David, 1985) how the generation and diffusion of new technology may be linked, but here we concentrate on diffusion *per se*.

Governments have largely attempted to speed up the diffusion of new technologies. Two routes have been used. The first is by information provision policies, e.g. the Agricultural Extension Scheme in the United States and certain aspects of the Microprocessor Applications Programme in the United Kingdom. The second is by the use of subsidies, e.g. the favourable leasing terms offered to Japanese robot users. In this paper we are interested not only in whether such policies will speed up diffusion but also whether their impact is welfare improving, for as we argue below, there may be a limit to the desirable speed of take up of new technology.

Reprinted from the *Economic Journal*, Conference Supplement, March 1986, pp. 142–50, by kind permission of Blackwell Publishers.

Our analysis is conducted within the framework of a model that integrates the two main prevailing theoretical approaches to diffusion (see Stoneman, 1983). The first approach is that diffusion is a reflection of the information propagation or learning process with firms adopting a technology as they come to learn of its existence. This literature has a strong tradition of using epidemic learning models which we follow below. The second approach allows that potential buyers of technology differ from each other in the benefits they can gain from use of the technology and diffusion proceeds as ownership is driven down the benefit distribution. Recent advances which our model reflects also consider that diffusion should be modelled as a process of supply and demand interaction (Stoneman and Ireland, 1983) and following Rosenberg (1976), that expectations are important in the diffusion process (Stoneman and Ireland, 1986; David and Olsen, 1984). Within the context of the model we proceed to investigate the impact of government policies which either directly stimulate the supply of information or are based on the use of financial incentives to produce faster diffusion. Our aim is to ask (a) whether and/or under what conditions such policies will affect the speed and extent of diffusion and (b) whether and/or under what conditions the impacts of these policies can be considered to be socially desirable. Our results indicate that the market structure of the industry supplying the new technology is crucial in determining the impact of the policy initiatives. Under competitive supply both types of policies will speed up and extend diffusion, but information provision policies yield definite welfare gains whereas subsidy policies may not. Under conditions of monopolised supply the monopolist may react to render government information provision policies ineffective, but the subsidy policies will increase usage. However these subsidy policies under monopolised supply may only yield a welfare gain under certain conditions.

14.1. The Model

The model is adapted from Ireland and Stoneman (1984), and is made particularly simple by considering that there are only two time periods, $t = 1$, $t = 2$. Multi-period approaches to similar issues can be found in David and Olsen (1984) and Stoneman and Ireland (1986). We assume:

Assumption 1: The new technology is a new process that can be acquired by any potential user by the purchase of one unit of a new capital good.

Assumption 2: The population of potential adopters is of size N, and the adopters differ across some characteristic z that is independent of the use of the technology and is continuously distributed according to $f(z)$ with cumulative distribution $F(z)$.

Assumption 3: The benefit (gross of purchase cost) obtained in time t from the use of the new technology by an adopter with characteristic z is $h_t(z)$, $h'_t(z) > 0$, $t = 1, 2$ and $h_1(z)$ and $h_2(z)$ have perfect rank correlation.

Assumption 4: Knowledge on the existence of the technology is limited and independent of z. Defining α_t as the proportion of the population who know of the technology in time t, α_1 is exogenous, $0 \leq \alpha_1 \leq 1$, and α_2 is determined by epidemic learning such that

$$0 < \alpha_2 = G(\alpha_1, X_1, N) = \gamma + \alpha_1 + (1 - \alpha_1)\beta\frac{X_1}{N} \leq 1 \qquad (14.1)$$

where X_1 is the number of users of the new technology in period 1, γ represents exogenous learning between period 1 and 2, and β is an indicator of the effectiveness of the learning mechanism.

Assumption 5: All actors are considered to be rational profit maximisers and have perfect foresight on prices once knowledge of existence is obtained (for variations on this see Stoneman and Ireland, 1986). Define

X_t = number of users of the technology in time t.
$\hat{X}_t = X_t/\alpha_t$
p_t = supply price of one unit of the new capital good in time t.
s = proportional subsidy rate paid by government to an acquirer of new technology.
$\hat{p}_t = p_t(1 - s)$
z_t = characteristic level of the marginal adopter in time t.
r = discount rate.
$v = 1/(1 + r)$.

We may then write

$$X_t = \alpha_t N \int_{z_t}^{\infty} f(z)dz = \alpha_t[N - NF(z_t)], \quad t = 1, 2 \qquad (14.2)$$

thus

$$z_t = F^{-1}[(N - \hat{X}_t)/N] \quad t = 1, 2. \qquad (14.3)$$

Given Assumption 5, z_1 and z_2 will be determined such that (14.4) and (14.5) hold.

$$h_1(z_1) = \hat{p}_1 - v\hat{p}_2 \qquad (14.4)$$
$$h_2(z_2) = \hat{p}_2. \qquad (14.5)$$

Defining

$$g_t(X) = h_t\{F^{-1}[(N - X)/N]\} \qquad (14.6)$$

(14.3), (14.4), (14.5) and (14.6) imply

$$\hat{p}_1 - v\hat{p}_2 = g_1(\hat{X}_1) \qquad (14.7)$$
$$\hat{p}_2 = g_2(\hat{X}_2). \qquad (14.8)$$

Assumption 6: $g_t(X)$, $t = 1, 2$, is continuous and differentiable, $g_t'(X) < 0$, and $Xg_t(X)$ has positive first and negative second derivatives (i.e. $g_t(X) + Xg_t'(X) > 0$, $2g_t'(X) + Xg_t''(X) < 0$).

These conditions on $Xg_i(X)$ are equivalent to the standard assumptions that marginal revenue is positive but declining.

Assumption 7: In capital goods supply unit costs of production in periods 1 and 2 are c_1 and c_2, $c_1 > vc_2$, and suppliers have perfect knowledge of the demand environment (i.e. they know (14.7) and (14.8)).

Given profit maximisation we may immediately state that if the supply industry is perfectly competitive then $\hat{X}_1$ and $\hat{X}_2$ will be determined such that, using c superscripts for competition,

$$\hat{p}_1^c = g_1(\hat{X}_1^c) + vg_2(\hat{X}_2^c) = (1 - s)c_1 \tag{14.9}$$

and

$$\hat{p}_2^c = g_2(\hat{X}_2^c) = (1 - s)c_2. \tag{14.10}$$

A monopolist supplier will maximise (14.11) subject to (14.7) and (14.8)

$$\pi = p_1 X_1 + vp_2(X_2 - X_1) - c_1 X_1 - v(X_2 - X_1)c_2 \tag{14.11}$$

with a first order condition (14.12)

$$\hat{X}_2^m g_2'(\hat{X}_2^m) + g_2(\hat{X}_2^m) = c_2(1 - s). \tag{14.12}$$

From (14.12) it is clear that

$$\frac{d\hat{X}_2^m}{d\alpha_2} = 0. \tag{14.13}$$

Use of (14.13) with the other first order condition yields (14.14)

$$g_1(\hat{X}_1^m) + \hat{X}_1^m g_1'(\hat{X}_1^m) + v\hat{X}_2^m g_2(\hat{X}_2^m)G_2 = (c_1 - vc_2)(1 - s) \tag{14.14}$$

where $G_2 = (1 - \alpha_1)\beta/N$.

From (14.12), the monopolist supplier chooses second period output such that marginal revenue equals second period costs. The competitive industry has output determined with price equal to marginal cost, thus $\hat{X}_2^m < \hat{X}_2^c$. In the first period from (14.14) the monopolist chooses his output taking account of the effect that first period sales will have on second period demand through learning. If there were no learning $(G_2 = 0)\hat{X}_1^m$ would be determined such that first period marginal revenue would equal the opportunity cost of supplying in period 1 rather than 2. The competitive supplier determines output such that price is equal to this cost and thus, if $G_2 = 0$, $\hat{X}_1^c > \hat{X}_1^m$, implying that $X_1^c > X_1^m$, which in turn from (14.1) implies $\alpha_2^c > \alpha_2^m$ and therefore $X_2^c > X_2^m$. However, as $G_2 > 0$, the monopolist will take account of this in determining $\hat{X}_1$, and $\hat{X}_1^m$ will be greater than in the no learning case. Given (14.13) and (14.1) we define a value of β, $\beta^*(\alpha_1)$, such that from (14.14) as $\beta \lessgtr \beta^*(\alpha_1)$ so

$\hat{X}_1^m \lessgtr \hat{X}_1 c$. We call the case where $\beta < \beta^*(\alpha_1)$ the standard case and where $\beta > \beta^*(\alpha_1)$ the non standard case. We may note that the smaller is α_1 the smaller is β^*.

From (14.4), (14.5), (14.9), (14.10), (14.12) and (14.14), and recalling $g_t'(X_t) < 0$ we may summarise our result thus far as

$$h_2(z_2^m) = g_2(\hat{X}_2^m) > g_2(\hat{X}_2^c) = h_2(z_2^c) = c_2(1 - s) \tag{14.15}$$

and if $\beta < \beta^*(\alpha_1)$, the standard case, then

$$(1 - s)(c_1 - vc_2) = h_1(z_1^c) = g_1(\hat{X}_1^c) < g_1(\hat{X}_1^m) = h_1(z_1^m) \tag{14.16}$$

but if $\beta > \beta^*(\alpha_1)$, the non standard case, then

$$(1 - s)(c_1 - vc_2) = h_1(z_1^c) = g_1(\hat{X}_1^c) > g_1(\hat{X}_1^m) = h_1(z_1^m). \tag{14.17}$$

With a zero subsidy rate, from (14.15), (14.16) and (14.17) we see that under conditions of competitive supply the benefits obtained by the marginal adopters in periods 1 and 2 equals the opportunity cost of their provision. Under monopolised supply the benefits exceed the cost of provision in period 2. In period 1, if the learning effect is strong, $\beta > \beta^*(\alpha_1)$, the marginal adopter has benefits less than the opportunity cost of their provision, but in the standard case where $\beta < \beta^*(\alpha_1)$ the benefit of the marginal adopter exceeds the cost of provision.

Assumption 8: The welfare gain made by the eventual users of the products produced using the new technology are sufficiently small to ignore, distributional issues can also be ignored, and thus welfare W, generated during the diffusion process can be considered as the sum of the surpluses of capital goods suppliers and users. Thus

$$W = \alpha_1 N \int_{z_1}^{\infty} h_1(z)f(z)dz + \alpha_2 N \int_{z_2}^{\infty} h_2(z)f(z)dz - c_1\alpha_1 N[1 - F(z_1)]$$
$$- vc_2\alpha_2 N[1 - F(z_2)] + vc_2\alpha_1 N[1 - F(z_1)]. \tag{14.18}$$

From (14.18) we may immediately generate that for social welfare to be maximised it is necessary that

$$c_2 = h_2(z_2) \tag{14.19}$$

and ownership in period two should be extended to the point where the benefits to the marginal adopter just equals the cost of provision. One may note that with zero subsidy this condition is met under competitive supply. Also from (14.18), we may derive that as $\alpha_1 \rightarrow 1$ and $G_1 \rightarrow 0$, that welfare maximisation requires

$$h_1(z_1) = c_1 - vc_2 \tag{14.20}$$

i.e. that usage in period 1 should extend to the point where the benefits of the marginal adopter equals the opportunity cost of their provision. If $s = 0$, $\alpha_1 = 1$, (14.20) will hold under competitive supply.

Conditions (14.19) and (14.20) immediately indicate to us that in the area of technological diffusion the apparent maxim that often seems to underlie technology policy, that more and faster technological change is always better is only true up to some point. From a welfare maximising point of view, optimality implies limits.

14.2.   Information Provision Policies

In our model there are two routes by which more information may be represented, the first is an increase in α_1 the second an increase in γ. The former models information provision in period 1, the latter information provision in period 2. We shall consider the effect of such increases on the diffusion path and welfare.

We assume a zero subsidy rate, $s = 0$, and initially consider a perfectly competitive supply industry. From (14.16) and (14.17),

$$g_1(\hat{X}_1^c) = h_1(z_1^c) = c_1 - vc_2$$

$$g_2(\hat{X}_2^c) = h_2(z_2^c) = c_2.$$

Thus

(i) $\dfrac{dz_1^c}{d\alpha_1} = \dfrac{d\hat{X}_1^c}{d\alpha_1} = 0, \quad \text{implying} \quad \dfrac{dX_1^c}{d\alpha_1} > 0,$

(ii) $\dfrac{dz_2^c}{d\alpha_1} = \dfrac{d\hat{X}_2^c}{d\alpha_2} = 0$

and $\dfrac{d\alpha_2}{d\alpha_1} = G_1 + G_2 \dfrac{dX_1}{d\alpha_1} > 0, \quad \text{therefore} \quad \dfrac{dX_2^c}{d\alpha_1} > 0,$

(iii) $\dfrac{d\alpha_1}{d\gamma} = 0, \quad \text{therefore} \quad \dfrac{d\hat{X}_1^c}{d\gamma} = \dfrac{dX_1^c}{d\gamma} = \dfrac{dz_1^c}{d\gamma} = 0,$

(iv) $\dfrac{d\alpha_2}{d\gamma} > 0, \quad \text{therefore} \quad \dfrac{d\hat{X}_2^c}{d\gamma} = \dfrac{dz_2^c}{d\gamma} = 0, \dfrac{dX_2^c}{d\gamma} > 0.$

These results indicate that under conditions of competitive supply the extra information provided in periods 1 and/or 2, increases the intensity of use of the new technology within unchanged margins. The marginal adopters in periods 1 and 2 have the same benefits, but a greater proportion of intra-marginal adopters make use of the technology as information increases. Without formal analysis we may immediately note that this will be welfare improving. Each user has benefits greater than or equal to the opportunity cost of their provision and thus the increased number of users will lead to an increase in welfare. Thus under competition, information provision increases usage and welfare.

With monopolised supply, given $s = 0$, we know from (14.13) that $\dfrac{d\hat{X}_2^m}{d\alpha_2} = 0$. From (14.14) we obtain

$$\frac{d\hat{X}_1^m}{d\alpha_1}[2g_1'(\hat{X}_1^m) + \hat{X}_1^m g_1''(\hat{X}_1^m)] + \hat{X}_2^m vg_2(\hat{X}_2^m)G_{21} = 0.$$

By assumption $G_{21} < 0$, and $2g_1'(\hat{X}_1^m) + \hat{X}_1^m g_1''(\hat{X}_1^m) < 0$, thus $\dfrac{d\hat{X}_1^m}{d\alpha_1} < 0$. As $\hat{X}_1^m$ declines, $h(z_1^m)$ increases, we cannot however sign $\dfrac{dX_1^m}{d\alpha_1}$, and therefore $\dfrac{d\alpha_2}{d\alpha_1}$, or $\dfrac{dX_1^m}{d\alpha_1}$. However we can state that $\dfrac{dz_2}{d\alpha_1} = \dfrac{d\hat{X}_2^m}{d\alpha_1} = \dfrac{dh(z_2)}{d\alpha_1} = 0$. The lack of precision on movements in X_1^m, X_2^m and α_2 means that we cannot make any definitive welfare statements. The point we can make is that a monopolist supplier will not act passively when the government intervenes. The monopolist's reactions in pursuing maximum profits in the light of government policy may well counteract the intent of that policy.

The impact of a change in γ is simpler. Given $\dfrac{d\alpha_2}{d\gamma} > 0$ and $\dfrac{d\hat{X}_2^m}{d\alpha_2} = 0$, we can immediately derive that

(1) $\quad \dfrac{d\hat{X}_1^m}{d\gamma} = \dfrac{dz_1^m}{d\gamma} = \dfrac{dX_1^m}{d\gamma} = \dfrac{d\alpha_1}{d\gamma} = \dfrac{d\hat{X}_2^m}{d\gamma} = \dfrac{dz_2^m}{d\gamma} = 0$

(2) $\quad \dfrac{dX_2^m}{d\gamma} > 0$

and increased information in period 2 increases the number of intra-marginal adopters without affecting the characteristic of the marginal adopter. Given that under monopoly $h_2(z_2^m) > c_2$, this must represent an increase in welfare. The rationale for this result is that in period 2 the monopolist has no incentives to manipulate usage to stimulate learning as there are no future periods. He will thus not behave to counteract the policy. However, as his prices remain unchanged, but usage increases, he will receive higher profits from the policy. Under competition of course there were no excess profits being made.

14.3. Subsidisation Policies

Subsidisation policies have two effects, the incentives cause movement down the benefit distribution thus extending usage and this extra usage generates changes in information further stimulating use. We model considering that the subsidy rate is the same in periods 1 and 2. Differential subsidies could be allowed but little extra insight is generated.

Under competition the effect of the subsidy is clear. From (14.15), (14.16), (14.17) and (14.1) we have that

(1) $\quad \dfrac{d\hat{X}_1^c}{ds} > 0, \ \dfrac{dz_1^c}{ds} < 0, \ \dfrac{dh(z_1^c)}{ds} < 0, \ \dfrac{dX_1^c}{ds} > 0,$

(2) $\quad \dfrac{d\alpha_2}{ds} > 0, \ \dfrac{d\hat{X}_2^c}{ds} > 0, \ \dfrac{dX_2^c}{ds} > 0, \ \dfrac{dz_2^c}{ds} < 0, \ \dfrac{dh(z_2^c)}{ds} < 0.$

The subsidy extends first period usage down the benefit distribution, usage increases and α_2 increases. In the second period there is therefore greater intra-marginal use in addition to the induced movement down the benefit distribution. The subsidy will therefore increase usage. The welfare impacts of these changes are that, given that under no subsidy $\hat{X}_1^c$ and $\hat{X}_2^c$ are determined by the equality of marginal benefits and the opportunity cost of provision, then:

1   the movements down the benefit distribution in both periods will imply welfare losses; but
2   the increased intensity of use in the second period implies a welfare gain.

The net effect cannot be signed. Thus although the policy would achieve the aim of increased usage it would not necessarily increase welfare.

Under monopoly, from (14.12) we obtain

$$\frac{d\hat{X}_2^m}{ds}[2g_2'(\hat{X}_2^m) + \hat{X}_2^m g_2''(X_2^m)] = -c_2$$

and by assumption 6, $\dfrac{d\hat{X}_2^m}{ds} > 0$. From (14.14), given $G_{22} = 0$ by (14.1), we obtain

$$\frac{d\hat{X}_1^m}{ds}[\hat{X}_1^m g_1'(\hat{X}_1^m) + 2g_1'(\hat{X}_1^m)] + vG_2\frac{d\hat{X}_2^m}{ds}$$

$$[g_2(\hat{X}_2^m) + \hat{X}_2^m g_2'(\hat{X}_2^m)] = -(c_1 - vc_2).$$

By assumption 6 the first square bracketed term is negative, from (14.12) the second square bracketed term is positive thus $\dfrac{d\hat{X}_1^m}{ds} > 0$. This in turn implies

$$\frac{dX_1^m}{ds} > 0, \quad \frac{dz_1^m}{ds} < 0, \quad \frac{dh(z_2^m)}{ds} < 0. \quad \text{Given} \frac{d\alpha_2}{ds} > 0 \quad \text{and} \quad \frac{d\hat{X}_2^m}{ds} > 0,$$

$$\text{then} \quad \frac{dX_2^m}{ds} > 0, \quad \frac{dz_2^m}{ds} < 0, \quad \frac{dh(z_2^m)}{ds} < 0.$$

Usage is extended in periods 1 and 2 by movements down the benefit distribution and also in period 2 by increased intra-marginal use. The objective of increased use is thus achieved. The welfare impact of these changes depends on whether the case is standard or nonstandard. In both cases the increased intra-marginal use in period 2 will, if the subsidy is not large enough to reduce $h_2(z_2^m)$ below c_2, generate increased welfare. Also as $h_2(z_2^m)$ is driven towards c_2 down the benefit distribution further increases in welfare are generated. However in period 1, as z_1 is reduced the benefit of the marginal adopter is reduced. In the standard case this benefit is above opportunity cost $(c_1 - vc_2)$ and thus welfare is increased. In the non standard case the benefit of the marginal adopter is below opportunity cost and thus the further movement down the benefit distribution will imply a negative welfare contribution. We can only be sure that welfare will be increased by the provision of a subsidy under monopoly in the standard case.

14.4.   Conclusion

Government diffusion policies have been of two types – information provision and subsidy. The intent of these policies has been to increase the take up of new technology. We have argued, however, that more extensive use of a technology is not necessarily welfare improving. When the industry supplying the new technology is competitive we illustrate that information provision policies increase use and welfare, but subsidisation policies although increasing use may not increase welfare because such policies encourage use by firms for whom benefits are exceeded by the cost of their provision. Under monopoly supply information provision policies may be counteracted by the monopolist's reaction and thus their impact is unclear. Subsidy policies will on the other hand, under monopoly, increase use. Such policies will also increase welfare if the learning mechanism fits what we label a standard case.

Note

1   The research in this paper was undertaken with financial support from the Technological Innovation Programme of the Centre for Economic Policy Research at Stanford University. We wish to thank James Mirless for his comments on an earlier draft.

References

David, P.A. (1985) 'New technology diffusion, public policy and industrial competitiveness', paper presented at the Symposium on Economics and Technology, March 17–19, Stanford University.

David, P.A. and Olsen, T. (1984) 'Anticipated automation: a rational expectations model of technological diffusion', Centre for Economic Policy Research, Publication No. 24 (CEPR, Technological Innovation Program Working Paper No. 2), Stanford, April.

Ireland, N. and Stoneman, P. (1984) 'An integrated approach to the economics of technological change', paper presented at the Warwick Summer Workshop on the Economics of Technological Change, July.

Rosenberg, N. (1976) 'On technological expectations', *Economic Journal*, 86, 523–35.

Stoneman, P. (1983) *The Economics Analysis of Technology Change*, Oxford: Oxford University Press.

Stoneman, P. and Ireland, N. (1983) 'The role of supply factors in the diffusion of new process technology', *Economic Journal*, 93, 65s–77s.

Stoneman, P. and Ireland, N. (1986) 'Technological diffusion, expectations and welfare', *Oxford Economic Papers*, 38, 283–304.

Chapter fifteen

The Role of Regulation, Fiscal Incentives and Changes in Tastes in the Diffusion of Unleaded Petrol

Co-written with Giuliana Battisti

15.1. Introduction

Public opinion polls and other surveys (e.g. INRA, 1992) suggest that environmental consciousness among the British public is both extensive and has grown in recent years. This would lead one to expect that environmentally friendly, or green, consumer products would be experiencing growing market shares. However, in a companion paper (Wong *et al.*, 1996) that looks at the opinions of the suppliers of green consumer products based upon their experience of the UK market, we are led to conclude that, at the current time, consumers are unwilling to trade off greenness against other product performance aspects or against price, and that as a result, apparent green consciousness is not being reflected in major changes in the patterns of consumer expenditure. It also appears that where green products have become dominant, this has been through the impact of government regulation and intervention rather than through the working of free market forces reflecting changed consumer preferences.

In this paper we explore these issues further using economic and econometric, as opposed to survey, methodologies to investigate the spread of the use in the UK of a particular green product, unleaded petrol.[1] Unleaded petrol first appeared on the UK market in June 1986. By May 1995 unleaded petrol held a 60 per cent market share. This is a classic reflection of a diffusion process and as such the theoretical underpinnings of our approach rely extensively on the diffusion literature.

In order to use unleaded petrol a car (and it is primarily cars rather than commercial vehicles that use petrol, the latter mainly use diesel) must be technologically capable of doing so (not all cars currently can use unleaded petrol). Cars with catalytic converters can

Reprinted from *Oxford Economic Papers*, 52, 326–56, 2000, by kind permission of Oxford University Press.

only use unleaded petrol (leaded petrol destroys the converter). In addition, for the consumer to purchase unleaded petrol, it must be available at petrol stations.

The prime objective of this paper is to explore the relative importance of the following factors in the determination of the spreading of unleaded fuel: changes in consumer tastes, i.e. the greening of consumer attitudes; supply side factors, i.e. unleaded petrol availability; government regulation (e.g. rules on the fitting of catalytic converters to cars); and other government intervention, i.e. fiscal incentives to encourage the use of unleaded fuel (leaded and unleaded petrol in the UK have attracted different rates of duty). One may then draw some policy implications.

In the next section we discuss in more detail the nature of the diffusion process of unleaded fuel in the UK, supplier behaviour, and the fiscal and regulatory environment. In section 15.3 we develop a theoretical model of consumer behaviour relating to choice of fuel type. In section 15.4 we proceed to estimate the model. The results are discussed in section 15.5 with conclusions drawn and policy discussed in section 15.6.

15.2.   The Market for Unleaded Fuel in the UK

Unleaded petrol (specification RON 95) was launched in the UK in June 1986 by Esso. Other suppliers soon followed this lead. Premium Super Unleaded was launched in March 1989. In fig. 15.1 we plot the availability of unleaded fuel measured by the proportion of petrol stations that sell unleaded fuel (all data sources are discussed in appendix 15A). From approximately 1 per cent of stations in January 1987 this had reached 50 per cent by early

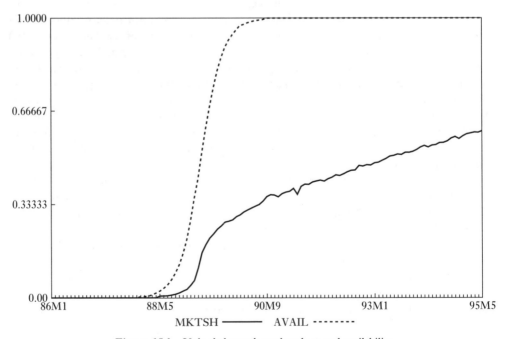

Figure 15.1   Unleaded petrol: market share and availability

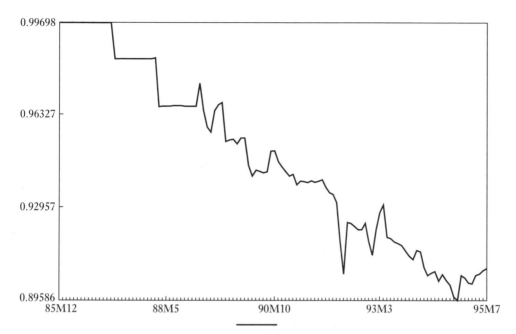

Figure 15.2   Ratio of prices of unleaded to leaded fuel

1989 and almost 100 per cent by mid-1990.[2] Throughout the diffusion process leaded fuel has been available at 100 per cent of stations.

In fig. 15.1 we also plot the market share of unleaded fuel which is minimal through to mid-1987 and then begins to rise reaching 20 per cent by mid-1989, 50 per cent by early 1993 and 60 per cent by May 1995, our last observation.

Prior to March 1987 leaded and unleaded fuel were subject to the same rate of duty, but from that date the rate on unleaded fuels has always been less than on leaded (from 95 per cent of the leaded rate in March 1987 the unleaded duty fell to 87 per cent of the leaded rate at the end of the sample period). In appendix 15A we show that the relative price of unleaded to leaded fuel is primarily determined by these changes in duty and is thus largely the result of government fiscal policy rather than other factors. We plot the ratio of unleaded to leaded prices in fig. 15.2.

At any point in time the petrol driven car stock will be made up of: cars with catalytic converters that must use unleaded fuel; cars that are capable of using unleaded fuel but do not have to; and cars that cannot use unleaded fuel. In line with European Commission mandates the UK government regulated that from October 1989 all new car models would have to be capable of running on unleaded petrol and from October 1990 all new cars sold in the UK (including imports) must be capable of using unleaded fuel. It was further regulated that from January 1993 all new cars sold in the UK must incorporate catalytic converters and thus of necessity must use unleaded fuel. In fig. 15.3 we plot the share of each type of car in the total UK car stock over time.

The diffusion process for unleaded fuel will reflect two factors: (i) changes in consumer choices of fuel type given the composition of the car stock; and (ii) changes in the composition

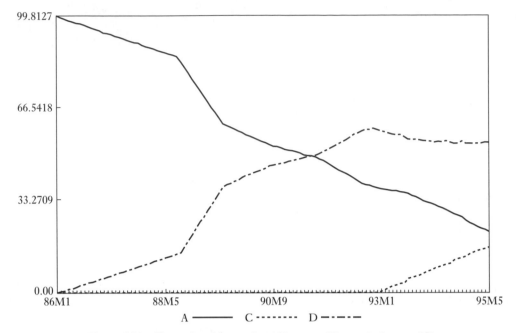

Figure 15.3 Share of total car stock unable to use (A), required to use (C), and capable of using (D) unleaded petrol

of the car stock. Consumer choice of fuel type is of course only relevant to owners of cars that have the capability of using either leaded or unleaded fuel (i.e. cars that do not have to use leaded fuel and do not have a catalytic converter).

Between December 1986 and May 1995 the proportion of cars in the total car stock capable of using both fuels increased from 5 per cent to 59 per cent. The share of unleaded petrol in total petrol sales increased from 0 per cent to 60 per cent. Given that in May 1995 18 per cent of cars had catalytic converters, this increase in market share is equivalent to an increase in the propensity to buy unleaded fuel by the owners of cars that can use either leaded or unleaded fuel from 0 per cent to 71 per cent (based upon the assumptions that all types of cars undertake the same annual mileage and yield the same miles per gallon). Although such an estimate is approximate because of the assumptions upon which it is based, the figures suggest that there was a major change in consumer choices over the study period. The factors that brought about such a major change are analysed in the next section.

Changes in the composition of the car stock can come about in two ways: (i) a car can be adapted, i.e. converted, to use unleaded fuel or (ii) a new car can be purchased with the capability (or requirement) of using unleaded fuel. Although it appears reasonable to argue that consumers would not buy a new car solely to be able to use unleaded fuel, conversions, which may be reasonably cheap,[3] could be undertaken in order to use such fuel. The composition of the car stock may thus, to some degree, reflect consumer's preferences over which fuel to use. Unfortunately we were unable to obtain any data on conversions and thus we are unable to precisely model the composition of the car stock. In modelling consumer choice over fuel type in the next section we thus assume that the composition of the car stock is given exogenously. However in section 15.4 when drawing some implications of our results for the relative importance of different factors in the diffusion process we do allow for such endogeneity.

15.3.   The Theory of Consumer Diffusion

The majority of the literature in economics on the diffusion of new technologies is concerned with new process technologies and/or with durable goods (see for example the survey by Stoneman and Karshenas, 1995). Unleaded fuel, however, is neither a consumer durable nor a producer good. Explicit modelling of the diffusion process for such a good is less common. In the marketing literature (e.g. Mahajan and Wind, 1986), such goods are often studied but the majority of that work relies upon the Bass (1969) epidemic diffusion model. As Davies (1979) has shown, the epidemic model has many deficiencies, for example, it relies upon an assumption of an homogeneous population. For present purposes the model is also rather limited in that it considers that diffusion is solely the result of information spreading whereas we consider that diffusion has a much wider set of determinants. Although it has not been much used in the extant diffusion literature (which may be precisely because that literature concentrates upon durable goods) we prefer to use a model developed by Deaton and Muellbauer (1980, 261–9) (henceforth D&M). This model is basically a version of the linear expenditure system (LES), it reflects the diversity of factors that impact on the diffusion process and is admirably suited to analysing the purchasing patterns of non durables.

The LES however has its critics. The model is, for example, strongly separable and imposes quite strong restrictions on consumer preferences (see the discussion in D&M Ch. 5.3). It is, however, precisely the properties that derive from this that make the model so tractable in the current circumstances. The key property of the model that provides tractability in the analysis below is that for a given consumer, the share of income expended upon petrol is independent of the price of petrol. This considerably facilitates the aggregation over consumers that is required in the derivation of the aggregate diffusion curve.

If the share of income expended upon petrol is invariant to the price of petrol then each consumer will exhibit a unit elasticity of demand for petrol. Although there is some evidence that a unit elasticity may have some empirical support (Berndt, 1991, for example estimates the elasticity of the demand for fuel by households to be unity) there is not an extensive body of empirical literature to which one can turn for verification of this property of the model. We are thus inclined to view the constant budget share implication of the model as a working hypothesis that happens to be very convenient for current purposes.

Putting aside regulatory issues, the factors that may affect changes over time in the demand for a new non durable consumer good are: (i) changes in preferences; (ii) changes in prices; (iii) changes in income; (iv) changes in information; (v) changes in product performance; (vi) lending and borrowing decisions.

Of the above six factors we address the first five but abstract from the last on the grounds that the product with which we are concerned will only form a small part of total consumers' expenditure and as such the lending/borrowing decision is not of critical importance.

Within a heterogeneous population consider consumer i with income Y_i who owns a car that can use either unleaded fuel, product 1, or leaded fuel, product 2. We assume that the performance characteristics of leaded fuel are known with certainty. Let this performance (or in this context quality) be household specific and indicated by $\mu_{i2}(t)$. With unleaded fuel, however, being a new product, the performance characteristics are not known with certainty. Let the estimate of performance in time t by consumer i be $\mu_{i1}(t)$. We assume that as time proceeds the estimate of the performance of specification 1 changes via learning following a path yet to be specified.

In time t the consumer purchases $x_{i1}(t)$ and $x_{i2}(t)$ of the two specifications at prices $p_1(t)$ and $p_2(t)$ respectively and expends the balance $y_i(t)$ of income, $Y_i(t)$, on a composite commodity with a price of unity.

Following D&M, with some modification, we write the expected utility function for consumer i as (15.1)

$$Uit = \{[h_i(t) + a_i(t)\mu_{i1}(t)]x_{i1}(t) + b_i(t)\mu_{i2}(t)x_{i2}(t)\}^{\sigma i} \cdot y_{it}^{\Omega i} \tag{15.1}$$

where $a_i(t)$ and $b_i(t)$ are factors that reflect tastes and σ_i and Ω_i are parameters. The element $h_i(t)$ represents the utility gained by consumer i from the extra information on the performance of product 1 generated from the consumption $x_{i1}(t)$ (see Grossman et al., 1977). The inclusion of this term allows that consumers might purchase product 1 purely in order to learn about it.

The consumer is assumed risk neutral and as such maximises (15.1) subject to the budget constraint (15.2)

$$Y_i(t) = y_i(t) + p_1(t)x_{i1}(t) + p_2(t)x_{i2}(t) \tag{15.2}$$

D&M show that, within this framework, at a point in time the consumer will buy either product 1 or product 2 but not both simultaneously. If

$$\log p_1(t) - \log\{h_i(t) + a_i(t)\mu_{i1}(t)\} - \log p_2(t) + \log b_i(t) + \log \mu_{i2}(t) < 0 \tag{15.3}$$

consumer i will purchase product 1.

We assume: (i) that the true performance of product 1 in time t is given by $\mu_{i1}^*(t)$; (ii) that over time $\mu_{i1}(t)$ tends to $\mu_{i1}^*(t)$; (iii) that as $\mu_{i1}(t)$ tends to $\mu_{i1}^*(t)$ the value of $h_i(t)$ tends to zero; and (iv) that this process can be modelled in a simple way such that

$$\log\{h_i(t) + a_i(t)\mu_{i1}(t)\} = \log a_i(t) + \log \mu_{i1}^*(t) + f(t) \tag{15.4}$$

where the function $f(t)$ reflects both the approach of $\mu_{i1}(t)$ to $\mu_{i1}^*(t)$ and the declining value of information as time proceeds and experience accumulates. $f(t)$ may be positive or negative – the contribution of $h(t)$ will always be positive but $\mu_{i1}(t)$ may approach $\mu_{i1}^*(t)$ from above or below.

Following D&M, we model the heterogeneity of the population by assuming that $(\log a_i(t) + \log \mu_{i1}^*(t))$ and $(\log b_i(t) + \log \mu_{i2}(t))$ differ across the population by consumer specific error terms, i.e.

$$\log a_i(t) + \log \mu_{i1}^*(t) = \log a(t) + \log \mu_1^*(t) + e_{i1} \tag{15.5}$$

$$\log b_i(t) + \log \mu_{i2}(t) = \log b(t) + \log \mu_2(t) + e_{i2} \tag{15.6}$$

Substitution from (15.4), (15.5), and (15.6) into (15.3) yields the condition for consumer i choosing product 1 as (15.7)

$$(\log p_1(t) - \log p_2(t)) - (\log \mu_1^*(t) - \log \mu_2(t))$$
$$- (\log a(t) - \log b(t)) - f(t) < e_{i1} - e_{i2} \tag{15.7}$$

which has been written to emphasise that the condition takes account of differences between products 1 and 2 in prices, performance, and contributions to utility.

Following D&M assume that e_{i1} and e_{i2} have independent Weibull distributions, then the probability that a consumer with a car that can use unleaded petrol, chosen at random, will actually use unleaded petrol, defined as $\Phi(t)$, is given by (15.8)

$$\Phi(t) = \Pr\{e_{i1} - e_{i2} > g(t)\} = 1/(1 + \exp(c + g(t))) \tag{15.8}$$

where

$$g(t) = (\log p_1(t) - \log p_2(t)) - (\log \mu_1^*(t) - \log \mu_2(t))$$
$$- (\log a(t) - \log b(t)) - f(t) \tag{15.9}$$

and c is a parameter reflecting the value of $\Phi(t)$ in time zero.

Although eq. (15.8) is the central prediction of the model the data available to us are not appropriate to estimating this equation directly. To estimate (15.8) we require data upon the proportion of the cars that may use either type of fuel that actually use unleaded fuel in each time period. Such data are not available. The data available to us refer instead to the prices, quantities sold and thus the total sales value of the two different types of petrol across the whole market encompassing therefore not only purchases by owners of cars that can use both types of fuel but also purchases by owners of cars with catalytic converters and cars that must use leaded fuel.

In order to model the total market for petrol we need to first analyse the expenditure on fuel by owners of each type of car and then to sum over all owners (cars). From the first order conditions on the utility maximisation we may derive that if j ($j = 1, 2$) is the fuel specification purchased by consumer i (be that consumer an owner of a car that must, can or cannot use unleaded fuel) then that consumer's expenditure on fuel in time t, $p_j(t)x_{ij}(t)$, is given by (15.10)

$$p_j(t)x_{ij}(t) = \sigma_i Y_i(t)/(\Omega_i + \sigma_i) \tag{15.10}$$

The implications of (15.10) are that the model predicts that the consumer's expenditure on fuel is: (i) as discussed above, invariant with respect to the price of fuel; (ii) independent of any of the parameters in (15.8) that determine the fuel type choice when the consumer has a car that can use either type of fuel; but (iii) dependent upon the consumer's income and the elasticities of the utility function with respect to the quantities of fuel and other goods purchased. The first two of these jointly further imply that an individual's expenditure on fuel is independent of the type of car owned and the type of fuel used in that car.[4] Thus if consumers were identical in terms of $Y_i(t)$, Ω_i and σ_i, the model would predict that all consumers spent the same amount on fuel independent of car type and as such the share of unleaded fuel sales in total fuel sales would simply equal the share in the total car stock of all cars that are using unleaded fuel.

However, although we can see no reason why the parameters of the utility function should differ consistently across owners of different types of cars, it may be that consumers with higher incomes may own newer cars and those with lower incomes older cars. Given that newer cars are more likely to have catalytic converters and older cars are more likely to be unable to use unleaded fuel it might thus be that owners of cars with catalytic converters spend more on fuel and owners of cars that can only use leaded fuel spend less on fuel. To allow for this possibility, define $Y(t)$, $Y_C(t)$ and $Y_D(t)$ as the average incomes of all car owners, owners of cars with catalytic converters and owners of cars that may use either type of fuel respectively. Recalling that the fuel type choice by owners of cars that can use either fuel is independent of income level, using (15.10), we may then immediately write[5] that

$$M(t) = \delta C(t) + \alpha D(t)\Phi(t) \tag{15.11}$$

where $M(t)$ = the market share of unleaded petrol in total petrol sales in time t; $C(t)$ = the proportion of the total petrol driven car stock with catalytic converters at time t; $D(t)$ = the proportion of the total petrol driven car stock that can, but does not have to, use unleaded petrol (i.e. cars capable of using unleaded fuel but without catalytic converters) at time t; $\Phi(t)$ = the probability that an owner of a car that can use either type of fuel uses unleaded petrol and given by (15.8) above; $\delta = Y_C/Y$ is the ratio of the average income of owners of cars with catalytic converters to the average income of all car owners; and $\alpha = Y_D/Y$ is the ratio of the average income of owners of cars that can but do not have to use unleaded fuel to the average income of all car owners.

We assume that δ and α are constant over time. If it is in fact the case that owners of different types of cars have different average income levels a reasonable expectation would be to find that $\delta \geq 1$ but we have no prior expectation on the value of α. After substitution from (15.8) and (15.9) we may write (15.11) as (15.12)

$$M(t) = \delta C(t) + \alpha D(t)/\{1 + \exp(c + (\log p_1(t) - \log p_2(t)) - (\log \mu_1^*(t)$$
$$- \log \mu_2(t)) - (\log a(t) - \log b(t)) - f(t))\} \tag{15.12}$$

We make two further modifications to this formulation.

1   The theory predicts that $g(t)$ in (15.8) carries a unit coefficient. We allow more generally that this coefficient is β and test whether β is unity.
2   We are unable to separately model or identify through available data the three terms in $(\log \mu_1^*(t) - \log \mu_2(t)) - (\log a(t) - \log b(t)) - f(t))$. We thus introduce a composite term $F(T)$, where T is time since unleaded petrol was launched on the UK market, as a proxy for these three terms (also implicitly incorporating the parameter β as discussed immediately above). The actual form of $F(T)$ is to be determined empirically but given the components of the model summarised by $F(T)$ we do not necessarily expect the function to be monotonic. Introducing these two modifications yields eq. (15.13)

$$M(t) = \delta C(t) + \alpha D(t)/\{1 + \exp(c + \beta(\log p_1(t) - \log p_2(t)) + F(T))\} \tag{15.13}$$

For purposes of interpretation one should note that eq. (15.8) predicts that as $g(t)$ tends to (minus) infinity $\Phi(t)$ tends to unity. If, however, there are some consumers who will never use unleaded fuel even if their car is capable of using such fuel, the limit of $\Phi(t)$ will be less than unity. To the degree that there is such an effect it will be reflected in α in (15.13). Thus even if the average fuel purchases by owners of cars that can, but do not have to use unleaded fuel, do not differ from average fuel purchases across all consumers, it is possible that α will be less than unity.[6]

Equation (15.13) summarises the impacts on the diffusion of unleaded fuel from: regulation, which will primarily be reflected in the impact of changes in the composition of the car stock i.e. $C(t)$ and $D(t)$; fiscal incentives, which will be reflected in the impact of changes in the relative price of leaded and unleaded fuels; and other factors summarised in $F(T)$. These other factors encompass, differences in the actual performance of the two types of fuels ($\log \mu_1^*(t) - \log \mu_2(t)$), learning about the two types of fuels ($f(t)$), and differences in consumer tastes relating to the two fuels, i.e. consumer greenness ($\log a(t) - \log b(t)$). We have no evidence to suggest that performances of the two fuels are different or have been changing over time thus below we refer to change in $F(T)$ as simply changes in tastes and learning.

Equation (15.13) is in fact a standard logistic curve of a type commonly found in the diffusion literature (see for example Stoneman, 1983). It has been frequently observed that diffusion patterns in the majority of cases may be summarised by an S shaped diffusion path. The logistic diffusion curve predicts that the adoption of new technology will follow such an S shaped path over time and as such we consider the logistic curve to be an advantageous prediction of the model.

In the diffusion literature it is common practice to proceed from this point using a linear transformation of the logistic diffusion curve for estimation purposes rather than the logistic curve itself, it being assumed that the error term is additive to the transformed equation (this tradition can be traced back to Griliches, 1957). To work with the logistic transformation rather than with the multivariate non linear form is also common practice in the econometric literature (see Harvey, 1989). Define

$$X(t, \delta, \alpha) = \{\delta C(t) + \alpha D(t) - M(t)\} / \{M(t) - C(t)\} \tag{15.14}$$

where $X(t, \delta, \alpha)$ (using 15.8) equals $(1 - \Phi(t))/\Phi(t)$ and may be interpreted as the ratio of the probability of using leaded petrol to the probability of using unleaded petrol for a typical consumer with a vehicle that may (but does not have to) use unleaded fuel. From (15.13) and (15.14) we may then write that

$$\log X(t, \delta, \alpha) = c + \beta (\log p_1(t) - \log p_2(t)) + F(T) + u'(t) \tag{15.15}$$

where $u'(t)$ is the error term. Allowing $F(T)$ to take the form

$$F(T) = a + \tau_1 T + \tau_2 \log T \tag{15.16}$$

which imposes neither linearity nor monotonicity and as such is particularly suited to the theoretical underpinnings of the model, and substituting into (15.15) yields the estimating equation, (15.17)

$$\log X(t, \delta, \alpha) = (a + c) + \beta(\log p_1(t) - \log p_2(t)) + \tau_1 T + \tau_2 \log T + u'(t) \qquad (15.17)$$

The advantage of using (15.17) rather than (15.13) is that in common with many non-linear relationships, the untransformed logistic form is rather difficult to handle. This is particularly the case when, as below, lagged values and other dynamic adjustments are entered into the model.

15.4.   Estimation and Results

The data we use to generate our estimates[7] relate to the UK, are monthly and cover the period from January 1987–May 1995. The data sources are reported upon in appendix 15A.

Prior to estimation we first explored whether the diffusion process was likely to have been supply constrained. This is an issue that is of interest in its own right but is also important to the estimation of eq. (15.17), for, if there have been supply constraints, then estimates of a single equation demand side model (which (15.17) is) would be biased.

In fig. 15.1 we plot the market share of unleaded petrol and its availability at petrol stations. It is clear that post early 1988 availability was much greater than market share. Prior to early 1988 availability and market share are much smaller although in each month the proportion of petrol stations selling unleaded exceeded the market share of unleaded. Given especially that motorists have a choice of where to purchase petrol and thus, if they wish, may select stations that sell unleaded petrol, this has led us to conclude that market share was never constrained by availability. We thus consider that the estimates of eq. (15.17) that we report below do not suffer from any bias due to supply constraints. However to further verify this we have undertaken a number of experiments in which terms measuring availability[8] have been added into eq. (15.17) and these terms were never significant (these results have not been reported in detail).

To estimate eq. (15.17) we need to measure $X(t, \delta, \alpha)$ as defined by eq. (15.14). Although $D(t)$, $M(t)$ and $C(t)$ are given by the data sources the definition of $X(t, \delta, a)$ includes two parameters α and δ that are not known to us. We proceeded by deriving initial values for (α, δ) by using non-linear least squares[9] on eq. (15.13). Despite the sensitivity of the NLS algorithm to the initial values assumed and some residual autocorrelation we observed a number of robust results and in particular that δ, the coefficient of $C(t)$ consistently equalled one and that α was consistently estimated as around 0.9. Initial estimates of eq. (15.17) were thus produced taking (α, δ) as $(0.9, 1)$. Using the non nested testing procedure suggested by Davidson and Mackinnon (1981), i.e. the Jay test, and the Cox extension of the likelihood ratio test we then checked in each model specification against alternative values for the (α, δ) pair (allowing α and δ to vary in intervals of 0.05). For space reasons we do not report the values of the test statistics, but in each case $(0.9, 1)$ produced the best diagnostic indicators and goodness of fit. Looking for brevity in presenting the results below, we thus limit the presentation to only those results in which $\delta = 1$ and α takes the value of 0.9.

Our initial estimates of eq. (15.17) using OLS consistently showed autocorrelation. Given that our preliminary analysis (see n. 9) indicated that the basic logistic cure was the appropriate functional form, we read this as indicating that eq. (15.17) did not appropriately specify the dynamic structure of the model. As Granger (1995) states, such problems are common in economics. Theoretical models rarely fully specify dynamic response structures.

As we had no particular expectations as to what the dynamics would be in this case, we looked for the most suitable dynamic adjustment process empirically, using a step by step procedure. We thus undertook many experiments using different dynamic specifications of eq. (15.17). These experiments led us to conclude that an error correction model (ECM) was the most fruitful approach to employ and it is upon results from this specification that we concentrate. We note that to the best of our knowledge ECM techniques have not previously been employed in the estimation of diffusion models.

Our analysis of the ECM proceeds by first establishing the order of integration and the time series properties of the relevant variables. We then specify and estimate an unrestricted ECM specification. Finally we apply the Johansen ML cointegration procedure and the restricted ECM as a further test.

The concept of cointegration was first introduced by Engle and Granger (1987) who define that the components of a vector $x(t)$ are said to be cointegrated of order (d, b) if (i) all components of $x(t)$ are $I(d)$, integrated of order d, and (ii) there exists a vector α (non-zero) such that the linear combination $Z(t) = \alpha x(t)$ is integrated of order $(d - b)$ where $b > 0$. If these conditions hold then α is called the cointegrating vector. In other words, given a simple regression model ($y(t) = wx(t) + z(t)$) the long run relationship between y and x may be represented by their co-integrating static regression $z(t) = y(t) - wx(t)$ and $z(t)$ should be stationary, $I(0)$ (see Granger, 1986; Granger and Weiss, 1983). $z(t)$ measures the deviation of $y(t)$ from its equilibrium value in time t and is known as the equilibrium error or the error correction term. It represents the adjustment made to the system each time a shock causes it to deviate from its equilibrium value. The co-integration vector is the vector of the coefficients of the co-integrating equation (in this case 1, $-w$).

The commonest version of the ECM is specified in terms of levels and first differences and for our model can be written as

$$D \log X(t) = \beta' D(\log p_1(t) - \log p_2(t)) + \tau_1' + \tau_2' D \log T + m'[\log X(t - 1)$$
$$- \beta(\log p_1(t - 1) - \log p_2(t - 1)) - a - \tau_1(T - 1)$$
$$- \tau_2 \log (T - 1)] + n_1(t) \tag{15.18}$$

where D is the first difference operator, the square bracketed term is the cointegrating equation, $(\beta'; \tau_1'; \tau_2')$ and $(\beta; \tau_1; \tau_2)$ are the short and long run coefficients respectively, a is the long run intercept, m' is a parameter measuring the short run impact of deviations from the long run equilibrium on changes in the dependent variable, and $n_1(t)$ is a well behaved error term.

For this model to be relevant it is necessary that the variables of interest are integrated of order 1, i.e. are $I(1)$. However our preliminary analysis of the time series properties of the relevant variables (see appendix 15B) shows that apart from the non-linear trend, the variables of interest in the model, $\log X(t, \delta, \alpha)$, for different (δ, α) pairs, and $(\log p_1(t) - \log p_2(t))$, were stationary in their second difference (i.e. they are $I(2)$) and not their first difference (as required by an ECM in levels and first differences). If a variable is $I(2)$ then that variable is stationary in its second difference. In the literature there are many example of $I(1)$ processes but few where the variables are $I(2)$ – although price series are often found to be $I(2)$. The finding that our variables are $I(2)$ requires that we take a slightly different approach to the ECM than the common method detailed above.

We specify an ECM in terms of levels, first and second differences (Johansen 1992a, 1992b, 1995, Juselius 1994) and we may then rely upon the Granger representation theorem (Granger, 1986; Granger and Weiss, 1983) which states that if our variables are cointegrated the ECM is a valid representation of their relationship (and vice versa). Given that the variables of interest are $I(2)$ we may, using (15.17) specify two relevant cointegrating relationships, one in first differences and one in levels

$$z(t-1) = D \log X(t-1) - \beta'D(\log p_1(t-1) - \log p_2(t-1))$$
$$- \tau_1' - \tau_2'D \log (T-1) \tag{15.19}$$

$$q(t-2) = \log X(t-2) - \beta(\log p_1(t-2) - \log p_2(t-2))$$
$$- a - \tau_1 - \tau_2 \log(T-2) \tag{15.20}$$

For (15.19) and (15.20) to hold it is necessary that the residual of the relevant cointegrating equation is stationary. We find that this is not the case for (15.20) and as such there is no empirical evidence for the existence of $q(t-2)$, indicating that our variables are cointegrated only in their first difference. We may thus ignore $q(t-2)$ and write the ECM as (15.21)

$$DD \log X(t) = \beta''DD(\log p_1(t) - \log p_2(t)) + \tau_2''DD \log T$$
$$+ m''[D \log X(t-1) - [\beta'D(\log p_1(t-1) - \log p_2(t-1)$$
$$- \tau_1' - \tau_2'D \log(T-1)] + n_2(t) \tag{15.21}$$

where D is the first difference operator and DD the second difference operator, the square bracketed term is the cointegrating equation, $(\beta''; \tau_2'')$ and $(\beta'; \tau_1'; \tau_2')$ are the short and long run coefficients respectively, m'' is the parameter measuring the short run impact of deviations from the long run equilibrium on changes in the dependent variable, and $n_2(t)$ is a well behaved error term.

Alternatively, exercising the option to leave the intercept term outside the co-integrating equation, and tidying up the representation of the parameters, we may write (15.21) as (15.22), the unrestricted reduced form ECM

$$DD \log X(t) = \Theta_0 + \Theta_1 DD(\log p_1(t) - \log p_2(t)) + \Theta_2 DD \log(T)$$
$$+ \Theta_3 D \log X(t-1) + \Theta_4 D(\log p_1(t-1) - \log p_2(t-1))$$
$$+ \Theta_5 D \log(T-1) + n_2(t) \tag{15.22}$$

As explained above eq. (15.22) has been estimated for different (δ, α) pairs. Our best results arise from the pair $(1, 0.90)$. The resulting OLS estimates are presented in column 1 of table 15.1. The diagnostic statistics for these estimates are good. From the estimates of the coefficients $\Theta_i(i = 1 \ldots 5)$ we may calculate that: the short run estimates of β and τ_2 equal $\Theta_1 = 0.52$ and $\Theta_2 = -104.5$ respectively; $m'' = -\Theta_3 = 0.85$; the long run estimates of β and τ_2 equal $\Theta_4/m'' = -\Theta_4/\Theta_3 = 0.82$ and $\Theta_5/m'' = -\Theta_5/\Theta_3 = -12.0$ respectively; the long run estimate of τ_1 is given by $\Theta_0/m'' = -\Theta_0/\Theta_3 = 0.11$. A Wald test of the non-linear restriction that the long run price coefficient is unity yields chi$^2 = 0.571$ and we are unable

Table 15.1   Estimates

	(1)	(2)
Estimation method	Unrestricted ECM	Restricted ECM
Dependent variable	DD log $X(t)$	DD log $X(t)$
α	0.90	0.90
Intercept	0.11	−0.057
	(2.51)	(−2.93)
$D \log X(t-1)$	−0.85	
	(−8.55)	
$D(\log p_1(t-1) - \log p_2(t-1))$	0.695	
	(3.18)	
$D \log(T-1)$	10.2	
	(3.60)	
$DD(\log p_1(t) - \log p_2(t))$	0.52	0.436
	(8.55)	(3.931)
$DD \log T$	−104.5	−128.73
	(−3.31)	(−6.891)
Error correction term $(t-1)^*$		−0.94
		(−9.077)
R^2	0.48	0.47
F	17.42	28.339
s.e.	0.155	0.16
DW/h	2.096	2.004
$PFT\dagger$		
$\chi^2(16)$	23.445	21.12
$F(16,77)$	1.4653	1.3201
Chow-test$\ddagger$		
$\chi^2(v_1)$	13.256	7.9225
$F(v_1; v_2)$	2.2094	1.9806

* The error correction term takes the form $z(t) = D \log X(t) - 0.14 - 0.718 * D(\log p_1(t) - \log p_2(t))$ + 12.97 $* D \log T$.
$\dagger$ Predictive failure test.
$\ddagger$ Test for the stability of the regression coefficients with (6,87) and (4,89) degrees of freedom for the unrestricted and restricted model respectively.

at a 5 per cent level of significance to reject the hypothesis that the long run price coefficient is unity (the value that a pure version of the theory would suggest).

As a further test we have also estimated the same relationship with a restricted autoregressive vector (the restricted ECM model) by substituting the ML Johansen co-integrating residual into the unrestricted ECM (see table 15.1 column 2) which is estimated by OLS at a second stage. This method (see Johansen and Juselius, 1990) overcomes potential problems of bias that are inherent to the first stage OLS estimation in the more common Engle and Granger (1987) procedure. Also, given that OLS estimates can be the result of a linear combination of more than one solution (see Banerjee et al., 1993) and thus the estimates of the adjustment process might not be unique, the Johansen procedure has the advantage of enabling us to test which of the possible solutions is the most representative of the underlying adjustment process.

The restricted ECM may be written as

$$DD \log X(t) = \theta_1 DD(\log p_1(t) - \log p_2(t)) + \theta_2 DD \log(T) - mz(t-1) + n_3(t) \quad (15.23)$$

where m measures the short run impact of the error correction term on $DD \log X(t)$ and $n_3(t)$ is a well behaved error term. As in the unrestricted ECM we find no evidence that the variables are cointegrated at levels and as such we have excluded any term in $q(t-2)$. Using this approach, with again (δ, α) equalling $(1, 0.90)$ we estimate the long run cointegrating relationship (with the deterministic trend being reintroduced in to $z(t-1)$) as (15.24)

$$D \log X(t) = 0.14 - 12.97 D \log T + 0.718 D(\log p_1(t) - \log p_2(t)) \quad (15.24)$$

The estimates of the other parameters of the model[10] are presented in column 2 of table 15.1 and imply short run estimates of β and τ_2 equal to 0.50 and -128.73 respectively and $m = 0.95$. The associated adjustment vector under this specification is $(-0.875; 0.06891; -0.1577e - 4)$ corresponding to $(D \log X; D(\log p_1(t) - \log p_2(t)); D \log T)$. The adjustment coefficients on $D(\log p_1(t) - \log p_2(t))$ and $D \log T$ are sufficiently small to suggest that these variables are determined exogenously to the system and thus we can reliably draw the inferences that we do below.

The diagnostic statistics for these estimates are good. ML tests lead to the rejection of the hypothesis of both first and higher order autocorrelation of the residuals. Traditional tests for cointegration have also been applied; CRDW = 0.79, DF = -5.773 and ADF = -4.8846. Comparing these values with the critical values tabulated by Engle and Yoo (1987) and Sargan and Bhargava (1983) (at the 5 per cent significance level 0.48, -3.93 and -3.75 respectively) we can reject the hypothesis of no cointegration and thus via the Granger representation theorem (Granger, 1986; Granger and Weiss, 1983) we cannot reject the hypothesis that the ECM is a valid representation of the relationship. We have also undertaken a number of predictive failure tests (see table 15.1) and are unable to reject the hypotheses that the regression coefficients are stable over time. The estimates indicate an insignificant intercept (as expected given that (15.22) contains no intercept other than the deterministic trend which is already included in (15.19)). All other variables are significant.[11]

The cointegrating relationship (15.24) states that long run changes in the ratio of the probability of using leaded petrol to the probability of using unleaded petrol for a consumer with a vehicle that may (but does not have) to use unleaded fuel, $D \log X(t)$, is made up of two parts (i) $0.14 - 12.97 \log T$, which is the change in the trend term reflecting changing tastes and learning and (ii) $0.718 D(\log p_1(t) - \log p_2(t))$ which is the effect of changes in relative prices over time. Our estimation method does not enable us to generate estimates of the levels of the trend and relative price terms. In fig. 15.4 we plot $D \log X(t)$ and the two terms reflecting changes in the trend and relative prices. $D \log X(t)$ has a mean value of -0.065 i.e. the above defined probability declines at 6.5 per cent per month on average over the sample period, takes its largest negative values in 1988 and 1989, and generally declines in size as the diffusion proceeds. The term reflecting changes in tastes and learning starts as a large negative (indicating that changes in tastes were making a positive contribution to the use of unleaded fuel) and then approaches zero becoming slightly positive for $T > 93$. The term reflecting the effects of changes in relative prices mainly cycles around zero although significant positive contributions to increases in the probability of using unleaded fuel are made in March or April each year when the Budget changing fuel duties

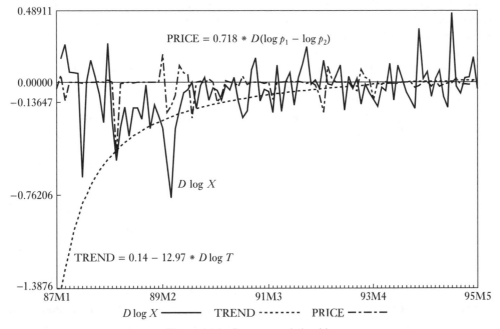

Figure 15.4 Long-run relationships

was traditionally delivered. We calculate that at the sample means the trend effect takes a value of -0.197 while the price effect takes a value of -0.0165 and thus at the sample means the trend effect is 12 times as large as the price effect.

Overall these estimates indicate: (i) changes in relative prices have impacted positively on changes in the use of unleaded fuel with the elasticity of the probability of buying such fuel to relative prices, β', being not significantly different from unity in the long run (based upon tests applied to the unrestricted ECM model) as the theory would suggest; (ii) changes in tastes and learning as reflected in changes in the trend term also have impacted positively on changes in the probability of buying unleaded fuel, these effects being considerably larger than the effects of changes in relative prices; (iii) our best estimates of the coefficients δ and α are 1 and 0.9 respectively. These two parameters were introduced to allow for differential fuel expenditures across different groups of car owners. However, given that $\delta = 1$ and that α will also reflect there being a group of car owners who will never voluntarily use unleaded fuel, this indicates little evidence in favour of the hypothesis that differential fuel expenditures across car types are significant.

15.5.   Discussion

The objectives of this paper were to explore the relative importance of the following factors in the determination of the spread of unleaded fuel: supply side factors i.e. unleaded availability; government regulation; other government intervention i.e. fiscal incentives; and learning and changes in consumer tastes.

On the basis of both data patterns and estimates of supply constrained models of consumer demand, in our view, the availability of unleaded petrol was not a constraint on the diffusion process. Clearly this does not mean that it was not important, for if the fuel were not available diffusion could not have proceeded. In fact availability played an enabling role.

In order to explore the relative importance of the other factors in the diffusion process we build upon the results derived in the previous section.[12] Using (15.14), defining $m(t)$, $c(t)$, $d(t)$, and $x(t)$ as the growth rates of $M(t)$, $C(t)$, $D(t)$, and $X(t)$ respectively, setting $\delta = 1$ and $\alpha = 0.9$ as estimated above and representing $x(t)$ by the long term cointegrating relationship (15.24) we may derive (15.25)

$$
m(t) = c(t)\frac{C(t)}{M(t)} + d(t)\left(\frac{M(t) - C(t)}{M(t)}\right) + \left(\frac{M(t) - C(t)}{M(t)}\right)\left(\frac{M(t) - C(t) - 0.9D(t)}{0.9D(t)}\right)
$$

$$
\times (0.14 - 12.97D \log T) + \left(\frac{M(t) - C(t)}{M(t)}\right)\left(\frac{M(t) - C(t) - 0.9D(t)}{0.9D(t)}\right)
$$

$$
\times (0.718D(\log p_1(t) - \log p_2(t)) + e(t)) \tag{15.25}
$$

Equation (15.25) illustrates that the rate of growth of the market share of unleaded petrol can be split into five components: (i) the effects of growth in the share of the car stock with catalytic converters (the first term on the right hand side of (15.25)); (ii) the effects of the growth of the share of the car stock that can but does not have to use unleaded fuel (the second term on the right hand side of (15.25)); (iii) the effect of changes in the trend term reflecting the impact of changes in tastes and learning on the propensity of owners with a choice to buy unleaded fuel (the third term); (iv) the effects of changes in relative prices on the propensity of owners with a choice to buy unleaded fuel (the fourth term); and (v) an error term $e(t)$ representing short term deviations from the long term cointegrating relationship and structural errors. In fig. 15.5 we plot against time for the whole sample period, $m(t)$, the growth of the market share of unleaded fuel, and each of the first four identified components.

The time profile of the diffusion of unleaded petrol may be split into three separate periods: from the start of the process to September 1989 when no regulations were in force; from October 1989 to December 1992 when all new models (and from October 1990 all new cars) sold in the UK had to be capable of using unleaded fuel; and from January 1993 when all new cars sold in the UK had to incorporate catalytic converters and thus of necessity use unleaded fuel. From fig. 15.5 we observe that the growth rate of market share is fastest from 1986 through to late 1989, the first period, averaging 16 per cent per month. In this period the growth rate of market share was also volatile, peaking at 47 per cent per month (one may also note that it is in this early part of the sample that the error term $e(t)$ is largest, i.e. when the four identified factors are least able to explain the growth of market share). The main factors driving market share growth in this first period were growth in the share of cars capable of using unleaded fuel (contributing on average 4.9 per cent per month to the growth rate), followed by changes in tastes and learning, given the car stock composition, contributing on average 1.3 per cent per month to the growth rate. The contribution of changes in relative prices to the growth of market shares (given the car stock composition) was minimal. In the second period of the diffusion, although market share has continued to

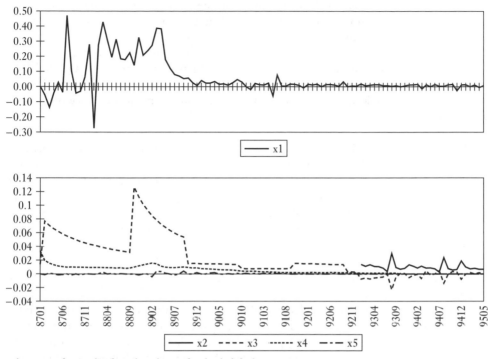

x1 = rate of growth of market share of unleaded fuel
x2 = contribution of growth of share of cars with catalytic converters
x3 = contribution of growth of share of cars that may (but do not have to) use unleaded fuel
x4 = contribution of changes in tastes
x5 = contribution of changes in relative prices

Figure 15.5   The rate of growth of market share and its components

increase, its growth rate was much smaller than in the first period and less volatile. The contribution of growth in $D(t)$ and changes in tastes and learning were both smaller than in the first period but their relative importance has not changed. Again changes in relative prices made little contribution. In the third period the growth rate of market share has reduced further. Tastes and relative prices contribute very little to changes in market share (given the car stock composition) but the growth of cars with catalytic converters begins to have a positive effect on the growth of market share contributing on average 1 per cent per month, however this is offset by a decline in the impact of the growth of the share of cars that can use either type of fuel.

Figure 15.5 basically illustrates that it is changes in the composition of the car stock that has been the major driving force in the diffusion process and not changes in tastes or relative prices. However, it is possible that consumers may have decided to convert their car to use unleaded fuel or to buy cars that may or must use unleaded fuel as a reaction to changing prices and tastes and thus that the car stock also reacted to changing prices and tastes. Until now this possibility has been ignored (the car stock being taken as exogenous) but it does provide an indirect route by which relative prices and tastes could have affected the growth of market shares. Thus, although we are unable to precisely model car stock composition, we undertake some counter factual exercises that help to indicate the potential sizes of the relative impact of regulations and consumer choice on the car stock composition.

The first obvious point is that prior to October 1989 there were no regulations and as such the regulatory impact on the car stock would have been zero. Post October 1989 we may gain some measure of the impact of regulation by setting up two counter factual scenarios of what would have happened in the absence of the regulations. We proceed by assuming that:

1   In the absence of the 1993 regulation the 1989 regulation would have stayed in force, no cars would have had catalytic converters, but the propensity of owners with the choice to use unleaded fuel would have followed the same path as actually followed. On the counter factual path therefore those cars that in reality were fitted with catalytic converters would instead have had the choice between leaded and unleaded fuel. We may then write (assuming $\delta = 1$ and $\alpha = 0.9$) that the counter factual market share, $M_{cf1}(t)$, is given by (15.26)

$$M_{cf1}(t) = \alpha(D(t) + C(t))/(X(t) + 1) \tag{15.26}$$

2   In the absence of the 1989 regulation and the 1993 regulation the share of cars with the choice between leaded and unleaded fuel would have remained constant at the September 1989 level of 38.7 per cent, $C(t)$ would have equalled zero for all t, but the propensity of owners with the choice to use unleaded fuel would have followed the same path as actually followed. The resulting counter factual market share, $M_{cf2}(t)$, may be written as (15.27)

$$M_{cf2}(t) = 38.7(M(t) - C(t))/D(t) \tag{15.27}$$

These are rather severe assumptions for the counter factuals and will tend to maximise the impact of regulations. As such the estimates that we produce should be taken as indicating the maximum possible contributions of such regulation (and of course the minimum contribution of other factors).

We could proceed by imposing these counter factual assumptions on to figure 15.5 and illustrate the resulting changes in the growth of market shares and the contributions of different factors. Qualitatively the results are obvious e.g. for $M_{cf2}(t)$ the contribution of $d(t)$ is reduced to zero for all months post September 1989. Instead we find it more enlightening to work on the levels of market shares rather than the growth rate. In order to do this, in calculating counter factual market shares, $1/(X(t) + 1)$ is measured[13] by its realised value of $(M(t) - C(t))/\alpha D(t)$. In table 15.2 we present the resulting estimates of the actual and various counter factual market shares.

Labelling the market share in the absence of regulation as the base market share we are then able to calculate the impact of the 1989 and 1993 regulations as in table 15.3.

Two particular points in these results merit some comment. First it may be surprising that the impact of the catalytic converter regulation is so small and much smaller than the share of cars with catalytic converters. This is because we have assumed that such cars under the counter factual might still use unleaded fuel (in fact 71 per cent of drivers with

Table 15.2 Actual and counter factual market shares

	Sept 1989	Dec 1992	May 1995
Actual	24.9	47.1	59.6
$M_{cf1}(t)$	24.9	47.1	55.9
$M_{cf2}(t)$	24.9	29.8	27.7

$M_{cf1}(t)$ indicates what market share would have been if the 1993 regulations had not been introduced and the 1989 regulations had still been in place. $M_{cf2}(t)$ indicates what market share would have been had neither regulation been in place.

Table 15.3 Percentage point increases in market share due to different factors

	Jan 87–Sept 89	Sept 89–Dec 92	Dec 92–May 95	Jan 87–May 95
Base effects	24.9	4.9	−2.1	27.7
1989 regulations	0	17.3	10.9	28.2
1993 regulations	0	0	3.7	3.7
Total	24.9	22.2	12.5	59.6

the choice actually used unleaded fuel in May 1995). Secondly we find that the base effects are negative between December 1992 and May 1995. This results because our estimate of the propensity of car owners that have the choice to use unleaded fuel calculated as $(M(t) - C(t))/\alpha D(t)$ declines over the period. Although this is surprising it is consistent with our econometric estimate of the growth of the trend term $F(T)$ which is positive for all t after September 1993. Essentially what is happening is that as drivers convert from cars that may use unleaded to cars that must use unleaded those that remain with the choice show a decreasing propensity to use unleaded fuel.

The estimates in tables 15.2 and 15.3 indicate that the May 1995 market share of unleaded fuel just over half is due to regulation and just under half is due to base effects. In terms of growth of market share therefore we may state that regulations have effectively doubled the rate of growth of the market share of unleaded fuel over the sample period. However such regulations had no impact in the initial stage of the diffusion process but were the dominant factors in the latter two stages. In the last two stages base effects were small.

Having removed the effects of regulations, the base effects in tables 15.2 and 15.3 reflect the impacts on market shares arising from (i) the direct effects of relative prices and tastes on the propensity to buy unleaded fuel (given the car stock composition), (ii) the indirect effects of relative prices and tastes on the composition of the car stock, and (iii) any unexplained residual effects. Given the construction of $M_{cf2}(t)$, in the second and third stages of the diffusion process the base effects estimated in table 15.3 define the indirect effects of changes in prices and tastes to be zero. The base effects that are estimated for these two stages will thus basically reflect the direct impact of changes in tastes and learning. The data in table 15.3 confirm what we have already shown in fig. 15.5 – these effects are small.

In the first stage of the diffusion process the base effects are much larger. Setting aside any unexplained residual effects the growth of market share in this first stage can only reflect the direct and indirect effects of changes in tastes, learning and relative prices. During this first diffusion stage therefore, relative prices, tastes and learning had a major impact upon market shares. However we have already shown in fig. 15.5 that the direct effects of changes in prices and tastes in this stage are small relative to the car stock composition effects. Given that these car stock composition effects reflect the indirect impact of changes in tastes and relative prices, we may conclude that it was mainly in this period and primarily through the car stock composition, that tastes and relative prices impacted on market shares.

Bringing these results together we may state, given the counter factuals that we have assumed, that: (i) about half of the May 1995 market share of unleaded fuel is due to regulations, primarily the October 1989/90 regulation; (ii) the direct impact of changes in relative prices on the growth of market share has been minimal throughout the diffusion process; (iii) the direct impact of changes in tastes and learning to the growth of market shares averaged 1.3 per cent per month through to October 1989 but then declined and was largely exhausted by mid to late 1992; (iv) growth in the share of cars capable of using unleaded fuel in the absence of regulation was a major factor driving the diffusion process pre-October 1989, contributing on average 4.7 percentage points to the monthly growth rate of market share; (v) this change in the composition of the car stock pre-October 1989 was largely driven by changes in tastes and relative prices (although we cannot separate out the two impacts) and represents the main indirect impact of such on market shares.

15.6.   Conclusions and Policy Implications

In this paper we have explored the diffusion of unleaded petrol in the UK during 1987–95. This diffusion process was driven by two main sub processes (i) the growing share of cars capable of using or having to use unleaded fuel (car stock composition effects) and (ii) the increasing probability that owners of cars that may use unleaded fuel actually use such fuel (fuel type choice effects). We were primarily interested in the roles that have been played in the overall diffusion process through these two routes by changes in consumer preferences, fuel availability and government intervention via fiscal incentives and regulation.

We find that:

1   The diffusion process was enabled by the availability of unleaded fuel but never constrained by it.
2   Car stock composition effects were the dominant factors in explaining the growth of the market share of unleaded fuel. The contribution of fuel type choice effects was always relatively small and such effects were largely exhausted by early 1992.
3   The main determinant of fuel type choice effects was changes in tastes and learning as opposed to changes in relative prices. The latter reflected differential duty rates to leaded and unleaded petrol and thus fiscal incentives to the use of unleaded fuel had only a minor impact upon fuel type choice. Given (2) this is consistent with the findings of the sister paper based on survey data (Wong et al., 1996) which suggests that although

the greening of consumer preferences may have once had a significant impact they are no longer a major force in the diffusion process.

4   The main determinants of the car stock composition prior to October 1989 were changing tastes and prices (although we were unable to measure their importance relative to each other). Through this route and in the period to October 1989 the impact of changes in tastes and learning and prices was almost four times the impact through fuel type choice effects.

5   Post-October 1989 car stock composition was impacted upon by two regulations, the first requiring that from October 1989 all new models sold and from October 1990 all new cars sold in the UK had to be capable of using unleaded fuel, the second requiring that from January 1993 all new cars sold should be fitted with catalytic converters and thus must use unleaded fuel. We find that by May 1995 the market share of unleaded fuel is approximately twice what it would have been in the absence of these regulations but the contribution of the 1993 regulation was much less than that of the 1989 regulation.

The policy maker concerned with changing consumer expenditure patterns in order to encourage environmental friendliness has a number of options available. The first is to do nothing. In this case that would have meant that the diffusion process would have been determined by (i) private decisions made upon unleaded fuel availability and (ii) the impact of changes in consumer tastes and learning working through both the car stock composition and through fuel type choice effects. Our results suggest that if no policy action had been taken then such effects would have led to an increased demand for unleaded fuel such that (in the absence of availability constraints) the market share of unleaded fuel would have reached a maximum of 30 per cent in December 1992 (a maximum because we cannot be precise as to the measure of the impact that the fiscally induced fuel price differential had upon the car stock composition). The potential for further such free market induced demand growth was largely exhausted by this date and at this level.

Whether such demand would have been satisfied by a free market is another matter. As we discussed in n. 2, the petrol suppliers stated in interview that the fiscal incentives to buyers of unleaded fuel in the 1987 Budget encouraged them to make unleaded petrol more widely available. Moreover the availability of unleaded fuel in the UK was driven by a European Commission mandate (85/210/EC) that unleaded petrol had to be available nationwide from October 1989. If availability had not been so widespread then the diffusion process may well have been constrained and the market share of unleaded fuel have been less.

Rather than doing nothing and relying upon market forces, the policy maker may use several different policy instruments to stimulate the diffusion of an environmentally friendly product. The first instrument is fiscal incentives. These were used in the UK to create a price differential between leaded and unleaded petrol varying over time from 5 to 13 per cent of the price of leaded fuel. Recently the UK government have offered a similar fiscal incentives to encourage the use of 'clean' diesel fuel and thus seemingly the instrument is still believed to be powerful. The price incentive will impact upon demand through both the car stock composition and through fuel type choice. We have shown that the size of the impact through the latter route was always small. We are unable to precisely quantify the former effect except that it may have been greater than the latter (our results suggest that the impact of changes in tastes and learning and changes in prices jointly had greater car stock composition effects than fuel type choice effects, but we cannot separate out the effects re the former). The results are thus somewhat sanguine as to the efficacy of fiscal incentives in stimulating the demand for unleaded fuel. Of course this may be because the fiscal incentive was not sufficiently large and a larger incentive would have had a greater impact. However, if this is done by making unleaded fuel absolutely cheaper rather than just relatively cheaper, our model predicts that more fuel will be purchased and thus there must come a stage where the incentive is self defeating in environmental terms. One may also note as stated above that the fiscal incentives to buyers of unleaded fuel in the 1987 Budget encouraged suppliers to make unleaded petrol more widely available. Thus the incentives may have worked indirectly by preventing availability constraints.

The second policy instrument available to the policy maker is regulation. Here there have been three significant policies introduced in the past. The first was the implementation of the European Commission mandate (85/210/EC) that unleaded petrol had to be available nationwide from October 1989. This may not have been necessary if the petrol suppliers would have made the product available anyway, but we do not know whether that would have been the case or not. The second regulation was the 1989/1990 regulation concerning the capability of new cars to use unleaded fuel. We estimate that this increased the market share of unleaded fuel by 28 percentage points in 1995 (when the market share was 59.6 per cent). The third regulation requiring all new cars sold after January 1st 1993 to have catalytic converters, we calculate added only 3.7 percentage points to the market share of unleaded fuel by May 1995.

These results suggest to us that as far as unleaded petrol in the UK was concerned, regulations have been by far a more effective instrument in stimulating the desired shift to an environmentally friendly product than have price incentives. However government intervention in general has been successful in raising the level of use of such fuel from around a 30 per cent market share (assuming no supply constraints) to a market share in 1995 of around 60 per cent.

With the 1993 regulation in place, over time as old cars are replaced, all cars will have to use unleaded fuel and as such the market share of such fuel will eventually go to 100 per cent. The policy maker may (and seemingly does) want to speed up this process. The same policy instruments are still available. Further price incentives could be employed, but our results suggest these will be largely ineffective. In fact, regulations are to be used again. A further European directive is in place that will require that leaded fuel will no longer be available (apart from a very few outlets servicing owners of classic cars) from the year 2000. Reducing the availability of leaded fuel to zero will clearly generate a 100 per cent market share for unleaded fuel.

Appendix 15A   Data Sources

The variables used above are defined and sourced as follows:

1   T measured as the number of months from June 1986, the launch date for unleaded petrol in the UK.
2   Total petrol driven car stock in the UK. Monthly data sourced from Society of Motor Manufacturers and Traders Limited, *Monthly Statistical Review*.

3   Proportion of the total number of petrol driven cars in the UK with catalytic converters ($C(t)$).
     Measured by cumulative new petrol driven car registrations from January 1993 sourced from
     Society of Motor Manufacturers and Traders Limited, *Monthly Statistical Review*, divided by
     total petrol driven car stock in the UK.

4   Proportion of total car stock that can use unleaded petrol ($B(t)$), sourced from Department of
     Transport, *Transport Statistics 1994*, based on annual survey of car drivers conducted by Lex plc.
     This provides 6 yearly observations from Autumn 1988 to Autumn 1993. We assume that the
     January 1986 value for this variable is zero. Given that all cars registered after October 1989 can
     use unleaded petrol we are also to extend the series to 1995 using monthly new car registrations.
     Monthly data is obtained by linear extrapolation.

     Given the extrapolations involved in generating this series and its importance to the results
     derived above we have compared the resulting data against the UK figures in a pan European
     data set constructed and supplied to us by Dr Z. Samaras of the Faculty of Engineering, Aristotle
     University, Thessalonika, Greece. These data are calculated using a completely different method
     developed on behalf of the European Commission and based on emissions data. The resulting
     series are very similar with the same turning points and similar market shares at each date.

5   Proportion of petrol driven car stock that can (but does not have to use) unleaded petrol. This is
     calculated as $B(t) - C(t)$.

6   Retail price of leaded petrol ($p_2(t)$). Measured by the price in pence per 100 litres inclusive of tax
     and duty of four star (RON 96) leaded fuel. Available on a monthly basis from January 1987 to
     July 1995 from the Institute of Petroleum.

7   Retail price of unleaded fuel ($p_1(t)$). Measured by the price in pence per 100 litres inclusive of tax
     and duty of RON 95. Available on a monthly basis from the Institute of Petroleum for the period
     January 1989 to July 1995. For the period January 1987–December 1988 the price of unleaded
     fuel was predicted from the price of leaded fuel and the rates of duty applied (sourced from
     OECD statistics). After experimentation we concluded that the price of leaded and unleaded fuel
     were related for the period from 1/89 to 6/95 according to

$$p_2(t) = m(t) + b_1 p_1(t) + b_2(D_2 - D_1)(1 + VAT) + e(t)$$

     where $m(t)$ is a stochastic drift ($m(t) = m(t - 1) + u(t)$) and $u(t)$ is an error term (see Harvey,
     1989), $D1$ and $D2$ are the rates of duty on leaded and unleaded petrol respectively, VAT is the
     rate of value added tax and $e(t)$ is an error term. We estimated the coefficients (with t statistics)
     and the intercept (with q-ratio) as: $m(t) = 0.022(1.00)$; $b_1 = 0.970(6.91)$; $b_2 = 0.973(43.64)$. The
     forecasting performance of the model was good, as were all the diagnostics and goodness of fit.
     These estimates have been used to backward forecast $p_1(t)$ for the period from 1/87 to 12/88.

8   Consumption of unleaded petrol, $V_1(t)$, measured as inland deliveries of unleaded petroleum
     products/motor spirits in 1000t. Available on a monthly basis 1/86 to 5/95 from Eurostat *Energy
     Monthly Statistics* and Department of Trade and Industry, *Energy Trends* aggregating data relat-
     ing to RON 92, RON 95, and RON 98 specifications. The statistics report zero consumption
     before July 1987. This seemed unrealistic, and thus we allow monthly consumption for each
     month prior to July 1987 to be equal to one, which also facilitates the taking of logs.

9   Consumption of leaded petrol, $V_2(t)$, measured as inland deliveries of leaded petroleum products/
     motor spirits in 1000t. Available on a monthly basis 1/86 to 5/95 from Eurostat *Energy Monthly
     Statistics* and Department of Trade and Industry, *Energy Trends* aggregating data relating to
     RON 92, RON 95, and RON 98 specifications.

10   Market share of unleaded petrol $M(t)$. Measured as $p_1(t)V_1(t)/(p_1(t)V_1(t) + p_2(t)V_2(t))$.

11   Availability of unleaded petrol, measured as the proportion of all retail petrol stations that sell
     unleaded petrol. Data sourced from Institute of Petroleum and available at 24 arbitrary points in
     time over a six year period. The logistic curve

$$\text{Avail} = 1/(1 + \exp(12.004 - 0.33t))$$
$$(11.8) \quad (-16.5)$$
$$R^2 = 0.98$$

has been fitted to the data to extrapolate monthly values for the period from 1/87–5/95.

Appendix 15B   Time series properties

In this appendix we present the results of our analysis of the time series properties of $\log X(t, \delta, \alpha)$ and $(\log p_1(t) - \log p_2(t))$. To save space, rather than present results for all (δ, α) pairs considered, we only present results for $\log X(t, \delta, \alpha) = \log X(t, 1, 0.9)$, the variant of $\log X(t, \delta, \alpha)$ used in the results presented above. The results show that $\log X(t, 1, 0.9)$ and $(\log p_1(t) - \log p_2(t))$ are stationary in their second difference (i.e. they are $I(2)$) and not their first.

In table 15B.1 we present the results of the analysis of the order of integration of the variables. The procedure refers to the Augmented Dickey–Fuller tests, with unknown data generating process, of unique and multiple unit roots (see Harris, 1995). The ADF testing procedure moves from the most general specification of a stochastic trend (non-stationarity) against the alternative of a deterministic trend (stationarity) down to more restricted specifications until the null hypothesis is rejected. The critical values (see table 15B.2) pertain to each of seven different models, since the distributions of the statistics obtained depend not only on the data-generation process of the variables, but also on the

Table 15B.1   ADF test of unit root and multiple unit root tests and CRDW test

	lag	t_β	F_β	t	t_μ	F_μ
$DD(\log P_1(t) - \log P_2(t))$	0				−2.260	2.184
$D(\log P_1(t) - \log P_2(t))$	3	−3.06	5.088	−3.06*	−1.298	3.96‡
$DD \log X$‡	6				−2.424	2.940
$D \log X$‡	0	−0.673	5.23	−0.673*	2.592	5.156

	t	t_τ	Ho	Ha	CRDW	Ho
$DD(\log P_1(t) - \log P_2(t))$	−2.260*	−1.704	$I(2)$	$I(1)$	2.11*	$I(1)$
$D(\log P_1(t) - \log P_2(t))$	1.298	−1.60	$I(1)$	$I(0)$	0.21	$I(1)$
$DD \log X$‡	−2.424*	−1.956*	$I(2)$	$I(1)$	0.88*	$I(1)$
$D \log X$‡	2.59†	−2.081	$I(1)$	$I(0)$	0.005	$I(1)$

Reject the null hypothesis at * 5 per cent and † 10 per cent levels respectively;
‡ $\log X(t, \delta, \alpha) = \log X(t, 1, 0.9)$.

Table 15B.2   Critical values of the ADF* and CRDW† tests

SL‡	τ_β	M_β	t§	τ_μ	M_μ	$t^{(d)}$	τ_τ	CRDW
0.5	−3.54	5.47	−1.65	−2.89	3.86	−1.65	−1.95	$R_L = 0.252$; $R_U = 0.645$
0.10	−3.15	6.49	−1.28	−2.58	4.71	−1.28	−1.61	$R_L = 0.373$; $R_U = 0.538$

* Source: Fuller (1976), Dickey and Fuller (1981); † Source: Sargan and Bhargava (1983);
‡ significance level (SL); § critical values of the t–distribution for N $\rightarrow \infty$.

Table 15B.3 Augmented Dickey–Fuller tests of unit roots

Steps and models	Null hypothesis Ho: I(1); Ha: I(0)	Test statistic	Critical values
$\Delta y_t = \mu_\beta + \gamma_\beta t + (\rho_\beta - 1)y_{t-1} + \Sigma\psi\Delta y_{t-1} + u_t$	$\rho_\beta = 1$	τ_β	Fuller (1976)
$\Delta y_t = \mu_\beta + \gamma_\beta t + (\rho_\beta - 1)y_{t-1} + \Sigma\psi\Delta y_{t-1} + u_t$	$(\rho_\beta - 1) = \gamma_\beta = 0$	ϕ_β	D&F (1981)
$\Delta y_t = \mu_\beta + \gamma_\beta t + (\rho_\beta - 1)y_{t-1} + \Sigma\psi\Delta y_{t-1} + u_t$	$\rho_\beta = 1$	t	Standard Normal
$\Delta y_t = \mu_\mu + (\rho_\mu - 1)y_{t-1} + \Sigma\psi\Delta y_{t-1} + u_t$	$\rho_\mu = 1$	τ_μ	Fuller (1976)
$\Delta y_t = \mu_\mu + (\rho_\mu - 1)y_{t-1} + \Sigma\psi\Delta y_{t-1} + u_t$	$(\rho_\mu - 1) = \gamma_\mu = 0$	ϕ_μ	D&F (1981)
$\Delta y_t = \mu_\mu + (\rho_\mu - 1)y_{t-1} + \Sigma\psi\Delta y_{t-1} + u_t$	$\rho_\mu = 1$	t	Standard Normal
$\Delta y_t = (\rho_\tau - 1)y_{t-1} + \Sigma\psi\Delta y_{t-1} + u_t$	$\rho_\tau = 1$	τ_τ	Fuller (1976)

Table 15B.4 Augmented Dickey–Fuller tests of multiple unit roots

Step and model	Null hypothesis Ho: I(2); Ha: I(1)	Test statistic	Critical values
$\Delta^2 y_t = \mu_\beta + (\rho_\beta - 1)\Delta y_{t-1} + \Sigma\psi\Delta^2 y_{t-1} + u_t$	$\rho_\mu = 1$	τ_μ	Fuller (1976)
$\Delta^2 y_t = \mu_\beta + (\rho_\beta - 1)\Delta y_{t-1} + \Sigma\psi\Delta^2 y_{t-1} + u_t$	$(\rho_\mu - 1) = \gamma_\mu = 0$	ϕ_μ	D&F (1981)
$\Delta^2 y_t = \mu_\beta + (\rho_\beta - 1)\Delta y_{t-1} + \Sigma\psi\Lambda^2 y_{t-1} + u_t$	$\rho_\mu = 1$	t	Standard Normal
$\Delta^2 y_t = (\rho_\tau - 1)\Delta y_{t-1} + \Sigma\psi\Delta^2 y_{t-1} + u_t$	$\rho_\tau = 1$	τ_τ	Fuller (1976)

model with which we investigate it. Table 15B.1 also contains the results of the CRDW test (see Sargan and Bhargava, 1983), based on the usual Durbin-Watson statistic. Tests based on the DF distributions (see Dickey, 1976 and Dickey and Fuller, 1979) and the non parametric test developed by Phillips and Perron (1988) yield similar results but are not reported here for space reasons.

Table 15B.3 and 15B.4 outline the testing procedure for the presence of respectively two and one unit roots (see Dickey and Pantula, 1987; Dickey and Fuller, 1981 and Fuller, 1976).

Acknowledgements

The research contained in this paper has been funded by the Economic and Social Research Council as part of the Global Environmental Change Initiative. We would like to give credit to William Turner who undertook much of the early data collection for this paper prior to his untimely death, and to Veronica Wong who is a collaborator on the ESRC project.

Notes

1   This paper is the first of three papers. Whereas here we explore the diffusion of unleaded petrol in the UK, in Battisti and Stoneman (1998) we undertake an Italian–UK comparison and in Stoneman and Battisti (1998) we undertake a wider pan-European comparison. The other two papers postdate this work and are built upon and cross refer to the model and econometric methods first detailed in this paper. The discussion section in this paper on the relative import-ance of the different effects in the diffusion process is unique. In this and the other papers it is assumed throughout, without argument, that unleaded petrol is more environmentally friendly than leaded petrol. We do not enter the debate on this issue.

2   The modelling of the availability of unleaded fuel is itself an interesting issue. It is not however an issue we address in this paper. Given that we do not find that availability was a binding constraint on the diffusion process the estimates of the demand model will not be biased as a result of this omission. Our discussions with the petrol suppliers indicated that the provision of tax incentives in the 1987 Budget was a major stimulus to the availability of unleaded fuel. We have also undertaken some experiments to explore whether the launch of premium super unleaded affected the diffusion process and our results indicated that it did not.

3   Although a referee has suggested that it may have been expensive. Casual personal observation suggests that the cost of conversion varied from a few pounds to a few hundred pounds depending upon the car.

4   The implication of this result is that if the consumer changes from a car using leaded fuel to one using unleaded fuel, or converts a given car to do so, then although unleaded fuel is cheaper, his/her total expenditure on fuel will remain constant. For given miles per gallon this implies that after switching to unleaded fuel the utility maximising driver will choose to travel further. This is not particularly 'green', but is consistent with the standard economic assumption that the demand curve is downward sloping and thus if travel is cheaper the consumer will demand more. Of course economics does not consider that in reaction to a price change that demand will always change to keep expenditure constant, but that has been discussed at the beginning of this section.

5   In seminar presentations of this paper it has often been noted that the market share equation presented as (15.11) below does not explicitly take account of the possibility that newer cars (in particular cars with catalytic converters) have higher fuel efficiencies than older cars because of technological advances. Higher fuel efficiencies can be modelled in the above framework by allowing a_i and/or b_i to decrease with the age of the vehicle (i.e. a gallon of petrol yields greater utility as fuel efficiency increase). From (15.10) however it is clear that the model predicts that expenditure on fuel is independent of a_i and b_i (car owners choose to do more miles if they can get greater miles per gallon) and as such the market share equation is unaffected by the possibility of differential efficiencies.

6   A referee on an earlier version of this paper disputes the possibility that some drivers, given the choice, will never use unleaded fuel. However in diffusion analysis it is quite common to find that the asymptote of the diffusion curve is not 100 per cent usage of a new technology. Possible rationales in this case may be ignorance of the fuel capabilities of cars bought second hand, irrationality and prejudice.

7   The packages mainly used in the estimation process have been SPSS, STAMP, TSP, and MFIT.

8   Availability may also act as an information spreading mechanism and thus may be one of the factors modelled within $F(T)$. We have not, however, attempted to separate out such a factor.

9   Although the NLS estimates still showed some residual autocorrelation and thus the results are not strictly valid we were also unable to reject the hypothesis that when $\log p_1(t)$ and $\log p_2(t)$ were entered into (15.13) as separate variables (rather than as $\log p_1(t) - \log p_2(t)$) then their coefficients are of equal but opposite signs, as the model predicts. We have done some hypothesis testing of this result in the ECM specification and the result still holds. Using NLS we also checked whether the theoretical prediction of the model that the diffusion curve is logistic was supported by the data by comparing the results from fitting a univariate logistic curve against log linear and Gompertz curves. The performance of the logistic curve ($R^2 = 0.99$) was superior. Although further use of non-linear estimation techniques was possible, we decided that there were too many problems applying error correction techniques to non linear models and thus such techniques were put aside in favour of the logistic transformation.

10   We have also estimated an ECM model with a partial adjustment mechanism incorporated in the model (see Bardsen, 1989, and Bewley, 1979). The unrestricted version yielded a very low value for the Durbin h statistic whereas the restricted estimates showed insignificant coefficients upon the intercept and $DD(\log p_1 - \log p_2)$. The presented results are thus preferred.

11 To date we have not been able to test the hypothesis that the long run estimate of β is signific-
    antly different from unity, but we are encouraged that in the unrestricted model one cannot
    accept the hypothesis.
12 One of the referees of this paper has a residual concern with our procedures at this point. He/she
    points out that in the analysis above we have been unable to identify a long run relationship
    between the variables in levels, only in terms of changes (or growth rates). Although it is accepted
    that the way we proceed to put numbers on and interpret (15.25) reflects this, the referee argues
    that our procedures do not correspond to the model in eq. (15.14). We do not accept this point,
    but after some interchanges have not been able to resolve the issue.
13 We take this route to the measurement of $X(t)$ rather than using our econometric estimates for
    our econometric analysis only enables us to predict the growth of $X(t)$ and not its level.

References

Banerjee, A., Dolado, J., Galbraith, J. and Hendry, D.F. (1993) *Co-Integration, Error Correction and the Econometric Analysis of Time Series*, Oxford University Press, Oxford.

Bardsen, G. (1989) 'The Estimation of Long Run Coefficients from Error Correction Models', *Oxford Bulletin of Economics and Statistics*, 51, 345–50.

Bass, F.M. (1969) 'A New Product Growth Model for Consumer Durables', *Management Science*, 15, 215–27.

Battisti, G. and Stoneman, P. (1998) 'The Diffusion of Unleaded Petrol: An Anglo Italian Comparison', *Labour*, 12, 255–78.

Berndt, E.R. (1991) *The Practice of Econometrics: Classic and Contemporary*, Addison Wesley, Reading, MA.

Bewley, R.A. (1979) 'The Direct Estimation of Equilibrium Response in a Linear Model', *Economics Letters*, 3, 357–61.

Davidson, R. and Mackinnon, J. (1981) 'Several Tests for Model Specification in the Presence of Alternative Hypotheses', *Econometrica*, 49/3, 781–93.

Davies, S. (1979) *The Diffusion of Process Innovations*, Cambridge University Press, Cambridge.

Deaton, A. and Muellbauer, J. (1980) *Economics and Consumer Behaviour*, Cambridge University Press, Cambridge.

Dickey, D.A. (1976) 'Estimation and Hypothesis Testing for Non-stationary Time Series', PhD dissertation, Iowa State University, Ames, IA.

Dickey, D.A. and Fuller, W.A. (1979) 'Distribution of the Estimators for Autoregressive Time Series with a Unit Root', *Journal of the American Statistical Association*, 74, 427–31.

Dickey, D.A. and Fuller, W.A. (1981) 'Likelihood Ratio Statistics for Autoregressive Time Series with a Unit Root', *Econometrica*, 49, 1057–72.

Dickey, D.A. and Pantula, S.G. (1987) 'Determining the Order of Differencing in Autoregressive Processes', *Journal of Business and Economic Statistics*, 15, 455–61.

Engle, R. and Granger, C. (1987) 'Co-Integration and Error Correction: Representation, Estimation and Testing', *Econometrica*, 55, 251–76.

Engle, R. and Yoo, B.S. (1987) 'Forecasting and Testing in Co-Integrated Systems', *Journal of Econometrics*, 35, 143–59.

Fuller, W.A. (1976) *Introduction to Statistical Time Series*, John Wiley & Sons.

Granger, C. (1986) 'Developments in the Study of Co-Integrated Economic Variables', *Oxford Bulletin of Economic and Statistics*, 48, 213–28.

Granger, C.W.J. (1995) 'Modelling Nonlinear Relationships Between Extended-Memory Variables', *Econometrica*, 63/2, 265–79.

Granger, C. and Weiss, A.A. (1983) 'Time Series Analysis of Error Correction Models' in S. Kalin, T. Amemiya, and L.A. Goodman (eds), *Studies in Econometrics, Time Series and Multivariate Statistics*, Academic Press, New York, NY.

Griliches, Z. (1957) 'Hybrid Corn: An Exploration in the Economics of Technological Change', *Econometrica*, 25, 501–22.

Grossman, S., Kihlstrom, R. and Mirman, L. (1977) 'A Bayesian Approach to the Production of Information and Learning by Doing', *Review of Economic Studies*, 44/3, 533–47.

Harris, R. (1995) *Using Co-integration Analysis in Econometric Modelling*, Prentice Hall-Harvester Wheatsheaf, London.

Harvey, A. (1989) *Forecasting Structural Time Series Models and the Kalman Filter*, Cambridge University Press, Cambridge.

INRA (1992) *Europeans and the Environment in 1992*, Report Produced for the Commission of the European Communities Directorate General XVII, Bruxelles.

Johansen, S. (1992a) 'Testing Weak Exogeneity and the Order of Co-integration in UK Money Demand', *Journal of Policy Modelling*, 52, 313–34.

Johansen, S. (1992b) 'A Representation of Vector Autoregressive Processes Integrated of Order 2', *Econometric Theory*, 8, 188–202.

Johansen, S. (1995) 'A Statistical Analysis of Cointegration for I(2) Variables', *Econometric Theory*, 11, 25–9.

Johansen, S. and Juselius, K. (1990) 'Maximum Likelihood Estimation and Inference on Co-Integration with Applications to the Demand for Money', *Oxford Bulletin of Economics and Statistics*, 52, 169–210.

Juselius, K. (1994) 'On the Duality Between Long-Run Relations and Common Trends in the I(1) Versus I(2) Model. An Application to Aggregate Money Holdings', *Econometric Reviews*, 13/2, 151–78.

Mahajan, V. and Wind, Y. (1986) *Innovation Diffusion Models of New Product Acceptance*, Ballinger, Cambridge, MA.

Phillips, P.C.B. and Perron, P. (1988) 'Testing for a Unit Root in Time Series Regression', *Biometrica*, 75, 335–46.

Sargan, J. and Bhargava, A. (1983) 'Testing Residuals from Least Squares Regressions for Being Generated by the Gaussian Random Walk', *Econometrica*, 51, 153–74.

Stoneman, P. (1983) *The Economic Analysis of Technological Change*, Oxford University Press, Oxford.

Stoneman, P. and Battisti, G. (1998) 'Fiscal Incentives to Consumer Innovation: The Use of Unleaded Petrol in Europe', *Research Policy*, 27, 187–213.

Stoneman, P. and Karshenas, M. (1995) 'The Diffusion of New Technology' in P. Stoneman (ed.), *Handbook of the Economics of Innovation and New Technology*, Basil Blackwell, Oxford, 265–97.

Wong, V., Turner, W. and Stoneman, P. (1996) 'Marketing Strategies and Market Prospects for Environmentally Friendly Consumer Products', *British Journal of Management*, 7, 263–81.

Part V

Extensions, Applications and Implications

Chapter sixteen
Diffusion Analysis: The Wider Implications

16.1. Introduction

The majority of this book has been concerned with illustrating the nature of the diffusion process, exploring the understanding of why the adoption of new technology takes time and addressing the policy implications. In this, the last substantive section of the book, some wider issues are addressed. In particular the material considers how the realization that technology adoption takes time impacts on the analysis of major economic phenomena.

Technological change impacts on all areas of economic activity and thus, for example, prices, quantities produced, investment, labour supply, incomes, the distribution of income, exports, imports, economic welfare are all affected by technological change. It is thus obvious that to understand such phenomena it is necessary to properly model the technological change process.

The main thrust of the diffusion literature is to emphasize that when new technologies appear on the market those technologies are rarely adopted by all potential users instantaneously. Instead there is a period of time, often a long period, during which the technologies spread across their potential markets. This applies to both producer and consumer technologies. It would thus seem obvious that if one is to understand and properly model the impact of technological change on economic phenomena then account ought to be taken of the diffusion process. However, the incorporation of diffusion processes within much of economic analysis is really quite limited. For example, as was argued in the very first chapter of the book, even in new growth theory, which emphasizes the role played by technological change in growth, diffusion phenomena have largely been ignored.

It is much more common in the literature to consider R&D as an appropriate indicator of technological change. But R&D is a measure of the generation of new technologies rather than a measure of the use of new technologies. But it is through the use of technology that the impacts will arise. Exploring use would mean exploring the diffusion of technology.

The subsections that follow therefore consider for several different areas of enquiry how economic analysis has been or can be adapted to incorporate diffusion analysis. In the following three chapters we provide some specific examples of research that does exactly this.

16.2.   Output and Productivity Growth

One particular area where the role of technological change has been studied more than most is in the determination of output and productivity growth. Here, there are large theoretical and empirical literatures of which the most extensive, especially on the empirical side, explores the determinants of productivity growth. Early work (e.g. Solow, 1957) has been superseded by more sophisticated analyses of the impact of technological change on output and productivity at the firm, industry and economy wide level (see, for example, Griliches, 1995). However, in nearly its entirety, such literature, if it is specific as to how technological change is to be considered, relies on research and development expenditures as an indicator. As stated above, however, R&D is a measure of the input to the generation of new technology rather than a measure of the use of new technology, and as such may not be ideal.

The literature that does diverge from this standard model tends to be of two types. First, there is a literature that looks at the impact of particular new technologies upon productivity. A common example explores the impact of computerization or IT on productivity (e.g. Lichtenberg, 1993). Such literature tends to explore the productivity paradox in which 'computers are seen everywhere except in the productivity statistics'. This work of necessity tends to relate productivity growth to the use of new technology to see the extent of any impact. The methodology thus allows for use and diffusion rather than R&D to be generating the impact. However, nearly all such literature considers the use of new technology as an exogenous variable. Very rarely is the use of new technology endogenized in such models, and even more rarely is it endogenized through a specific diffusion model.

The second literature that tends to allow for a diffusion process is that relating to convergence (see for example Jones, 1998, pp. 56–65). This literature, growing out of the early new growth theories, explores whether laggard countries in the productivity stakes converge relatively or absolutely to the leading economies. The main underlying suggestion is that laggard countries will be experiencing a technological gap relative to leading countries and this gap provides a pool of technologies that the laggard countries can diffuse. As they do so they will catch up with the leader. Again however, such analysis rarely considers or uses explicit modelling of the diffusion process to characterise the catch up (although see Sala-i-Martín and Barro, 1995). In fact most of the empirical versions of this literature relates the rate of growth of a country in a period to the initial productivity gap and any diffusion process is part of the 'black box' of the catch up process.

Kwon and Stoneman (1995) is one of few published papers that explicitly considers diffusion modelling in the context of productivity growth. Here the productivity growth of firms is related to the use of several new technologies, but importantly, the use of the new technologies is made endogenous via a diffusion model. Another useful reference is Soete and Turner (1984) which relates the macroeconomic rate of technical change to diffusion at the micro level.

16.3.   International Trade

The analysis of international trade has, more than many areas in economics, considered technological change to be of great importance (a good source for an overview of the literature is Krugman, 1995). More than that, it has also emphasized that there are international diffusion processes. Thus, for example, the early work of Posner (1961) and Vernon (1979) emphasizes how there are international diffusion processes by which new technology is transmitted from country to country. The work of Krugman (1979) on North/South models has illustrated not only how the prosperity of the North arises from a technological lead over the South but also how technology will be diffused from North to South and as the South catches up the gap between North and South will be closed (with the North becoming relatively poorer and the South relatively richer). The Krugman analysis illustrates how the North will only maintain its relative prosperity if it generates and uses new technology faster than it is diffused in to the South. Similarly the work of Grossman and Helpman (1991) illustrates the role that international diffusion of technology plays in new growth theoretic modelling of open economies.

At the empirical level, however, there is less emphasis on diffusion phenomena. We have discussed empirical analysis of convergence above. There is also a literature looking at the impact of technological change on imports and exports. A good example is Soete (1989). Much of this literature represents technological change or relative technological performance by patent indices. Patent indices are, however, a measure of new technology generated and not new technology used. Thus, in such analysis, diffusion has played only a minor role.

It is also fair to state, however, that diffusion analysis itself has relatively ignored international diffusion especially at the empirical level. Although there are specific literatures looking, for example, at the role of transnational corporations in the transfer of new technologies between countries, there are very few empirical studies of international diffusion of particular technologies. There are studies that compare the diffusion processes of particular technologies across countries, but this is not the same as studying the worldwide diffusion of a technology in which each country is a separate unit of observation. Useful references include Dunning and Usui (1987), Eaton and Kortum (1999) and Dekumpe *et al.* (1997).

16.4.   The Trade Cycle

The trade cycle is a particular economic phenomenon that has been the subject of analysis almost since the birth of economics as a subject. Currently the level of interest is rather muted, with it even being claimed in some quarters that the trade cycle is dead. Much of the dispute in this field has centred upon whether the trade cycle is exogenous or endogenous to the economic system – that is, is it the result of exogenous shocks to a generally stable system or is it the case that by their nature economies will always experience cyclical levels of activity? In the analysis, many different lengths of cycles have been claimed to exist, some with short periodicity and some with long periodicity. It is with respect to the long cycles, known as Kondratieff cycles, with periods of 40–50 years peak to peak, that technological change has been considered to play a major role.

The impact of technological change on such cycles is generally considered to arise from the appearance and diffusion of new 'general purpose technologies' as defined above, or new technological paradigms. Examples might be steam power, electricity, IT etc. The fullest story of how the impact arises is still to be found in Schumpeter (1934). In outline, the argument is that from a steady state position the availability of a new general purpose technology encourages profit seeking 'entrepreneurs' to use that technology for the first time. They generate profit increases. These profit increases signal to and encourage other firms to also use the new technology. As use extends there is growing pressure on factor prices and output prices that further encourages other firms to use the new technology. The expansion in investment is supported by increased lending and money supply expansion in the economy. The increased profit makes such lending profitable. The increased level of economic activity also has multiplier effects on investment and demand and generally the rate of economic activity in the economy expands. This expansion is also allied with increased speculation on capital markets. Both the nature of the diffusion process and this speculation sows the seed of the downward part of the cycle. As the use of the new technology becomes universal there is lesser demand for new capital goods and thus the driving force of the boom is removed. Also as the real economy turns down, the speculative activity tends to collapse leading to a further negative impact on the level of economic activity. Jointly they force the economy back into recession. Only once another new technology appears will the economy start to climb out of recession again.

There has been some empirical exploration of the role of technological change in the Kondratieff cycle, for example Freeman and Soete (1997, pp. 18–22 and 64–74). However, as far as is known, there is no empirical analysis that explores such issues explicitly considering the nature of the diffusion process and endogenizing that process, although the more theoretical work of Aghion and Howitt (1996, 1997 and 1998) is very relevant.

16.5.   Household Behaviour

The analysis of household behaviour concerns both the demand for consumer goods and thus consumption behaviour and also labour supply. The diffusion of consumer technologies has been discussed above, but the impact more generally of technological change on consumer spending and labour supply has not been discussed to any extent.

The general issue of technological change and household behaviour is related to old literatures in which it was feared that because of declining marginal utility, as household consumer expenditures become larger with increasing income levels, eventually a point of satiation would be reached. At this point households would not value greater consumption and thus the demand for goods would stop growing and also as income was not valued households would not wish to increase labour supply and thus labour supply would stop growing. Growth in the economy would thus cease. Whether this is a realistic scenario is not the main point. The crucial issue is that technological advance will prevent such an outcome. As new household technologies appear this will increase the marginal utilities of expenditure. This in turn will encourage household expenditure to grow as the new technologies are diffused and also labour supply to increase as the marginal utility of income increases. Technological advance thus will prevent stagnation.

On a theoretical level the work of Katsoulacos (1986) explores this link between technological change, household expenditure and labour supply. No empirical work relating labour supply or total household expenditure to technological change or the diffusion of new technology is known to me.

A second approach to exploring the relevance of diffusion to household behaviour is best told by casual empiricism. For most of the twentieth century there has been an increasing supply of new and/or improved household technologies such as vacuum cleaners, washing machines, fridges, freezers, dishwashers, lawn mowers, cleaning agents, for example washing powders and polishes, and other related products, such as disinfectants. One might even consider advances in contraception as a major new technology in these terms. These technologies have both substituted for domestic servants for the wealthier classes and also considerably reduced the need for labour services in the home. Jointly the effect has been to considerably increase the labour services that could be sold on the open labour market, particularly female labour. Although one cannot say whether the diffusion of these technologies generated the increase in the female labour supply on the market or whether women's desire to work outside of the home led to the diffusion of such technologies, the effect is that there should be a close relationship between the diffusion of such new household technologies and the labour market. In addition, of course, as households change from one to two income households one would expect to see changes in spending patterns.

A closely related issue concerns health technologies. With advances in medical technologies over the last 150 years, life expectancy has increased and perhaps more importantly the average physical abilities of the population have also increased. This has had impacts on both the labour supply and also on the age composition of the population, and via these through to spending habits, leisure occupations, saving habits etc. Thus as new health technologies are diffused through households one might expect to see further impacts on spending and labour supply.

We do not know of any studies that empirically explore such linkages either with or without endogenizing the diffusion process.

16.6.   Government Expenditure

As a final example one might consider government expenditure and activity. In this area the potential impacts of technological change are again large. For example, one might consider how new defence or military technologies impact on government spending. Arms races based on new technologies are a characteristic of the twentieth century (and not only the twentieth century). As new military technologies diffuse across different nations, spending on such technologies changes.

Another example might be the impact of IT on government activity. Essentially with improvements in IT technology and reductions in cost, both the ability of government to perform certain tasks is improved and the cost of performing tasks is also reduced. Thus, for example, as administration with respect to social security payments, vehicle licensing, tax implementation, and criminal records is increasingly computerized, the possibilities of doing new things is raised. The impact could be that the relationship between government and its citizens and the involvement of government in private sector economic activity can be changed considerably. Again we know of no specific work that explores such issues.

16.7.   The Next Three Chapters

In the next three chapters three papers are reproduced that illustrate how the explicit incorporation of a diffusion based approach to modelling can inform the analysis of three topics not yet discussed. In chapter 17 a diffusion based approach to modelling the impact of new technology on firm performance is presented. Chapter 18 explores the impact of technology on employment using a diffusion based approach. Chapter 19 presents a diffusion based approach to modelling gross investment determination.

Chapter 17, originally published as Stoneman and Kwon (1996) is closely related to the literature on the impact of technological change on productivity and especially to Kwon and Stoneman (1995). In this case, however, firm performance is measured by profitability. The paper has a number of points worthy of note.

1   The work specifically addresses the impact of technological change on firm performance relating that impact to the adoption of technologies rather than measures of the generation of technologies (R&D).
2   The paper looks at all adopters of the new technologies and not just first adopters as in other literatures.
3   A multiple technology stance is taken.
4   The impact of adoption of technology on the performance of non-adopters is specifically modelled.
5   Within the work the diffusion process is endogenized via an encompassing diffusion model.

The results show that (1) in most cases the use of new technology leads to increased profits, (2) that increase declines as the number of users increases, (3) the profits of non using firms declines as usage extends, (4) there are cross technology effects.

This research is also useful for another reason. The model is constructed by essentially inverting a standard diffusion model. The diffusion model argues that expected profit gains drive adoption. In this research, therefore, actual profit gains are related to adoption. As a result the findings of the paper can also be considered as a test of alternative theories of diffusion. In this particular study evidence is found to support both rank and stock approaches to diffusion.

Chapter 18, originally published as Waterson and Stoneman (1985), looks at the impact of technological change on employment. This is a topic that has been widely discussed in economics for more than a century and one that is ripe for further modelling using diffusion analysis. A survey of the literature can be found in Petit (1995). This particular paper is included because it analyses the time path of employment in an industry as diffusion of a new technology proceeds. It is this emphasis upon the diffusion path that is the main reason for inclusion. It should be noted, however, that in this paper the diffusion path is determined exogenously. This could be improved upon. The main finding of the paper, however, is an important one. It is found that the relationship between industry employment and the use of new technology is generally not monotonic. As the use of new technology extends, often, employment first starts to fall, but as usage extends further, employment starts to increase. This implies that employment at the end point of the diffusion process is not a good predictor of employment levels during the process. This further implies that a comparative statics comparison of employment levels at the beginning and end of the diffusion process will give a misleading prediction as to employment during the diffusion process. A further implication is that if in looking at the impact of technology on employment one ignores the time intensive nature of the diffusion process by, for example, looking at the relationship between employment and R&D, then it is possible that the predictions of the model would be in error.

Chapter 19 contains material that has not been published before although that material is closely related to Stoneman and Kwon (1998 and 2000). The underlying rationale of this work is two fold. First, it is noted that to a large extent the theory and modelling of gross investment has often, mistakenly in our view, ignored technological change. Secondly, there ought to be a close relationship between diffusion modelling and the modelling of investment, for both are concerned with expenditure on new capital goods. In this chapter, therefore, gross investment is modelled, building on the theory of diffusion. The adoption of individual capital goods is explicitly modelled via a diffusion approach and then gross investment is derived by summing over capital goods available. The model predicts that gross investment will, *inter alia*, be related to the rate at which new technologies appear, as proxied by, for example, R&D, and the determinants of the speed of diffusion. A notable outcome of the approach is that technological change enters the gross investment function quite naturally using this approach. The empirical work gives strong support to the basic hypotheses modelled.

References

Aghion, P. and Howitt, P. (1996) 'A Model of Growth through Creative Destruction', in G. Grossman, (ed.), *Economic Growth: Theory and Evidence*, Vol I, Cheltenham: Elgar.

Aghion, P. and Howitt, P. (1997) 'A Schumpeterian Perspective on Growth and Competition', in D. Kreps and K. Wallis (eds.), *Advances in Economics and Econometrics: Theory and Application*, Vol 2, Cambridge: Cambridge University Press.

Aghion, P. and Howitt, P. (1998) 'On the Macroeconomics Effects of Major Technological Change', *Annales d'Economie et de Statistique*, 49/50, 53–75.

Dekumpe, M.G., Parker, M.P. and Savory, M. (1997) 'Globalization: Modelling Technology Adoption Timing Across Countries', INSEAD Working Paper, 97/75/MKT.

Dunning, J. and Usui, M. (eds.) (1987) *Structural Change, Economic Interdependence and World Development*, Vol 4, New York: St Martin's Press.

Eaton, J. and Kortum, S. (1999) 'International Technology Diffusion: Theory and Measurement', *International Economic Review*, 40(3), 537–70.

Freeman, C. and Soete, L. (1997) *The Economics of Industrial Innovation*, 3rd edition, London: Pinter.

Griliches, Z. (1995) 'R&D and Productivity: Econometric Results and Measurement Issues', in P. Stoneman (ed.), *Handbook of the Economics of Innovation and Technological Change*, Oxford: Basil Blackwell, 52–89.

Grossman, G.M. and Helpman, E. (1991) *Innovation and Growth in the Global Economy*, Cambridge, MA: MIT Press.

Jones, C. (1998) *Introduction to Economic Growth*, New York: W.W. Norton & Co.

Katsoulacos, Y. (1986) *The Employment Effect of Technical Change*, Brighton: Harvester Press.

Krugman, P. (1979) 'A Model of Innovation, Technology Transfer and the World Distribution of Income', *Journal of Political Economy*, 89, 253–66.

Krugman, P. (1995) 'Technological Change in International Trade', in P. Stoneman (ed.), *Handbook of the Economics of Innovation and Technological Change*, Oxford: Basil Blackwell, 342–65.

Kwon, M.J. and Stoneman, P. (1995) 'The Impact of Technology Adoption on Firm Productivity', *Economics of Innovation and New Technology*, 3, 219–33.

Lichtenberg, F. (1993) 'The Output Contributions of Computer Equipment and Personnel: A Firm Level Analysis', NBER Working Paper No. 4540. Cambridge, MA.

Petit, P. (1995) 'Employment and Technological Change', in P. Stoneman (ed.), *Handbook of the Economics of Innovation and Technological Change*, Oxford: Basil Blackwell, 366–408.

Posner, M. (1961) 'International Trade and Technical Change', *Oxford Economic Papers*, 13, 323–41.

Sala-i-Martín, X. and Barro, R.L. (1995) 'Technological Diffusion, Convergence and Growth', Yale Economic Growth Center, Discussion Paper No. 735, June.

Schumpeter, J.A. (1934) *The Theory of Economic Development*, Cambridge, MA: Harvard University Press.

Soete, L. (1989) 'The Impact of Technological Innovation on International Trade Patterns', *Research Policy*, 16, 101–30.

Soete, L. and Turner, R. (1984) 'Technology Diffusion and the Rate of Technical Change', *Economic Journal*, 94, 612–23.

Solow, R. (1957) 'Technical Change and the Aggregate Production Function', *Review of Economics and Statistics*, 57, 312–20.

Stoneman, P. and Kwon, M.J. (1996) 'Technology Adoption and Firm Profitability', *Economic Journal*, 106, 952–62.

Stoneman, P. and Kwon, M.J. (1998) 'Gross Investment and Technological Change', *Economics of Innovation and New Technology*, 7, 221–43.

Stoneman, P. and Kwon, M.J. (2000) 'Gross Investment and Technological Change: A Diffusion Based Approach', in R. Barrell, G. Mason and M. O'Mahoney (eds.), *Productivity Innovation and Economic Performance*, Cambridge: Cambridge University Press, 199–216.

Vernon, R. (1979) 'The Product Cycle Hypothesis in a New International Environment', *Oxford Bulletin of Economics and Statistics*, 41, 255–67.

Waterson, M. and Stoneman, P. (1985) 'Employment, Technological Diffusion and Oligopoly', *International Journal of Industrial Organisation*, 3, 327–44.

Chapter seventeen

Technology Adoption and Firm Profitability

Co-written with Myung Joong Kwon

The objectives of this paper are to explore the determinants of the returns to the adoption of new process technologies theoretically and empirically and to calculate some measure of that return.[1] The paper thus represents a contribution to the literature on the return to technological change. This is a field of both major policy concern and also extensive academic interest. However, most of the literature on the return to technological change measures the return to R&D (see, for example, Mairesse and Sassenou, 1991). R&D is not a good proxy for the use of new process technology (which will be largely purchased from outside the firm rather than being generated from within). There is a growing literature on the return to innovation i.e. the return to the first user of new technology (see for example, Geroski *et al.*, 1993), however, to obtain a complete picture of the return to technological change one must look at the returns achieved by all users, not just the first. It is this task that is attempted in this paper. As a by product of the approach taken the paper also provides an indirect test of the empirical validity of a number of different hypotheses relating to the technological diffusion process and also Schumpeterian hypotheses relating to the impact of technology adoption by other firms on the profits of non-adopters.

The paper is built around the theory of diffusion; however, because any one technology alone may not be sufficiently 'important' to have a measurable impact on a firm's profit (Stoneman and Kwon, 1994) we take a multi technology stance and address the simultaneous impact of the adoption of a number of different technologies. Diffusion theory, as synthesised in Karshenas and Stoneman (1993), hypothesises that the profit gain to the firm from the adoption of new technology will depend upon the characteristics of the firm (rank effects), the number of other adopters (stock effects), and the firm's position in the order of adoption (order effects). Endogenising dates of adoption we generate a reduced form equation relating the profit gain from adoption to the above factors plus information asymmetries (epidemic effects), the costs of adoption and expectations of changes therein. This equation is then estimated using panel data relating to a sample of firms in the UK engineering industry over the period 1983–6, embodied hypotheses are tested and estimates of the returns to adoption are calculated.

Reprinted from the *Economic Journal*, 106, 952–62, 1996 by kind permission of Blackwell Publishers.

17.1.   Theory

Define $\pi_i(\tau)$ as the pre tax gross profits of firm i in time τ, $g_{ij}(t_{ij}, \tau)$ as the annual gross profit gain to the firm in time τ from the adoption of technology j, $j = 1, \ldots, m$, at time t_{ij}, $\tau \geq t_{ij}$, and $\pi_{i0}(\tau)$ as counter factual profits where no new technologies have been adopted. Assume that the several technologies are neither complements nor substitutes[2] in the production process. We may then immediately specify that

$$\pi_i(\tau) = \pi_{i0}(\tau) + \Sigma_j D_{ij}(\tau) g_{ij}(t_{ij}, \tau), \tag{17.1}$$

where $D_{ij}(\tau)$ are dummy variables equal to 1, if firm i owns technology j in time τ and zero otherwise.

For firm i in industry k we assume that $\pi_{i0}(\tau)$ is a function of vectors of firm and industry characteristics $(\mathbf{C}_i(\tau), \mathbf{C}_k(\tau))$ and $\mathbf{N}_k(\tau)$, a vector of the number of users of the different new technologies in industry k at time τ. Formally

$$\pi_{i0}(\tau) = \pi_{i0}[\mathbf{C}_i(\tau), \mathbf{C}_k(\tau), \mathbf{N}_k(\tau)]. \tag{17.2}$$

The elements of $\mathbf{N}_k(\tau)$ are expected to impact negatively on $\pi_{i0}(\tau)$. This may be rationalised on Schumpeterian grounds – as more firms use a new technology industry average costs fall which in turn will lead to lower prices and lower profits for non-users. A formal model of such a process can be found in Waterson and Stoneman (1985).

We further assume, following Karshenas and Stoneman (1993), that $g_{ij}(t_{ij}, \tau)$ is given by

$$g_{ij}(t_{ij}, \tau) = g_j[\mathbf{C}_i(\tau), \mathbf{C}_k(\tau), N_{jk}(t_{ij}), \mathbf{N}_k(\tau)], \tag{17.3}$$

thereby allowing that the returns to the adoption of technology j are determined by: firm and industry characteristics (rank effects); the number of adopters of technology j in industry k at the date of adoption, $N_{jk}(t_{ij})$ (an order effect, having assumed that there are no cross technology order effects); and the number of other users in industry k at time τ of each of the new technologies, $\mathbf{N}_k(\tau)$ (stock effects). We expect $g_{j3} < 0$, and that the derivatives of g_j with respect to each of the elements of $\mathbf{N}_k(\tau)$ will be negative.

The date of adoption of technology j by firm i, t_{ij}, is an endogenous variable. Following Karshenas and Stoneman (1993), for a present value maximising firm, at the optimal date of adoption of technology j the net benefit of waiting further before adoption is zero.[3] We allow, however, that the actual adoption date may differ from the optimal date on account of information deficiencies. Defining T_j as the date at which technology j first appeared on the market, we follow the logic of the epidemic diffusion model and assume that the difference between the actual and optimal date is determined by $\Phi_j(t_{ij} - T_j)$ and thus is the smaller (in absolute value) the later that adoption occurs. If $\Phi_j > 0$ adoption is 'too early' whereas if $\Phi_j < 0$ adoption is 'too late'.

Define α_j as the number of units of technology j required per unit of output (i.e. a Leontief technology), $S_i(\tau)$ as the output of the firm in time τ, and $P_j(\tau)$ as the (quality adjusted) cost per unit of acquiring technology j in time τ. Assume (initially) that when a firm adopts a technology that all its capacity is converted at that time (there is no intra firm diffusion process). The cost of adopting technology j in time τ is then $\alpha_j S_i(\tau) P_i(\tau)$. We may then specify, assuming that at the date of adoption the firm takes no account of expected future changes in output and that the derivatives of the g_j function are time invariant constants, that at the date of adoption

$$g_{ij}(t_{ij}, t_{ij}) = \alpha_j r S_i(t_{ij}) P_j(t_{ij}) - \alpha_j S_i(t_{ij}) p_j(t_{ij}) + g_{j3} n_{jk}(t_{ij})/r + \Phi_j(t_{ij} - T_j), \qquad (17.4)$$

where $p_j(t_{ij})$ and $n_{jk}(t_{ij})$ are the perfect foresight expectations at time t_{ij} of changes in $P_j(t_{ij})$ and $N_{jk}(t_{ij})$ respectively and r is the interest rate/discount rate.

Using a Taylors series expansion, we specify that the profit gain to the firm in time τ from the adoption of technology j at time t_{ij} equals the profit gain at time t_{ij} plus the change in the profit gain between τ and t_{ij} resulting from changes in firm and industry characteristics and the number of other users of the technology since the date of adoption. We also allow that $g_{ij}(t_{ij}, \tau)$ is related to $(\tau - t_{ij})$, the number of years since the technology was adopted by the firm to account for the previously ignored intra firm diffusion process and possible learning by using effects, and thus write

$$g_{ij}(t_{ij}, \tau) = g_{ij}(t_{ij}, t_{ij}) + [\delta g_{ij}(t_{ij}, \tau)/\delta \tau] d\tau + \beta_j(\tau - t_{ij}), \qquad (17.5)$$

where β_j is a parameter.

Defining g_{jh} and g_{jq} as the derivatives of the g_j function with respect to the elements of the $\mathbf{C}_i$ and the $\mathbf{C}_k$ vectors (C_{ih} and C_{kq}) respectively, assuming for empirical simplicity that the derivatives of g_j with respect to different elements of $\mathbf{N}_k(N_{jk})$ are the same for each technology and equal to g_{j4}, and summing over technologies j yields (17.6).

$$\pi_i(\tau) = \pi_{i0}[\mathbf{C}_i(\tau), \mathbf{C}_k(\tau), \mathbf{N}_k(\tau)] + \Sigma_j[D_{ij}(\tau)(\alpha_j r S_i(t_{ij}) P_j(t_{ij}) - \alpha_j S_i(t_{ij}) p_j(t_{ij})$$

$$+ \Sigma_h\{g_{jh}[C_{ih}(\tau) - C_{ih}(t_{ij})]\} + \Sigma_q\{g_{jq}[C_{kq}(\tau) - C_{kq}(t_{ij})]\}$$

$$+ g_{j3} n_{jk}(t_{ij})/r + g_{j4}\Sigma_j[N_{jk}(\tau) - N_{jk}(t_{ij})] + \Phi_j(t_{ij} - T_j) + \beta_j(\tau - t_{ij})]. \qquad (17.6)$$

Equation (17.6) is the basic estimating equation used below, although, in order to operationalise the model, it is further assumed that $\pi_{i0}(\tau)$ and $g_{ij}(t_{ij}, \tau)$ are linear in their arguments, and for completeness we also include terms $\beta_j' D_{ij}(\tau), j = 1, \ldots, m$, which pick up whether ownership *per se* yields a profit gain.[4]

The hypotheses incorporated in (17.6) suggest that a firm's gross profits at time τ will be negatively related to the number of users of each technology at time τ, $\mathbf{N}_k(\tau)$, and that, for each technology adopted by the firm by time τ, extra profits will be earned, the amount extra being positively related to the cost of acquisition of the technology, $\alpha_j r S_i(t_{ij}) P_j(t_{ij})$, and negatively related to: the change between τ and t_{ij} in the number of users of each technology, $\Sigma_j[N_{jk}(\tau) - N_{jk}(t_{ij})]$, via the stock effect; the expected change in the number of users of the technology at the date of adoption, $n_{jk}(t_{ij})$, via the order effect; and changes in the expected cost of acquisition at the date of adoption, $\alpha_j S_i(t_{ij}) p_j(t_{ij})$. The impact of firm and industry characteristics and changes in such characteristics between τ and t_{ij} (i.e. rank effects) on profits is characteristic specific. Similarly the sign of the impact of epidemic learning, $\Phi_j(t_{ij} - T_j)$, and intra firm diffusion, $\beta_j(\tau - t_{ij})$, for each j, cannot be predicted *a priori*.

17.2.   Data Sources and the Measurement of Variables

The main data source used for estimating equation (17.6) is two surveys of technology adoption in nine Minimum List Headings industries in the UK engineering and metalworking sector undertaken by the Centre for Urban and Regional Development Studies (CURDS) at the University of Newcastle upon Tyne (see Alderman *et al.*, 1988). These surveys provide data by establishment upon: the dates, between 1965 and 1986, of first adoption of four different technologies (computer numerically controlled machine tools (CNC), coated carbide tools (CCT), microprocessors used in process operations (MIC) and computers for administrative purposes (COMP)); employment in 1970, 1975, 1981 and 1986; and R&D employees in 1981 and 1986. We were able to match profits data from Lotus Datastream to construct a panel data set containing 105 (single establishment) firms for the period 1981–6.

Following the standard industrial economics literature and taking account of data availability, we specify the relevant industry characteristics determining base level profits and the profit gains to adoption to be: a measure of industry size, real total sales, M, which accounts for the state of demand (and the inclusion of which nets out any requirement to include industry price); the five firm concentration ratio, CR; and the real wage rate, w (all sourced from *Business Monitor*). We expect the base level of profits to be positively related to $M(\tau)$, and negatively related to $w(\tau)$, but are agnostic as to whether $CR(\tau)$ will impact positively or negatively (primarily because most of our sample firms are not amongst the five largest in their industry and thus the impact of an increase in the size of the largest five may have opposing effects). We consider similarly that the sign of the impact of changes in CR between τ and t_{ij} on the profit gain from adoption is uncertain and that the impact of changes in w between τ and t_{ij} on the profit gain from adoption will be technology specific (depending on whether the new technology is relatively labour saving or using). We expect changes in the $M(\tau)$ to have a positive impact on the profit gain from adoption.

Largely on the grounds of data availability only two firm characteristics have been included, firm size, S_i, and the firm's R&D, R_i (both sourced from the survey data). The inclusion of these two characteristics is consistent with the standard industrial economics literature, the latter acting, *inter alia*, as a proxy for product innovation. We expect both to impact positively on the base level of profits and for changes in both between τ and t_{ij} to impact positively on the profit gain. Firm size, S_i, may also act as a good proxy for unobservable difference across firms that may well impact upon profitability. In the absence of full sales data, firm size has been measured by employment.[5] The nature of the survey data has necessitated that $S_i(\tau)$ be measured by employment of the firm in 1986 (and $S_i(\tau)$ is thus a non-time varying covariate) whereas size of the firm at the date of adoption of a technology j, $S_i(t_{ij})$, is measured by employment of the firm in whichever year out of 1970, 1975, 1981 or 1986 was closest to the date of adoption. Similarly, given the survey data available, we measure R&D in time τ, $R_i(\tau)$, by R&D employees in 1986 (and thus $R_i(\tau)$ is also a non-time varying covariate)[6] and R&D at the date of adoption of technology j by R&D in 1981 or 1986, depending on which date is closest to the date of adoption.

The theory is a real model and thus all nominal variables (basically profits, wage rates and the costs of acquiring the technologies) are deflated by the retail price index[7] (sourced from *Economic Trends*). The interest rate should also be a real rate i.e. the nominal rate minus the rate of expected price inflation. To model the variables $r\alpha_j S_i(t_{ij})P_j(t_{ij})$, $j = 1, \ldots, m$, we introduce two separate groups of terms in the regression: $\alpha_j r_n S_i(t_{ij}) P_j(t_{ij})$, where r_n is the nominal rate of interest; and $-\alpha_j p^e S_i(t_{ij}) P_j(t_{ij})$, where p^e is the perfect foresight expected rate of inflation over the period $(t_{ij}, t_{ij} + 1)$, and $S_i(t_{ij})$ is as measured above. If it is the real rate that affects the technology adoption decision and the expected rate of inflation is the perfect foresight rate then we expect these two sets of terms to have estimated coefficients (α_j) that are of the same (absolute) value.

The terms $g_{j3} n_{jk}(t_{ij})/r$ for each j also include the real interest rate. Here r is the discount factor that capitalises to the adoption date the loss of profit that derives from delaying adoption and moving down the order of adoption. We amalgamate this interest rate in to the coefficient and proceed using $n_{jk}(t_{ij})$ as the explanatory variable.

The variables $p_j(t_{ij})$ and $n_{jk}(t_{ij})$ are represented by the actual changes in prices and actual changes in the number of users in the interval $(t_{ij}, t_{ij} + 1)$. Data on $P_j(t_{ij}), j = 1, \ldots, 4$, has been collected from various sources. We have calculated quality adjusted price series for both computers and microprocessors (details available from the authors upon request) but for other technologies we were unable to quality adjust.

17.3. Estimation Methods and Results

On the grounds of brevity details on data characteristics and sample statistics have not been included but are available on request from the authors. It is however worth noting that of the sample of 105 firms, by 1986, 61 had adopted CNC, 78 COMP, 39 MIC and 52 COT, with 93 of the firms having adopted at least one of the four technologies. Some adoptions of each of the technologies occurred in every year from 1965 to 1986.

Many estimation experiments were undertaken, but again on the grounds of brevity, only the preferred results are discussed in detail. Presented in table 17.1 (where the D operator is used to indicate the change in a variable between t_{ij} and τ) these are based on a panel data set covering 105 firms for each of the years 1983 to 1986 yielding 420 observations in total. The adoption dates of the technologies (t_{ij}) by this sample of firms vary between 1965 and 1986. The results exclude firm specific effects, industry dummies and time dummies (which were not significant over this sample) and were produced using a Robust estimator which achieves almost OLS efficiency in situations where the error term is independently but not normally distributed (Hamilton, 1991).[8] The software package STATA was used to produce the estimates.

The other empirical experiments undertaken included:

1 Using a larger sample encompassing the 1981–6 as opposed to the 1983–6 period. However, a Chow test indicated a structural break between the 1981–2 and 1983–6 periods. Given the uniqueness of the recessionary conditions 1981–2 and our inability to refine the model to account for this structural break only the results for the later period are presented.

2 We experimented at length with the inclusion of fixed effects. However, the two non-time-varying covariates (firm R&D and firm size in 1986) cannot be included in addition to fixed effects.[9] The decision to exclude the fixed effects was based upon the view that fixed effects are a measure of our ignorance and using the R&D and size data helps reduce the extent of this ignorance (in addition, specifically including firm size may proxy for those omitted variables that may be labelled 'unobservables').

Table 17.1 Regression results: robust estimation

Constant	$M(\tau)$	$w(\tau)$	$CR(\tau)$	S_i	R_i
560.58	19.97	-0.005	-6.89**	0.47*	9.04**
(1.05)	(0.44)	(-0.1)	(-3.64)	(1.64)	(1.97)

	CNC	Computer	Micro processors	Carbide Tools
$N_j(\tau)$	8.74*	-3.66**	-1.75	-13.83**
	(1.85)	(-2.44)	(-0.25)	(-4.04)
$D_{ij}\Sigma N_j$	2.23	1.8	-4.11**	1.15
	(1.3)	(0.89)	(-3.23)	(0.8)
$D_{ij}rP_jS_i$	0.05**	0.025**	0.4*	-4.48**
	(2.32)	(5.18)	(8.02)	(-3.76)
$D_{ij}p^eP_jS_i$	-0.05**	-0.01*	-0.07**	3.34**
	(-3.44)	(-1.87)	(-4.6)	(3.84)
$D_{ij}DM$	-594.8**	651.7**	38.03	-36.2
	(-2.33)	(3.62)	(0.08)	(-0.14)
$D_{ij}Dw$	0.15	0.10	0.03	-0.05
	(1.19)	(1.62)	(0.18)	(-0.77)
$D_{ij}DCR$	12.16	-0.67	33.68	-3.12
	(0.81)	(-0.05)	(1.54)	(-0.26)
$D_{ij}DS_i$	2.94**	0.76*	1.17	1.15**
	(3.58)	(1.75)	(1.1)	(3.85)
$D_{ij}DR_i$	14.92	-24.1*	20.03**	-11.9
	(1.5)	(-1.95)	(2.9)	(-0.78)
$D_{ij}n_j$	35.5**	-1.16	46.4**	21.4
	(2.47)	(-0.1)	(2.37)	(1.00)
$D_{ij}p_jS_i$	1.93*	0.026**	8.75**	-56.1**
	(1.83)	(6.00)	(9.12)	(-5.97)
$D_{ij}(t_{ij} - T_j)$	22.4	-28.6	58.5*	-54.7
	(0.55)	(-0.67)	(1.69)	(-1.28)
$D_{ij}(\tau - t_{ij})$	-53.2	-168**	87.66	-31.7
	(-0.56)	(-2.64)	(0.58)	(-0.45)
D_{ij}	-506.6	1051.6	-883.7	1516
	(-0.66)	(0.84)	(-1.63)	(1.36)

The D operator is used to indicate a difference between τ and t_{ij}.
Number of observations 420.
$F_{64,335} = 31.76$ (testing the hypothesis of all coefficients = 0).
$\chi^2 = 2.25$ (testing the hypothesis of autoregressive conditional heteroscedasticity).
Estimated first serial order autocorrelation of error term $e(i, t) = 0.003$: LM statistic $(\chi^2) = 3.6$.
$R^2 = 0.85$.
t-statistics in parentheses: ** 5 per cent significance level, * 10 per cent significance level.

3 Further experiments encompassed the inclusion of a lagged dependent variable[10] reflecting persistence effects. However, the structure of our model is one where past technology adoptions impact on today's profits rather like a persistence effect and thus in many ways the lagged dependent would reflect the technology adoption effects that the model is already built to capture. Thus the lagged dependent was excluded.

4   A number of estimates were produced including industry dummies. It should be noted that as modelled the coefficients in the model are the same for each industry. To model industry specificity fully would require multiplying the number of coefficients by nine (the number of industries) which goes beyond the capabilities of the data set. Thus experiments were undertaken with the inclusion of industry dummies. This, as a general rule, made insignificant the industry variables already included and thus table 17.1 excludes industry dummies.

Turning to the preferred results in table 17.1 and looking first at the diagnostic statistics, a White test (White, 1980) and a test of autoregressive heteroscedasticity suggested by Engle (1982) both reject the hypothesis of heteroscedastic residuals. An LM test for the joint significance of a set of estimated autocorrelation terms enabled us to reject the hypothesis of serially correlated disturbances. The hypothesis that all coefficients in the regression are zero is rejected by the F test. An LR test also indicates that the specified model is superior to a stripped down model that included on the RHS only the expression for the base level of profits plus dummies for adoption of each of the technologies, thereby indicating the general validity of the modelling of the profit gains from adoption. The estimated R^2 is 0.85. This fully loaded model contains 62 regressors and a general observation on the results is that, in most cases, where a variable is significant its coefficient is of the sign expected *a priori*.[11]

The model relates the base level of profits, or the profits of a non-user, $\pi_{i0}(\tau)$, to firm and industry characteristics and the number of users of the four technologies under consideration. The five characteristics variables all carry coefficients of a sign consistent with the discussions above and concentration, firm size and R&D are all significant, at least at the 10 per cent level. Three of the four $N_j(\tau)$ variables carry the expected negative coefficient. Three of the four $N_j(\tau)$ terms are significant at the 5 per cent level and using an F-test we were able to reject the joint hypothesis that the four $N_j(\tau)$ terms carry zero coefficients.

We have hypothesised that gross profit gains will be positively related to the annual rental costs of the technologies acquired (represented by the two terms $D_{ij}rP_jS_i$ and $D_{ij}p^eP_jS_i$). The first set of these terms should carry positive coefficients, the second set negative coefficients, which is so for each of the four technologies except carbide tools. Seven of the eight variables are significant at the 5 per cent level, and the eighth at the 10 per cent level. We have also tested whether these two sets of terms have estimated coefficients (α_j) that are of the same (absolute) value but of opposite signs and the hypothesis is rejected. We may thus conclude that it is more efficient to include the nominal interest rate and the expected rate of inflation as separate terms rather than incorporating them in one term measuring the real rate of interest.

The cost of the technologies also appear in the price expectations terms $D_{ij}p_jS_i$. The hypothesis is that expected changes in the cost of acquisition will have a negative impact upon the profit gain. Although across the four technologies three of the coefficients are significant at the 5 per cent level (and the joint hypothesis of zero coefficients can be rejected) only the coefficient for carbide tools is of the expected sign and we thus reject the hypothesis of a negative technology price expectations effect.

The rank effects are represented by the terms $D_{ij}DM$, $D_{ij}Dw$, $D_{ij}DCR$, $D_{ij}DS_i$ and $D_{ij}DR_i$. $D_{ij}Dw$ and $D_{ij}DCR$ do not impact significantly on the profit gain. This may be the result in the former case of having to use industry rather than firm level wage rates, and in the latter case is consistent with the findings of Karshenas and Stoneman (1993) on the impact of concentration on the adoption probability. An F-test indicated that one cannot reject the joint hypothesis that all coefficients on $D_{ij}Dw$ and $D_{ij}DCR$ are zero. The coefficients upon $D_{ij}DS_i$ are of the correct sign for all j and significant for three of the four technologies. The coefficients upon $D_{ij}DM$ and $D_{ij}DR_i$ are of the correct sign for two of the four technologies in each case, and significant for two of the four technologies in each case. In each case, however, only for one technology is the coefficient both significant and of the correct sign. Separate F-tests enabled us to reject the joint hypotheses that each of these three groups of variables ($D_{ij}DS_i$, $D_{ij}DM$ and $D_{ij}DR_i$) carry zero coefficients. Overall one may argue that there are rank effects in the determination of the profit gain from adoption, the most effective measure of which appears to be firm size. This would be consistent with much of the literature that argues that firm size has a positive impact upon the probability of adoption.

The stock effects terms, $D_{ij}\Sigma N_j$, are hypothesised to carry negative coefficients. For only one technology was the coefficient significant but for that technology the coefficient is of the correct sign. Using an F-test we were able to reject the joint hypothesis that the four stock terms carry zero coefficients. There are therefore significant stock effects.

The other effects included in the model are intra firm or learning by using effects, $D_{ij}(\tau - t_{ij})$, order effects $D_{ij}n_j$, epidemic effects, $D_{ij}(t_{ij} - T_j)$ and constant terms $D_{ij}(\tau)$, $j = 1, \ldots, 4$. Using a series of F-tests we are unable to reject the hypotheses that each of these effects carry zero coefficients.

On the basis of these results we cannot reject the hypotheses that (i) the profit of a non-adopting firm declines as other firms use new technologies (ii) the profit gain from adoption is determined by rank and stock effects (iii) the cost of acquisition impacts positively on the profit gain from adoption. We do, however, reject the hypotheses that the profit gain from adoption is determined by expected changes in the cost of acquisition, intra firm diffusion effects, order effects and epidemic effects.

We have calculated the absolute values of the elasticities of firm profits with respect to each of the regressors at the sample means. The elasticity of profits with respect to N_j averages 0.45 across the four j; with respect to $D\Sigma N_j$ averages 0.11; the main rank effect (DS_i) averages an elasticity of 0.1; the cost of acquisition effects exhibit elasticities in the 0.4–0.8 range. One may therefore conclude that the effects that we have argued to be supported by the estimation are also quantitatively significant.

From these coefficient estimates we have calculated the implied profit gains from the adoption of each technology at the sample means. A useful background observation is that non–adopters in the sample have mean profits of £536,541 whereas the mean profits of the firms that adopt one or more of the technologies is £820,229. The estimates are that the annual gross profit gain from adopting CNC is £57,500, computers £71,540, carbide tools £640 and microprocessors a loss of £58,320. (We observe that for microprocessors the epidemic coefficient is significant and positive implying that the technology was adopted 'too early'. The negative estimated return could be related to this early adoption. We also note that in the early 1980s there was considerable media hype over microprocessors that could have induced firms to adopt too early.) We also calculate that a firm adopting one or more of the four technologies exhibit an annual profit gain equal to 11 per cent of the mean profit of the whole sample or 8.7 per cent of the profits of adopting firms.

17.4.   Conclusions

Understanding the determinants of and measuring the returns to technological change are of major interest to both academics and policy makers. Unfortunately the existing literature tends to concentrate upon the returns to R&D, whereas the benefits from technological change only arise with adoption. Measuring the returns to adoption has, as far as is known to the authors, been largely ignored in the past.

On the basis of the technological diffusion literature we have argued that the profit from adopting a new technology will be related to rank, stock, order and epidemic effects. A theoretical model is constructed that reflects this argument and an empirical version of that model is estimated upon data relating to the adoption of four different technologies in the UK engineering industry.

The estimates indicate that we cannot reject the hypotheses that: the profit gain of a non-adopting firm declines as other firms use new technologies; the profit gain from adoption is determined by rank and stock effects; and the cost of acquisition impacts positively on the profit gain from adoption. We do however reject the hypotheses that the profit gain from adoption is determined by expected changes in the cost of acquisition, intra firm diffusion effects, order effects and epidemic effects.

At the sample means it is calculated that a firm adopting one or more of the new technologies realised an annual gross profit gain equivalent to 11 per cent of the mean profit of sample firms.

Notes

1   The work reported in this paper has been financed by a grant from the Economic and Social Research Council on The Impact of Technology Adoption on Firm Performance. We wish to thank participants in seminars at York and Warwick Universities. The authors alone are responsible for any errors that may remain.

2   Although interactions are allowed to occur through the product market with the return to the adoption of technology j by the firm being related to the number of other adopters of j and other technologies. Relaxation of the technological independence assumption would severely complicate the analysis. An approach without this assumption may be taken in which technology states are identified, each technology state corresponding to ownership of some combination of the j technologies available. Such an approach, we calculate, would increase the number of regressors in the empirical work by 130.

3   This rather terse description of the theory and the leanness of the paper as a whole reflects the need for brevity. A fuller version of this paper which spells out the theory and empirics at greater length is available from the authors upon request.

4   It has been suggested by referees that a reformulation of the model in terms of rates of return on either capital or sales may have some advantages. Although not totally accepting this view, data are not available for the sample used below on either sales or capital stock that would enable us to operationalise such a model.

5   The use of sales data would have reduced the sample size by approximately one third. We tested whether the use of employment as opposed to sales data induced any bias in the estimates and rejected the hypothesis.

6   We also experimented with the use of R_i (1981), but this did not significantly affect the results.

7   Over the sample period the PPI and the RPI move very much together.

8   This estimator does not allow for the potential endogeneity of variables such as R&D and firm size. To address such potential endogeneity would suggest that perhaps we should use an instrumental variables estimator. Given, however, that these are non-time varying covariates and given the limits of our data set we were unable to identify appropriate instruments in the data set. Estimates using R&D and firm size in 1981 instead of 1986 were produced as a means of overcoming the problem but the results were not materially affected.

9   If the non-time varying covariates are excluded and fixed effects are included the results in general show coefficient estimates with the same signs as in table 17.1 but the estimated standard errors are inflated. If fixed effects and industry effects are both included collinearity problems become extreme.

10 In general we found that a lagged dependent variable carried a coefficient of about 0.5 but its inclusion led to widespread insignificance elsewhere.

11 The results presented do include a number of coefficients that are not significantly different from zero at the 5 per cent or 10 per cent level. We do not consider this in itself a particular problem. Our main interest is in testing the basic hypotheses, and as such, the crucial issue is not so much whether individual coefficients are or are not significant but whether groups of variables that represent a particular hypothesis jointly contribute significantly to explaining the dependent variable. The results of such tests are reported in the main text. However, we have undertaken a number of experiments in the search for a more parsimonious representation of the data and results can be produced, using for example stepwise regression, where only significant variables are included. We have not, however, presented such results for it was found that using an F-test, the decisions whether or not to exclude a set of variables depended upon the order in which the variables were excluded.

References

Alderman *et al.* (1988) 'Patterns of innovation diffusion,' Technical Report no. 12, CURDS, University of Newcastle upon Tyne.

Engle, R. (1982) 'Autoregressive conditional heteroskedasticity with estimates of the variance of United Kingdom inflations,' *Econometrica*, 987–1009.

Geroski, P., Machin, S. and Van Reenan, J. (1993) 'The profitability of innovating firms,' *Rand Journal of Economics*, 24(2), 198–211.

Hamilton, L.C. (1991) 'How robust is robust regression,' *Stata Technical Bulletin*, 2, 21–6.

Karshenas, M. and Stoneman, P. (1993) 'Rank, stock, order and epidemic effects in the diffusion of new process technologies: an empirical mode,' *Rand Journal of Economics*, 24(4), 503–9.

Mairesse, J. and Sassenou, M. (1991) 'R&D and productivity: a survey of econometric studies at the firm level,' *STI Review*, 8, 9–43, Paris, OECD.

Stoneman, P. and Kwon, M.J. (1994) 'The diffusion of multiple process technologies,' *Economic Journal*, 104, 420–31.

Waterson, M. and Stoneman, P. (1985) 'Employment, technological diffusion and oligopoly,' *International Journal of Industrial Organisation*, 3(3), 327–44.

White, H. (1980) 'A heteroskedasticity – consistent covariance matrix estimator and a direct test for heteroskedasticity,' *Econometrica*, 48, 817–38.

Chapter eighteen

Employment, Technological Diffusion and Oligopoly

Co-written with Michael Waterson

18.1. Introduction

One of the more topical subjects for economic debate at the present time concerns the impact of new technology on employment. Recent published work. Neary (1981) and Sinclair (1981), for example, and unpublished work, e.g., Katsoulacos (1984), has extended our understanding of the process involved at both the micro and the macro levels. We contend, however, that this work may be at best telling only part of the story, and at worst misleading, for it concentrates on comparing employment before and after adoption of an innovation by the whole industry. A common observation on the technological change process is that diffusion of new technology takes time,[1] in fact often a considerable length of time. If it is the case that results obtained through analysis of the endpoints (which we dub comparative statics results) are not only quantitatively but also qualitatively different from those generated by considering the transition path,[2] then to rely on such comparative static modelling is misleading.

The purpose of this paper is to examine the employment effects of technological change during the diffusion process within an oligopolistic industry. Some process innovations are so widely applicable that the assumption of perfect competition might be more appropriate, but for an important number of others, the demanding industry is best thought of as oligopolistic.[3] The employment effects are examined only within the context of a very simple model which neglects supply side influences and factor price effects and which involves particular functional forms. Within this simple structure though, we are able to capture two important connected influences at work – forces which so far appear not to have been investigated, but which are the key to our results. The first of these influences is the relative importance of expansion and composition effects in the determination of labour demand. The second influence comes from exit during the diffusion process.

In the section which follows the framework of the model is outlined. Then in the next two sections the path of employment as diffusion proceeds is spelled out, first assuming no exits then allowing for that complication. The paper closes with some concluding remarks.

Reprinted from the *International Journal of Industrial Organisation*, 3, 327–44, 1985 by kind permission of Elsevier Science.

18.2. A Theoretical Framework

One question which immediately arises when considering an oligopolistic industry is how to model the distribution of existing firm sizes. Since the number of firms is definitely not large, problems arise in asserting that firms are distributed in size according to some continuous density function such as the lognormal. Thus a probit diffusion model, for example like that used by David (1969), Davies (1979) and Stoneman and Ireland (1983), is not particularly appropriate. On the other hand, any choice of discrete size distribution would appear somewhat arbitrary.

For the purposes of simplicity, in this paper we adopt the simplest possible size distribution, namely that all firms are of equal size. In fact, the framework used in the discussion below is closely related to that employed by Reinganum (1981). It may be recalled that in Reinganum's model there is a homogeneous-product oligopoly in which the firms adopt Cournot–Nash conjectures regarding the diffusion game. Despite identical firms, a diffusion process occurs because two factors interact. Early innovation brings about greater benefits in terms of higher profits, but early innovation also implies higher process introduction/adjustment costs. Hence once one firm has innovated it will not pay another to do so until introduction costs fall somewhat, and so on. Such a process might be considered implicitly to lie behind the diffusion path that we take to be exogenously determined.

In order to facilitate analytical solutions, we take the case (as in Reinganum's section 18.3) where cost and demand functions take on simple linear forms. We choose demand to be represented by the inverse function relating price (p) to outputs (q_i),

$$p = a - bQ = a - b\sum_i q_i, \quad i = 1, 2, \ldots, n, \quad a, b > 0. \tag{18.1}$$

Total costs for a firm are assumed to be

$$C = c_k q_i + f_k, \quad k = 0, 1, \quad c_k, f_k > 0. \tag{18.2}$$

Here the subscript k differentiates between those who have adopted and those who have not adopted the innovation (1 and 0, respectively) at any point in time. The dynamic aspects of the process are implicit rather than explicit functions of time in our model, and we do not use an explicit form for the time–cost tradeoff function, though later in the paper, despite this, we have a few remarks on timing.

As far as employment is concerned, we again make heroic simplifications. We assume that the process improvement which is followed in our diffusion path is Hicks-neutral. Marginal costs as in (18.2) above are of course implicitly functions of factor prices [though not output, given the simple form of (18.2)]. Hence, assuming two representative variable factors of production labour, the one which is our concern, and capital, say, we may write the marginal costs relationship

$$c_1(w, r) = \theta c_0(w, r), \quad \theta < 1, \tag{18.3}$$

where w and r are the respective factor prices.[4] Hence, using the derivative property of the cost function, firms' demands for labour per unit of output before and after adoption are related thus:

$$l_1(w, r) = \theta l_0(w, r).$$ (18.4)

Of course, the firm's employment of labour may either rise or fall after adoption, depending upon the extent of the expansion in output which is engendered. Industry employment once all firms have adopted similarly may rise or fall. We wish to stress not the eventual effects (on which see, for example, Dobbs et al., 1983) but the employment path through the diffusion process.

Upon adoption of the innovation then, the horizontal marginal and average variable cost functions shift down by the proportion θ. The question of what happens to fixed costs is left open for the present. Many innovations would fit the pattern of increasing fixed costs while reducing marginal costs, though not all would. The eventual number of firms in the industry will presumably be determined by the breakeven number together with the conditions of entry (barriers to entry) obtaining, and following complete diffusion, numbers in the industy could either rise or fall.

The final question concerns potential entrants at an early stage. For example, it might be the case that the early adopters were new firms without substantial investments in existing technology. Then subsequently, (some) existing firms would adopt. Few additional insights are generated by considering this extension of the model and our analysis of it is confined to some remarks at the end of section 18.4.

18.3. The Path of Employment, Disregarding Exit

Let us first consider the situation where the identity of each firm in the industry prior to innovation is preserved throughout the diffusion (and there is no entry or exit). At any point along the innovation path there are m firms who have adopted and $(n - m)$ who have not. Both maximise profits which, using (18.1) and (18.2), are

$$\Pi_i = \left(a - b \sum_i q_i \right) q_i - c_k q_i - j_k.$$ (18.5)

In doing this, firms make Cournot conjectures on price and output.

The first-order maximisation condition[5] for those who have adopted (which are all identical) is

$$a - b[mq_1 + (n - m)q_0] - bq_1 - c_1 = 0,$$

while for those who have not, we have

$$a - b[mq_1 + (n - m)q_0] - bq_0 - c_0 = 0.$$

Solving these equations for the two values q_0 and q_1, at the point where m have adopted and $(n - m)$ have not, we find

$$q_0(m, n - m) = \frac{a - (m + 1)c_0 + mc_1}{b(n + 1)},$$ (18.6)

$$q_1(m, n - m) = \frac{a + (n - m)c_0 - (n + 1 - m)c_1}{b(n + 1)},$$ (18.7)

from which it may be noted that both q_0 and q_1 fall as m rises. However,

$$q_1(m, n - m) - q_0(m, n - m) = (c_0 - c_1)/b > 0;$$ (18.8)

a firm's output increases on adoption.

Total output can be written[6]

$$Q(m, n - m) = mq_1(m, n - m) + (n - m)q_0(m, n - m)$$

$$= \frac{m(a - c_1) + (n - m)(a - c_0)}{b(n + 1)}.$$

But then it may be noted that

$$Q(m, n - m) = \left(\frac{n - m}{n}\right)Q(0, n) + \frac{m}{n}Q(n, 0).$$ (18.9)

Also, industry price is

$$p(m, n - m) = \frac{a + (n - m)c_0 + mc_1}{n + 1}$$

$$= \left(\frac{n - m}{n}\right)p(0, n) + \frac{m}{n}p(n, 0).$$ (18.10)

Hence in this simple model, both industry output and price over the diffusion period are a simple linear combination of initial and final positions; output being an increasing and price a decreasing function of m. However, employment does not follow a linear relationship.

Using the assumptions embodied in (18.4), we may evaluate industry employment at any point as

$$L(m, n - m) = l_0[(n - m)q_0(m, n - m) + \theta mq_1(m, n - m)].$$ (18.11)

Substituting from (18.6) and (18.7) and employing the assumption that $c_1 = \theta c_0$ yields

$$L(m, n - m) = \frac{l_0}{b(n + 1)}[(n - m)(a - c_0) + \theta m(a - c_1) + (\theta - 1)(c_0 - c_1)m(n - m)].$$

We may derive that

$$L(0, n) = \frac{l_0 n}{b(n + 1)}(a - c_0)$$ (18.12a)

and

$$L(n, 0) = \frac{l_0 n}{b(n+1)} \theta(a - c_1).$$ (18.12b)

Hence,

$$L(m, n - m) = \frac{n - m}{n} L(0, n) + \frac{m}{n} L(n, 0) - \frac{(1 - \theta)^2 m(n - m) c_0 l_0}{b(n+1)}$$ (18.13)

and

$$L(n, 0) - L(0, n) \equiv \Delta L = \frac{l_0 n}{b(n+1)} (1 - \theta)[c_0 \theta - (a - c_0)].$$ (18.14)

Using (18.14) we can make some initial statements concerning the comparative statics exercise of whether employment will have increased or decreased after technology has improved. Thus if $\theta > (a - c_0)/c_0$, employment increases, if $\theta < (a - c_0)/c_0$, employment decreases. Also given $\theta < 1$, if $a > 2c_0$, then $\theta < (a - c_0)/c_0$ and employment will decrease for any θ. These initial results are not surprising. The condition that $\theta > (a - c_0)/c_0$ (given $\theta < 1$) is equivalent to the condition that the marginal revenue curve cuts the horizontal axis to the right of competitive output, and thus that at all outputs less than competitive output levels, industry marginal revenue is positive and the industry elasticity of demand is greater than unity in absolute value. Given a linear demand curve, the combination of Hicks-neutral technical change with a demand elasticity greater than unity has been shown by Katsoulacos (1984) to yield employment gains.

The effect of changes in θ on ΔL is not so clear. Again using (18.14), we find

$$\text{sign } \frac{\partial \Delta L}{\partial \theta} = \text{sign}(a - 2\theta c_0).$$

Therefore, if $\theta > a/2c_0$ then terminal employment increases with θ, and if $\theta < a/2c_0$, terminal employment decreases with θ. Clearly if $a > 2c_0$ and $\theta < 1$, terminal employment must decrease as θ increases. We may also note the impact of changes in n on $L(n, 0)$, $L(0, n)$ and ΔL. As n increases both $L(n, 0)$ and $L(0, n)$ increase, and moreover ΔL increases.

Results pertaining to the endpoints of the diffusion path are not at the focus of our interest. We mainly wish to investigate the sequence of employment levels as m tends from zero to n along the diffusion path. From (18.13) we may derive that

$$\frac{\partial L(m, n - m)}{\partial m} = \frac{l_0 c_0 (1 - \theta)}{b(n+1)} \left[\theta - \left(\frac{a - c_0}{c_0} \right) - (1 - \theta)(n - 2m) \right].$$ (18.15)

The sign of this expression clearly is determined by the term in square brackets. From (18.15), $\partial^2 L / \partial m^2 > 0$, thus the square bracketed term increases with m. We may then delineate three cases. Case A involves employment continuously increasing, that is, where $\partial L(0, n) / \partial m > 0$. Case C occurs when employment falls continuously, so that the square

Table 18.1 Cross-classification of diffusion and comparative static cases

	$a < 2c_0$			$a > 2c_0$	$\partial L/\partial m$
	$1 > \theta \geqq a/2c_0 > \dfrac{a-c_0}{c_0}$	$1 > a/2c_0 > \theta > \dfrac{a-c_0}{c_0}$	$1 > \dfrac{a-c_0}{c_0} > \theta$	$\dfrac{a-c_0}{c_0} > 1 > \theta$	
$\theta - (1-\theta)n > \dfrac{a-c_0}{c_0}$	$L(n,0) > L(0,n)$ $\partial \Delta L/\partial \theta > 0$ Case A				> 0
$\theta + (1-\theta)n > \dfrac{a-c_0}{c_0} >$ $\theta - (1-\theta)n$	$L(n,0) > L(0,n)$ $\partial \Delta L/\partial \theta < 0$ Case B.1	$L(n,0) > L(0,n)$ $\partial \Delta L/\partial \theta > 0$ Case B.2	$L(n,0) < L(0,n)$ $\partial \Delta L/\partial \theta > 0$ Case B.3	$L(n,0) < L(0,n)$ $\partial \Delta L/\partial \theta > 0$ Case B.4	negative becoming positive as m increases
$\theta + (1-\theta)n < \dfrac{a-c_0}{c_0}$				$L(n,0) < L(0,n)$ $\partial \Delta L/\partial \theta > 0$ Case C	< 0

bracketed term never becomes positive even if $m = n$, i.e., $\partial L(n, 0)/\partial m < 0$. The third case, case B, exists when the quantity in square brackets changes in sign as m increases. Thus case B involves $\partial L(0, n)/\partial m < 0$, $\partial L(n, 0)/\partial m > 0$. We may identify the three cases by the following conditions:

Case A: $\theta - (1 - \theta)n > (a - c_0)/c_0$,

Case B: $\theta + (1 - \theta)n > (a - c_0)/c_0 > \theta - (1 - \theta)n$,

Case C: $\theta + (1 - \theta)n < (a - c_0)/c_0$.

Given the comparative statics results and these sequence results we can now completely define the effects of technical change on $L(m, n - m)$ both during the diffusion and during the post diffusion for different parameter values. Of the twelve potential parameter combinations arising and listed in table 18.1, we may note that case A is restricted to the first column since $\theta \leqq a/2c_0$ is equivalent to $2\theta - 1 \geqq (a - c_0)/c_0$, which is in turn necessary for A. Similarly, by observing that $\theta + (1 - \theta)n > 1$, we may restrict C to the final column. For each of the six feasible combinations we provide an alpha-numeric for identification purposes.

Using table 18.1 we may observe that for a high cost industry ($a < 2c_0$), for high values of θ, ($\theta > a/2c_0$), equivalent to a small technological advance, we are in case A. As technological advance is more rapid we move to case B.1, then B.2, then B.3. As θ is declining, in cases A and B.1, $L(n, 0) - L(0, n)$ is increasing, but as θ declines further, $L(n, 0) - L(0, n)$ decreases, becoming negative in case B.3. Figure 18.1(a) plots the relation between $L(n - 0) - L(0, n)$ (i.e., ΔL) and θ. We may further note that as $n \to \infty$, case A disappears since the θ that satisfies $\theta - (1 - \theta)n > (a - c_0)/c_0$ tends to unity, leaving only cases B.1–B.3.

In a low cost industry ($a > 2c_0$), for high θ (small technological advances) case C is relevant, and as θ falls case B.4 becomes relevant. In both C and B.4, $L(n, 0) - L(0, n) < 0$, and declines as θ falls. As $n \to \infty$, the θ that satisfies $\theta + (1 - \theta)n = (a - c_0)/c_0$ tends to unity and thus only case B.4 is relevant for large n. Figure 18.1(b) shows the relationship between ΔL and θ, for the low cost case.

In figure 18.2, we plot the sequence of $L(m, n - m)$ against m for the different cases. Figure 18.2(a) assumes $a < 2c_0$, figure 18.2(b) assumes $a > 2c_0$.

Implicitly, if not explicitly, most partial equilibrium studies have assumed that the comparative static effect on the industry as a whole is a good guide to the sequence effect,[7] that is, if employment rises as a result of new technology, for example, it will rise continuously along the path of adoption. Our results show, however, that the implicit assumption of monotonicity in the sequence of factor demands is a property only of cases involving small technological changes or low n, and that as θ becomes small or n large, the various case B's involving non-monotonicity represent the rule rather than the exception. The implicit assumption therefore seems misleading and our results illustrate the importance of considering the diffusion profile more explicitly.

The rationale for our results concerning potential non-monotonicity is as follows. As new technology is introduced into the economy two countervailing effects are at work on labour demand. Firstly, industry output is increasing, thereby generating higher demands for labour (the expansion effect). Secondly, labour per unit of output is falling as output is transferred to relatively non-labour intensive firms as a result of firms switching to the new technology, resulting in a lower demand for labour (the composition effect).

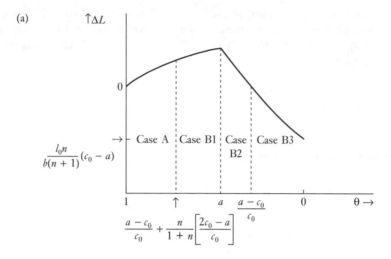

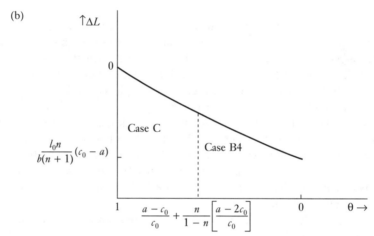

Figure 18.1   Terminal employment levels and the extent of technological advance
(a), $a < 2c_0$; (b), $a > 2c_0$.

From eq. (18.11) we may write labour demand as

$$L(m, n - m) = l_0 Q(m, n - m) + (\theta - 1)l_0 m q_1(m, n - m). \tag{18.16}$$

Therefore we have, as an alternative to (18.15),

$$\frac{\partial L(m, n - m)}{\partial m} = l_0 \frac{\partial Q(m, n - m)}{\partial m} + (\theta - 1)l_0 \frac{\partial (m q_1(m, n - m))}{\partial m},$$

whereby the change in demand is split into the two component parts, the first being the expansion effect, the second the composition effect. The first term, from (18.9), is a positive constant. The second term is always negative but declines in absolute value as m increases.

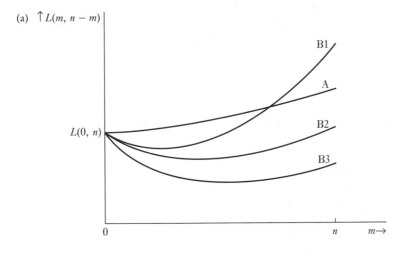

(a) $\uparrow L(m, n - m)$

$L(0, n)$

(b) $\uparrow L(m, n - m)$

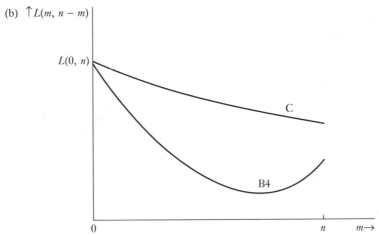

$L(0, n)$

Figure 18.2   Sequential employment levels. (a) $a < 2c_0$; (b), $a > 2c_0$.

Thus, if for low m the expansion effect outweighs the composition effect, employment increases continuously (case A). If for high m the composition effect outweighs the expansion effect, employment continually decreases (case C). The various case B's arise when for low m the composition effect outweighs the expansion effect but as m increases the smaller absolute size of the composition effect becomes outweighed by the expansion effect.

We may also observe that as the diffusion proceeds industry concentration changes. Initially, because early adopters, having lower costs than non-adopters, achieve larger market shares, concentration (as measured by the Herfindahl index appropriate to the Cournot case) rises,[8] and with it the industry price–cost margin. Later, as more firms have adopted, concentration begins to fall, and so does the price–cost margin, because later increases in output are accompanied by greater equalisation of firms' market shares.

To discuss the dynamics of the employment process further requires some assumption about the relationship between m and time.

A common observation regarding diffusion curves is that m follows a sigmoid curve when plotted against time. Thus whilst $dm/dt > 0$ throughout d^2m/dt^2 will initially be positive but will later become negative. From (18.15) we may derive that

$$\frac{\partial^2 L}{\partial t^2} = \frac{\partial L}{\partial m}\frac{d^2 m}{dt^2} + \frac{2(1-\theta)^2 c_0 l_0}{b(n+1)}\frac{dm}{dt}.$$

Then given our assumptions about the time derivatives we may derive the implications for the employment path:

(a)   In case A where $\partial L/\partial m > 0$, $\partial^2 L/\partial t^2$ can change sign only once and employment may follow a sigmoid path with $\partial^2 L/\partial t^2$ going from positive to negative as time proceeds.

(b)   In case C where $\partial L/\partial m < 0$, the term $((\partial L/\partial m)(d^2 m/dt^2))$ will initially be negative until $d^2 m/dt^2$ changes sign to make it positive. Only one change in sign (from negative to positive) is thus possible for $\partial^2 L/\partial t^2$.

(c)   In case B where $\partial L/\partial m$ is initially negative and then positive, a number of changes in sign of $\partial^2 L/\partial t^2$ are possible, and L is unlikely to follow a simple sigmoid shape when plotted against time.

18.4.   The Effect of Firm Exit and Entry

So far we have said nothing on problems of entry and exit. We are particularly interested in the case of the forced exit of non-adopters as noted by Reinganum (1981) which will generate for us our second important influence on labour demand. We must also consider the possibility that the $L(m, n - m)$ generated in the model above may involve $q_0(m, n - m)$ becoming negative, which will occur whenever $p \leq c_0$. It is to these issues that we now turn.

As diffusion proceeds, non-adopters continuously become worse off (assuming input prices remain unchanged). To see this, observe that since $\Pi_0 = (p - c_0)q_0 - f_0$,

$$\frac{\partial \Pi_0}{\partial m} = (p - c_0)\frac{\partial q_0}{\partial m} + q_0\frac{\partial p}{\partial m} < 0,$$

using (18.6) and (18.10).[9] Hence firms may leave the industry at some point in the diffusion process.

At this stage it is important to distinguish two situations – that where price fails to cover old technology average total cost and that where it fails to cover old technology average variable cost. Once the latter point ($p = c_0$) is reached, immediate exit is inevitable. However, if the fixed costs are avoidable by ceasing production (e.g., local authority rates, standard charges for electricity, machinery on rental contracts, etc.) then exit will occur when price has fallen to average total cost, that is, when $\Pi_0 = 0$, which point is reached before price falls to average variable cost.

Define a new technology, by analogy with Arrow's (1962) terminology, as a drastic innovation if for some $m = m^d < n$, market price will not cover old technology average variable costs,[10] i.e.,

$$p(m^d, 0) \leqq c_0. \tag{18.17}$$

For such a drastic innovation, it is clear that all non-adopters will produce zero output for $m \geqq m^d$. We may show that case C involves a non-drastic technology. For case A the technology is always drastic. For cases B.1–B.4 the technology may be drastic or non-drastic.

Allow first that exit does not occur until price equals average variable cost, then at $m = m^d$ the $n - m^d$ non-adopting firms will all have zero output and are assumed to leave. It is easy to show that

$$Q(m^d, 0) = Q(m^d, n - m^d),$$

$$p(m^d, 0) = p(m^d, n - m^d),$$

$$L(m^d, 0) = L(m^d, n - m^d),$$

and

$$\Pi(m^d, 0) = \Pi(m^d, n - m^d).$$

From this point on in the diffusion as we allow m to increase from m^d to n, the departed firms will re-enter on the back of new technology. Industry employment for $m \geqq m^d$ will then be given by $L(m, 0)$ and we may easily confirm that

$$\partial L(m, 0)/\partial m > 0.$$

Thus in the case of drastic innovations the paths detailed assuming no exit apply only until $m = m^d$, from which point $L(m, n - m)$ follows $L(m, 0)$, where

$$L(m, 0) = \frac{l_0 \theta m}{b(m+1)}(a - c_1).$$

In figure 18.3 we illustrate the resulting employment path over the whole diffusion for a particular example.[11] The solid lines represent the case presently under consideration where exit of non-adopters occurs when $p(m, 0) = c_0$. We see that with the chosen parameter values $L(m, n - m)$ falls until $m = 4$. If we continued to plot it, the curve would start to rise at $m = 4.5$. At $m = 4$, $p(m, 0) = c_0$ so that $n - m$, the number of producing non-adopters, falls to zero; hence from this point on employment is given by the $L(m, 0)$ curve, with employment gradually rising as firms re-enter the industry. Thus, in the case where exit only occurs when price fails to cover average variable costs, those declines in employment indicated by considering $L(m, n - m)$ alone may be yielding an overestimate of the employment reduction.

Turning to the second situation, if exit occurs before price fails to cover average variable costs because fixed costs can be avoided (in which situation all cases, A, B.1–B.4 and C, may involve exit), non-adopters will exit at some m, say $\hat{m} < m^d$. It is easy to show that

$$Q(\hat{m}, 0) < Q(m, n - m),$$

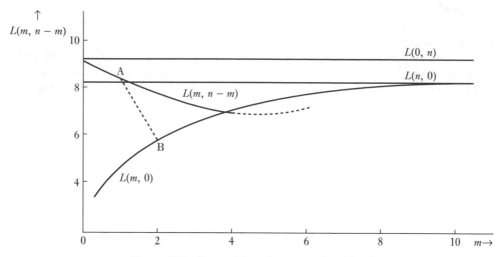

Figure 18.3   Sequential employment paths with exit

and *a fortiori* that

$$L(\hat{m}, 0) < L(m, n - m).$$

In this case exit will occur when price fails to cover average *total* costs. Thus if Π^0 reaches zero for some $\hat{m} < m^{\mathrm{d}}$, non-adopters exit at $\hat{m}$ and employment will fall from $L(\hat{m}, n - \hat{m})$ to $L(\hat{m}, 0)$, which will represent a considerable fall if $\hat{m}$ is significantly below m^{d}. As these non-adopters re-enter m increases and employment will follow the path of $L(m, 0)$.

This case is also illustrated in figure 18.3. We have set $f_0 = 0.5$; consequently upon adoption by a second firm, all non-adopters would have zero profits and would leave the industry. Employment will then fall from A to B in figure 18.3. As these firms re-enter, employment will follow the $L(m, 0)$ path. As can be seen, with exit prior to m^{d}, i.e., in the presence of avoidable fixed costs, reductions in employment are made more severe over some part of the diffusion path than consideration of $L(m, n - m)$ would suggest. It is this employment reduction that is the second influence referred to in our introduction.

In the case illustrated, the behaviour of profit is also interesting. If all firms except one leave, on adoption by a second firm, both firm and industry profits increase dramatically. The second firm may thus adopt quickly. Similarly the third adopter also achieves high profits and may do likewise.

Whatever the dynamics, though, a fall in employment below that considered in $L(m, n - m)$ can be predicted in this case where exit occurs at $\hat{m} < m^{\mathrm{d}}$. Therefore, importantly, even if the parameters are such as to suggest cases A or C as being relevant, the employment path may still not be monotonic once the exit possibility has been taken into consideration.[12]

One further implication of our results is that a relatively oligopolistic industry or an industry with high existing entry barriers, where prices are relatively high and profits high, has a cushion of profits for non-adopters that will act to smooth the transition.

Finally, let us talk of entry. It should be obvious that if entry occurs, the final level of employment will depend positively on the number of entrants. The potential for entry will depend upon the fixed costs of the new technology and the requirement that $\Pi_1 > 0$. But suppose now that new entry occurs prior to any exit. It is easy to show that when m firms have entered, we obtain as an alternative to (18.16) the following:

$$L(m, n) = l_0[Q(m, n) + (\theta - 1)mq_1(m, n)],$$

so that

$$\frac{\partial L}{\partial m}(m, n) = l_0 \left\{ \frac{\partial Q(m, n)}{\partial m} + (\theta - 1)\frac{\partial[mq_1(m, n)]}{\partial m} \right\}.$$

The first term in braces is positive whilst the second is negative since here $\partial[mq_1(m, n)]/\partial m = q_1(n + 1)/(m + n + 1) > 0$, but $\partial^2(mq_1)/\partial m^2 < 0$. In words, there is a growing composition effect to offset the expansion effect, which former effect tails off though it does not actually decline. Therefore the analysis of section 18.3 is modified slightly. However, things are more complex than this since if new firms enter this will tend to reduce the value of m associated with the exit of non-adopters. Thus to some extent new entry will also occasion exit.

18.5.   Concluding Remarks

The model developed above is obviously rather crude and is not intended to be a precise mirror of reality. Despite this, we would argue that the forces identified as giving rise to a period of relatively low employment during the diffusion process are more general than the specific functional forms employed and that these forces have not received sufficient attention.

The first force we identified was the interaction of expansion and composition effects which could produce non-monotonic time paths for employment with initial reductions followed by later gains. The behaviour was the more likely the greater the technological advance or the more competitive the industry. However, the reduction in employment thus generated is limited by a zero output minimum for non-adopters. If non-adopters leave the industry at the point where price fails to cover average variable cost, then at this point employment is at a minimum and as the firms re-enter using new technology employment begins to rise. If, however, firms leave the industry earlier, when price falls below average total cost, then at this point there is a reduction in employment to a level below that indicated on the path neglecting exit, after which employment starts to rise again. The potential for exit to reduce employment is the second force we have identified.

Of course, we do not in practice see exit and re-entry as a common phenomenon following process innovation. Even so, firms' market shares do fluctuate according to productive efficiency somewhat, and firms quite frequently do abandon production in particular segments of a market for a period, although this can often be disguised by their engaging in merchanting activities. In practice also there are factors which tend to make big fluctuations in firms' labour forces unlikely – e.g., problems of re-hiring skilled workers and institutional factors such as redundancy payments. Thus the pressures we have identified may manifest themselves in other forms.

We may also mention other limitations of our analysis, for example, the assumption of a symmetric size distribution of firms,[13] a linear demand curve and an unchanging new technology. All of these in principle are capable of being relaxed in the search for greater realism. Such a relaxation may well be a profitable exercise, but here we have pursued simplicity to illustrate the main forces at work, and we leave the development of the model to more complex worlds for another occasion.

Finally, there are two fairly general if rather negative lessons we would like to draw from our analysis. First, studying the diffusion path brings out the point that 'technological unemployment' is much more likely than comparative static predictions would suggest. Hence firms will face difficulties in managing change efficiently yet equitably. Second, and connected with the above, predictions of employment paths in the face of technical change would appear extremely difficult – initial falls in employment can be reversed. Neither the effect on the first few firms to adopt, nor the predicted eventual effect is a good guide to the employment path which will actually be experienced.

Acknowledgements

We should like to thank Paul David and Morton Kamien for helpful comments at an early presentation of this work during the Warwick Summer Workshop on the Economics of Technological Change.

Notes

1 Based upon the cross-section of 22 process innovations studied by Davies (1979, esp. ch. 5) we may note that it would be an exceptionally swift process which diffused throughout an industry in ten years and, in addition, that many innovations have not diffused to their final extent even after 30 years.

2 For some exploratory comments on employment during transition, see Stoneman (1983, pp. 158–9).

3 To take some examples from Davies (1979), shuttleless looms and tufted carpets might be examples of the former, while automatic track lines in car production and the basic oxygen process in steel production would be cases of oligopolistic demanders. Our conception of oligopoly has perfect competition as a limiting case.

4 It is assumed that the quantities of both factors may be varied without difficulty. Actually, little would alter in the model if there were only one variable factor, labour.

5 Our restrictions on the functional forms are sufficient for the second-order conditions to be satisfied.

6 We write $Q(m, n - m)$ meaning total output when m have adopted and $(n - m)$ have not. The notation is slightly at variance with Reinganum's.

7 Stoneman (1975) was critical of this assumption in a general equilibrium framework but the topic appears not to be treated in partial equilibrium analyses.

8 In general the Herfindahl appropriate to this situation is, given $S = pQ$, $H = mS_1^2 + (n - m)S_0^2$, so it must rise, at least at first.

9 Of course, m takes on only integer values, but all we wish to do is establish monotonicity.

10 With the obvious related definition of non-drastic.

11 The actual values used were $c_0 = 10$, $a = 20$, $\theta = 0.75$, $n = 9$, $b = l_0 = 1$, $f_0 = 0.5$ and the result is a case on the borderline between B.3 and B.4.

12 This may again be seen by utilising a particular example. Take the case (an example of 'A') where $c_0 = 10$, $a = 12$, $\theta = 0.95$, $n = 9$, $b = l_0 = 1$ and $f_0 = 0.02$. Given these values, the innovation becomes drastic before $m = 2$, at which point $L(m, 0) < L(m, n - m)$, as can be verified by straightforward calculation.

13 Consider for a moment the question of asymmetry in costs prior to innovation. It is certainly true that the diffusion path of employment will differ depending on whether it is the firms with lower or those with higher costs which adopt the innovation first. To see this within a very simple framework, take the case of a duopoly where, prior to innovation, firm A's costs are $\phi(< 1)$ times firm B's. Suppose then initially either than firm A's costs drop to $(2\phi - 1)$ times B's *or* that B's costs drop to the level of A's. In both scenarios, industry output increases as a result to

$$Q' = 2(a - \phi c_0^{B})/3b,$$

where c_0^{B} refers to B's initial unit costs. In the first case employment may be found (e.g., from (18.17)) as

$$L' = l_0 Q' + (2\phi - 2)l_0 q'_A$$
$$= \phi l_0 Q' + (1 - \phi)l_0(Q' - 2q'_A) < \phi l_0 Q',$$

where q'_A is A's output in this scenario. In the second case, employment is $\phi l_0 Q'$. Thus employment falls to a greater extent over the first stage of the path in the first case and the path is more likely to be non-monotonic. The problem is, which case is the more likely? Are those with higher costs more inclined to search for improvements or instead are those who are more efficient also more likely to be aware of potential cost-saving devices? The lesson we wish to draw from this is solely that there seems to be no reason in general why having an asymmetric industry structure at the start should overturn the non-monotonicity possibility. The same goes for the linear demand assumption.

References

Arrow, K.J. (1962) Economic welfare and the allocation of resources for invention, in: National Bureau of Economic Research, *The rate and direction of inventive activity*, Princeton University Press, Princeton, NJ.

David, P.A. (1969) *A contribution to the theory of diffusion*, Memo no. 71, Center for Research in Economic Growth, Stanford University, Stanford, CA.

Davies, S. (1979) *The diffusion of process innovations*, Cambridge University Press, Cambridge.

Dobbs, I.M., M.B. Hill and M. Waterson (1983) Industrial structure and the employment consequences of technical change, Newcastle Discussion Papers in Economics no. 72. Oct.

Katsoulacos, Y. (1984) The employment effect of product & process innovation: A theoretical study, Ph.D. thesis, University of London, London.

Neary, P. (1981) On the short-run effects of technological progress, *Oxford Economic Papers* 33, 224–233.

Reinganum, J.F. (1981) Market structure and the diffusion of new technology, *Bell Journal of Economics* 12, 618–624.

Sinclair, P. (1981) When will technical progress destroy jobs, *Oxford Economic Papers* 33, 1–18.

Stoneman, P. (1975) The effect of computers on the demand for labour in the United Kingdom, *Economic Journal* 85, 590–606.

Stoneman, P. (1983) *The economic analysis of technological change*, Oxford University Press, Oxford.

Stoneman, P. and N.J. Ireland (1983) The role of supply factors in the diffusion of new process technology, *Economic Journal* 93, suppl., 66–78.

Chapter nineteen

Technological Opportunity, Technological Diffusion and Gross Investment: An Inter-Industry Approach

Co-written with Myung-Joong Kwon

19.1. Introduction

The prime objective of this paper is to explore empirically the role played by technological change in the determination of gross investment at the level of the industry.[1] The paper is original in two main dimensions. First, although the suggestion that technological change should impact on gross investment has a long history (for example, Keynes, 1936 in *The General Theory* considers how changing technological opportunities will impact on investment) the issue has not been much discussed and even more rarely empirically addressed. Secondly, in approaching the main issue we construct a model of the determination of gross investment that builds on the literature on the diffusion of new technology. To the best of our knowledge, although the modelling of technological diffusion (for a survey see Stoneman and Karshenas, 1995) is concerned with the time path of demand for particular new technologies (especially new process technologies embodied in individual capital goods) the obvious link from this literature to models of gross investment has never been theoretically or empirically exploited. Building on the diffusion literature not only enables one to theoretically derive an investment function that incorporates terms in technological opportunity but also provides a particularly rich approach that places the exploitation of technological opportunity at the very heart of investment modelling. The basic hypothesis that we derive and test is that expansions in technological opportunity will have a positive impact on gross investment.

Studies of the link between technological change and investment experienced a brief renaissance in the heyday of vintage growth models in the 1970s (Stoneman, 1983 provides a survey of the literature through to the early eighties). Recently, new growth theory, as exemplified in the work of Romer (1990), has brought the topic centre stage by emphasizing how investment is driven by the appearance of new technologies produced in the research sector.[2] Lach and Schankerman (1989) have explored the link between investment and technological change using a dynamic factor demand model. Although the theoretical approach and the concept of technological opportunities used differ considerably from those used here, they do find that, for a sample of US firms, R&D (their measure of technological change) Granger causes investment but investment does not Granger cause R&D.[3] Nickell and Nicolatsis (1996) have also looked at the R&D investment link (in this case using UK data). Again their approach is very different from that employed here but they find that R&D expenditure does encourage investment in most industries and that there are no positive effects in the other direction.

The existing literature thus suggests that technological opportunities are a potentially important but under-researched determinant of gross investment. By building on the diffusion literature the analysis presented here provides a clearer picture of the nature of the link between technological change and investment and also utilizes a richer menu of indicators of technological change than in these earlier contributions.

One might also note that if technological change is an important determinant of gross investment then there are a number of policy implications. In various countries at various times there have been government fiscal incentives to encourage firms to undertake gross investment. The economic rationale for these incentives has rarely been clear. In particular it has not always been possible to provide a standard market failure argument in favour of government incentives. Since Arrow (1962) it has been argued that market failure is endemic to technological change. If it can be established that gross investment is, to a significant degree, the result of investments in new technology, then it is much more likely that there will be market failure in the determination of investment spending.

The next section of the paper explores more fully the relationship between gross investment and technological change, theoretically derives an industry level gross investment function explicitly incorporating a term in technological opportunities and moves to an empirical specification via a discussion of measurement issues. In section 19.3 data and estimation methods are addressed. In section 19.4 the results of estimating the model on a sample of 23 three digit UK manufacturing industries over the 1968–90 period are presented and discussed. In section 19.5 conclusions are drawn and policy issues are briefly considered.

19.2.   Gross Investment and Technological Change, Issues and Modelling

19.2.1.   Introduction

The standard approach to modelling investment (see for example Nickell, 1978) is to define a capital aggregate and to then model the changing demand for that aggregate over time. When technical change is introduced into such a framework (Denny and Nickell, 1991 is a rare example of such) it is usually via a total factor productivity term being entered into the production function from which the investment function is derived. In our view such an approach is inappropriate to modelling the link between technological change and investment. A total factor productivity term captures very little of the complexity of technological change and the prior definition of a capital aggregate means that such an approach can only imperfectly represent the changing nature and number of capital goods that are being introduced over time. This latter point was recognized early in the growth literature and led to the development of vintage models. Although vintage models are more appropriate they have their own problems. In particular they rely on the assumption that investment in a time period is always in the latest technologies. The diffusion literature (see Stoneman and Karshenas, 1995) shows that generally this assumption cannot be empirically verified.

In order to more adequately link investment to technological change we first adopt the Schumpeter (1934) definition of innovation or technological change as encompassing new products, new processes, new raw materials, new management methods and new markets (although we ignore this last type). We further argue (1) that technological change is continuous and (2) that in order to introduce new technologies firms will have to undertake capital expenditures. Although this is most obvious for new process technologies, which will generally be embodied in new capital goods, the introduction of new products or new raw materials may well also involve the introduction of new plant and machinery. We associate a particular capital good with each technology and represent changing technological opportunities by a changing list of capital goods upon the market.

Given the changing menu of technological possibilities the firm decides at each moment in time whether to acquire a particular capital good (technology). The analysis of such decisions is the realm of the literature on technological diffusion. That literature proceeds by analysing the differing dates of adoption of particular technologies by different firms rather than the composition of the capital good acquisitions of a particular firm at a moment in time, but the issue is identical. In this paper we proceed following this diffusion-orientated route. In particular we first model a single firm's optimal date for adopting a given technology. We then aggregate across the firms in the industry to determine the industry's intertemporal pattern of ownership of that technology which, taking first differences, enables us to generate an expression for gross investment in that technology at each time t. We then sum across all technologies available to obtain an expression for total gross investment across all technologies at time t. Clearly this aggregative structure is very different from that assumed in the standard approach and moreover the changing nature of technological possibilities is at the heart of the analysis. Another implication of this approach is that it implies that at any particular point in time different firms will have capital stocks made up of different capital goods, installed at different times and embodying different technologies. Even if there were no other reason this is sufficient to ensure that firms should be considered to be heterogeneous.

Karshenas and Stoneman (1993) identify rank, stock, order and epidemic approaches to diffusion modelling in the literature. In a series of papers (Karshenas and Stoneman, 1993; Stoneman and Kwon, 1994, 1996) the empirical validity of the different approaches have been explored. The one result that is common to all these papers is that the rank approach to diffusion has consistent empirical support but the degree of support for the various other approaches is limited. This paper therefore concentrates on a rank model of diffusion.

Based on the work of David (1969) and Davies (1979), in the rank or 'probit' approach to diffusion, the differing dates of adoption of new technology by profit maximizing firms in an industry is explained by differences in the gross benefits from adoption. These in turn depend on firm characteristics (these characteristics being considered independent of the adoption of the technologies being modelled). If issues of intertemporal arbitrage are (temporarily) set aside, the models predict that at time t only those firms for whom the expected gross returns from adoption exceed the cost of adoption will be users of the new technology.

However, acquisition costs fall over time and, as they do so, the usage of technology extends to other firms.[4] Firm size is the characteristic with the greatest degree of empirical validation (larger firms enjoying higher gross returns from the adoption of new technology than smaller firms) and it is on this firm characteristic that we concentrate. The dependence of returns on firm output can be interpreted either strictly as reflecting scale economies (the standard rank model interpretation) or one might think that the level of firm output is a reflection of many other characteristics of the firm. In particular one might argue that the level of firm output will reflect other technologies adopted in the past.

However, in such models firm size (or output) is taken as a variable that is exogenous to the adoption of new technology. It could of course be argued that firm size will change as a new technology is adopted and thus output ought to be considered an endogenous variable. This alternative approach is the basis of the stock and order diffusion models which, as stated in the text, have much less empirical support. Our past empirical work has led us to believe that the adoption of any *one* technology is probably, of itself, not sufficiently important to affect the firm's level of output (see, for example, Karshenas and Stoneman, 1993) and thus when modelling the adoption of individual technologies it is reasonable to assume that the output of the firm at the date of adoption is predetermined. This is still consistent with the possibility that output in time t is related to past adoption activities.

Explicitly, at time t allow there to be a number of new technologies, $m_k(t)$, available to firms in industry k. Assume that: (1) when a firm adopts a new technology it fully equips itself, that is, there is no intra-firm diffusion process;[5] (2) all technologies are of the Leontief type requiring an investment in a specific capital good j ($j = 1 \ldots m_k(t)$) of α_j per unit of output; (3) all technologies are of the 'one hoss shay' type and thus throughout their life are of constant efficiency; and (4) the physical life of all capital goods is greater than their economic life. These assumptions rule out both investment to replace physically worn out capital goods in order to maintain production capacity[6] and *ex post* substitution investment of the traditional kind.[7] Further assume that: (5) the $m_k(t)$ technologies available are neither complements nor substitutes[8] in the production process and thus are completely additive; (6) that investment is irreversible; (7) that the firm is a price taker in the market for new capital goods; and (8) the price in the output market, $P_k(t)$, is independent of the firm's adoption decisions which is consistent with either the firm's output level being independent of its adoption decision or with the firm being small relative to the whole industry.

First we consider a world in which the (planned) output of each firm in the industry is constant at $q_i(t)$ in time t. Then in a subsequent analysis we consider the issue of changing output levels. If output is constant, given the assumptions made above, the only investment taking place is investment for the purposes of introducing new technologies (capital goods). We thus label investment under the fixed output assumption as adoption investment and consider this in the next subsection. That investment induced by changes in (planned) output we label expansion investment and consider in the following subsection.

19.2.2.   Adoption investment

Following an approach to the specification of the rank model as presented in greater detail in Stoneman and Kwon (1994, 1996), define the annual gross benefit in time t to firm i in industry k from the use of technology j as $g_{ijk}(t)$, determined as

$$g_{ijk}(t) = g_j(q_i(t), P_k(t), \mathbf{C_k(t)})\tag{19.1}$$

where k is the industry identifier (and which, when obvious, is suppressed below), $P_k(t)$ is the industry price, $\mathbf{C_k(t)}$ is a vector of other industry characteristics (discussed in more detail below) and the partial derivatives are signed as $g_{j1} \geq 0$, $g_{j2} \geq 0$ (higher firm output and higher prices mean greater returns), $g_{j3} \leq 0$. $P_k(t)$, the price of output, is introduced partly as an indicator of the state of industry demand, but may also be considered as reflecting at least partly the stock effects that we are not explicitly modelling (the greater is the number of users of new technologies in the industry the lower will be industry price).

Defining $P_j(t)$ as the cost of acquiring a unit of technology j in time t, the total cost of adopting technology j in time t for firm i to produce output $q_i(t)$ will be $P_j(t) \cdot \alpha_j \cdot q_i(t)$. Following Karshenas and Stoneman (1993), thus precluding the need to present all the details of the optimization here and thereby saving space, we may state that for a value maximizing firm, the optimal adoption date for technology j, t_{ij}^*, may be defined as that date when the net benefit from waiting further before adoption is equal to the net cost of waiting. With constant output, expected changes in $q_i(t)$ are zero at the date of adoption and the optimality criterion may then be written as (19.2).

$$rP_j(t_{ij}^*) \cdot \alpha_j \cdot q_i(t_{ij}^*) - p_j(t_{ij}^*) \cdot \alpha_j \cdot q_i(t_{ij}^*) - g_j(q_i(t_{ij}^*), P_k(t_{ij}^*), \mathbf{C_k(t_{ij}^*)}) = 0\tag{19.2}$$

where r is the interest/discount rate[9] and $p_j(t)$ is the expected change at time t in the cost of acquisition of a unit of technology j in the time interval $(t, t + dt)$ (modelling an intertemporal arbitrage effect). The sum of the first and last terms on the left-hand side of (19.2) represent profits foregone by waiting whereas the second term represents the gains from waiting as the cost of acquiring the new technology falls. In essence (19.2) states that marginal revenue equals marginal cost appropriately defined.

From (19.2) one may define a critical or threshold value of q for each technology j at each time t, $q_{jk}^*(t)$, which is assumed unique, where

$$q_{jk}^*(t) = G(rP_j(t), p_j(t), P_k(t), \mathbf{C_k(t)})\tag{19.3}$$

If the firm's output exceeds $q_{jk}^*(t)$ it is value enhancing for the firm to use technology j whereas if its output is less than $q_{jk}^*(t)$ it is not value enhancing to do so. Equation (19.3) thus identifies the threshold value of output in time t above which it will be desirable for the firm to use technology j. We assume that the firm installs technology j at the first date that it is desirable to do so, i.e. at the first date that $q_{ik}(t) \geq q_{jk}^*(t)$, which is equivalent to the date at which $t = t_{ij}^*$.

Although changes in $P_k(t)$ and $\mathbf{C_k(t)}$ may offset the effect, the expectation is that $rP_j(t) - p_j(t)$ will fall over time (see Ireland and Stoneman, 1986) leading to reductions in $q_{jk}^*(t)$ over time. We thus proceed on the assumption that $q_{jk}^*(t)/q_{ik}(t)$ is non increasing for all i and t.[10]

As data upon the prices of individual capital goods, $P_j(t)$, is not available to us we follow Meijers (1994) and assume that the price of capital good j will move in line with the general price of capital goods, $P^c(t)$, but will decline relative to the latter the longer technology j has been on the market. Specifically, defining τ_j as the date at which technology j first appears on the market, it is assumed that (19.4) holds

$$P_j(t) = \Phi_j \cdot P^c(t) \cdot \exp(-\theta_j(t - \tau_j)) \tag{19.4}$$

where Φ_j and θ_j are parameters. Substituting from (19.4) into (19.3) for both $P_j(t)$ and $p_j(t)$ enables us to rewrite (19.3) as (19.5)

$$q_{jk}^*(t) = H(rP^c(t), p^c(t), P_k(t), \mathbf{C_k(t)}, t - \tau_j) \tag{19.5}$$

where $p^c(t)$ is the expected change at time t in $P^c(t)$ over the time interval $(t, t + dt)$ and $H_1 \geq 0, H_2 \leq 0, H_3 \leq 0, H_4 \leq 0$, and $H_5 \leq 0$.

In order to generate an expression for industry level gross adoption investment in technology j define $Q_k(t)$ as total industry output in time t and $F(q_{ik}(t))$ as the proportion of output in industry k produced in time t by firms of size greater than $q_{ik}(t)$. The proportion of industry output produced on technology j in time t is then given by $F(q_{jk}^*(t))$ and total industry output produced on technology j, defined as $N_{jk}(t)$, is given by

$$N_{jk}(t) = Q_k(t) \cdot F(q_{jk}^*(t)) \tag{19.6}$$

Given the working assumption that $q_i(t)$ is constant for all t we may also consider that $Q_k(t)$ is constant for all t[11] and from (19.6) changes in total industry output produced on technology j may be written as (19.7), where D is the first difference operator,

$$DN_{jk}(t) = Q_k(t) \cdot DF(q_{jk}^*(t)) \tag{19.7}$$

Nominal industry adoption investment in technology j, written as $I_{jk}^A(t)$ and previously defined as investment undertaken in time t to equip firms to produce their (constant) output levels with technology j, is then given by (19.8).

$$I_{jk}^A(t) = \alpha_j \cdot P_j(t) \cdot DN_{jk}(t) = \alpha_j \cdot P_j(t) \cdot Q_k(t) \cdot DF(q_{jk}^*(t)) \tag{19.8}$$

In order to obtain total industry adoption investment in time t, $I_k^A(t)$, we sum the investments in individual technologies (equation 19.8) over the $m_k(t)$ independent technologies available upon the market.

Substituting from (19.4) for $P_j(t)$, the summation of (19.8) over j yields (19.9)

$$I_k^A(t) = P_c(t) \cdot Q_k(t) \cdot \Sigma_j\{\exp(\log \alpha_j + \log \Phi_j - \theta_j(t - \tau_j)) \cdot DF(q_{jk}^*(t))\} \tag{19.9}$$

Using the approximation that $\exp(x) = 1 + x$, and defining $\log \alpha_k$, $\log \Phi_k$ and $\theta_k(t - \tau_k)$ as the averages over $j = 1 \ldots m_k(t)$ of $\log \alpha_j$, $\log \Phi_j$ and $\theta_j(t - \tau_j))$ respectively, we may then write (19.9) as (19.10)

$$RI_k^A(t) = Q_k(t) \cdot m_k(t) \cdot DF_k^*(t) \cdot \exp(\log \alpha_k + \log \Phi_k + \theta_k(t - \tau_k)) \tag{19.10}$$

where $RI_k^A(t)$ is defined as total real adoption investment, that is, the value of adoption investment in time t divided by the price of capital goods in time t, $I_k^A(t)/P_c(t)$, and $DF_k^*(t)$

is the geometric mean over $j = 1 \ldots m_k(t)$ of the change in $F(q_{jk}^*(t))$, that is, $DF(q_{jk}^*(t))$, in time t.

One should note that (19.10) includes $m_k(t)$, the number of technologies available for adoption in time t. This has appeared essentially because we have summed the individual technologies over $m_k(t)$. The inclusion of this term establishes the proposition that is essential to the paper – that technological change or technological opportunities impacts positively on total gross adoption investment.

In order to move to the estimation of (19.10) we need to be more precise as to the specification of $DF_k^*(t)$. This is the geometric mean over j of changes in the proportion of industry output produced by firms with output greater than $q_{jk}^*(t)$. In equation (19.5) we implicitly detail the determinants of $q_{jk}^*(t)$. Using (19.5) we define an approximation[12] such that $DF_k^*(t)$, is related to the determinants of $q_{jk}^*(t)$ such that (19.11) holds.

$$\log DF_k^*(t) = b_0' + b_1 DrP^c(t) + b_2 Dp^c(t) + b_3 DP_k(t) + b_4 \mathbf{DC_k(t)} + b_5 D(t - \tau_k) \quad (19.11)$$

where b_0' is a constant that may be zero, $b_1 < 0$, $b_2 > 0$, $b_3 > 0$, $b_4 \lesseqgtr 0$ and $b_5 > 0$. This approximation allows that, as the theory suggests, if the price of capital goods fall, the expected increase in the price of capital goods is greater, industry price is higher, capital goods on average have been on the market longer, or industry characteristics move in an appropriate direction, then, for each j, critical firm size will be reduced and thus the (geometric) mean over j of the proportion of industry output being produced on new technologies will rise. Taking logs of (19.10) and using (19.11) then yields (11.12)

$$\log RI_k^A(t) = b_{0k}(t) + \log Q_k(t) + \log m_k(t) + b_1 DrP^c(t) + b_2 Dp^c(t)$$
$$+ b_3 DP_k(t) + b_4 \mathbf{DC_k(t)} \quad (19.12)$$

where

$$b_{0k}(t) = b_0' + \log \alpha_k + \log \Phi_k + \theta_k(t - \tau_k) + b_5 D(t - \tau_k)$$

Conceptually equation (19.12) reflects that total industry gross adoption investment will increase: (1) as the benefit/cost ratio of adopting new technologies increases because then more firms will adopt new technologies; (2) as industry output increases because the required expenditure needed to equip firms to produce this output will be greater and; (3) as the total number of technologies available for purchase increases because more technologies will be invested in. In (19.12) changes in the benefit/cost ratio are represented by *changes* in $rP^c(t)$ (the rental cost of capital which enters with a negative effect), $p^c(t)$ (expected changes in the cost of acquisition which enters with a positive effect), $P_k(t)$ (the price of output which enters with a positive effect) and $\mathbf{C_k(t)}$ (industry characteristics). The number of technologies upon the market enters through the term in $\log m_k(t)$ with a coefficient of unity and output enters through $\log Q_k(t)$ also with a coefficient of unity. The constant term (of indefinite sign) reflects, for the industry, average capital requirements per unit of output (over the technologies available), the reductions in the price of capital goods as they age, and the average age of technologies on the market and changes therein. One may note that this constant may be time varying.

19.2.3. Expansion investment and total investment

Thus far we have assumed that firms have constant levels of output and thus that industry output is constant. These are limiting assumptions. In reality we might expect there to be changes in firm and industry output levels and this would lead to further investment. For brevity we call such induced investment expansion investment. Total investment will then equal the sum of adoption investment and expansion investment. To allow for changes in firm and industry output levels consider initially a variant of (19.7). When industry output is allowed to change, the change in total output produced using technology j in industry k can be written as (19.7′)

$$DN_{jk}(t) = Q_k(t) \cdot DF(q_{jk}^*(t)) + DQ_k(t) \cdot F(q_{jk}^*(t)) \tag{19.7′}$$

where the second term allows for output expansion. Multiplying by the cost of capital good j per unit of output, and defining total (adoption plus expansion) nominal gross investment in technology j in industry k as $I_{jk}(t)$, we may then write that

$$I_{jk}(t) = \alpha_j \cdot P_j(t) \cdot Q_k(t) \cdot DF(q_{jk}^*(t)) + \alpha_j \cdot P_j(t) \cdot DQ_k(t) \cdot F(q_{jk}^*(t)) \tag{19.13}$$

and summing over j write that total real gross investment in industry k $(RI_k(t))$ is given by

$$RI_k(t) = \Sigma_j[\alpha_j \cdot Q_k(t) \cdot DF(q_{jk}^*(t))] + \Sigma_j[\alpha_j \cdot DQ_k(t) \cdot F(q_{jk}^*(t))] \tag{19.14}$$

This may be written as

$$RI_k(t) = \Sigma_j[\alpha_j \cdot Q_k(t) \cdot DF(q_{jk}^*(t))]\{1 + \Sigma_j[\alpha_j \cdot DQ_k(t) \cdot F(q_{jk}^*(t))]/$$
$$\Sigma_j[\alpha_j \cdot Q_k(t) \cdot DF(q_{jk}^*(t))]\} \tag{19.15}$$

Taking logs and approximating $\log(1 + x)$ by x yields that

$$\log RI_k(t) = \log RI_k^A(t) + \{DQ_k(t)/Q_k(t)\} \cdot \Sigma_j[\alpha_j \cdot F(q_{jk}^*(t))]/\Sigma_j[\alpha_j \cdot DF(q_{jk}^*(t)]$$
$$\tag{19.16}$$

In principle the second term in (19.16) could be expanded more precisely in terms of the model. However, to do so would be to accept that this approach to modelling expansion investment is satisfactory whereas in fact there are several significant problems. First, the second term in (19.16) is defined over $q_{jk}^*(t)$, but this has been modelled on the assumption that the firms' output level was assumed to remain constant. Secondly the factors that influence decisions on which capital goods to use to expand capacity may be different from those that affect replacement decisions, for example, the latter depend on the increase in profit relative to currently installed technology whereas the former depends only on the absolute profitability of the new technology. Thirdly this approach takes no account of the possibility of the churning of firm sizes such that for a given level of industry output some firms will be growing, some firms declining. Nor does it account for the possibility of firm entry to and exit from the industry so that the number of firms is changing. Finally, no account is taken of the argument that it is planned changes in output that affect expansion investment and that with our fixed coefficients assumptions output expansion can only follow and not lead investment.

Rather than trying to precisely model these arguments in the context of the model we proceed in a more ad hoc manner. We assume first that the realized growth rate of output is a valid proxy for the planned growth rate of output. Secondly we assume that the functional form of the relationship between $\log RI_k(t)$ and $DQ_k(t)/Q_k(t)$ in (19.16) is still acceptable, but that in the light of the arguments above we reduce the term $\Sigma_j[\alpha_j \cdot F(q_{jk}^*(t))]/\Sigma_j[\alpha_j \cdot DF(q_{jk}^*(t))]$ to a single parameter $\Omega_k(t)$ that in principle may be time and industry specific. Finally we introduce a parameter $\beta_k(t)$ into (19.16) to allow for churnover, entry and exit (which in general may be independent of the growth of industry output). This then enables us to write (19.17).

$$\log RI_k(t) = \log RI_k^A(t) + \beta_k(t) + \Omega_k(t) \cdot DQ_k(t)/Q_k(t) \tag{19.17}$$

In operationalizing (19.17) we further allow for an asymmetry between periods of output expansion and periods of output reduction. We argue that if (planned) output is decreasing expansion investment will be zero rather than negative. We thus measure $DQ_k(t)$ by the increase in real output since the previous peak if positive, and otherwise zero.

19.2.4. Further dynamic structures

The model constructed above, through the theory of diffusion, already contains a considerable dynamic structure. However, it is common in investment modelling to include a lagged dependent variable to allow for further dynamic effects (see, for example, Hay and Liu, 1998) and then to test for the significance of that variable. In the current context such extra dynamic effects may arise *inter alia* because (1) the modelling of adoption decisions centres on optimal adoption dates in meeting which firms may incur adjustment costs, and (2) the diffusion modelling is demand orientated (see Karshenas and Stoneman, 1995) and there may be ordering and delivery lags. From the *static* relationship (19.17), introducing a lagged dependent variable and using (19.12) yields (19.18).

$$\log RI_k(t) = \beta_k(t) + b_{0k}(t) + \log Q_k(t) + \log m_k(t) + b_1 DrP^c(t) + b_2 Dp^c(t)$$
$$+ b_3 DP_k(t) + b_4 \mathbf{DC_k(t)} + \Omega_k(t)DQ_k(t)/Q_k(t) + \sigma \log RI_k(t-1) \tag{19.18}$$

Prior to operationalizing equation (19.18) we detail the specification and measurement of $m_k(t)$ and $\mathbf{C_k(t)}$. This is the purpose of the next two subsections.

19.2.5. Technological opportunities

The number of new technologies available to firms in industry k, or technological opportunities, $m_k(t)$, cannot be measured directly and thus we proceed by using a number of proxy indicators. The technological opportunities that are available to firms in an industry arise from a number of different sources. The most obvious source is research and design efforts within the industry. Subject to decisions on the lag structure we proxy this by the values of: industry R&D, RD_k; the number of patents granted to firms in industry k, PT_k; the number of (new) trademarks registered and advertised in industry k, TR_k; and the number of innovations produced in industry k, IP_k. These variables will reflect the broad range of product, process and other innovations generated from within the industry itself. However technological opportunities may also arise from the activities of other industrial sectors or overseas. This is more difficult to measure. Our proxy variable is the number of innovations used in (but not necessarily originating in) industry k, IU_k. The inclusion of these various different measures of technological opportunities over and above R&D is one of the main empirical differences between the work reported here and the analysis of Lach and Schankerman (1989) and Nickell and Nicolatsis (1996). It is assumed that $m_k(t)$ is log linearly related to the values of the five proxy variables, positively in each case. For completeness, industry level fixed effects (i.e., industry dummies) are also included to account for other industry specific omitted factors that are not picked up by the above proxy variables.

19.2.6.   Industry characteristics

The elements of the vector $C_k(t)$ are industry level factors that will affect the return to the adoption of new technology. Partly on the grounds of data availability, but also following standard Industrial Organization (I-O) arguments and the existing diffusion literature, we specifically include as relevant industry characteristics, labour costs, measured by $W_k(t)$, the industry average wage in time t, and two indicators of market structure or the degree of competition, the five firm concentration ratio, $CR_k(t)$, and the number of firms in the industry, $NF_k(t)$. These variables enter the investment equation in first difference form. The existing diffusion literature is somewhat agnostic as to what signs these variables should carry. If (on average) new technologies are labour saving relative to previous technologies, higher wages will increase the return to new technologies, increase adoption rates and increase investment. However, if new technologies (on average) are labour using, then higher wages will reduce the returns to adoption and reduce investment. In the absence of detailed knowledge on the relative labour saving of new technology one cannot predict the sign on $DW_k(t)$ a priori. The sign of the impact of market structure is similarly uncertain. As discussed in Karshenas and Stoneman (1993) neither theory nor existing empirical evidence provides convincing support for any particular sign. We are thus also agnostic a priori as to the signs to be expected on $DCR_k(t)$, and $DNF_k(t)$. It has also been suggested to us that there may be effects on investment from the degree of unionization, the importance of skilled labour,[13] the degree of international competition etc. We thus also include industry specific effects (i.e. industry dummies) to capture such omitted characteristics. These effects will also pick up any effects arising from the differing compositions of existing capital stock across industries.

   Assuming that the industry characteristics enter the investment function in a linear form, taking account of the proxies for $m_k(t)$, and including time dummies (to pick up both the average age of technologies upon the market, $(t - \tau_k)$, and potential variations in macroeconomic conditions which may affect the returns to the adoption of new technology) the final, estimating, equation may then be written (for brevity excluding any lagged effects of right hand side variables) as (19.19)

$$\log RI_k(t) = \beta_{0k}(t) + \sigma \log RI_k(t-1) + \log Q_k(t) + \mu_1 \log RD_k(t)$$

$$+ \mu_2 \log PT_k(t) + \mu_3 \log TP_k(t) + \mu_4 \log IP_k(t) + \mu_5 \log IU_k(t)$$

$$+ b_1 DrP^c(t) + b_2 Dp^c(t) + b_3 DP_k(t) + \beta_1 DW_k(t) + \beta_2 DCR_k(t)$$

$$+ \beta_3 DNF_k(t) + \Omega_k(t) DQ_k(t)/Q_k(t) + u_i(t) \tag{19.19}$$

where $\beta_{0k}(t)$ includes all constant terms, industry specific and time effects and $u_i(t)$ is the error term.

19.3.   Data and Estimation Methods

The sample is panel data on 23, three digit, UK manufacturing industries over the period 1968–90. Data sources and sample characteristics are detailed in appendix 19. The data set is complete except that data on innovations used and produced is only available for the 1968–83 period which leads us to define two different samples for estimation purposes below. The first includes innovations used and produced as an indicator of technological opportunity but covers only the 1968–83 period, the second covers the whole period but innovations used and produced are excluded. Non-stationarity in the data was tested for using a unit root test (see Im et al., 1995, for the unit-root test)[14] and it was found for both samples that there is stationarity.

Initial explorations of the data led us to conclude that $\log Q_k(t)$ and $DQ_k(t)/Q_k(t)$ are highly collinear. Although we experimented with the removal of the former variable we proceed here instead by replacing $\log Q_k(t)$ by $\log P_k(t)$ on the argument that industry price would be a good proxy for industry output. This removes the collinearity problem. Given that $\log Q_k(t)$ was expected to carry a coefficient of unity we expect $\log P_k(t)$ to carry a negative coefficient.

The model specification allows for industry-specific and time-specific effects. We represent these by allowing that (19.19) contains a constant β_0 with the error term $u_i(t)$ being respecified as $e_i(t) + e_k + e_t$ where $e_i(t)$ is the standard error term, e_k picks up industry-specific effects and e_t time-specific effects. Given this specification and the presence of the lagged dependent variable in the estimating equation we estimate (19.16) by generalized method of moments (GMM) using two period lagged instruments (see Bond and Blundell, 1998 for a discussion of the factors determining the choice of the length of lag to be used for instruments). This eliminates the industry-specific effects (and the constant, β_0) through first differencing and overcomes the problem of inconsistent estimates resulting from correlations between the lagged dependent variable and $e_i(t-1)$ and possibly $e_i(t)$. The e_t terms are represented by time dummies in the first difference specification.

The model as specified in equation (19.19) contains a number of right-hand side variables that may be considered as either endogenous or at least contemporaneously determined with investment. For example, and of particular relevance in that we are attempting to explore the impact of technological change upon investment, $DQ_k(t)/Q_k(t)$ may be an endogenous variable in that technological change can affect industry output. As firms introduce new technologies (be they new process technologies, new products, new raw materials, or new management methods) one might well expect industry costs to fall or product quality to improve and thus industry output to grow. This argument would suggest that $DQ_k(t)/Q_k(t)$ may well be a function of industry adoption investment. Such arguments could, however, also be extended to other variables. We have thus instrumented our right-hand side variables using another set of variables that are not included in (19.19), namely the industry real wage, the industry concentration ratio, the number of firms in the industry, all lagged two periods, as well as two period lagged values of the independent variables themselves. For both samples, Lagrange Multiplier (LM) tests and Sargan tests cannot reject the hypothesis that the instruments used are valid.

Thus far we have left open the question of the lag structures on the technological opportunity variables. It would seem reasonable to argue that current investment would depend on the current stock of knowledge rather than current period additions to the stock of knowledge (which would affect future investment). This might suggest that lagged values of the technological opportunities variables might be more appropriate than current values. Introducing lags would also help to overcome any problems of contemporaneous determination with investment. After considerable experimentation the results we report include RD and IP with one period lags and TR and IU without lags. The patent variable PT (measured by the number of UK patents in industry k registered in the US in time t) was removed as it was never significant. The insertion of more extended lag structures did not improve the performance of the relevant variables (thus suggesting either that flow additions to the stock of technologies are more important or that flow variables are a relevant proxy for the stock). One period lags on RD and IP are consistent with it taking at least a year for the results of the firm's own expenditure on technology generation to yield results capable of being incorporated in its own capital stock. On the other hand IU is a measure of the number of innovations actually being introduced into the firm from outside and as such it is appropriate that there is no lag. TR carrying no lag may mean that investment in a new technology and obtaining a trade mark for it are contemporaneous activities, which may also be appropriate.

Finally, before moving to the estimates themselves, the theory developed above potentially allows that some of the parameters of the estimating equation are time varying. We have estimated the model assuming that all parameters are constant over time and have then tested the validity of this assumption. A series of LM tests rejected the hypothesis that the parameters are changing over time and thus this is not discussed further below.

19.4. Results

Two samples have been identified for estimation purposes. Sample A includes innovations used and produced as an indicator of technological opportunity but covers only the 1968–83 period, sample B covers the whole 1968–90 period but innovations used and produced are excluded. Variables are defined in table 19.1 with the expected signs of the coefficient also indicated. Both static and dynamic versions of equation (19.16) were estimated but given that the dynamic version nests the static version and the lagged dependent variable was

Table 19.1   Definitions of variables

Variable	Definition [expected sign]
$\log RI_k(t)$	Log of gross investment in plant and machinery, buildings and vehicles in industry k in time t (£million) divided by the price index of capital goods (1985 = 100) in industry k in time t.
$\log P_k(t)$	log of price in industry k in time t (1985 = 100) [−]
$\log RD_k(t-1)$	log of R&D in industry k in time $t-1$ in 1985 prices (£million) [+]
$\log TR_k(t)$	log number of trademarks registered at the UK Patent Office to firms in industry k in time t [+]
$\log IP_k(t-1)$	log number of innovations produced in industry k in time $t-1$ [+]
$\log IU_k(t)$	log number of innovation used in industry k in time t [+]
$DrP^c(t)$	$r(t+1)P^c(t+1) - r(t)P^c(t)$, where $r(t)$ is the real interest rate in time t (nominal rate minus the actual rate of inflation) and $P^c(t)$ the real price of capital goods in industry k in time t (1985 = 100) [−]
$Dp^c(t)$	$p^c(t+1) - p^c(t)$ where $p^c(t) = P^c(t+1) - P^c(t)$ [+]
$DP_k(t)$	$P_k(t+1) - P_k(t)$, where $P_k(t)$ is real price of output in industry k in time t (1985 = 100) [+]
$DW_k(t)$	$W_k(t+1) - W_k(t)$, where $W_k(t)$ is the real wage index in industry k in time t (1985 = 100) [?]
$D\,CR_k(t)$	$CR_k(t+1) - CR_k(t)$, where $CR_k(t)$ is the five firm concentration ratio in industry k in time t [?]
$DNf_k(t)$	$NF_k(t+1) - NF_k(t)$, where $NF_k(t)$ is the number of firms in industry k in time t [?]
$DQ_k(t)/Q_k(t)$	The change in real output since the previous peak in industry k in time t as a percentage of real output in industry k in time t if positive, otherwise zero [+].

always significant in the dynamic version we only present results on the dynamic version. DPD (see Arellano and Bond, 1988, 1991) was used to produce the GMM estimates. The preferred estimates are presented in table 19.2. Heteroscedastic consistent t-statistics are presented in parentheses with significance at the 5 per cent level indicated by ** and at the 10 per cent level by *. To save space coefficient estimates relating to time dummies are repressed; however, the time dummies are found to be jointly significant.

The diagnostic indicators of the estimates are good in that using Wald tests we can reject the hypotheses that (1) jointly all coefficients are zero, (2) that the time dummies are not significant and (3) that the instruments are invalid. A Sargan test cannot reject the validity of our instruments at the 5 per cent significance level.

For both samples we observe that: (1) the lagged dependent variable is highly significant (with a coefficient that is reasonably stable across the two samples) and thus the dynamic model is to be preferred to a static model; (2) the constant is never significant in these estimates which is consistent with it being removed via the first differencing employed; and (3) $\log P_k(t)$ is also significant at the 5 per cent level for both samples and carries the

Table 19.2 Regression estimates

Variables	Sample A 1968–1983	Sample B 1968–1990
Constant	−0.03 (−0.61)	−0.0047 (−0.08)
Log $RI_k(t-1)$	0.71 (15.07)**	0.80 (26.6)**
Log $P_k(t)$	−0.75 (−2.01)**	−0.69 (−2.04)**
Log $RD_k(t-1)$	0.013 (1.92)**	0.029 (2.78)**
Log $TR_k(t)$	0.04 (0.39)	0.136 (1.66)*
Log $IP_k(t-1)$	0.013 (3.52)**	–
Log $IU_k(t)$	0.001 (0.44)	–
$DrP^c(t)$	0.073 (1.76)*	0.059 (1.06)
$DP^c(t)$	0.23 (1.64)*	0.30 (1.88)*
$DP_k(t)$	0.002 (2.4)**	0.003 (3.61)**
$DW_k(t)$	0.0003 (0.26)	−0.001 (−1.42)
$DCR_k(t)$	0.003 (0.89)	0.0003 (0.10)
$DNF_k(t)$	0.000013 (0.47)	0.00003 (1.28)
$DQ_k(t)/Q_k(t)$	0.73 (4.27)**	1.14 (6.24)**
Wald test (χ^2) for significance of time dummies	36.96	88.1
Sargan test for instrument validity	221.32	247.2
Wald test for $\mu_1 = \mu_2 = \mu_3 = \mu_4 = \mu_5 = 0$	16.5	44.3
Wald test for $b_1 = b_2 = b_3 = \beta_1 = \beta_2 = \beta_3 = 0$	12.1	20.2
Wald test for all coefficients = 0	335.5	985.9
Number of observations	322	483

expected negative coefficient (which is again reasonably stable across the two samples). It should be recalled that $\log P_k(t)$ was entered to represent $\log Q_k(t)$ and picks up the effect of industry output on gross investment.

The variables representing technological opportunity are $\log RD_k(t-1)$, $\log TR_k(t)$, $\log IP_k(t-1)$ and $\log IU_k(t)$. In sample A both industry R&D and the innovations produced variables are significant at the 5 per cent level. For sample B where the innovation variables are excluded both industry R&D (at 5 per cent) and trade marks registered (at 10 per cent) are significant. In each case the variables carry the expected positive coefficients. A Wald test rejects the hypothesis (at 5 per cent), for both samples, that the technological opportunities variables jointly have no impact on gross investment. These results confirm that technological opportunity impacts positively on industry gross investment. From the estimates using sample B we may calculate the long-run elasticity of gross investment to technological opportunity as measured by RD_k and TR_k as 0.825. The impact is thus quantitatively significant.

Of those variables that we have incorporated as determinants of the speed of diffusion, the change in the rental cost of capital $D(r(t) \cdot P^c(t))$ is significant at the 10 per cent level in sample A but is not significant for sample B. It also carries the wrong sign in both samples. However $Dp^e(t)$ (the change in the expected change in the price of capital) is significant at the 10 per cent level in both samples and carries the expected sign. The change in industry price, $DP_k(t)$, carries the expected positive coefficient and is also significant, at the 5 per cent level, for both samples. However, the impact of the industry characteristics variables are very imprecisely estimated, none of the three being individually significant. A Wald test enables us to reject the hypothesis (at the 10 per cent level) that jointly these diffusion related variables do not impact on gross investment.

Finally, as stated above, expansion investment is included in this model through the term in $DQ_k(t)/Q_k(t)$, measuring the growth of industry output. $DQ_k(t)/Q_k(t)$ carries the expected positive coefficient and is also significant at the 5 per cent level in both samples.

These results confirm that: (1) this approach to modelling gross investment has empirical support; (2) technological opportunity impacts on gross investment; (3) jointly those variables that impact upon the diffusion speed behave as expected; and (4) the dynamic version of the model with its assumed adjustment lags is to be preferred to a static formulation.

19.5. Discussion and Conclusions

Existing literature, especially the empirical literature, has largely ignored the role that technological change might play in investment determination, although there is an undercurrent implying that it is reasonable to argue that technological change does have a role. In this paper, in contrast, we place technological change at the heart of the modelling of gross investment.

Gross investment is treated as made up of two separate parts defined as adoption investment and expansion investment. The former, encompassing investment undertaken to introduce new technologies given firms' planned output levels, is modelled utilizing the theory of technological diffusion providing a unique combination of two related fields of study that have previously developed independently. It is allowed that firms are being offered over time a changing number of technologies in which they may invest. These technologies are assumed additive. Theoretically an optimal adoption date for each technology by each firm is derived, aggregation across technologies yields an expression for total adoption investment by the firm and a further aggregation across firms yields total adoption investment by the industry. It is predicted that gross adoption investment will be the greater (1) the larger the number of technologies available, (2) the faster is the diffusion speed and (3) the larger is the industry output to be equipped with new technology.

Adding expansion investment, defined as investment undertaken to increase capacity and modelled as a function of the growth in industry output, the resulting expression for total gross investment has been estimated on a panel data set of 23 UK manufacturing industries covering the period 1968–90. The empirical results confirm that: the proxies used to measure technological opportunities (R&D, trademarks registered and innovation counts) impact positively and significantly on gross investment; those factors that determine the speed of diffusion jointly impact as predicted; industry output (proxied by price) and the growth in industry output also impact on gross investment as predicted; and there are adjustment lags in the process.

Our estimates are sufficiently well defined to enable us to argue that technology effects are quantitatively important (with a direct elasticity of investment to technological change close to unity) and thus that models of investment that exclude technological opportunities may well suffer from mis-specification. Of more importance, however, and perhaps this is our major finding, the empirical estimates are consistent with the view that gross investment may be successfully modelled via an approach built on the foundations of the analysis of technological diffusion. This approach does much more than just add a technological change or opportunities term into a standard investment function. Technological change is placed at the heart of the model of investment and as such the role of technological change is endemic to the model rather than additional.

Viewing gross investment as (at least in part) reflecting the process of new technology diffusion provides a route by which one may also approach the (micro) economics of investment policy. Although to date the theory and empirics of diffusion policy has not merited extensive discussion (see Stoneman and Diederen, 1994 for an accessible survey), the extant literature does provide a number of insights into why a free market economy may under-invest in the diffusion of new technology and thus also provides a market failure rationale for government policies to stimulate gross investment (of course the rationale is not itself a sufficient reason for intervention, it must also be shown that intervention will be effective). The policy literature extends beyond the diffusion models used here, and *inter alia* suggests the following factors that may lead to sub optimal diffusion speeds: information deficiencies; information and other non appropriable externalities; market power effects in capital good supply; incomplete insurance markets; and inefficient capital markets. Such factors provide a justification of, for example, tax incentives to investment, risk sharing policies or information provision policies. The realization that technological change plays a major role in the gross investment process thus provides a rationale for policy intervention that is much more soundly based than the view that commonly underlies arguments in support of stimulating gross investment – that is, that more would be better.

Appendix 19A

Gross fixed investment, industry output, the five-firm concentration ratio and the number of firms in an industry are sourced from *Business Monitor*. The price of capital, output prices and wages were sourced from *The Monthly Digest of Statistics*, and the retail price index, the rate of inflation and the interest rate from *Economic Trends Annual Supplement*. Industry R&D data were supplied by the OECD, the number of patents granted in the US to UK firms by the *US Department of Commerce*, and the number of trademarks advertised and registered by the Patent Office. Data on the number of innovations produced and used was provided by the Science Policy Research Unit (SPRU). This was only available for the 1945–83 period. The availability of annual data determined the range of industries (23 industries) and time period (1968–90) of the sample. Where necessary monetary variables were converted to real variables using the retail price index (1985 = 100) as deflator.

With the R&D data it was necessary to interpolate for missing years in order to create a complete time series. The interpolation method used was a simple linear one. For example, to interpolate for the years between R1 and R4, we used $R2 = R1 + 1 * (R4 - R1)/3$ and $R3 = R1 + 2 * (R4 - R1)/3$.

Given the variety of sources for the data used, construction of the data set involved a certain amount of mapping from the original (different and changing) classifications into the industry classifications used here. Tables 19A.1 and 19A.2 provide the details. Table 19A.3 presents sample statistics.

Table 19A.1   Sample industries and the mapping of data (R&D and patents)

Sample industry	R&D data (OECD industry classification)	Patent data (US Patent Office industry classification: sequence numbers in bracket)
1. Iron and steel	Ferrous metal	Primary ferrous products (19)
2. Non-ferrous metals	Non-ferrous metals	Primary and secondary non-ferrous metals (20)
3. Non-metallic minerals	Stone, clay and glass	Stone, clay, glass and concrete products (17)
4. Chemicals	Sub-total chemical minus petroleum refineries	Chemicals and allied products (6, 7, 8, 9, 11, 12, 13, 14)
5. Metal goods	Fabricated metal products	Fabricated metal products (21)
6. Mechanical engineering	Machinery	Machinery (except electrical) (22, 24, 25, 26, 29, 30, 31, 32, 53)
7. Office machinery	Office machinery and computer	Office computing and accounting machines (27)
8. Electrical engineering	Sub-total electrical group	Electrical and electronic machinery (35, 36, 38, 39, 40, 42, 43)
9. Motor vehicles	Motor vehicles	Motor vehicles and motor vehicles equipment (46)
10. Ships and other vessels	Ships	Ship and boat building and repairing (49)
11. Aerospace equipment	Aerospace equipment	Aircraft and part, guided missiles, space vehicles (47, 54)
12. Other vehicles	Sub-total other transport minus motor vehicles and ships	Railroad, motorcycles, bicycles and parts, miscellaneous transportation equipments (50, 51, 52)
13. Instrument engineering	Instruments	Professional and scientific instruments (55)
14. Manufactured food	Food, drink and tobacco	Food and kindred products (1)
15. Alcoholic drinks	Food, drink and tobacco	Food and kindred products (1)
16. Tobacco	Food, drink and tobacco	Food and kindred products (1)
17. Textiles	Textiles and clothing	Textile mill products (2)
18. Clothing and footwear	Textiles and clothing	Textile mill products (2)
19. Timber and furniture	Wood, cork and furniture	All other SIC's products (59, 60)
20. Paper and board	Paper and printing	All other SIC's products (59, 60)
21. Printing and publishing	Paper and printing	All other SIC's products (59, 60)
22. Rubber and plastics	Rubber and plastics	Rubber and miscellaneous plastics products (16)
23. Other manufacturing	Sub-total	All other SIC's products (59, 60)

Table 19A.2 Sample industries and the mapping of data (prices and wages)

Sample industry	Price of capital	Price of product	Wage
1. Iron and steel	Iron and steel	Metal manufacturing	Metal manufacturing
2. Non-ferrous metals	Non-ferrous metals	Metal goods N.E.S. industries	All manufacturing
3. Non-metallic minerals	All manufacturing industries	Non-metallic minerals	Bricks, pottery, glass and cement
4. Chemicals	Chemical, paint, ink	Chemical	Chemical and allied industries
5. Metal goods	Metal goods	Metal goods	Metal goods
6. Mechanical engineering	All manufacturing industries	Mechanical engineering	Mechanical engineering
7. Office machinery	All manufacturing industries	Instrument engineering	Instrument engineering
8. Electrical engineering	Electrical engineering	Electrical and electronic engineering	Electrical engineering
9. Motor vehicles	Vehicles	Motor vehicles and parts	Vehicles
10. Ships and other vessels	Ship-building	Vehicles engineering	Shipbuilding and marine engineering
11. Aerospace equipment	All manufacturing industries	All Manufacturing industries	All manufacturing industries
12. Other vehicles	Vehicles	Motor vehicles and parts	Vehicles
13. Instrument engineering	All manufacturing industries	Instrument engineering	Instrument engineering
14. Manufactured food	Food	Food manufacturing	Food, drink and tobacco
15. Alcoholic drinks	Drink and tobacco	Food, drink and tobacco	Food, drink and tobacco
16. Tobacco	Drink and tobacco	Food, drink and tobacco	Food, drink and tobacco
17. Textiles	Textile, leather and clothing	Textile	Textile
18. Clothing and footwear	Textile, leather and clothing	Footwear and clothing	Clothing and footwear
19. Timber and furniture	All manufacturing industries	Timber and wooden furniture	Timber and furniture
20. Paper and board	Paper, printing and publishing	Paper, printing and publishing	Paper, printing and publishing
21. Printing and publishing	Paper, printing and publishing	Paper, printing and publishing	Paper, printing and publishing
22. Rubber and plastics	All manufacturing industries	Rubber and plastics	All manufacturing industries
23. Other manufactures	Other manufactures	Other manufactures	Other manufactures

Table 19A.3   Sample statistics (means and standard deviations (SD))

Variable	Mean	SD	Min.	Max
$\log RI_k(t)$	4.27	1.11	1.44	6.48
$\log Q_k(t)$	8.89	0.95	6.00	11.05
$\log P_k(t)$	6.23	0.10	5.84	6.47
$\log RD_k(t)$	4.15	2.93	−11.51*	7.88
$\log PT_k(t)$	4.60	1.33	1.61	7.73
$\log TR_k(t)$	6.10	0.66	4.33	7.53
$\log IP_k(t)$	−1.96*	5.67	−11.51*	3.97
$\log IU_k(t)$	−2.00*	5.51	−11.51*	3.43
$DrP^c(t)$	0.021	0.45	−1.35	2.82
$Dp^c(t)$	−0.00051	0.089	−0.42	0.35
$DP_k(t)$	−0.73	19.30	−62.70	95.60
$DW_k(t)$	14.79	13.66	−18.70	48.60
$DCR_k(t)$	−0.20	3.78	−26.00	22.00
$DNF_k(t)$	40.04	476.96	−6250	2103
$DQ_k(t)/Q_k(t)$	0.02	0.06	0	0.99

* Where industry R&D, or the number of innovation used and produced were zero, we set values to 0.00001 in order to take logs.

Notes

1   The work reported upon in this paper has been supported by a grant from the Economic and Social Research Council. In a companion paper, Stoneman and Kwon (1998), the link between investment and technological change is analysed using firm level data. It is shown in that paper that at the firm level there is considerable support for the view that technological change impacts positively on gross investment. Compared to that work, this paper, as well as considering a different aggregative level and a modified theoretical approach, also provides an improved treatment of investment undertaken to increase capacity and further refinements of the econometrics to take due account of the possible endogeneity of regressors. We are grateful for the comments of referees on an earlier version of this paper, but all errors that may remain are the sole responsibility of the authors.

2   It is worth noting that although new growth theory has been a stimulant for this work, in the majority of that literature it is assumed that diffusion of new technologies is instantaneous. All the empirical evidence (see Stoneman and Karshenas, 1995) suggests that diffusion is far from instantaneous. This paper in fact exploits the time intensiveness of the diffusion process to model gross investment.

3   In complete contrast to the early work of Schmookler (1966) on technological change which argues for the reverse causality.

4   This approach is deterministic and uncertainty is not treated explicitly. Although in some recent work we have been able to explicitly incorporate uncertainty in a diffusion model (see, for example, Toivanen et al., 1996) it has not yet proved possible to operationalize that model and to use it for empirical purposes. As a result the recent work on real options (see for example, Dixit and Pindyck, 1994) that has so impacted on the investment literature is not explicitly addressed in this paper.

5   This assumption is of dubious empirical validity. In Stoneman and Kwon (1996), however, we do have some difficulty in identifying intra-firm diffusion effects. Also relaxation of the assumption generates considerable further complexity.

6   This does not rule out the possibility that when new technologies are introduced these technologies lead to the scrapping of existing technologies. However, as we are only interested in gross investment (and not net investment) the scrapping decision is not of particular interest to us.

7   Of course substitution may still be occurring if new technologies being installed have different capital labour ratios than old technologies.

8   This assumption considerably simplifies both the modelling and the empirical analysis. In two papers Stoneman and Kwon (1994) and Stoneman and Toivanen (1997) we have explored the role of complementary and competing technologies in the diffusion process. These papers illustrate that some complementarities between technologies may well exist and will affect the diffusion process. However, whereas it is practical to consider such interconnections when a small number of specific technologies are being analysed it is impractical to take account of such considerations when all technologies are being considered and no details are available on the particular technologies being diffused at any point in time.

9   In deriving (19.2) discounted gross profit gains are summed over an infinite horizon. It is possible under the stated assumptions that the technology may be made economically obsolescent at some (unknown) prior time by a later superior technology. Following Ireland and Stoneman (1986) one may argue that this is consistent if the discount rate is implicitly assumed to include the hazard of future obsolescence.

10 The purpose of this assumption is to rule out the case where the firm installed technology j at a previous date but since that time changes in the threshold value or the firm's output have made ownership sub optimal. In such circumstances (1) the proportion of industry output produced on capital good j would no longer be simply related to $q_{jk}^*(t)$ and (2) investment by the firm would not occur if at some later date it again met the adoption criterion. To the extent that such events do happen they must be considered as incorporated into the error term in the model. The assumption also guarantees that in (19.7) below $DF(q_{jk}^*(t))$ is always non-negative and this considerably simplifies the aggregation. One may note that in our empirical work we have verified that the parameter estimates produce declining values for the average threshold level.

11 Note that this implies that there is no entry or exit from the industry. We discuss this further below.

12 We have explored several approaches involving the explicit specification of the firm size distribution combined with explicit forms for (19.5) but as we have no good reasons to select particular forms in preference to others we instead proceed more directly through this approximation.

13 A referee has pointed out to us that there may be significant complementarities between the use of skilled labour and the use of new technologies. We accept this argument. The literature also suggests that some of the quasi rents from innovation may go to labour, especially skilled labour and as such the skilled labour ratio might impact on investment (see for example Van Reenan, 1996). The measurement of skilled labour intensity is, however, a problem for us and the full complexity of this reasoning is not incorporated in our formulation. We consider, instead, that the impact of skilled labour intensity will partly be picked up by the fixed effects but also, as higher skills will command higher wages, the wage variable may also act in a similar way.

14 We are grateful to Dr Y. Shin for sending us the unit root test programme.

References

Arrelano, M. and Bond, S. (1988) 'Dynamic Panel Data Estimation using DPD: A Guide for Users', Institute for Fiscal Studies, Working Paper no. 88/15.

Arrelano, M. and Bond, S. (1991) 'Some Tests of Specification for Panel Data: Monte Carlo Evidence and an Application to Employment Equations', *Review of Economic Studies*, 58, 277–98.

Arrow, K.J. (1992) 'Economic Welfare and the Allocation of Resources for Inventions', in R.R. Nelson (ed.), *The Rate and Direction of Inventive Activity*, Princeton, NJ: Princeton University Press.

Bond, S. and Blundell, R. (1998) 'GMM Estimation with Persistent Series: an application to production functions'. A paper presented at a Conference on Productivity and Competitiveness, National Institute for Economic and Social Research, London.

David, P.A. (1969) *A Contribution to the Theory of Diffusion*, Stanford Center for Research in Economic Growth, Memorandum No. 71.

Davies, S. (1979) *The Diffusion of Process Innovations*, Cambridge: Cambridge University Press.

Denny, K. and Nickell, S.J. (1991) 'Unions and Investment in British Industry', *Economic Journal*, 102, 874–87.

Dixit, A. and Pindyck, R. (1994) *Investment and Uncertainty*, Princeton, NJ: Princeton University Press.

Hay, D. and Liu, S. (1998) 'The Investment Behaviour of Firms in an Oliogopolistic Setting', *Journal of Industrial Economics*, XLVI, 79–100.

Im, K.-S., Pesaran, M. and Shin, Y. (1995) 'Testing for Unit Roots in Heterogeneous Panels', DAE Working Paper series No. 9526, Cambridge University.

Ireland, N. and Stoneman, P. (1986) 'Technological Diffusion, Expectations and Welfare', *Oxford Economic Papers*, 38, 283–304.

Karshenas, M. and Stoneman, P. (1993) 'Rank, Stock, Order and Epidemic Effects in the Diffusion of New Process Technology', *Rand Journal of Economics*, 24(4), 503–28.

Keynes, J.M. (1936) *The General Theory of Employment Interest and Money*, London: Macmillan.

Lach, S. and Schankerman, M. (1989) 'Dynamics of R&D and Investment in the Scientific Sector', *Journal of Political Economy*, 97(4), 880–904.

Meijers, H. (1994) *On the Diffusion of Technology in a Vintage Framework*, Maastricht: Maastricht University Press.

Nickell, S. (1978) *The Investment Decision of Firms*, Welwyn Garden City: Cambridge University Press.

Nickell, S. (1981) 'Biases in Dynamic Models with Fixed Effects', *Econometrica*, 49, 1417–26.

Nickell, S. and Nicolatsis, D. (1996) 'Does Innovation Encourage Investment in Fixed Capital', Discussion Paper No. 309, Centre for Economic Performance, LSE, London, October.

Romer, P. (1990) 'Endogenous Technological Change', *Journal of Political Economy*, 571–602.

Schmookler, J. (1966) *Invention and Economic Growth*, Cambridge, MA: Harvard University Press.

Schumpeter, J.A. (1934) *The Theory of Economic Development*, Cambridge, MA: Harvard University Press.

Stoneman, P. (1983) *The Economic Analysis of Technological Change*, Oxford: Oxford University Press.

Stoneman, P. and Diederen, P. (1994) 'Technology Diffusion and Public Policy', *Economic Journal*, 104, 918–30.

Stoneman, P. and Karshenas, M. (1995) 'Technological Diffusion', in P. Stoneman (ed.), *Handbook of the Economics of Innovation and Technological Change*, Oxford: Basil Blackwell.

Stoneman, P. and Kwon, M.J. (1994) 'The Diffusion of Multiple Technologies', *Economic Journal*, 164, 420–31.

Stoneman, P. and Kwon, M.J. (1996) 'The Impact of Technology Adoption on Firm Profitability', *Economic Journal*, 107, 952–62.

Stoneman, P. and Kwon, M.J. (1998) 'Gross Investment and Technological Change', *Economics of Innovation and New Technology*, 7, 221–43.

Stoneman, P. and Toivanen, O. (1997) 'The Diffusion of Multiple Technologies', *Economics of Innovations and New Technology*, 5(1), 1–18.

Toivanen, O., Diederen, P. and Stoneman, P. (1996) 'Technology Adoption under Uncertainty', mimeo, University of Warwick.

Van Reenan, J. (1996) 'The Creation and Capture of Rents: Wages and Innovation in a Panel of UK Companies', *Quarterly Journal of Economics*, III, 195–226.

Chapter twenty
Future Research Agendas

20.1. Introduction

The final chapter of a book of this kind can be used as a summarizing chapter and/or be more forward looking and talk of possible future research agendas. Given the way this book has been constructed with a considerable amount of summary material already presented, here the former is played down in favour of the latter. Largely, the purpose of the chapter is to discuss future research agendas and thus summaries of existing material are only presented to the extent that they are needed to do this.

The material is presented under four headings related to the four parts of the book, theory, empirics, policy and applications. However, even more than in the rest of the book, the views expressed are very personal.

20.2. Theory

The theory discussion in part II of the book considered various theoretical approaches to the modelling of diffusion processes and several underlying factors that would lead to the adoption of technology being time intensive. On the demand side these factors related to information deficiencies, differences between firms, order effects, stock effects, network effects and risk and uncertainty. In addition to these demand-side effects, supply-side issues were explored endogenizing the pricing of new technology, quality changes, the degree of product differentiation etc. This literature is now quite rich and diverse.

However, there do seem some obvious ways in which the literature can be extended. Although it may well be that some new underlying rationale for the time intensity of the diffusion process may be offered in the future, that is difficult to predict. Within the context of existing approaches, however, there are a number of clearer issues that need to be researched further.

1   In many ways the epidemic approach to diffusion is now very dated. The principle involved, that information deficiencies and improvements in knowledge are basic to the

diffusion process is not disputed. However, it is clear that any such analysis has to be undertaken in the context of an uncertain world, which has not always been the case in the past. It is also clear that the analysis of information issues has to be considered in a world where active search is possible and it is not just assumed that firms gather information passively. In any such analysis it is crucial to also consider that the externalities that one firm's adoption yields in terms of information to other firms may well impact on the firm's decision as to when to adopt and this will need to be explicitly modelled. It may even be that because of such externalities firms will deliberately try to protect the information that they get from adoption and thus prevent the externality arising. In general the epidemic story needs to be fully reconsidered in a more decision theoretic and behavioural context.

2   For simplicity much diffusion theory has not explicitly considered uncertainty. This is a severe limitation. Modern writings on real options have illustrated how significantly uncertainty affects decision rules on adoption. As yet, however, real options approaches have not been extensively used in the analysis of diffusion. There is considerable scope here for further work.

3   One of the points emphasized in the text above is that realized adoption patterns are the result of the interaction of supply and demand factors and not the result of demand factors alone. However, the supply demand interaction literature is very limited. In particular there seems to be a requirement to consider the role of alternative assumptions in such models relating to the cost of producing new technologies (perhaps this could be explicitly endogenized through modelling the suppliers' R&D expenditures), changes over time in the number of suppliers (perhaps again to be endogenized) and also product differentiation issues (also endogenized). The material presented above really only scratches the surface of what could be done in this area.

4   Diffusion models of the different kinds analysed here tend to have been developed independently. Thus, for example, the rank model assumes that firms have perfect information but are different whereas the epidemic models assume that firms are the same but have imperfect information. There seems to be a need to build encompassing models, so that, for example, one would have a model with both imperfect information and firms with different characteristics. This is not as simple as it sounds. For example, in the stock model firm size is endogenous whereas in the rank model it is usually taken as exogenous. However, it is only by building encompassing frameworks that it will be possible to fully explore how the different diffusion drivers interact (there is also a need for encompassing models for empirical purposes).

5   The material presented in the theory section above talked little of the international diffusion of technology. This is largely because there is very little literature that provides a satisfactory approach to understanding how and why technologies spread from country to country. In the trade literature there are discussions of the roles of transnational corporations in this process, but no modelling frameworks that reflect or even stand up against the models provided for analysing diffusion within firms, industries or economies. There is clearly scope here for advances to be made.

6   Finally we can list a number of other areas where there is scope for improvement: the role of product differentiation in technology diffusion has largely been ignored; although the analysis of networks, standards and compatability has grown apace in recent years, explicit application to the analysis of the diffusion process is still limited; intra-firm

diffusion has been a poor relation in diffusion analysis and little analysed; there are still significant gaps as regards finance issues and the diffusion of technology; there is also still considerable scope for analysis of the diffusion of organizational innovations, especially the interaction between such innovation and technological innovation; and finally, reflecting perhaps a personal bias, it is important to be aware that other subject areas such as marketing, geography and sociology, also explore diffusion issues, and it would seem there is considerable scope for some cross fertilization of ideas here.

20.3. Empirical Analysis

To a large extent empirical analysis on diffusion is limited by data availability. This is an area where it is not common for government statistical agencies to collect data on a regular basis and thus the researcher is often forced to use private sector data (from say market research organizations) or undertake the costly and time consuming task of original data collection. There is always value to new data. In addition, there have been few attempts in the literature to bring together data series collected from different sources and at different times. Thus, for example, there would seem to be some advantage in jointly analysing the diffusion of particular technologies in different countries using individual locally collected data sets.

As we have illustrated above much of the econometric analysis of diffusion phenomena is now rather dated and the tools that were used, although appropriate to their time, have been superseded. There is a need for much of the econometric work on diffusion to catch up with recent econometric advances. To date, such issues as, for example, the preliminary analysis of time series, cointegration, sample attrition and fixed effects have not been fully considered in the literature.

At a general level as well, the literature in the past has tended to too often consider individual models applied to individual diffusion examples. There is a need for comparative testing of different diffusion models. In an ideal world there would be encompassing models that nested alternative frameworks, and the application of such encompassing models would be an ideal approach. Considerably more should be done in this area.

Specific topics that have been largely or completely ignored in the empirical literature include: risk and uncertainty; the supply side; demand and supply interaction; intra-firm diffusion; international diffusion; product differentiation; finance; and network and standards effects. There is considerable scope here for further work.

20.4. Policy

Diffusion policy has been the poor relation in the development of a body of work on technology policy. There is considerably more work on R&D related issues than diffusion related issues. This is unfortunate given that the benefit of technological change only arises as technologies are diffused. The importance of diffusion issues is now, more than has been the case in the past, near the top of policy makers' agendas and thus further understanding of diffusion policy would be most timely.

In research terms there are several requirements:

1   The linking of policy to explicit theorizing on welfare optimality is most important. Too often it has been assumed that more or faster is always better but this will not always be so.
2   There is a need to link policy advice to the findings in the literature on the importance of different diffusion drivers. If the empirical literature suggests that information factors are not a major force driving diffusion then an information based policy would be inappropriate.
3   Thus far the theory of diffusion policy is in its infancy. There is much more to be done here in terms of the needs for intervention and the effects of specific policy instruments.
4   Finally, there is a need for more evaluation studies to be undertaken. Policies have been introduced in many countries aimed at stimulating the use of new technology. Good econometric analysis of their impact is required.

20.5.   Applications

The importance of diffusion phenomena has largely been played down by economics in general. As we have illustrated above, technological change impacts on all areas of economic activity, and understanding diffusion is a key part of understanding the process of technological change as a whole. If one is fully to understand how economies behave it is thus important that diffusion issues are more fully appreciated.

Part V of the book presented some examples of how consideration of diffusion factors can yield insight into the determination of important economic phenomena. At the same time the limited scope of such applications was discussed. There is clearly much room and considerable need to extend this literature. Particular obvious areas where more can be done, to mention just a few, are growth theory, the analysis of productivity growth and firm performance, international convergence, employment and investment.

In fact, it is precisely because of a belief that technological change is important in the determination of all economic phenomena that it is studied. It is also precisely because diffusion is such an important part of the technological change process that diffusion is studied. It would thus seem logical to fully explore the role of diffusion processes in the economy. In this book it has been shown that there is now a considerable body of knowledge regarding the determinants of diffusion processes, although there is still much to learn. It would be a rewarding way to close the circle if a fuller realization and illustration of the importance of diffusion processes in the world economy were to be available.

Index